About the Author

Rob Buckhaven had always wanted to make a career out of what he loved doing, hence his working life is centred around drinks. As Drinks Columnist for the *Metro* newspaper, Rob has the perfect excuse to regularly try out new tipples and flavours, tasting his way through the good, the bad and the ugly so his readers don't have to. He's been award-shortlisted for it as well, justifying the distinction he received in his wine and spirit MBA from the INSEEC Business School in Bordeaux. When he isn't writing, Rob is training sommeliers, hospitality industry professionals and everyday drinks enthusiasts, and can also be found hosting tasting theatres at food and drink shows around the country. He does much of his tasting from his home in West London, where he lives with his long-suffering, though well-watered, fiancée Tom.

The Alcorithm™

Rob Buckhaven

MICHAEL JOSEPH
PENGUIN
Est. 1936

MICHAEL JOSEPH

UK | USA | Canada | Ireland | Australia
India | New Zealand | South Africa

Michael Joseph is part of the Penguin Random House group of companies
whose addresses can be found at global.penguinrandomhouse.com

Penguin
Random House
UK

First published 2021
001

Copyright © Rob Buckhaven, 2021

The moral right of the author has been asserted

The Alcorithm™ and Alcorithm™ are trademarks owned by Rob Buckhaven

Set in Bembo and Grotesque
Design by Here Design Ltd
Colour origination by Altaimage Ltd
Printed and bound in Latvia by Livonia Print

The authorized representative in the EEA is Penguin Random House Ireland,
Morrison Chambers, 32 Nassau Street, Dublin D02 YH68

A CIP catalogue record for this book is available from the British Library

ISBN: 978–0–241–50519–9

www.greenpenguin.co.uk

Penguin Random House is committed to a
sustainable future for our business, our readers
and our planet. This book is made from Forest
Stewardship Council® certified paper.

*This book is dedicated to my parents, Simon and Charlotte,
my sister Katie, and Tom, my partner*

Contents

Introduction

You know the well-known saying 'If a book doesn't exist, write it yourself'? Me neither. Maybe I'm getting confused with 'If you want a job done, do it yourself'. Either way the first adage conveniently sums up why I wrote *The Alcorithm*, and while I'm grateful that nobody had written this book before me, it was a bit inconvenient from a research point of view. There wasn't anything available that looked at drinks from the angle of their flavours, so ironically the book I really needed to help me research this book was, well, this book.

Uniquely for a drinks book *The Alcorithm* leads by flavour, using our style preferences to guide us towards our new favourite beverages. It's based around the algorithm 'If you like this, you'll love that', found on streaming platforms to recommend movies, songs or books we might like based on our behavioural patterns. As your personal drinks algorithm, *The Alcorithm* will guide you through the gamut of flavour styles from floral and fruity to smoky and spicy, leading you to the drinks in which you can find them, from wine, beer, cider, tequila and vodka through to tea, coffee, mixers and everything in between. I mean, who knew that mature Champagne had flavours of black truffle and mocha coffee, that if you like a Pornstar Martini you might also be fond of Japanese sake, or that fans of Scotch Islay Malt Whisky may be down for sipping a cup of smoky Lapsang Souchong tea?

The Alcorithm is a light-hearted but highly informative go-to reference guide, aimed at anyone who likes a drink, to 'choose your own adventure' through the drinks universe via flavours and discover new beverages they may never have considered before. No two journeys should be the same in theory, and the idea of someone finding their new favourite drink via *The Alcorithm* makes me disproportionately excited.

Functionality-wise *The Alcorithm* is divided into two sections: Part One is based around ten flavour headings, from floral to spicy, while Part Two contains 300 drink references that illustrate where those flavours are found. The ingenious idea, if I say so myself, is to start in Part One by dipping straight into the flavour headings. For example, if 'Creamy Sweet' flavours float your boat, then check out the 'Vanilla and Clove-Spiced Toffee Apple' pairing. This will signpost you to drinks that share those flavours, such as Cask-Aged Cider, complete with its corresponding page number in Part Two. When you've flipped over to Cask-Aged Cider in the second section, you can read about its background, production method and how its flavours are formed, along with a 'sip list' of drinks that share its flavours, like Georgian Orange Wine. Likewise, jump over to Georgian Orange Wine and you can either stay in the drinks section to learn about other similarly styled beverages or be guided back to its formative flavours in Part One. You will find that most drinks are referenced in two or more flavour categories to reflect their complex network of flavour cues. This is designed to give the reader more to get their teeth into. Thus the possibilities for adventure are broad and varied, all powered by your own unique and personal flavour preferences.

With a drinks ocean that's ever-expanding, choppy and noisy, I believe we need *The Alcorithm* in our lives more than ever. It's no wonder that we cling to certain beverages like a life raft, pushing away new drinks like Rose did to Jack in *Titanic*. Abandoning a tried and tested tipple to branch out to something unfamiliar requires a giant leap of faith and a fair bit of cash, particularly without any decent rationale as to why we might like it. We're embarking on a potentially perilous voyage that requires a trustworthy guide to remove some of the risk factor, which is just what *The Alcorithm* is designed to do.

Computerised algorithms are clever, don't get me wrong; they detect patterns through our buying habits, building on them and adapting their recommendations as our tastes evolve. They have their limitations, though, lacking consideration for the crucial emotional side of the process. Automated recommendations generally work on the basis of 'If you like this wine, you'll love . . . this other wine', without recognising that similar nuances can be found in cocktails or liqueurs. I guess it's called artificial intelligence for a reason; without wanting to brag, *The Alcorithm* is based on 'real intelligence' and is powered by my experience of recommending drinks through my newspaper column and face-to-face, with a developed understanding of people's individual flavour preferences.

Getting acquainted with the flavours we like and dislike is a subjective and personal quest in its own right, involving a massive amount of psychology and our own human experience. It's no surprise given that our perceptions of flavour are processed in the part of our brain that deals with emotions, motivation and behavioural responses: the limbic system *[Glossary, p. 17]*. While taste is built on the five pillars of salty, sweet, bitter, sour and umami, flavour is the full sensory experience that is processed in the olfactory bulb behind the nose, and it combines aroma, taste, texture and temperature. In a plot twist, we also taste via our eyes, the visuals triggering our minds to search through the Rolodex of our past associations and sketch out the likely flavours in a drink before a drop even touches our lips.

Then there's autosuggestion *[Glossary, p. 15]*. I mean, if someone tells me I should be sensing a raspberry note, I may as well be drinking liquidised raspberries, as that's all I end up tasting. Describing a drink as raspberry-flavoured is one thing, but who doesn't want to know what makes a raspberry taste the way it does in the first place? Surely it can only enrich our sipping experience to know whether our drink shares flavour compounds with the foodstuff it's being compared to, or whether our beverage contains molecules that mimic raspberries' red-fruity, violet and woody notes, which collectively add up to the flavour of raspberry?

Early on in his career Heston Blumenthal tried to put together the definitive food-matching algorithm by breaking down the chemical composition of foods into a molecule database, but he concluded in a 2010 article in *The Times* that 'any foodstuff is made up of thousands of different molecules, that two ingredients have a compound in common is a slender justification for compatibility'. I'd have to reluctantly agree, though I do find it fun to identify molecular connections and to learn how food flavours can be replicated in drinks via a network of completely separate flavour compounds that have no connection to one other.

In my capacity as a drinks writer I recommend drinks of all shapes and sizes to anyone who will read my column. I also happen to be a flavour maniac, zoning in when I'm chewing my food or sipping a drink, probably looking like a masticating, slurping shell of a human, my eyes turned skyward, sporting an intensely baffled expression while wildly scrawling on anything with pages. I sound like a catch, though in my mind I'm doing a roll call of flavours and playing a game of Snap with their descriptive associations.

I can trace my deep fascination for flavours back to when I started out in the drinks industry, ahem, years ago. I would take a sip of something and describe it as tasting of 'russet pear skin' rather than simply 'pear', or 'Royal Gala' instead of 'red apple'. Am I pretentious? Yes, but I like to think there was more to it, that in some way I grasped, or was at least interested in, the unique characteristics of the subcategories of foodstuffs I was using to describe the booze and was digging into their textures, tastes, aromas and flavours, dreaming of one day writing a book about them.

While I'd love to say that *The Alcorithm* basically wrote itself, in reality it took months of planning, more than twenty Excel spreadsheets, lists full of hundreds of potential booze flavours whittled down and finely tuned into ten chapters segmented by flavour style. The practical research part, where I tasted my way through the flavour combinations, was a highlight, though more challenging than you'd think, being occasionally counter-intuitive and requiring multiple samplings of each drink 'just to make sure'. One can never be too thorough!

The flavour combinations I've allocated to each drink are based on my assessment of some of their formative nuances and my knowledge of the subject. I include popular double-act flavour descriptors like strawberries and whipped cream, along with many more off-the-wall combinations. Anyone for kerosine and nectarine? My drinks selections include popular classics through to more esoteric tipples, all designed to showcase the flavour combinations in bottled form. I back up with science where I feel it's relevant, and, trust me, there was a lot more science in the first draft – we're talking hundreds of lengthy compound names that I eventually removed on the basis that if I couldn't pronounce them, they shouldn't be in there. That's because *The Alcorithm* isn't a science book but an entertaining (hopefully) reference guide, leading us by the taste buds for a frolic through flavours to discover the drinks we might like.

Here's the last thing I'll say before we get into the book: there's a fair bit of information in *The Alcorithm* if you're looking for it, but I've intentionally formatted it into short, snappy paragraphs to make it as user-friendly as possible. This hopefully means it caters to those who want to be guided by flavours to discover their new favourite drinks, and learn some fascinating factoids about them along the way.

Rob Buckhaven
London, May 2021

Acknowledgements

Where do I start? That takes me back to what I said to my beloved fiancée, Tom, at the beginning of the writing process. My first acknowledgement therefore has to go to Tom, who has listened to me incessantly, provided a shoulder when I needed it, has been an ever-present source of encouragement and great ideas and who hasn't left me *yet*, which speaks highly to his character.

My parents, Simon and Charlotte, and my sister Katie have always been my biggest fans, as I am theirs – they are my best friends, my rocks in life and throughout this process, and I love them beyond words. Without them I wouldn't have the confidence in my abilities and *The Alcorithm* wouldn't exist, pure and simple.

My scientific consultant, Dr Ian Whitehead, must come next; his advice, collaboration on *The Alcorithm*'s format, boundless enthusiasm, availability to chat through anything at any time has been incredible. Ian not only helped school me in the tenets of flavour science via his encyclopaedic knowledge on the subject but also on how to communicate it engagingly to the masses.

I am almost lost for words for how to thank my editor at Penguin Michael Joseph, Ione Walder, which isn't like me. Ione's patience, enthusiasm, empathy and guidance, not to mention just being a lovely human being, has been a constant reassurance and major part of how *The Alcorithm* has turned out so aligned with the ideas we initially discussed.

A big thank-you to Cathryn Summerhayes, my literary agent at Curtis Brown, along with Jess Malloy. They have made the process feel like a partnership, offering me their support and guidance each step of the way.

As a consultant on the cocktails within the book, bar owner, mixologist and friend Chris Dennis was ready to help and happy to impart his knowledge, at a time when he was busy with his own projects, for which I am extremely grateful.

Tony Milanowski, for taking the time to read through the first proofs and give your expert feedback, thank you.

Mark and Sarah Driver, who have supported me from the very start of *The Alcorithm*, gave me the crucial time I needed to write. I won't forget your kindness.

John, Teddy and Adrian, thank you for all your encouragement. Theodore and Rufus, for being my two lovely nephews.

Clara, my bestie, thank you for supporting me always.

My gratitude to Here Design for absolutely nailing *The Alcorithm*'s design brief.

Glossary

Acetic
Acetic acid/vinegar

Anethole
A compound with a sweet taste, obtained from anise or fennel oils

Anthocyanin
Compounds responsible for red, blue and purple pigmentation in fruit, veggies, cereal and flowers

Autoclave Oven
An apparatus for steaming or 'cooking' agave piñas under high pressure in Tequila and Mezcal production

Autosuggestion
The repetition of verbal messages as a way to influence behaviour

Benzaldehyde
A compound with an almond-like aroma found in the essential oil of almond, cherry and apricot kernels

Bergamottin
A fragrant compound found in the rind of pomelos, grapefruits and bergamot oranges, which has a citrusy-floral aroma

Brettanomyces
A common yeast found in wines and vineyards that grows naturally on fruit skin, bringing aromas of barnyard, horse stable and plasters into fermented beverages

Camphoraceous
Showing similar aromatic characteristics to those of camphor

Capsaicin
An extremely pungent compound that provides the 'burn' in chilli peppers

Carotenoids
Red, yellow and orange pigments found in plants and certain animal tissues

Carvone
A compound found naturally in spearmint (R-carvone), caraway, and dill (S-carvone)

Cations
Positively charged ions that link to negatively charged 'anions', hence sodium (cation) and chlorine (anion) give us sodium chloride, aka table salt

Cinnamaldehyde
The compound that gives cinnamon its sweet, spicy flavour and fragrant aroma

Citral
A compound with a strong lemon-like aroma, which is found naturally in the essential oils of lemon, orange and lemongrass

Clavelin Bottle
A squat 62cl bottle that traditionally houses Vin Jaune from the Jura region of France

Colloidal System
When one substance is dispersed through another substance without combining to form a solution

Column Still
A variety of distillation 'still', consisting of two industrial-looking columns that produce a high-alcohol, clean and neutral spirit like vodka. Also called the 'Coffey Still' or 'Continuous Still'

Conching Process
A process used in chocolate manufacture in which the flavours and textures are

refined by warming and grinding the cocoa mass, either in a 'concher' or between rollers

Cuminaldehyde
A compound found in cumin, eucalyptus, anise and beef, which has a pungent green-herbal and spicy aroma and flavour

Cuve-close
A sparkling wine production method where the second fermentation takes place in a closed pressurised tank not a bottle, as practised in Prosecco. Also known as the 'Charmat Method'

Cynarin
A major compound constituent of the artichoke that inhibits our taste receptors, making subsequent flavours taste sweet

Diacetyl
A compound present in most beers and many wines, which is produced by microorganisms and imparts buttery flavours

Dimethyl Sulphide
A pungent sulphurous compound that is a by-product of fermentation with an aroma veering from cooked corn and seashore to mushrooms, nuts and cabbage depending on its concentration

Dosage
A solution of sugar, wine and sometimes grape must that is added to sparkling wine just before the cork goes in – allowing sweetness to be adjusted according to the desired style

Drupe
Any fruit consisting of an outer skin, a pulpy middle layer and a hard woody outer shell usually enclosing a single seed, like a plum, peach, cherry or almond

Dunnage Warehouse
A traditional warehouse used for storing the barrels in whisky production, typically with a slate roof, stone walls and an earthen floor. Barrels are stacked three high

Enzyme
A protein produced by a living cell that acts as a catalyst to cause biochemical reactions, while not being changed itself in the process

Ester
A class of fragrant organic compounds usually formed from an acid and an alcohol

Esterification
The condensation reaction between an alcohol and an acid to bring about an ester

Estragole
A compound found in the essential oil of tarragon and basil with the aroma of anise

Eugenol
The main compound of cloves' essential oil, which is also found in plants such as bay, allspice, cinnamon leaf and oak

Flavedo
The coloured outer peel of citrus fruits, also known as the 'zest'

Fructose
A sugar that's sweeter than sucrose that is found especially in honey and fruit

Gamma-decalactone
A compound with an intense peachy aroma, particularly formative in the flavours of peach, apricot and strawberry

Geraniol
A compound found in the essential oil of fruit, roses and herbs like lemongrass

and lavender with a characteristic rose-like aroma and a sweet floral and citrusy flavour

Gingerol
The most abundant compound in root ginger, with a 'sting' that mirrors its more pungent relatives, capsaicin, which is found in chilli pepper, and piperine, which is found in black pepper

Glycerine/glycerol
A viscous flavourless liquid that is a by-product of fermentation, which provides texture to beverages like wine

Glycyrrhiza Root
Liquorice root, which contains glycyrrhizin, a compound fifty times sweeter than sugar, along with anethole, which is responsible for liquorice's anise flavour

High Crack
A cooking term meaning that the sugar syrup has reached a stage in which it becomes brittle and cracks when you attempt to bend it

Hojun
A Japanese term for full-bodied, rich and full of umami flavours. Usually used in reference to sake

Hotrienol
A compound with a fresh green, fruity and floral-like flavour that is found in green tea and citrus fruit

Hydrophobic
Liquids, such as oils, that repel water, separating from it when combined, literally meaning 'water-fearing'

Ionones
Aroma compounds found in a variety of essential oils, from roses and violets to raspberries – an alpha and beta-ionone together have aromas of Parma violet, rose petal, raspberry, orris and cedarwood

Ions
Electrically charged atoms that carry a positive or negative electrical charge; positive is called a 'cation', negative is called an 'anion'

Koji
A Japanese mould used to ferment rice and soya beans in sake, shōchū, miso and soy sauce production

Lactones
A group of flavour compounds found in tropical fruit, strawberries, mushrooms and milk products, usually with intense fruity aromas of coconut, peach and apricot, also known as cyclic esters

Lactose
A sugar present in milk that is broken down in our bodies by an enzyme called lactase in the small intestine into glucose and galactose. Lactose-intolerant people lack sufficient lactase

Lignan
A group of chemical compounds, whose name derives from the Latin word for 'wood', that are found in plants and trees and which impact on the flavour of barrel-aged beverages

Lignin
A substance that forms the chief part of woody tissue in trees and plants

Limbic System
The part of the brain involved in emotion, behaviour, memory formation and processing our perception of flavour

Limonene
A compound in the essential oil of citrus

fruits that is found in their rind. It has a flavour similar to the citrus fruit from which it is derived

Linalool

A compound with a floral, woody and citrusy aroma reminiscent of lavender and bergamot oil that occurs naturally in many fruits, flowers and spices

Maderise

The process of heating and oxidising a wine while it's in barrel, which is predominantly used in the production of madeira from where the term originates

Malic Acid

An acid present in green or unripe apples, grapes and other fruits, which contributes to their sour taste

Malolactic Fermentation

A process used in winemaking to convert sour malic acid into softer-tasting buttermilk-like lactic acid by inoculating the wine with a bacteria

Maltol

A compound with a malty, caramel-like candied flavour that is produced through the baking or roasting process. It is found in breads, cocoa, coffee, malt and nuts

Megastigmatrienone

A compound formed during the ageing of wines and spirits with a pronounced tobacco aroma

Monofloral

A style of honey made entirely, or almost completely, from the nectar of one type of flower

Pellicle

A super-thin skin or membrane found on nuts and mushroom caps

Phenol

A broad category of compounds that may be welcome or undesirable in drinks, bringing notes that can include cloves, smoked vanilla, black pepper, horse box, raspberry and thyme

Phenolics

The term for the collective phenol-influenced flavours in beverages

Pinene (Alpha)

A terpene compound with a woody, green, pine-like aroma that can resemble turpentine

Pomace

The pulpy residue remaining after fruit has been crushed in order to extract its juice

Pyrazine

Compounds found naturally in vegetables like bell peppers, asparagus and peas, which also bring those primary flavours to wines like Sauvignon Blanc, Cabernet Sauvignon and Carménère. Pyrazines formed by heat take on secondary nutty and roasty flavours

Rancio

A term that literally translates as 'rancid', which is used to describe the caramel, fig, coffee and spiced notes of wines that have undergone a process of oxidative ageing

Residual Sugar

The grape sugars left in a wine once the alcoholic fermentation has finished, which are measured in grams per litre

Rhizome

An underground horizontal stem or 'creeping rootstalk', which strikes new roots out of their nodes down into the soil

Rotundone

A peppery-flavoured compound found in the essential oil of black pepper and herbs like marjoram, basil and thyme. Also found on the skin of certain grapes like Syrah

SCOBY

An acronym for 'symbiotic colony of bacteria and yeast'. Used predominantly in the fermentation and production of black or green tea kombucha

Sotolon

A powerful flavour compound with an aroma of fenugreek and maple syrup. It imparts a nutty, toasted aroma to wine, particularly dessert wines that have undergone noble rot

Sur Lie/Lees

French term for wine that's been aged on its dead yeast cells, or lees. Mainly used for white and sparkling wines to enrich them

Tepache

A lightly fermented drink made from pineapple peels and brown sugar and seasoned with powdered cinnamon

Terpenes

The largest group of volatile compounds found in the essential oils of plants, especially conifers and citrus trees. Used in the wild to repel pests and attract pollinators

Thiol

Sulphur-containing compounds (also known as Mercaptans) that exist in trace amounts in grape berries, which are triggered by fermentation to deliver flavours ranging from fruity and earthy to mineral and garlicky

Thujone

An anise-odorous compound famously present in wormwood, which in high doses can be psychoactive and hallucinogenic

Valencene

A compound contributing to the aroma component of citrus fruits, particularly the orange

Violet-leaf Aldehyde

A compound with a cucumber-like flavour that is found in green vegetables, tea, molluscs, cereals and musk melons

Volatile Acidity

Pungent compounds in a wine, caused by bacteria and yeast that manifest as the aroma of vinegar and fermented fruit

Whisky Lactone

The collective name for aromatic compounds found in oak-aged whisky, cognac and wine, which infuse flavours of coconut, celery, cloves and sweet vanilla via the barrel staves

Yuzunone

A compound that significantly contributes to the flavour of yuzu, found in the essential oil of its rind

Flavours

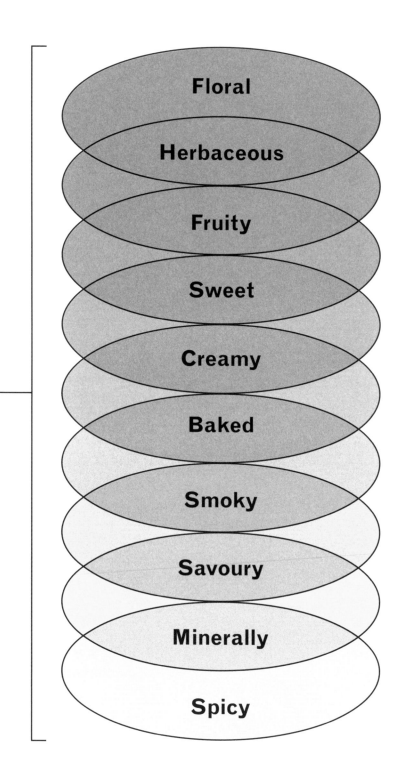

Flavours

Floral

Herbaceous

Fruity

Sweet

Creamy

Baked

Smoky

Savoury

Minerally

Spicy

If you like . . . **Floral**, *you'll love . . .*

Fruity Floral

Elderflower

If it's good enough for Prince Harry, it gets its own section in my book; heck, I've even included his wedding cake's combination of lemon and elderflower. Technically a blossom, elderflower couldn't get more English if it sang 'God Save the Queen' while delivering a floral-fruity trumpet fanfare. It's largely down to rose oxide, a compound unsurprisingly found in roses, plus the lime-blossomy hotrienol *[Glossary, p.17]*, a major source of elderflower notes in **Loire Sauvignon Blanc** *[White Wine, p.130]*. We'd instantly recognise elderflower's unique aroma in any line-up, from **Elderflower Cordial** *[Mixers, p.258]* through to **St Germain** *[Flower Liqueur, p.209]*.

<u>Elderflower & Cantaloupe Melon</u> Cantaloupe is the breakout star of the melon mafia, beloved for that unctuously sweet, juicy flesh that contains more complex volatile aromas than other varieties. These qualities come courtesy of esters *[Glossary, p.16]* for its appley notes, and a compound called violet-leaf aldehyde *[Glossary, p.19]* for melon and cucumber, which mesh with elderflower's floral, creamy, musky and honeyed nuances in **Elderflower Cordial** *[Mixers, p.258]*. This is a common flavour combo in **English Bacchus** *[White Wine, p.125]*, **Junmai Ginjo** *[Sake, p.242]*, **Pornstar Martini** *[Vodka, p.232]* and Japanese melon liqueur, **Midori**, which twins the two flavours in its signature **Melon Ball Drop** cocktail *[Fruit Liqueur, p.184]*.

<u>Elderflower & Cereal</u> I'm one of those people who whacks Cornflakes in the oven to release those toasty, grainy notes we love to crunch for breakfast. Science-wise, baked flavours are brought to us by the reaction of browning ingredients via heat. Cereal's nuttiness is neatly contained in a particular compound that also moonlights in fresh bread, steamed jasmine rice, buttered popcorn and the flavours of **Genever** *[Gin, p.228]*. Given elderflower's floral-savoury flavour profile, it's no wonder there's a fast friendship brewing with cereal, shown in a crystalline **French Wheat Vodka** *[Vodka, p.233]*, an **Australian Pale Ale** or cold **Belgian** and **Bavarian Wheat Beer** *[Beer, pp.237, 241]*.

<u>Elderflower & Lemon Sherbet</u> Sherbet lemons are living proof that we never really grow up. It just doesn't get old, the sherbet hitting our tongue, citric acid causing our saliva glands to gush, the bicarbonate of soda creating the coveted fizz. It's basically our childhood in a lozenge. Limonene *[Glossary, p.17]* from this sassy citrus confection schemes with elderflower's leading floral-herbal compound, bringing about a right royal pairing, as per the floral-citrus flavours in **St Germain** *[Flower Liqueur, p.209]* or the cocktails **Necromancer** *[Anise Liqueur, p.221]* and **Melon Ball Drop** *[Fruit Liqueur, p.184]*. It's also not a stretch to say that **Italian Limoncello** *[Fruit Liqueur, p.184]* buzzes with lemon sherbet and elderflower exuberance.

Elderflower & Red Cherry There's a shedload going on in a cherry; it's almond-like, woody and faintly floral with a lick of creamy cinnamon. Interestingly the red cherry shares compounds with elderflower, which explains their pally partnership. It's a full house of flavour compounds, with a couple of standouts in the form of a chemical that brings a sweet-floral bouquet and another for its woody almond-skin notes. Compounds bringing in freshly clipped grass notes, rose and allspice also firmly feature, with **Beaujolais** *[Red Wine, p.146]* and **Kirsch** *[Fruit Liqueur, p.183]* playing a particularly strong red cherry and elderflower game.

Elderflower & Yellow Peach Unpacking peach's aroma compounds requires a team of highly trained concierge staff, since there's around forty of them. Compunds, not staff. The headline compound behind that patented peachiness, also present in apricots and strawberries, is gamma-decalactone; try saying that after a few wines *[Glossary, p.16]*. Whether it's a fuzzy or shaved peach, we're talking about that yellow flesh, which has more acidic bite and airy florals than the white variety. What with peach's creamy profile and elderflower's honey and lychee leanings, we're looking at you **Bellini** *[Sparkling Wine, p.120]* or **Peach Schnapps** *[Fruit Liqueur, p.183]*, as a neat way of finding both flavours in a glass.

If you like . . . **Floral**, *you'll love . . .*

Intense Floral

Rose

Valentine's Day relies on rose's pronounced flouncy aromas to rise over our frisky pheromones. Luckily, to pick up a rose's scent we need the equivalent of half a teaspoon in an Olympic-sized swimming pool, so a little goes a long way. Rose oxide brings aboard the sweet florals among hundreds of compounds found in roses, with another one packing a citrus uppercut to aromatic **Argentinian Torrontés** *[White Wine, p.123]*. Rose oxide also resides in lychee, a floral-tropical melting pot of a fruit, which explains why **Alsace Gewürztraminer** *[White Wine, p.126]* is bursting with those rose and lychee notes.

Rose & Black Cherry It's a small world when it comes to the uncanny flavour connections shared by rose and black cherry. Our fruity friend contains four compounds made up of bitter almond, sweet clove, rose and citrus notes, which all moonlight in rose oil. Talk about double-dipping. Black cherry has the benefit of a warming smidge of cinnamon spice, and even the fruit's blossom shares a pine-like compound with rose for yet another cosy connection. **Maraschino** and **Cherry Brandy** are our go-to cherry and rose-flavoured beverages *[Fruit Liqueur, pp.180, 185]*.

Rose & Dark Chocolate You can't make this stuff up: chocolate's roasty notes contain the same chemical that gives roses their fragrance. Who knew? Cocoa beans are chock-a-block with a compound also found in rose and violet, though chocolate's intoxicating waft is also built from chemicals found in less appetising items like potato crisps, cooked meat, raw beef fat, cooked cabbage, human sweat, earth, cucumber and honey. Believe it or not, this grizzly shopping list produces a nutty, earthy, woody, floral, spicy masterpiece, aka chocolate, that is figuratively drizzled over rose petals in the form of **LBV Port** and **Metaxa 12-Star** *[Brandy, pp.169, 178]*.

Rose & Liquorice Granted, this is a Marmite match, though if you think liquorice is a bizarre partner to rose, tar was my original choice. Liquorice is the extract of the *Glycyrrhiza* root *[Glossary, p.17]*, best known for that chewy black confection containing a compound many times sweeter than sugar. It shares a key flavour component with eucalyptus, clove notes and those all-important aniseed compounds. Left to its own devices, rose can get a tad sweet and benefits from being balanced by liquorice's bitter notes, shown seamlessly in the guise of a rustic **Bandol Rosé** *[Rosé Wine, p.140]*, **Italian Barolo**, **Barbaresco** or the mature tones of an **Aged Red Burgundy** *[Red Wine, pp.152, 145]* or a **Vintage Port** *[Fortified Wine, p.170]*.

Rose & Plum Plum is a staple in red-wine tasting notes, it's a handy fruit for describing anything red-fruity and juicy, cue a plum-stashed **Californian Pinot Noir**, **Touriga Nacional**, **Châteauneuf-du-Pape** *[Red Wine, pp.161, 156, 147]* or a **Ruby Port** *[Fortified Wine, p.170]*. The European plum tastes like biting into a contradiction, with sweet flesh beneath a sassy outer skin. That unique flavour comes from fruity lactones *[Glossary, p.17]* which deliver intense stone-fruit notes, while another compound gives a rose and orange woodiness found in each of the above plummy beverages.

Rose & Violet Roses get around, just saying, or rather their intense flavour compounds do, with one even showing up in chocolate and violets. β-ionone is the badger *[Glossary, p.17]*: deep and woody, it gives violet its rosy, talcum-powdery profile, verging on something you'd smell in a boudoir or a bottle of **Argentinian Torrontés** *[White Wine, p.123]*, **LBV Port** *[Fortified Wine, p.169]* or Sicilian **Nero D'Avola** *[Red Wine, p.155]*. Balance is restored by the wild raspberry and tree-bark notes brought in by another of rose's compounds, a collaboration that crescendos in **Crème de Violette** *[Flower Liqueur, p.209]*, the fancy French liqueur full of pimped-up Parma Violets.

If you like . . . **Floral**, you'll love . . .

Rich Floral

Violet

Attention all Parma Violet fans: violets have been playing around with your emotions for years, sorry to break it to you. I don't know if you've noticed, but we don't get the same overwhelming odour fatigue from violets as we do from other intensely floral aromas, as our brain eventually stops registering it. Violets contain ionones *[Glossary, p.17]*, compounds that bind to our smell receptors, temporarily deactivating and reactivating them to make us think we're smelling a brand-new aroma. This Houdini-like trickery is a superpower, or superflower, that gives violets a disproportionately persistent fragrance.

Violet & Christmas Cake It's never too early to start feeding the Christmas cake with hard liquor until it's completely soused. Am I right? Those candied-fruit, spirity base notes and marzipan icing can only mean one season. Yuletide is a smorgasbord of festive smells and flavours, with a compound found in oranges at the fruity foreground, another one pumping out the clove and root-beer aromas, the peppery pine-wood notes from nutmeg and scores of sweet cinnamon bark and violet aromas. Crack open a premium ***Cream Sherry*** *[Sherry, p.171]* to capture most of the above notes and more.

Violet & Coconut Let's tackle the elephant in the room: coconut isn't actually a nut – it's a fruit with a hard covering enclosing a fleshy seed or a 'drupe' *[Glossary, p.16]*. Identity fraud aside, in all but its roasted form coconut's fragrant creaminess is down to milky lactone compounds *[Glossary, p.17]*. They may be subtle, but coconut's flavours run a broad spectrum of fruity, creamy, sweet, buttery, green and woody. In the beverage game 'whisky lactone' compounds *[Glossary, p.19]* infused by American oak impersonate coconut's aromas, with an added touch of violet that ***High-Rye Bourbon*** *[Whisky, p.250]* fans will be familiar with.

Violet & Coffee Coffee is a complex beast, bless it, with over a thousand compounds making up its impressive flavour portfolio. I'm not surprised, as looking at Nespresso's coffee pod selection I can well believe it. Sour, bitter and astringent notes can be triggered by caffeine, and not unlike violet, coffee plays with the odour receptors in our brain, removing our sensation of tiredness. The act of roasting beans activates coffee's bitter compounds, also releasing an aroma reminiscent of violets, often noted in super-aged ***Armagnac*** *[Brandy, p.175]* and roasty ***South African Pinotage*** *[Red Wine, p.157]*.

Violet & Eucalyptus Eucalyptus notes in ***Australian Cabernet Sauvignon*** *[Red Wine, p.143]* are like an episode of *Columbo*. Was it caused by neighbouring eucalyptus trees, a coincidental compound in the grapes, or both? Eucalyptol has been busted as the culprit; it's an organic compound that injects fresh, minty, medicinal notes into brawny Aussie reds, complementing their bitter violet base notes. Studies solved this as a case of MOG – material other than grapes – where eucalyptus leaves were falling on to the vines, their vapours coating the grapes and those aromas winding up in our wine. This flavour duo is also detected in a glass of ***XO Cognac*** *[Brandy, p.178]*, ***Crusted Port*** *[Fortified Wine, p.169]* and ***Gaillac Rouge*** *[Red Wine, p.149]*, without any MOG in sight.

Violet & Raspberry Our galaxy smells of raspberries, fact – ethyl formate is a chemical that's been detected at the centre of our galaxy by astronomers seeking the 'building blocks of life'. Here on Earth, ethyl formate runs rampant in raspberries and has a **White Rum**-like *[Rum, p.197]*, caramelised fruit aroma also found in rum itself. Raspberries share the compound β-ionone *[Glossary, p.17]* with violets and another dubbed 'the raspberry ketone', both savoured in **Crème de Violette** *[Flower Liqueur, p.209]*, **Argentinian Malbec**, a perfumed **Côte-Rôtie**, **Beaujolais** *[Red Wine, pp.143, 146, 148]* or the soft and crowd-pleasing notes of a **New Zealand Pinot Noir Rosé** *[Rosé Wine, p.142]*.

If you like . . . **Floral**, *you'll love . . .*

Soft Floral

Blossom

Blossom is an exciting little nuance to find in drinks, as technically it describes the flowers of any form of fruit tree. Aroma-wise, you'll sense an echo of the fruit in the title, now with the added bandwidth of flowers and herbs. This gives it a new versatility to buddy up to a wider array of styles and aromas. Without getting all school-chemistry-class about it, blossom contains super-aromatic compounds called terpenes *[Glossary, p.19]*, which broadcast blossom's floral-fruity flavours to our receptors like they're being blasted over local radio.

Apple Blossom & Coffee Apple flowers are all the rage; heck, you probably fished one out of your cocktail only last weekend. This blossom has a whitey-pink petal, with sweet aromatics that verge on rosy notes. It's no shocker that apples gravitate towards spice given their own petals contain a soupçon of cinnamon-adjacent compounds. Add in a chemical with a ridiculously long name that's virtually unpronounceable but actually smells like roasted coffee beans, and we have the flavour version of a high-five in an appley **Kenyan** cuppa *[Coffee, p.205]* or a roasty **Coffee Stout** *[Beer, p.239]*.

Cherry Blossom & Lemon Things don't get more blossomy than springtime in Japan. Fact. Aside from the visual splendour of Sakura petals falling like floral snow, cherry blossom's subtle perfume is down to floral-nutty compounds and a vanilla component, as sipped in a **Sakura Gin Bee's Knees** cocktail *[Gin, p.228]*. There's a whisper of rose and lilac with a teasing almond creaminess and a suggestion of lemons and limes, as delivered in **Daiginjo** *[Sake, p.242]* and **French Wheat Vodka** *[Vodka, p.233]*. Cherry blossom also shares a chemical with lemon peel oil, seamlessly linking the two flavours with an added pop of pine. *[Cocktail Recipe, p.229]*

Lemon Blossom & Sea Mist Punchy statement alert: lemon blossom is the happiest smell in the world. There, I said it. Way softer on the nostrils than the angular odours of the sour citrus fruit itself, lemon blossom contains the citrusy compound citral

[Glossary, p.15], plus another one that's found in lemongrass for a more fragrantly herbaceous **Margarita**-like moment *[Tequila, p.190]*. Match those aromas with the brisk minerality of fresh seaside air and that refreshing kick of marine algae sulphur, and we've basically got ourselves a floral-lemony **Pessac-Leognan** or the citrusy-saline tones of a **Galician Albariño**, **Italian Grillo**, **Portuguese Vinho Verde** and a **Soave Classico** *[White Wine, pp.128, 137, 135, 136, 135]* or a super-minerally **Vichy Catalan** *[Mixers, p.259]*.

Orange Blossom & Honey Just between us, orange blossom is allegedly one of the secret ingredients in **Coca-Cola** *[Mixers, p.260]*; it's also one of the most widely used floral oils in perfumery. As for honey, or 'buzz custard', as the crazy Silicon Valley guys call it, the pairing with orange blossom just works, as seen in **Curaçao** *[Fruit Liqueur, p.182]*, **Peruvian Coffee** *[Coffee, p.207]* and **Metaxa** *[Brandy, p.178]*. Linalool *[Glossary, p.18]*, a compound with a floral-citrus profile, looms large in both, which checks out, given honey's ties to botany, as sampled in a **Sakura Bee's Knees** cocktail *[Gin, p.228]*, **Condrieu** *[White Wine, p.127]* or **Moscato d'Asti** *[Sparkling Wine, p.121]*. **Drambuie** *[Whisky Liqueur, p.246]* is a slam-dunk for both flavours, a Scottish malt whisky liqueur blended with aromatic heather honey, sweet herbs and saffron.

Peach Blossom & Cream Soda Here's to the peaches and cream pairing we've all been waiting for. That said, peach blossom is more nutty than fleshy, but still has that sweet, creamy, floral aroma from lactone compounds *[Glossary, p.17]*. These hold the key to everything peach-like we've come to love and make an appearance in fruit from apricots to strawberries. Premium cream soda, with its vanilla forwardness, marshmallow and hint of menthol has never met a peach blossom pairing it didn't like. We're spoilt for choice, either a **Peach Martini**, a **Pornstar Martini** *[Vodka, pp.234, 232]* or a **Bellini** *[Sparkling Wine, p.120]* will smash this flavour combo. *[Cocktail recipes, pp.234, 233, 121]*

If you like . . . **Floral**, *you'll love . . .*

Sweet Floral

Jasmine

Entering your local Thai is all about that fragrant thwack of jasmine rice. Either that, or from a takeaway. You may even have a jasmine plant creeping outside the house somewhere, giving off an intoxicating floral aroma of a summer evening. This tiny white flower is generally lumped in with other 'white flower' flavours, which just doesn't do it justice. With a unique combo of super-sweet top notes and a herbaceous undercarriage, its punchy perfume is found in anything from **Sancerre** *[White Wine, p.131]* to Peruvian/Chilean **Pisco** *[Brandy, p.179]*.

Jasmine & Apricot There's nothing quite like lounging poolside with a glass of pink plonk. Kudos to **Provençe Rosé** *[Rosé Wine, p.141]*, our summer spirit animal, with a hub of floral-fruity flavours we just can't seem to sip enough of. Flavour-wise, one of jasmine's lactone compounds *[Glossary, p.17]* is known for its peachy-apricot note, so it's no accident jasmine and apricot play nicely together, also witnessed in the perfumed apricot notes of **Sancerre** and oak-aged **Roussane** *[White Wine, p.131, 130]*. Another key compound in jasmine is also found in spearmint, cinnamon and raspberries, so if you find any of these aromas in your vino, you're probably what's known as a 'super-taster'.

Jasmine & Caramel Everything goes with caramel – drizzle it over dirty socks and they'll taste spot on, allegedly. Caramel's 'brown', or cooked notes come from the caramelisation process of applying heat to sugar, as we've all learned the hard way from leaving anything sticky in the pan until its singed into insignificance. It's a similar story for toasting wine barrels, breaking down the wood's natural sugars via barrel-toasting to unleash caramel-flavoured compounds into the maturing liquid. Same again for roasting coffee beans or tea leaves; in fact, **Ethiopian Coffee** *[Coffee, p.205]* has that jasmine-caramel combo down to perfection, as does **Oolong Tea** *[Tea, p.201]*.

Jasmine & Clove Talk about the six degrees of separation: jasmine has a peachy-apricot aroma, while peach and clove share a formative flavour compound. Who knew? You'll recognise clove's tongue-tingling, mouth-numbing chemical eugenol *[Glossary, p.16]*, from nutmeg and cinnamon, though cloves have it in a much higher concentration. Given this flavour is also found in toasted oak barrels, we can see how it makes its way into wine, bringing in bittersweet nuances from the ageing process. An oak-aged **Roussanne** *[White Wine, p.130]* from the Rhône has that floral-spice combination that really nails the brief.

Jasmine & Hazelnut Like all passionate relationships, the 'opposites attract' theory also works for drinks, even in the case of flavour frenemies. What one lacks, the other brings to the bottle. Hazelnuts have a roasted earthiness thanks to a nutty flavour compound that's given a lift by jasmine's piccolo-solo floral notes. Like Nutella, hazelnut's leading chemical is also fatty-sweet, complementing jasmine's creamier side. Case in point with an aged **Meursault** *[White Wine, p.127]*, admittedly a wine for a special occasion, which is beautifully balanced by nutty-floral notes against a backdrop of lemon and buttered popcorn.

Jasmine & Mint A flavour power couple of the highest order, but don't just take my word for it, here's a smidge of science. Both jasmine and mint share an aromatic terpene compound called linalool *[Glossary, p.18]*, that majors on floral-citrus aromas. Linalool is used to lighten up heavy perfumes; oh, plus it's also found in cannabis plants. No connection to the latter but the northern Italian **Fiano di Avellino** *[White Wine, p.133]* is all about that wild-mint aroma, smushed underfoot in the garden while taking in that heady summer jasmine scent, also found in **Pisco** *[Brandy, p.179]* and the pronounced orange notes in **Cointreau** *[Fruit Liqueur, p.182]*.

Flavours

Floral

Herbaceous

Fruity

Sweet

Creamy

Baked

Smoky

Savoury

Minerally

Spicy

If you like . . . **Herbaceous**, *you'll love . . .*

Bitter Herbaceous

Bitter Greens

Maybe it's global warming, but it feels like the world is thawing out in favour of bitter flavours. Whether it's darker coffee roasts *[Coffee, p.204]*, **Amari** *[Amaro, p.222]*, **Vermouths** *[Fortified Wine, p.174]* or **Bitters** *[Mixers, p.100]*, change is certainly afoot. For want of a better term, I've gone with 'bitter greens' to include leafy veggies with a bitter edge and a herbaceous freshness. Granted, they're not all green, but Belgian endive, radicchio and escarole lettuce all rock the required bitterness, cleansing crunch and restorative bite that we're looking for.

Chicory & Green Olive Olives are a wild ride flavour-wise, prized for their salty-creamy credentials. From the same family as jasmine and lilac, they share a fair whack of aroma compounds with lavender, of all things. Brutally bitter when picked fresh off the tree, olives are cured in brine for months to make them palatable. This gives them a salty calling card, which enhances their apple, lavender, tea and honey notes and tag-teams chicory's creamy-leafed bitterness. The end result? The notes of fresh and briny **Fino Sherry** *[Fortified Wine, p.172]*, an umami-flavoured **Bloody Mary** *[Vodka, p.235]* or a gin-based **Dirty Martini** *[Gin, p.229]*. *[Cocktail Recipes, pp.235, 229]*

Chicory & Liquorice While the couple name for these two could be either 'chicorice' or 'liquory', their break-up would be more bitter than their combined flavour profile. To illustrate just how bitter chicory can be, its root is roasted and used as a coffee substitute; so far so mouth-puckering. Pairing super-bitter flavours together can be a car crash, requiring one of the parties to back down, which liquorice graciously does. It pulls out a salty-sweet note, offsetting chicory's quinine-like profile and drawing out its vanilla nuances, which is tried and tested in **Zucca Rabarbaro** *[Amaro, p.225]*, **Ricard**, **Pastis** and **Raki** *[Anise Liqueur, pp.218, 217 and 220]* or an **Italian Rosso Vermouth** *[Fortified Wine, p.175]*.

Endive & Honeysuckle Have you ever wondered what a triple threat smells like? Honeysuckle, that's what, a creeping flower that contains every flavour combination under the sun. For starters, it shares jasmine's signature compound for a sweet, floral moment, with a cut-grass greenness, faint orange-zest notes, vanilla and a dab of bitter almond. Actually that's more like a quintuple threat. Honeysuckle and endive are two sides of the same coin, working their bitter-floral magic to mirror the gentian-heavy flavours of a **White Negroni** cocktail *[Gin, p.227]*, also nuanced in a **Pale Ale** *[Beer, pp.237, 240]* and **Elderflower Cordial** *[Mixers, p.258]*. *[Cocktail Recipe, p.228]*

Escarole & Orange Orange is up there with vanilla, cherry and almond as the world's most popular flavourings. We're all familiar with juicy, floral, woody, vibrant orange flesh, while its peel's bitter, pine-like leanings are brought to us by a cocktail of citrusy, herbaceous compounds that are key to keeping orange's aromas finely balanced. Merged with escarole's leafy, bitter-fresh notes, we start to see the flavour blueprint for **Angostura Bitters** *[Mixers, p.258]*, a **Negroni**, **Averna** and **Aperol** *[Amaro, pp.224, 223, 222]* with their bittersweet orange, spicy, floral notes poured with a spritz of something sparkling. *[Cocktail Recipes, pp.225, 223]*

Radicchio & Pear If you're tasting candied pear drops in your white wine, send it back, though fresh pears are another thing entirely. Certain ester compounds *[Glossary, p.16]* kicked up during fermentation bring in the dreaded candied pear-come-acetate aroma, though ripe pears have a sticky, wine-like pulp with a grainy richness and tannin-roughened skin, delivering deep notes of aniseed and spice. Given that pome fruits are related to the rose family, floral aromas are a major flavour feature for pears, and **Vintage Perry** *[Perry, p.188]* radiates those fragrant, fruity notes combined with crisp, radicchio-like bitterness.

If you like . . . **Herbaceous**, *you'll love . . .*

Dried Herbaceous

Tea

Soap operas teach us that there's no drama that can't be solved by putting on the kettle and making a decent cup of tea. Grassy, fresh, floral, barky and astringent, tea's flavours depend on the level of leaf processing, from rolling and drying to fermentation. Whether it's bagged Earl Grey or peppermint leaves in a ball strainer, tea's herbal flavours can be sensed in beverages as eclectic as the bergamot tones of **Touriga Nacional** *[Red Wine, p.156]*, **Genever**'s echinacea *[Herb Liqueur, p.228]*, the dried-grassy tang of **Kombucha** *[Tea, p.200]*, **Mezcal Añejo**'s smoky richness *[Mezcal, p.193]* to **Crème de Menthe**'s *[Herb Liqueur, p.213]* punchy peppermint profile.

Earl Grey & Blueberry 'Half orange, half grapefruit, half lime' is how we'd describe bergamot if maths didn't exist. **Earl Grey**'s *[Tea, p.202]* most pungent flavour is brought into teabags by the essential oil of bergamot orange rind, which shares major aroma constituents with lavender, and is spotted in Portugal's signature black grape, **Touriga Nacional** *[Red Wine, p.156]*. Blueberries also share a floral side and bergamot-adjacent notes from their own clove-like compounds that emphasise Earl Grey's citrus, cedar and earthy coriander seed side, with stylistic similarities to **Ethiopian Coffee** *[Coffee, p.205]*.

Echinacea & Malted Biscuit Echinacea has more aliases than P-Diddy, or whatever he's called nowadays, from 'snakeroot' to my personal favourite 'hedgehog'. Flavour-wise, **Echinacea** *[Tea, p.204]* goes in hard on the florals, with a tingling pine-needle freshness that gives us flashbacks of juniper-based liqueur **Genever** *[Gin, p.228]*. Echinacea shares a compound with juniper for a herbal, balsamic moment, with shared peppery, minty, citrusy influences. Though it's not an obvious pairing, dunk in a malted biscuit for the burnt-sugar, toasted barley and candyfloss component of the above Dutch herbal libation courtesy of the compound, maltol *[Glossary, p.18]*.

Green Tea & Apple Cider Vinegar It's been called 'the elixir of life', which is slightly overdramatic, but then so is **Green Tea Kombucha** *[Tea, p.200]*. A mushroom tea–vinegar hybrid, kombucha is fermented by a bacteria that closely resembles an alien life form. **Green Tea** *[Tea, p.200]* majors on cut-grass aromas, crushed almonds over violet and jasmine notes. Though cider vinegar is largely unrecognisable from its original flavour source, apples share green tea's grassy compound, with acetic acid *[Glossary, p.15]* giving fermented tea its pugnacious sour taste that can act as a flavour stand-in for the kick of booze.

Peppermint Tea & Lemongrass Look past the peppermint in **Crème de Menthe** *[Herb Liqueur, p.213]* and you'll find yet more peppermint, sweet anise and lemongrass. This is minty menthol's moment, a compound found in higher doses within peppermint than in spearmint. Like the liqueur, **Peppermint Tea** *[Tea, p.202]* also majors on menthol and a kick of liquorice, with both flavours found in a lanky bottle of **Galliano** *[Anise Liqueur, p.219]*. You only have to smash a stalk of lemongrass to smell that its tart lemon component is balanced by floral, grassy, herbaceous and minty mannerisms, which also appear in **Fernet-Branca** *[Amaro, p.224]*.

Rooibos & Smoked Vanilla Not unlike a 'centring' juice cleanse, fermentation treats **Rooibos Tea** *[Tea, p.203]* to a honey and vanilla flavour makeover. Similarly, barrel-ageing agrees with **Añejo** *[Mezcal, p.193]*, switching it from an uncouth herbal youth to rich, smoked vanilla Scotch-a-like. Rooibos tea retains its smokiness, though fermentation strips away its awkward green astringency by bringing in caramel and vanilla notes, echoing the sweet and smoky tones of a **Rusty Nail** cocktail *[Whisky, p.247]*. Genuine vanilla is a spendy spice, so copies of this flavour are made from a compound found in cloves and a chemical housed in the anal glands of beavers, often with smoky, medicinal nuances.

Grassy Herbaceous

Cut Grass

Who hasn't trimmed their grassy border and fancied a glass of **Sauvignon Blanc** *[White Wine, pp.130, 136]*? The cut-grass aroma is the springtime starter pistol that heralds the holidays; and in drink speak, it usually means a herbaceous note. When grass is mown, it fires out a distress chemical to warn other plants, a potent cut-grass-odorous compound that's easy to pick up. Well, there's often pleasure with pain, I suppose, as a few lucky drinks share the very same grassy compound, from New Zealand's **Marlborough Sauvignon Blanc** *[White Wine, p.136]* through to **Tequila** *[Tequila, p.190]*.

Cut Grass & Acacia Honey Monofloral *[Glossary, p.18]* is the grand cru, nay, holy grail of the honey world. Seen as a superior specimen that takes on the aroma mannerisms of a single flower, acacia honey contains a compound found in medicinal plants such as eucalyptus, bringing in a fresh green note to balance out the sweetness. Throw in a honey-flavoured compound, nuances of cut grass, a hoppy note and a rosy aroma, and we start to spell out Peruvian/Chilean **Pisco** *[Brandy, p.179]*, **Oolong Tea** *[Tea, p.201]* and **Yellow Chartreuse** *[Herb Liqueur, p.214]* with their celebrated honey-like profile and fresh-herb complexity.

Cut Grass & Quince Beauty is on the inside for the quince; it may not look like much, yet this pocket pear has a floral perfume and inner woodiness its siblings could only dream of. I'm looking at you, apples and pears. Quince's flavour payout is provided by a unique compound that delivers a dessert trolley full of vanilla-custard, camomile, guava and bergamot flavours. No wonder quince is dubbed the 'honey apple' in Greek. **Sancerre** and **Reuilly Sauvignon Blanc** *[White Wine, pp.131, 130]* from the Loire have all the grassy and quince credentials we need in our lives.

Cut Grass & Salt-Roasted Almonds Funny how the humble almond goes from wallflower to wrecking ball at the click of a stove lighter. It's down to complex chemical reactions that happen during heating, offering almonds the benefit of a more interesting personality. Thermal-introduced compounds transform nuts, giving them rich chocolatey, toasty, smoky aromas with ramped-up pairing repertoires, over almonds' naturally sherry-like aroma with its lean, green, grassy edges. Bring salt into the equation and it's no shocker that the flavours mirror those of **Manzanilla** *[Sherry, p.172]*, the herbaceously saline notes of **Greco di Tufo** *[White Wine, p.134]* or the flavour kaleidoscope that is an **Orange Chenin Blanc** from South Africa *[Orange Wine, p.140]*.

Cut Grass & Toffee Toffee is caramel's brother from another mother. Brown sugar cooked at top whack to the 'high crack' stage *[Glossary, p.17]* has given toffee a brittle texture and brawnier flavours, found in the grassy-molasses mannerisms of a *Mojito [Rum, p.197]*, *Cynar [Amaro, p.224]*, a *Mint Julep [Bourbon, p.252]* and *Green Chartreuse [Herb Liqueur, p.213]*. Its compounds consist of the nutty, buttery, toasty, fruity-flavoured sort, which only intensify as the temperature soars. We can wind up finding notes ranging from mushroom, roasted almonds, vanilla and cinnamon through to hints of cut grass, a flavour playlist we find in *Rhum Agricole Blanc [Rum, p.199]*. *Reposado* and *Añejo Tequila [Tequila, pp.192, 190]* are the spirit equivalent of a herb-dusted toffee apple, made to be supped over ice like a *VS Cognac [Brandy, p.177]*.

Cut Grass & Yuzu With over 70 varieties of sour fruit, Japan wins at life. Yuzu is hands down their nation's favourite citrus, sitting somewhere between a grapefruit and a mandarin in stature and style. More floral than lemon, less bitter than grapefruit, yuzu has a stylistic flavour sideline in bergamot and lime. Majoring on a yuzunone *[Glossary, p.19]*, a compound not shared by any other citrus fruit, yuzu is prized for its super-aromatic skin, containing the citrus, grassy and floral notes we look for in a *Dry White Vermouth [Fortified Wine, p.174]* or a citrusy-herbaceous *Grapefruit IPA [Beer, p.240]*.

If you like . . . **Herbaceous**, *you'll love . . .*

Minty Herbaceous

Mint

The phrase 'cool as a cucumber' should really be reassigned to mint. As the chilled nemesis to chilli's red-hot compound, capsaicin *[Glossary, p.15]*, minty menthol triggers the cold receptors in our mouths, giving us minor brain freeze while sucking on a breath mint. Who knew? Peppermint's hefty menthol count makes it spicier than spearmint, which is milder and contains a sweeter compound that is found in caraway and dill. *Aged Bordeaux Cabernet Sauvignon*-dominated blends *[Red Wine, p.144]* have pronounced minty notes, thanks to a natural chemical that creeps in during maturation and also makes an appearance in eucalyptus.

Mint & Blackcurrant Forget mint, the proper pairing for cassis should be cat's pee. Cassis, blackcurrant's posh alias, actually features a compound found in feline urine, though we'll stick with mint for this section. *Aged Bordeaux Cabernet Sauvignon [Red Wine, p.144]*, has minty notes complemented by cassis, thanks to a specific compound also found in Sauvignon Blanc, which is no surprise as the grapes are related. This compound, called a thiol *[Glossary, p.19]*, is triggered by fermentation and ramps up with ageing, as also seen in *South African Cabernet Sauvignon [Red Wine, p.157]*, another jackpot for mint and cassis action.

Mint & Buttered Popcorn Minty breath and popcorn have all the makings of a nerve-racking first date. Sure, they seem like a bizarre pairing at first, though both in fact share deep-seated nutty, earthy aromas. That said, mint and popcorn come from opposite ends of the flavour spectrum, though notes of truffles and crushed nuts are apparent in both. Pyrazine compounds *[Glossary, p.18]* contribute these flavours to cooked popcorn; chuck on melted butter and we've added in roasted, fried notes as found in a **Mint Julep** cocktail *[Bourbon, p.252]*, which majors on smashed mint and corny **Wheated Bourbon** *[Bourbon, p.253]*. *[Cocktail Recipe, p.252]*

Mint & Dates So many 'date' jokes, so little time, though having said that I can't think of any. Dates and dried fruit are deceptively complex bundles of nectar, making our eyes spiral like pinwheels from a single nibble. Known as 'nature's candy', dates take on honeyed, caramel flavours from sun-drying, which concentrates their two-thirds sugar content. They come packing an insane amount of nutty, buttery, tangy flavours and a good amount of mint-like herbaceous tones, with nuances of dates and mint found in Hungary's luscious dessert wine, **Tokaji Aszú** *[Dessert Wine, p.165]*.

Mint & Lime Anyone who's met a **Mojito** *[Rum Cocktail, p.197]* knows that mint and lime are one of life's classic matches. They've got chemistry, quite literally, and together they disprove the phrase 'It's not easy being green', but how do they make it look so effortless? Lime is the most edgy and herbaceous member of the citrus family, containing a grassy compound also found in pine. This brings in a bitter-tart flavour that's greener, more balsamic and angular than lemon's. Menthol soothes lime's sting and creates an almost spiritual collaboration with **Rum**'s mellow spices *[Rum, p.195]*. *[Cocktail Recipe, p.198]*

Spearmint & Juniper Spirit guzzlers will be well versed in juniper, the hardest-working botanical in the gin blend. Juniper is also a descriptive word found in wine-tasting notes, replacing the term 'peppery' when flavours err on the spicy side. A seed with conifer-like green notes, juniper shares a major compound with mint and boasts a clean herbal profile that meshes with spearmint's minty-citrus flavours. Their combined pine and orange-peel powers draw out the floral, herbal and citrus flavours in **Argentinian Torrontés** *[White Wine, p.123]*, likewise minty-herbal **Strega**, **Galliano** *[Herb Liqueur, pp.215, 219]* and **Echinacea** *[Tea, p.204]*.

If you like . . . **Herbaceous**, *you'll love . . .*

Sweet Herbaceous

Bell Pepper

There's a brilliance to bell peppers that makes me wonder why we don't see any running the country. So much goes on under those bell-shaped bonnets of such complexity we could barely replicate it in a lab. The shades of green, yellow, orange and red mirror their stages of ripeness, each complete with its own aroma menu. For a quick slug of science, the grassy to roasty aromas are down to a pungent compound called the bell pepper pyrazine *[Glossary, p.18]*, also found loud and proud in wines like **Chilean Carménère** *[Red Wine, p.144]*.

Green Bell Pepper & Cut Grass Mention green bell peppers and winemakers will freeze like you're a newbie entering a Wild West saloon. It's a controversial odour in the world of red wine, where it can imply unripe fruit. True, the bell pepper pyrazine is one of the most powerful smells on Earth, so the slightest overkill can tip it over the edge. Done right, or white, though, and you're in grassy meadow heaven. Just take your pick of France's pyrazine-rich bounty in a **Pouilly Fumé** *[White Wine, p.129]*, **Chilean Carménère**, **Gaillac Rouge** or a **Chinon** *[Red Wine, pp.144, 149, 148]* for all the proof we need.

Orange Pepper & Vanilla No one expected me to bring flamingos, salmon and carrots into this, but I feel I have to. Whether it's their orange flesh or pink plumage, carotenoids *[Glossary, p.15]* are the compounds responsible for this striking rosy appearance. It's the same for the orange bell pepper, and please don't get me started on canaries or hens' egg yolks. Orange is the least common colour of the pepper Pantone references, and they also contain a creamy sweetness that almost swings towards vanilla, not unlike **Advocaat** *[Brandy, p.179]*, that retro brandy, egg and vanilla liqueur.

Red Pepper & Sesame Seed Red peppers must be exhausted – they run the aroma gamut from caramel-like to savoury and fruity. Their naturally pungent pyrazine compounds *[Glossary, p.18]* give off nutty, roasty aromas even in their raw state, mirroring flavours usually brought in by the cooking process. This is a notable case in point with sesame seeds, which become coffee-like, rubber-flavoured, meaty and caramelly when heat is applied. There's a massive flavour overlap between red peppers and sesame seeds; both have burnt-earth notes that replicate those of the Chinese super spirit, **Baijiu Sesame Aroma** *[Grain Liqueur, p.255]*, with its unique sesame-seed style.

Roasted Red Pepper & Samphire A salty lick of sea spray makes everything taste more complex. Just look at samphire, or sea fennel as it's more frequently name-checked. It's a succulent, not a seaweed, residing in coastal areas where it absorbs lashings of wave-delivered sodium, giving it that twist of saline that brings out its natural orange, pine, celery, fennel and lime-peel notes. Heck, it even houses vanilla and rosemary compounds, as if it needed it to be any more versatile, seasoning the caramelised red pepper notes in a rugged *Islay Malt Whisky* [Whisky, p.246].

Yellow Bell Pepper & Passion Fruit Give them a chance – some of the unlikeliest pairings are the most palate-pleasing, and this is one of those. This flavour duo share compounds rich in vanilla, cheese, vegetal and floral notes, both harbouring a milky-vegetal aroma if you dig your nose deep enough. The yellow bell pepper has a bright creaminess that meshes with passion fruit's gloopy tartness; you'll notice it as you take your next sip of New Zealand *Marlborough Sauvignon Blanc* [White Wine, p.136] or a *Pornstar Martini* [Vodka, p.232], when that instant thwack of the herbaceous gives way to the creamy-sour pop of passion fruit.

If you like . . . **Herbaceous**, *you'll love . . .*

Veggie Herbaceous

Fennel

For the love of liquorice, how do we pick between fennel and tarragon? It's a tight contest: fennel contains the compound anethole [Glossary, p.15], while tarragon is tied to closely related estragole [Glossary, p.16]. They're interchangeable, frankly, both boasting a fresh, herbaceous, unapologetically aniseed-like aroma many of us have encountered in drinks like *Pernod* and *Ouzo* [Anise Liqueur, pp.217, 218]. As one of the original ingredients in *Absinthe* [Anise Liqueur, p.216], fennel has quite the artistic heritage, also used in the drinks lexicon to describe general 'herbal' notes, along with mint and dill.

Fennel & Clove Fennel, clove and vanilla are all so aromatically linked they should have a three-way. Clove contains trace amount of vanillin – heck, one way of synthesising vanilla flavour is via clove oil. Known as the 'nail spice' because, well, it resembles a nail, clove's poker chips are all in on one compound, eugenol [Glossary, p.16], with a perfumed eucalyptus-like scent that has a sweetening effect on the tongue and is also shared by the anise-rich herb tarragon. Fennel and clove notes are well represented in *Belgian Wheat Beer* [Beer, p.237] or a shot of *Ouzo* [Anise Liqueur, p.218].

Fennel & Ginger Whether it's stem, cooked or candied, ginger delivers like Domino's Pizza. Gingerol [Glossary, p.17] is its headline compound, with a chemistry that's easy to manipulate by the way it's prepared. Raw ginger gives off a peppery warmth, cooking it brings in vanilla and clove-like notes, while drying it doubles down on the **Ginger Beer**-like spice *[Mixers, p.259]*, no surprise given gingerol *[Glossary, p.17]* is a relative of chilli peppers' super-hot active compound. Cooked ginger's warming spices work with a fennel pairing, especially bearing in mind **Black Spiced Rum**'s *[Rum, p.196]* vanilla-herbal molasses, which are also found in a **Dark 'n' Stormy** *[Rum, p.195]*.

Fennel & Green Apple We only have to picture a green apple and our mouths go all a-gush. It's a reaction to the combination of sour malic acid *[Glossary, p.18]* and sweet fruity notes brought on by green apple's natural sugars and ester compounds *[Glossary, p.16]*. Green apple crops up in tasting notes from **English Non-Vintage** *[Sparkling Wine, p.116]*, **Fino Sherry** *[Fortified Wine, p.172]* to **Clare Valley Riesling** *[White Wine, p.124]*, as code for a lip-smacking lean and green style. A cut-grass-odorous compound gives Granny Smiths' aroma and flavour a leafiness that leans into aniseed notes, cue **Verdejo** from Rueda *[White Wine, p.138]* or **Cava Brut Nature** *[Sparkling Wine, p.122]*, which are case studies in fennel and green apple nuances.

Fennel & Lemongrass Anything with the nickname 'barbed-wire grass' has got to have a sharp taste to it, surely? That said, lemongrass lacks lemon's acidic kick, majoring instead on citral *[Glossary, p.15]*, a milder floral-citrusy compound. Think about the fragrant balance of a Thai green curry and you've nailed the delicacy of lemongrass's citrus-fresh, grassy, woody complexity. Funnily enough, fennel shares a citrusy compound with lemongrass that makes matching the two a cakewalk, captured in herb-based **Aquavit** *[Herb Liqueurs, p.215]*, a **Dry-Hopped IPA** *[Beer, p.239]* **Pernod** and the **Absinthe**-based **Necromancer** cocktail *[Anise Liqueur, pp.217, 221]*. *[Cocktail Recipe, p.221]*

Fennel & Vanilla How do we know vanilla again? Oh yes, it's the most popular flavour on the planet. Vanillin is the major compound behind the flavour, with hundreds of others contributing spicy, floral, woody and fruity notes. Nowadays, vanilla is often synthesised from 'me too' chemicals that are bit players in nature but cheaper to work with than the genuine pods. **Mezcal Joven** *[Mezcal, p.193]* and retro herb liqueur **Galliano** *[Herb Liqueur, p.219]* both flex flavours of fennel and vanilla, the latter accompanied by orange juice in the retro **Harvey Wallbanger** cocktail. *[Cocktail Recipe, p.221]*

Flavours

Floral

Herbaceous

Fruity

Sweet

Creamy

Baked

Smoky

Savoury

Minerally

Spicy

If you like . . . **Fruity***, you'll love . . .*

Bitter Fruity

Grapefruit

Bitter is a funny old taste that can take us a while to acquire. Grapefruit is full of it; in fact, it's jam-packed with bitter-herbal, woody, musky, sulphurous and citrus flavours. Given the French word for lemon is actually based on the Greek word for 'cedar', it makes sense that citrus fruit centre around woody-pine aromas. Cue grapefruit's calling-card compound, with its unmistakable woody-cedar odour that makes up only 0.2 per cent of its flavour profile but blasts out musky grapefruit aromas we'd instantly recognise in a boozy line-up, from **New Zealand Rosé** *[Rosé Wine, p.142]* to **IPA** *[Beer, p.240]*.

Pink Grapefruit & Strawberry We're obsessed with the colour pink these days, whether it's hair, *Candy Crush*, **Cosmopolitan** cocktails *[Vodka, p.236]* or baby-pink wines like **New Zealand Pinot Noir Rosé** *[Rosé Wine, p.142]*. Pink grapefruit is blushed up by a natural pigment and contains far less of yellow grapefruit's bitter flavonoid compound and more of a mild-tangy sweetness with balsamic notes and minty inflections. These are warmly accommodated by strawberry's crowd-pleasing caramel, honey, butter and candyfloss flavour Rolodex, where you'll also find **Pink Gin** *[Gin, p.226]* and **Provence Rosé**, both under the letter 'P' *[Rosé Wine, p.141]*.

Ruby Grapefruit & Persian Lime This pairing just screams Mexico, so no wonder the **Paloma** *[Tequila, p.191]* is the most popular tequila cocktail over there. Trust Mexico to deliver bitter-on-sour-on-pepper flavours in one drink, though thankfully lime swoops in to soften grapefruit's edges with a sanding tool of pine and lilac, mimicking its partnership with cranberry in a vodka-based **Cosmopolitan** *[Vodka, p.236]*. That said, with bitterness largely bred out of the supermarket ruby grapefruit, nowadays a light muskiness is the only reminder that it is not a blood orange. *[Cocktail Recipes, pp.192, 236]*

Yellow Grapefruit & Juniper Juniper and grapefruit don't do small talk because they see each other so regularly in gin. Juniper has a bold freshness about it, and rightly so as the legally appointed premier gin botanical. Juniper berries major on a compound that gives them their pine resin and citrus flavour blueprint, with a bitterness that works better when matched with similar suspects. This pairing plays on their shared bitter-citrus connection, with juniper's lemony pine notes seeking out grapefruit's musky orange tang in a gin-based **Salty Dog** cocktail, **Genever** and a **Gin & Tonic** *[Gin, pp.227, 228, 226]* or an English **Dry White Vermouth** *[Fortified Wine, p.174]*. *[Cocktail Recipe, p.227]*

Yellow Grapefruit & Malt Mention 'malt' and we imagine beer, whisky or, in my case, a cup of Horlicks before bed. I know, I'm a riot. Most brewing malt smells like my nightcap, with a creamy, biscuity aroma courtesy of a compound called maltol *[Glossary, p.18]*. Grapefruit and malt notes are cracked open in **Dry-Hopped** and craft **IPA** *[Beer, pp.239, 240]*, thanks to the magic of hop-derived sulphurous compounds. One in particular, found in specific hops, is heavily associated with a grapefruit aroma, though brewers also infuse grapefruit directly into **Grapefruit IPA** *[Beer, p.240]*.

Yellow Grapefruit & Sea Air Am I pretentious? Probably, but I'm using 'sea air' instead of 'salt' to bring in those maritime associations. Salt blocks our flavour receptors, dulling our ability to sense bitterness so we perceive a ramp-up in sweetness, which works wonders on the bitter compound found in grapefruit's juicy vesicles. The faintest kick of marine algae aroma in sea air plays up to grapefruit's light sulphur tones in a lip-smacking glass of **Rueda Verdejo** *[White Wine, p.138]* or a bitter-saline **Paloma** cocktail *[Tequila, p.191]* and mirrors the saline-bitter notes in a **Salty Dog** cocktail *[Gin, p.227]* or a Sardinian **Vermentino** *[White Wine, p.135]*.

If you like . . . **Fruity**, *you'll love . . .*

Creamy Fruity

Peach

Cue the naughty peach emoji, as there's no delicate way of describing those sticky droplets of peach juice we love to lick off our skin, like preening felines. Peaches contain sweet, fatty compounds called lactones *[Glossary, p.17]*, giving them creamy, fruity, floral and almondy notes that match masterfully with anything dairy. These peachy, almond and coconutty compounds have the sensual flavour traits we clock time and again in **Sonoma Coast Chardonnay** *[White Wine, p.139]*, **Champagne Demi-Sec** *[Sparkling Wine, p.117]* and premium **Sake** *[Sake, p.242]*.

Flat Peach & Honeysuckle This sounds like the opener to a bad joke, but what's the difference between flat and regular peaches? One is sweeter and less acidic with subtle nuttiness and a floral perfume; the other is a regular peach. A shared compound emphasises flat peach and honeysuckle's citrus-floral notes, while both pump out stone fruit nuances that are captured in the creamy richness of an **English Blanc de Blancs** *[Sparkling Wine, p.116]*, a **Sonoma Coast** or **Australian Chardonnay**, a peachy-floral Rias Baixas **Albariño**, **Alsace Gewürztraminer** or a high-altitude **Argentinian Torrontés** *[White Wine, pp.139, 124, 137, 123, 126]*, a sticky **Tokaji Aszú** *[Dessert Wine, p.165]*, **Peach Schnapps** *[Fruit Liqueur, p.183]*.

Nectarine & Oolong Tea Anything is possible in a bottle of **Orange Wine** *[Orange Wine, p.139]*, a white wine left on its skins to draw in more flavour and colour, where aromas range from honey, nectarine, jackfruit, hazelnut and bruised apple to wood varnish, sourdough and dried orange. Nectarines and oxidised **Oolong Tea** *[Tea, p.201]* align aromatically with an **Orange Chenin Blanc** *[Orange Wine, p.140]*, the smoother stone fruit delivering more rose and orange notes than fuzzy peaches ever could. Aside from their honeyed sweetness and floral flourishes, nectarines house herbaceous hints that mirror Oolong tea's bittersweet, fermented notes of cut grass, honey, bark and jasmine.

Tinned Peach & Bitter Orange Zest Guzzling peaches out of a tin is apparently not the 'done thing'. Well, there goes my Friday night. Shame, as there's something quite bewitching about those buttery yoke-hued segments, shimmering in sugar syrup and citric acid. Pressure cooking before tinning brings in cooked-apple aromas and a herbaceous compound found in **Green Tea** *[Tea, p.200]*. Bitter orange's piney notes, hints of lavender and bergamot team up with syrupy tinned peaches to bring floral, herbaceous, citrus and mint flavours and aromas to **Speyside Single Malt Whisky** *[Whisky, p.247]*.

White Peach & Crème Brûlée Whatever our idea of pitch or peach-perfect is, the yellow-pulped fruit has a 'classic' tangy-sweet profile, while its paler counterpart is lower in acid, floral and sweeter. White peach's Champagne-hued flesh gives off heady jasmine tea aromas via fatty lactone compounds *[Glossary, p.17]*, becoming fast friends with vanilla-loaded double-cream custard. Crack a spoon into crème brûlée's toasty, nutty, burnt-sugar lid to release caramelised aromas that combine with white peach and vanilla custard like the unctuous foam of **Prosecco DOCG** or **Champagne Demi-Sec** *[Sparkling Wine, p.122,117]*.

Yellow Peach & Star Anise Those luscious, juicy yellow orbs that taste of summer are actually made up of a network of aromas including bitter almonds, cherries, lavender, roasted red peppers and roses. I'm talking about yellow peaches, and given their flavour complexity, it's no shocker that the warming tones of star anise should prove a match. Majoring on a liquorice-like compound, star anise delivers a brass band of aromas that veer from fresh, woody and medicinal to green-peppery and citrusy. In case you're wondering, spiced peach notes abound in **Junmai Ginjo** *[Sake, p.242]* and **Rueda Verdejo** *[White Wine, p.138]*.

If you like . . . **Fruity**, *you'll love . . .*

Crisp Fruity

Apple

With thousands of edible varieties, there's no one apple flavour or aroma. Starting with the tartest, Granny Smiths give a whoosh of malic acid *[Glossary, p. 18]* and a grassy compound for maxed-out greenness, while Braeburns have a sour-floral bite that smacks of ***Calvados*** *[Brandy, p. 177]*. On a good day, a semi-sweet Golden Delicious shows off honied tones from fruity ester compounds *[Glossary, p. 16]* and delivers aniseed aromatics in the guise of a nutty Golden Russet, while Royal Galas' creamy-berry notes reach a crescendo in ***English Blanc de Noirs*** *[Sparkling Wine, p. 116]*.

Baked Braeburn & Cinnamon Forget the one-dimensional Red Delicious, we love a mixed-flavour message and biting into a Braeburn gives us just that. Is it sweet? Nope, it's actually pretty sour; yet its skin brings us a warming kick of nutmeg and cinnamon. First comes the crunch, then the mouthfeel, the sweetness, a salty lick and then those subtle spices. A cinnamon-stick pairing builds on a Braeburn's spice-rack notes, preferably in a skin-on, oven-baked format. Cooked Braeburns retain their aromatics and lose much of the sour malic acid *[Glossary, p. 18]*, with their baked flavours resembling the nuances of a ***VSOP Calvados*** *[Brandy, p. 177]*.

Golden Delicious & White Pepper This school lunch-box staple is actually considered part of the 'fine apple fraternity' by the 'applearati'. The truth is, the Golden Delicious has some seriously honeyed junk in its trunk, so to speak, which is thanks to its high levels of fructose *[Glossary, p. 16]* and expressive ester compounds *[Glossary, p. 16]*. Mild white pepper plays nicely with the creamy notes of a Golden Delicious, adding a pinch of spice to ***Austrian Grüner Veltliner*** *[White Wine, p. 125]*, a wine well known for its triumvirate of honey, apple and white pepper flavours.

Golden Russet & Pear Cockney rhyming slang aside, apples and pears were the first fruits planted in Britain and share a compound with a pear-like flavour. Golden Russet is a cider-making clone of the Golden Delicious apple, with rough skin patches that make it susceptible to water loss, massively concentrating its flavours. Likewise, patches of russeting on the fruit's skin nudge in nuances of fennel and anise notes in certain pears, mirroring the spiced piquancy of an ***Austrian Grüner Veltliner*** and ***Roussanne*** *[White Wine, pp. 125, 130]*, ***English Heritage Cider*** *[Cider, p. 187]*, ***Vintage Perry*** *[Perry, p. 188]* and the orchard-fruit complexity of Italian ***Soave Classico*** and ***Sonoma Coast Chardonnay*** *[White Wine, pp. 135, 139]*.

Granny Smith & Lemon Welcome to 'sweet-tart central', a place where lemons and green apples collide in a Martini glass to create a seismically sweet-sour cocktail known as the *Appletini [Vodka, p.234]*. Granny Smiths have grassy-herbaceous notes that combine with sour malic acid *[Glossary, p.18]* to conjure up an almost citrusy twang, as picked out in the green apple-citrusy lines of *English Sparkling Non-Vintage [Sparkling Wine, p.116]*, *Cava Brut Nature [Sparkling Wine, p.122]*, a *Riesling Sekt [Sparkling Wine, p.120]*, a *Clare Valley Riesling*, a *Picpoul de Pinet* and the green-hued wines of *Vinho Verde [White Wine, pp.124, 129, 136]*. In a plot twist lemons also couple up with green apple, bringing a burst of pine and citrus that seek out apple's sweeter side, as sipped in a *Caipirinha* cocktail *[Cachaça, p.194]*. *[Cocktail Recipes, pp.235, 195]*

Royal Gala & Brioche Whether it's bread or pastry, we all know about apples' ties to baked goods. Orangey-pink-streaked Royal Galas have creamy, floral, berry-like notes with nuances of anise and watermelon. Their 'red apple' aromas are thanks to three key compounds, one of which is also responsible for bringing red-fruit notes into wine. This fruit basket of flavours works with brioche's sweet and oven-baked profile, which has a buttery compound from the yeast action, injecting bakery notes into the red apple-rich *English Sparkling Blanc de Noirs [Sparkling Wine, p.116]*.

*If you like . . . **Fruity**, you'll love . . .*

Floral Fruity

Cherry

Now we're chatting cherries, prepare to be spoilt for choice. From tart red, sweet black, sour morello to the marzipan-like Maraschino and tooth-disintegrating glacé, the cherry-flavoured beverage sphere veers from *Chianti* and *Gaillac Rouge [Red Wines, pp.153, 149]* to *Kirsch [Brandy, p.183]* and *Maraschino* cocktails *[Fruit Liqueur, p.180]*. In fact, cooking cherries with their stones intact brings out a bitter almond compound that's one of the fruit's formative flavours. There's a clove-adjacent, warming base note, while lavender and the citrusy-woody aromas are, well, the collective cherry on top.

Black Cherry & Raspberry Jam Next time you sip a *Chianti Classico* or a *Californian Pinot Noir [Red Wine, pp.153, 161]*, look out for black cherries and raspberry jam. They shouldn't be floating in the wine, mind you, it's the flavours of this fruity duo that loom large in Tuscan reds and other lucky beverages. Black cherries add a sprinkle of cinnamon, giving them deeper baritone notes than the red-skinned sopranos. Both fruits serve up rosy, violet, fruity and woody tones, while cooking with sugar dials down raspberry's cheek-hollowing tang, as witnessed in the reds of *Barolo* and *Primitivo*, American *Old Vine Zinfandel [Red Wine, pp.152, 155, 161]*, *Cherry Brandy [Fruit Liqueur, p.185]* and in the wine-like *Ethiopian Coffee [Coffee, p.205]*.

Maraschino Cherry & Damson Skin Authentic maraschino cherries should look like they've been lacquered in maroon lip gloss. Essentially unripe cherries soaked in a spirit that's distilled from their stems, stones and leaves, they take on a tipsy marzipan flavour tempered by an earthy sweetness. This process brings all the almond notes to the yard, via a compound found in cherry stones and damson skin. Woody-floral tones mesh with soused maraschinos to conjure up the brooding notes in a bottle of **Maraschino**, **Cherry Brandy**, **Sloe Gin** *[Fruit Liqueur, pp.180, 185, 181]* or a spicy Italian **Rosso Vermouth** *[Fortified Wine, p.175]*.

Morello Cherry & Almond Bakewell tarts make more sense now knowing that cherries and almonds are related. They share a compound that tastes squarely of cherries and bitter almonds that's used to flavour drinks ranging from **Cherry Coke** *[Mixers, p.260]* to **Amaretto** *[Nut Liqueur, p.253]*. Sour morello cherries are replicated in **Kirsch**, **Maraschino** *[Fruit Liqueur, pp.183, 180]*, **The Last Word** cocktail *[Herb Liqueur, p.216]*, **Armagnac** *[Brandy, p.175]*, **Sangiovese Rosé** *[Rosé Wine, p.142]* and **Amarone della Valpolicella** *[Red Wine, p.151]*, which are collectively the ultimate cherry and almond sippers.

Red Cherry & White Pepper Screw a pepper grinder blindfolded and you'll instantly pick up those warm, woody, medicinal notes we relish in mashed potato or, more appropriately, a glass of **Gaillac Rouge** *[Red Wine, p.149]*. White pepper lacks the black shell containing all the punchy volatile oils, giving us a milder flavour experience. Piperine is pepper's pungent compound, which shares floral-fruity oils with cherries that converge in **Campari** *[Amaro, p.223]*. Piperine is found in trace amounts within wine, and it champions the cherry notes in **Crozes-Hermitage**, **Frappato** *[Red Wine, pp.149, 154]* and **Syrah Rosé** *[Rosé Wine, p.141]* without overpowering them.

Sweet Cherry & Milk Chocolate We could learn a lot from chocolate and its almost unlimited flavour spectrum, depending on how it's been prepped. Its nutty, earthy, woody, floral and spicy flavours wouldn't seem out of place in a wine-tasting note; you only have to look at **Ruby Port** *[Port, p.170]*, premium **Montepulciano d'Abruzzo**, **Aglianico del Vulture** and **Central Otago Pinot Noir** *[Red Wine, pp.154, 151, 156]* to see that chocolate and sweet cherries are a jackpot flavour match. Cherries' buy-one-get-one-free almond nuances mesh with milk chocolate's malty, nutty, caramel notes and vibe sublimely with its creamy side.

If you like . . . **Fruity**, *you'll love . . .*

Juicy Fruity

Orange

Now for the orange segment, and if you see it as a basic flavour, think again. There are compounds in orange's pith, pulp and zest associated with pineapple, floral, woody, lemon and green-leaf notes. The sum of its parts is that sought-after 'Goldilocks' flavour zone that straddles both sweet and tart. Then there's spin-off characters, with mandarins, satsumas, blood and bitter oranges bringing their own box of tricks to boozy tipples and beyond, from **Italian Aperitivos** *[Amaro, p.222]* to **Orange Liqueur** *[Fruit Liqueur, p.182]*.

Bitter Orange & Butterscotch Bitter orange was born to be used in booze, just look at **Cointreau**, **Grand Marnier** and **Curaçao** *[Fruit Liqueur, p.182]* for some of its most celebrated roles. You only have to taste **Aperol Spritz**'s saccharine bitterness *[Amaro, p.222]* to appreciate that bitter orange has more pine flavours than its sweeter orange sibling, giving it greener edges that offset its soothing citrus and honey notes. Butterscotch sits midway between caramel and toffee, coaxing out the bergamot in bitter orange with its buttery embrace, as borne out in a **Sidecar** cocktail *[Brandy, p.176]* or **Bual Madeira** *[Fortified Wine, p.167]*.

Mandarin Orange & Lemon Sharing is caring, and any aromas not shared by mandarins and lemons aren't worth caring about. Mandarins are a sweeter subcategory of the orange, more herbal and spicier in character, with a floral-honied component we taste in a **Belgian Wheat Beer** *[Beer, p.237]*. As well as the usual citrus-fruit flavour suspects, mandarins have herbaceous side hustle with the thyme, pine and woody-flavoured compounds found in their rind. There's also a vanilla-like, coconutty note in mandarins that vibes with lemon in both a **Sidecar** cocktail *[Brandy, p.176]* and in **Cointreau** *[Fruit Liqueur, p.182]*. *[Cocktail Recipe, p.176]*

Seville Orange Marmalade & Grapefruit Seville is just a fancy name for the bitter kind of oranges, unpalatable when raw, that are made into marmalade by cooking them in sugar and water. Chuck grapefruit into the equation and it feels a bit like a battle of the bitters. Yet it's that sticky, pulpy, peely, pectin-rich marmalade that gives rise to aromas resembling **Aperitivos**, **Amari**, the **Negroni** *[Amaros, p.224]*, the tooth-loosening **Vin de Paille** *[Dessert Wine, p.164]* and the racy grapefruit and orange zesty outline of an **Italian Grillo** *[White Wine, p.135]*. *[Cocktail Recipe, p.225]*

Sweet Orange & Cinnamon Give me a whiff of orange and cinnamon and I'm mentally placing the angel on the Christmas tree while sipping a glass of **Mulled Wine**

[*Red Wine, p.150*]. That's because smell and emotion are processed in the brain's limbic system [*Glossary, p.17*], which is also involved in behaviour and memory formation, hence odours have memory associations. Orange's fatty, green, floral, woody, piney notes jive sublimely with cinnamon's essential oil, as harboured in a **Harvey Wallbanger** cocktail [*Anise Liqueur, p.220*]. **Pimm's** [*Fruit Liqueur, p.181*], with its summery cinnamon and orange notes, has stepped in to disrupt this wintery association, and, you know what, I'm here for it.

Valencia Orange & Cooked Ginger That photogenic fruit on the side of Tropicana cartons is a Valencia orange, with juice so stereotypically 'orangey' it almost tastes flavour-photoshopped. That's partly thanks to a compound called valencene [*Glossary, p.19*], found in these Florida-grown citruses. Valencia's cartoon-orange appearance and flavours are offset by base notes of earth and wood, which are complemented by ginger's citrus tones and a vanilla-like compound that's coaxed out by cooking root ginger. **Assyrtiko** [*White Wine, p.133*] from Greece is renowned for its fresh orange profile that's offset by a smidge of vanilla and zingy ginger.

If you like . . . **Fruity**, *you'll love . . .*

Sweet Fruity

Berries

If you think 'berries' is a broad heading, just wait until you see 'tropical'. Berries are staple references in tasting notes across the drinks' universe, with styles ranging from strawberries' unapologetically sweet-fruity compounds, raspberries' uniquely tart-floral flavours, cranberries' citrus adjacency, blueberries' floral-sour tones and blackberries' brambly red-wine-like edges. These diminutive flavour bombs run the gamut of drinks' styles, from the bright to the brooding, covering everything from Wimbledon-in-a-glass-style **Sparkling Rosé** [*Sparkling Wine, p.118*], **Aged Rhône Grenache** [*Red Wine, p.145*] through to Carrie Bradshaw's ubiquitous **Cosmopolitan** cocktail [*Vodka, p.236*].

Blackberry & Fig Face-planting into a hedgerow while picking blackberries is called 'suffering for your art'. That said, it's worth it to retrieve those matt-black drupelets that stain our lips purple with their vinous juice. Blackberries have dark-fruit notes, obviously, with a touch of spice and a hint of herbaceous from their ties to the wild. Figs give an echo of greenness, but major on syrupy florals that salute blackberries' dusky spices and merge to form the foundations of a Sicilian **Nero D'Avola** or a super-ripe Stateside **Old-Vine Zinfandel** [*Red Wine, pp.155, 161*].

Blueberry & Spearmint Bless those blueberries – everyone bangs on about their health benefits, but they've also got a lot to give flavour-wise. Once we get over the explosion of sourness on the first bite, there's spicy, floral and fruity notes to get stuck into. Part of the *Vaccinium* sour berry family, which includes cranberries, blueberries play a similarly strong citrusy game. Spearmint matches blueberries' citrus hand and reveals a shared woody-pine note from a compound called terpinene, which would explain why blueberry and mint are a classic flavour duo found in drinks like **Rioja Gran Reserva** and **Touriga Nacional** *[Red Wine, pp. 159, 156]*.

Cranberry & Lime Ah, **Cranberry Juice** enemas *[Mixers, p. 261]*, we've all done them. Taste-wise, that blood-red juice is so sour it shares a pH with lemon juice, though that's not the only connection to the citrus family. Pine-like flavours give cranberries a direct link to lime's bitter-sour green notes, alongside a medicinal-tasting compound found in eucalyptus for light nuances of first-aid kit. Cranberry skin is rich in mouth-puckering tannins, which combined with the piney splurge of citrus, gives cranberry and lime the wherewithal to nail it in a zesty **Cosmopolitan** cocktail *[Vodka, p. 236]*.

Raspberry & Black Truffle Once you deep-dive into black truffles, you'll almost wish you hadn't; the fungus, not the chocolate. Their aromas are built from sublime notes of butter, caramel, fruit and yoghurt to less appetising odours of cabbage, garlic and putrid vegetation. While a dusting of truffle is delightful over ravioli or when its earthy tones are picked out in a Pinot Noir, we're drawing the line at nuances of rotting cabbage. Dimethyl sulphide *[Glossary, p. 16]* is the compound known to pump flavours of truffle and raspberry into **Aged Rhône Grenache Noir** and **Barolo** *[Red Wine, pp. 145, 152]*, in a good way.

Strawberry & Whipped Cream There's a co-dependency going on here that a therapy session should remedy, and by that I mean my own affection for strawberries and cream. Eton Mess is a classic match for a reason, with ripe strawberries housing buttery and creamy flavours on top of their fruity, caramel, spiced and herbaceous notes. Pair these with fluffy whipped cream, replicated sublimely in a bottle of **New Zealand Pinot Noir Rosé**, **Provence Rosé** *[Rosé Wine, pp. 142, 141]*, **Rosé Champagne** or **English Blanc de Noirs** *[Sparkling Wine, pp. 118, 116]* and just like that, we've recreated Wimbledon.

If you like . . . **Fruity**, *you'll love . . .*

Tropical Fruity

Tropical Fruits

We could be munching them fresh on a Thai beach, slathering on their scents in a sun cream or sipping a glass of **Sauvignon Blanc** *[White Wine, p. 130]*; either way we experience tropical fruit notes on an almost daily basis. True, they share flavour compounds, but each fruit brings their own angle to boozy blends, from passion fruit's sulphurous tang, mango's resinous creaminess, banana's vanilla and clove notes, papaya's buttery muskiness to pineapple's ripe and spirity swagger. We can spot their flavours in everything from a **Pornstar Martini** *[Vodka, p.232]* to the dessert wines of **Sauternes** *[Dessert Wine, p.164]*.

Banana & Brown Butter Finding an unripe banana note in wine is like discovering a mouse in your muesli – it really shouldn't be there. More than a bit of banana aroma is considered a fault; it's the overkill of a particular ester compound *[Glossary, p.16]* from fermentation that brings in an odour verging on nail polish remover. You wouldn't catch that in a bottle of **Kentucky Straight** *[Bourbon, p.251]*, whose fans live for those rich rum-like, brown-skinned banana base notes in the blend, which remind us of a **Vintage Jamaican Rum** *[Rum, p.198]*. A sweet, clove-bestowing compound in super-ripe bananas finds its soulmate in the salted-caramel notes of brown butter, brought into Bourbon and **Bavarian Wheat Beer** by fermentation *[Beer, p.241]*.

Mango & Elderflower Mangos may as well open their own library, so extensive is their Dewey Decimal Classification of aromas and flavours. These joyfully smelling shelves would include nuances of peach, pear, guava, melon, coconut, plum and pine, without a shushing librarian in sight. True to form, a bountiful cocktail of compounds go into mango's uniquely sweet-resinous notes, which carry flavours of citrus, pineapple, coconut, peach, raspberry, sweat and pine needles that bind with elderflower's floral, creamy, musky, honied tones in the tropical flowery **India Pale Ale** *[Beer, p.240]*.

Papaya & Lavender Honey Like Aretha Franklin, **Moscato d'Asti** *[Sparkling Wine, p.121]* deserves a little respect, as it's too often confused with the brash bubbles of Asti, the sparkling formerly known as Asti Spumante. It's a treacle-floral meets tropical-floral pairing, and I'm here for it. Though unripe papaya starts out sweet and sweaty from a musky compound it shares with mustard seed and cabbage, it goes in a distinctly floral direction on ripening. Papaya's persona is largely down to a powerhouse compound full of floral, barky and citrus notes that also lives loud in lavender honey.

Passion Fruit & Vanilla Scooping out a passion fruit's rich, pulpy, tangy-sweet greeny-orange seeds is the tropical-fruit version of shucking an oyster or scraping a sea urchin. Lactone compounds *[Glossary, p.17]* issue passion fruit with a Swiss army knife of cheesy, vegetal and floral notes, so there's no shortage of pairing possibilities. Vanilla is everyone's pal but it's particularly tight with tropical fruit, using its mellow woody, spicy, floral and fruity skill set to soften passion fruit's tart, musky edges. The two flavours famously converge in the classic **Pornstar Martini**, or a **Passion Fruit Martini** if we're feeling prudish *[Vodka, p.232]*. *[Cocktail Recipe, p.233]*

Pineapple & Brown Sugar With flavours resembling a Polynesian-themed tiki bar, pineapples are almost **Pina Coladas** all by themselves *[Rum, p.199]*. Pineapple contains vanilla, rum, coconut and caramel-adjacent compounds, flavours also found in wine, sake, bourbon and rum. Pineapple ketone is a compound shared with strawberries and brings the essence of pineapple's aroma, which is mirrored in **Aged Japanese Single Malt** *[Whisky, p.245]*. Although there's no need for extra sugar on pineapple, have you ever tried the brown, slow-roasted caramel flavours in **Pineapple Rum** *[Rum, p.197]*, **Mezcal Joven** *[Mezcal, p.193]* or **Reposado Tequila** *[Tequila, p.192]*?

If you like . . . **Fruity**, *you'll love . . .*

Zingy Fruity

Lemon

Party in the pulp, business in the zest – that's one way of looking at lemons. That super-sour flesh is dominated by citric acid, hence us looking like a bulldog chewing a wasp when we suck on a segment. Citral *[Glossary, p.15]* is the compound that gives the flesh that lemony flavour, while the zest retains the essential oils with other key chemicals bringing a melee of citrus, lavender and pine notes with a hint of the herbaceous. Lemon is box office gold in drinks flavours, featuring in everything from light white wines to citrus-based cocktails.

Lemon & Fresh Pear Forgetting to qualify 'fresh pear' over 'pear' risks some serious side-eye from a wine producer. 'Pear' indicates pear drops in our plonk, and no one wants that; what we do want are those floral, woody, aniseed tones delivered by the fresh kind of fruit. Pears share lemon's pine and citrus aromas, with bitter-almond notes delivering all the hallmarks of a fridge-chilled **Italian Vermentino** *[White Wine, p.135]*, a **Crémant de Loire** *[Sparkling Wine, p.119]*, a fresh-fruity Chilean/Peruvian **Pisco** *[Brandy, p.179]*, sunny **South African Chenin Blanc** *[White Wine, p.137]*, **Elderflower Cordial** *[Mixers, p.258]* or a fruit-nuanced **Nicaraguan Coffee** *[Coffee, p.206]*.

Lemon & Juniper **Gin & Tonic** *[Gin, p.226]* is the Piccadilly Circus, nay, Times Square of frenetic citrus flavours; I mean, it comes garnished with a lemon for goodness' sake. Juniper berries brim with boldly bitter, evergreen, lemon and pine flavours, with compounds like limonene *[Glossary, p.17]* and pinene *[Glossary, p.18]* key to triggering those alpine-fresh aromatics. The flavour connections don't end there, with other resinous and turpentine-like compounds in common, which make juniper and lemon a herby, woody and spicy package deal. Try a gin-based **Tom Collins** or a **Dirty Martini** *[Gin, pp.230, 229]* to live your best lemon and juniper life. *[Cocktail Recipes, pp.239, 230]*

Lemon & Marzipan Essentially glammed-up almond paste with a slug of sugar, marzipan gives me flashbacks of party-balloon animals and Laser Quest. Anything almonds can do, marzipan does more sweetly, and it is used in tasting notes to describe drinks that tick the 'rich with a hint of bitter' boxes like *Amaretto [Nut Liqueur, p.253]*. A bitter compound in almonds cosies up to sucrose, giving us that bittersweet riposte to lemon's brightening sting. If that's your flavour wheelhouse, try an Italian *Soave Classico* on for size *[White Wine, p.135]*, or a Sake, specifically a *Daiginjo [Sake, p.242]*.

Lemon & Salt Like swallows and summer, salt and a lemon slice do not a *Tequila Slammer* make *[Tequila, p.192]*, though they do replicate the briny-citrusy intensity of a *Dirty Martini [Gin, p.229]*. The product of a particle war between positive cations *[Glossary, p.15]* and negative anions, salt is the superhero mineral that supresses the overly sour, showing the sweet side of challenging flavours. A *Margarita*'s lemon, lime and orange flavour combo would be too sour to sip without the balancing tones of salt to neutralise the citrus, so it seems so perfectly harmonised with a sodium-dusted rim. *[Cocktail Recipe, p.191]*

Lemon Zest & Apricot Note to self: treating apricots and peaches alike is a flavour faux pas. Apricots have a tart floral style, midway between a peach and a plum. Mansplanation over. That said, both are paid-up members of the rose family, hence the flowery influence with its teasing kick of cedarwood. Apricot has low-key nuances of almond and citrus peel, which swipe right on lemon's matching profile. Lemon zest and apricot flavours are fixtures in *Mosel Kabinett Riesling Trocken*, *Argentinian Torrontés*, an *Austrian Grüner Veltliner [White Wine, pp.132, 123, 125]* or *White Port* & Tonic *[Port, p.171]*, which is poured in Portugal like water.

Flavours

Floral

Herbaceous

Fruity

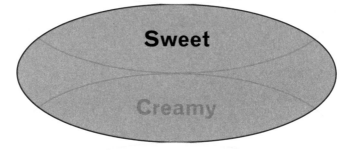

Sweet

Creamy

Baked

Smoky

Savoury

Minerally

Spicy

If you like . . . **Sweet**, *you'll love . . .*

Bittersweet

Liquorice

You could write a book about liquorice-flavoured drinks, and people have, ranging from French **Absinthe** right the way through to Lebanese **Arak**, Greek **Ouzo**, Turkish **Raki** and our flaming favourite, Italian **Sambuca** *[Anise Liqueur, pp.216, 219, 218, 220, 219]*. Liquorice has gone global, all centred around a couple of aroma compounds, anethole and estragole *[Glossary, pp.15, 16]*. That jet-black liquorice sweet-shop chew is naturally saccharine from a compound that's a whopping fifty times sweeter than sugar. Aroma-wise, liquorice is aniseed-like, earthy and burnt, with a deep-fried element and a medicinal tone from eucalyptol, a compound shared with, well, eucalyptus.

Liquorice & Black Cherry Talk about a gothic pairing . . . Though as a rule of thumb, darker cherries have a sweeter flavour with pigment from compounds that also colour the likes of purple carrots and blueberries. Worryingly, almond notes are inextricably linked to cherries – just snap a wild cherry twig and you'll get an almondy waft from cyanide compounds in its bark. Black cherries' woody, floral, cinnamon, rose and green notes link up with liquorice's medicinal aromas in the opaquely dense wines of **Madiran**, **Aged Bordeaux Cabernet Sauvignon**, Sicily's brooding **Nero D'Avola** *[Red Wine, pp.150, 144, 155]* and Spanish **Pacharán** *[Fruit Liqueur, p.186]*.

Liquorice & Dark Chocolate Both sitting on the intensely roasted side of the aroma spectrum, these two just 'get' each other. Chocolate's aroma kaleidoscope depends on the way it's prepped, with the fermentation and roasting of cacao beans bringing in compounds with an enormous breadth of odours, from malty, rosy, popcorn, potato, mocha, cheesy, sweaty, rum-like, roasted and caramel-like. Roasty, brown, bittersweet-flavoured compounds work hard in cocoa, with nutty, earthy flavours that merge with liquorice's burnt, sweet-tangy, menthol-like profile in the luscious Italian **Recioto della Valpolicella** *[Dessert Wine, p.166]*.

Liquorice & Lemon Thyme It's got to be like being beaten over the head with a liquorice stick, only with floral, herbaceous and citrus aromas drifting through **Ouzo**, **Raki**, **Arak**, **Pernod** and **Pastis** *[Anise Liqueur, pp.218, 220, 219, 217]*. Lemon thyme nails it as a flavour descriptor, building on thyme's herbaceous aromas with a soft lemony top note. Lemon thyme's compound, thymol, manipulates the brain into registering an icy blast where there is none, offsetting liquorice's all-encompassing sweet anise notes with cooling lemony-floral tones and a dab of bitterness, as illustrated in **Absinthe** *[Anise Liqueur, p.216]* or a **Sazerac** cocktail *[Whisky, p.248]*.

Liquorice & Prune Prunes need a better PR person; they're all too often associated with ageing, wrinkles and a slow digestive tract. Laxative properties aside, in wine dried-plum aromas are a game of two halves, veering from overripe Bordeaux reds to the deliriously deep and spicy notes in young *Argentinian Malbec*, *Aged Rhône Grenache* and *Amarone della Valpolicella* *[Red Wine, pp.143, 145, 151]*. We're looking at the latter here, where liquorice is often present as prunes' aroma chaperone, with a similarly sticky texture and a sweet-spicy profile brought in by compounds shared with Sichuan pepper, bizarrely, also expressed in *Sambuca* *[Anise Liqueur, p.219]*.

Liquorice & Smoked Bacon This pairing will grow on you, I promise. Think about it: bacon has sweetness and a fried, fatty, smoky profile, while liquorice has a bittersweet, deep-fried, smoky, medicinal persona. Not convinced? You will be when you get your gums around the bold savoury and smoky wines of Provence's *Bandol* *[Red Wine, p.145]*, which resembles a Malbec in the weights room. Cooking bacon kick-starts the thermal breakdown of fat molecules, releasing compounds that play off liquorice's burnt sweetness, not unlike devils on horseback, a meaty-herbal *Corbières* or a smoke-stacked *Pinotage* *[Red Wine, pp.148, 157]*.

If you like . . . **Sweet***, you'll love . . .*

Burnt Sweet

Caramel

Caramel is something of a chameleon, or caramelion if you will. From toffee and butterscotch to salted caramel, honeycomb toffee and dulce de leche, it's a versatile confection that works for both sweet and savoury-toothed types. It's all about the caramelisation process of sugar-on-heat action, which brings in those brown, roasty compounds that massively amp up the complexity of confectionery. Caramelised notes are readily discernible in richer-styled wines like *Port*, *Sherry*, *Madeira* *[Fortified Wines, pp.168, 171, 167]*, *Rivesaltes Ambré* and *Vin Santo* *[Dessert Wines, pp.164, 166]*.

Blonde Caramel & Dried Fig Sidle up to an *Aged Tawny Port* and you'll get a full-on whiff of dried fig and blonde caramel aromas; it's a similar story for a *Colheita*, *Vin de Paille* or a decent *Cream Sherry* *[Fortified Wine, pp.168, 169, 164, 171]*. Barrel-maturation brings in a compound with a punchy caramel aroma and a sweet, burnt flavour that injects fig and nut nuances into ageing ports and sherries, while actual dried figs have a golden caramel aroma thanks to complex thermal reactions. If that weren't enough, another compound delivers sackfuls of almond notes to dried figs, making up the three-in-one flavour deal of nuts, dried figs and caramel found in *Vintage Jamaican Rum* *[Rum, p.198]* and *VSOP Cognac* *[Brandy, p.177]*.

Dulce de Leche & Mango Don't mess with mangos – they have ties to the poison ivy family. Who knew? Flavour-wise, mangos are a contradiction, their fruity-resinous notes giving them a herbaceous edge over their tropical-fruit siblings with a spicy compound shared by basil and fennel. They're also brimming with lactone compounds *[Glossary, p.17]*, giving them a coconutty creaminess that complements dulce de leche's satiny, lactic, nutty complexity that's brought on by slow-cooking milk and sucrose. *Vin Santo [Dessert Wine, p.166]* with its partially dried grapes, is practically dulce de leche-drizzled segments of fresh mango in a glass.

Honeycomb Toffee & Turkish Delight Who doesn't crave this crumbly retro confection? Those brittle pumice stone-like pores of bitter-astringent treacly toffee. Honeycomb's baking soda party piece still elicits the awe it did in first-year physics, except now I appreciate its flavours in the form of an Australian *Rutherglen Muscat [Dessert Wine, p.162]*. Throw in one of the world's oldest confections, which happens to taste of boudoir, rose water and lemon pulp covered by a dusting of icing sugar, and the intense combo might require us to lie down in a darkened exotic bed chamber sipping a glass of similarly flavoured *Alsace Gewürztraminer [White Wine, p.126]*.

Salted Caramel & Lychee Salted caramel gives us a recognised condition close to heroin craving, called 'hedonic escalation'. The salty, fatty, sweet combination, Aristotle's 'golden mean' in flavour form, bypasses our body's usual response to being full, making us gannets for salted caramel. The addition of salt tempers caramel's sweetness, which is just as well now lychee's saccharine, rosy top notes have entered the equation in *St Germain [Flower Liqueur, p.209]*. Strawberry furanone, a compound found in twenty-five per cent of flavours, is like the sweet version of MSG and injects caramel notes into lychees for a flavour alliance witnessed in a moreish glass of *Rivesaltes Ambré [Dessert Wine, p.164]*.

Scorched Caramel & Cayenne Pepper Toss out the burnt gunk we absent-mindedly left in the pan that time, we want the well-stirred opaque nectar on the cusp of over-cooking, please. Scorching adds a roasty bitterness to caramel's flavour repertoire, bringing in additional browning compounds with flavours of nuts, butter, toast and fruit, thanks to increased oxidation of the sucrose molecules than for blonde caramel. *Malmsey Madeira [Fortified Wine, p.167]*, has a smidge of bitterness to stabilise its exceptional sweetness, with a pinch of cayenne pepper's earthy piquancy for further balance.

If you like . . . **Sweet**, *you'll love . . .*

Creamy Sweet

Vanilla

The Stan Lee of flavours, vanilla makes an appearance in almost every beverage in some form or other. Generalisation and Marvel movie reference, check. Loads of our favourite drinks are laced with vanilla notes, often brought in by barrel-ageing, from **Sherry** *[p.171]*, **Fortified Wine** *[p.167]* to **Whisky** *[p.243]*. In its natural podded form vanilla is packed with woody, balsamic, leathery, dried-fruity, herbal and spicy aromas. Its main compound, vanillin, is recreated on the cheap via anything from petrochemicals and plants through to a compound expressed from the castor sac on the back end of a beaver, true story.

Chantilly Cream & Yellow Peach Nothing bad ever comes from peaches, which are made up of milky compounds that love their play dates with dairy pairings. Chantilly is a jackpot match – essentially it's the la-di-da name for cream with vanilla essence. The compounds responsible for peaches' unique aroma are lactones *[Glossary, p.17]* with their pillowy, fatty, fruity, vanilla-like, creamy, buttery skill set, which are all found in a **Bellini** *[Sparkling Wine, p.120]*. Flavour-wise, yellow peach bites back with its floral-tangy baby teeth, echoing the fiery-smooth contradiction of **Southern Comfort** *[Whisky liqueur, p.249]*, the spirit of the Deep South. *[Cocktail Recipe, p.121]*

Mexican Vanilla & Cinnamon Vanillamon, aka my couple name for vanilla and cinnamon, resides on the sweeter side of the spice rack, with cinnamon's warming essential oil spicing up vanilla's aroma playlist like that naughty new friend at school. Both contain clove-like compounds; not that a good pairing relies on a shared chemistry, but it gives them a warming woody base note in common. Cinnamon's barky, floral, citrusy inflections complement Mexican vanilla with its spicier profile, and both aromas feature in sloe-berry-based **Pacharán** *[Fruit Liqueur, p.186]*, **Mexican Coffee** *[Coffee, p.206]*, **Pineau de Charentes** *[Dessert Wine, p.163]*, barrel-aged **Bual Madeira** *[Fortified Wine, p.167]* and **Tequila Reposado** *[Tequila, p.192]*.

Vanilla & Bitter Orange Forget the vanilla and orange creamsicle for kids and book the babysitter, we're talking 'adult' aromas here. Bitter orange is a slam-dunk in the grown-up notes of an **Old-Fashioned** or a **Manhattan** *[Bourbon, pp.252, 251]*, cocktails that demand the spicy tones brought in by bitter orange's cedar and minty flavour compounds. Barrel-aged bourbon exudes vanilla aromas that put a soft-focus filter over its spicy-piney, resin-heavy compounds, allowing bitter orange's persistent bergamot floral notes to fly freely, as they do in a **Grand Marnier** *[Fruit Liqueur, p.182]*, **Coca-Cola** *[Mixers, p.260]* and **Rwandan Coffee** *[Coffee, p.207]*. *[Cocktail Recipes, pp.253, 251]*

Vanilla & Clove-Spiced Toffee Apple It's Bonfire Night; you're waving a sparkler in one hand and a toffee apple in the other, try not to get them mixed up. I'd swap them both for a chilled bottle of **Cask-Aged Cider** *[Cider, p.186]* or a **White Port** & Tonic *[Fortified Wine, p.171]* any day; both of which combine sweet fruit with anise and nutty caramel notes. Jazz apples are a crunchy cross between Braeburns and Galas, with a sassy, floral mouthful that offsets its saccharine crystallised toffee coating. A dusting of warming ground cloves brings in a barky aroma reminiscent of falling leaves and open fires, which together with vanilla depicts a **Speyside** or **Japanese Single Malt** *[Whisky, pp.247, 245]*, **VSOP Calvados** *[Brandy, p.177]*, **Rooibos** *[Tea, p.203]* or a **Californian Pinot Noir** *[Red Wine, p.161]*.

Vanilla Pod & Roasted Pecan Let's be real, pecans are essentially more metrosexual-looking, less bitter-tasting walnuts. Sweet and nutty with buttery, peachy nuances when they're raw, the gloves come off when they're roasted, with caramelised, brown, coffee-like compounds swapping their chinos for tight leather trousers. With ramped-up nutty, chocolatey, burnt-caramel and dried-fruit aroma compounds that kick in from complex thermal reactions, paired with the bittersweet notes of vanilla pods, we've got ourselves the deep toasted-nut and earthy vanilla notes of an **Oloroso Sherry** *[Sherry, p.173]*, **Rioja Gran Reserva** *[Red Wine, p.159]*, **Nicaraguan Coffee** *[Coffee, p.206]* or **Malmsey Madeira** *[Fortified Wine, p.167]*.

If you like . . . **Sweet**, *you'll love . . .*

Floral Sweet

Honey

Here's a sweet story: honey is nature's original marker of 'place', with aroma mannerisms anchored to the plants that provided the pollen. Do different honeys share compounds? Absolutely. We're looking at naturally occurring molecules for those 'honeyed' characteristics, while individually manuka's cool herbaceous notes, clover's low-key spices, lavender's floral-woodiness, thyme's herbal-vanilla profile and citrus's fruit-led tones are nuances found in drinks as far-ranging as **Mead** *[Herb Liqueur, p.212]*, **Bénédictine** *[Herb Liqueur, p.212]*, and don't forget **Condrieu** *[White Wine, p.127]*.

Citrus Honey & Charentais Melon Describe a **Condrieu** *[White Wine, p.127]*, and I bet you'll mention melon and honey. Citrus honey is produced from the pollen of fruits like oranges, grapefruit and lemons, and is noted for marmalade-like aromas, floral nuances and a touch of bitterness. Charentais melons are smaller than cantaloupes and so intensely flavoured they're almost guava-like, for a tropical-citrusy meeting of minds that's also savoured in an **Auslese Riesling**, Cape **Chenin Blanc**

[White Wine, pp.131, 137], **Prosecco DOCG** *[Sparkling Wine, p.122]* and **Midori**'s syrupy mannerisms *[Fruit Liqueur, p.185]*.

Clover Honey & Gingerbread Mention honey and our minds automatically go to clover honey, the amber standard-bearer of cinnamon, nutmeg, caramel, maple syrup and plum flavours. Chemistry-wise, clover honey benefits from compounds known to shape the characteristic musky, citrus, floral, earthy 'honey' aroma. Honey is often used as gingerbread's sweetening agent, where it's combined with all the peppery dried ginger, warming cinnamon, creamy-fruity clove, citrus-zesty cardamom and woody nutmeg we'll find in a glass of sticky **Vin de Paille** *[Dessert Wine, p.164]* or **Irish Whiskey** *[Whisky, p.244]*.

Lavender Honey & Dried Rosemary I may be an advertiser's dream, but lavender honey is touted as one of the best in the world and I'm running with it. A sweet, herbal-floral infusion with a slightly medicinal quality thanks to a eucalyptus-adjacent compound called eucalyptol, lavender honey nails **Bénédictine**'s honey-herbal aroma persona *[Herb Liqueur, p.212]*. This is even more so with the help of dried rosemary, with which it shares camphor, that woody, balsamic, evergreen aroma compound found in potpourri, while in a balancing pincer movement lavender injects honey with floral, woody base notes.

Manuka Honey & Custard Apple There's serious buzz around manuka honey, even the Kardashians consume it by the vatful, allegedly. Prized for its antibacterial properties, it has twenty times the flavour compounds of regular honeys: medium-sweet, with earthy, menthol, eucalyptus, barley sugar and herbaceous notes. Meanwhile, custard apples exude tropical flavours midway between pineapples, bananas and strawberries, not bad for a fruit that looks like a globe artichoke crossed with a startled pangolin. Together with manuka's mentholated manoeuvres, we can trace the aroma outline of a **Traditional Mead** *[Herb Liqueur, p.212]* or an **Orange Chenin Blanc** from the Cape *[Orange Wine, p.140]*.

Thyme Honey & Granny Smith Like that friend you go to with a problem, honey is the anchor in flavour relationships, with a richness that tempers angular tastes. Look at green apple's sharp lines, that sour malic acid *[Glossary, p.18]* waiting to bust out of its bulging cell walls. Amber-hued thyme honey has a herbal, lilac, bitter-almond, violet, ginger, caramel, vanilla and rose aroma profile to mute Granny Smith's tang without extinguishing it, as slurped in a sweet-sour **Appletini** *[Vodka, p.234]*. Spicy compounds in thyme honey are key to bringing the honey-nutty, herbal and vanilla notes into a green-appley **Auslese Riesling** *[White Wine, p.131]*.

If you like . . . **Sweet**, *you'll love . . .*

Roasty Sweet

Chocolate

Biting down on a chocolate segment unlocks a world of flavour networks based around its processing journey. From astringent cocoa beans, fermentation dishes out fruity, rum-like aromas, while roasting throws in nutty, caramelly, malty, mocha, floral and earthy tones. There's also drying, winnowing, grinding, conching and tempering to think about, but we won't. With flavours ranging from harrowingly bitter high cocoa, balanced and bittersweet to vanilla ice cream in a bar, chocolate's flavour influence in booze stretches from **Stout** *[Beer, p.239]*, **Amarone** *[Red Wine, p.151]* to the **White Russian** cocktail *[Coffee Liqueur, p.208]*.

Bitter Chocolate & Burnt Toffee Appreciating a bitter taste in booze is all in the eye of the beer holder. In the case of chocolate the more roasting and higher the cacao content, the more it resembles licking the inside of an earthenware pot – in a good way. Take burnt toffee, its complex flavour compounds require those harsher roasting conditions to form. **Brown Porter**s are brimming with bitter chocolate and scorched-caramel flavours, sweeter than **Dry Stout** *[Beer, pp.238, 241]*, less spicy than **Coffee Tequila** *[Tequila, p.190]*, though less luscious than **Marsala Sweet Superiore Riserva** or **Pedro Ximenez Sherry** *[Fortified Wine, pp.168, 174]*.

Dark Chocolate & Molasses Nobody says 'all right, treacle' any more, thank goodness, but it was probably in reference to the honeyed golden syrup remaining from refining sugarcane. I'd be surprised if it were molasses, the bittersweet, sulphur-rich, tar-like syrup that's taken on brown notes with a balancing bitterness and an almost salty follow-up note. Compounds from the barley malting process, along with the occasional use of chocolate malt and sweetening via molasses, masterfully coax dark chocolate and black treacle flavours into **Chocolate Stout** *[Beer, p.239]*, echoed in the aroma of both **Mexican** and **Brazilian Coffee** *[Coffee, pp.206, 204]*.

Dark Chocolate Mousse & Plum Admittedly this isn't a combination I'd pick off a dessert menu, though I would in the context of a luscious Greek **Mavrodaphne de Patras** *[Dessert Wine, p.165]*. Imagine those citrusy, woody and floral notes in plum skin balanced by sticky, creamy, fragrant, lactone-rich pulp *[Glossary, p.17]*. The whipped-up, earthy, nutty richness of bittersweet cocoa nibs pick out plum's cherry and almond-like flavour compound, bringing in a praline base note also found in **Peruvian Coffee** *[Coffee, p.207]*, **Brown Ale** *[Beer, p.238]*, **Argentinian Malbec** and the choca-plummy wines of **Pomerol** and Uruguayan **Tannat** *[Red Wine, pp.143, 147, 160]*.

Ruby Chocolate & Violet If only someone would produce a pink chocolate with red-berry flavours. Oh, wait, Swiss chocolate maker Barry Callebaut already has. Supposedly the fourth chocolate style, it shares a bittersweet compound with cloves and strawberries and another with plucky flavours of raspberry, blackberry and violet. This story checks out, when you look at violet's rosy, powder-puff, bitter-barky nuances layered over ruby chocolate's candyfloss and cinnamon notes to match the intense flavour profile of a **Rosé Champagne** *[Sparkling Wine, p.118]*, an **Amarone** or a Riojan **Graciano** *[Red Wine, pp.151, 158]*.

White Chocolate & Mocha Cocoa purists eye-roll at the white stuff being classified as chocolate, but it's my favourite variety so it's staying in. That said, white chocolate is made from cocoa butter, the lighter, fatty, odourless content of cocoa beans, with most of its flavour derived from milk and vanilla, so I see their point. Super-sweet white chocolate lacks that balancing bitterness brought into regular chocolate via roasting, but that's corrected by coffee liqueur and cream in a **White Russian** cocktail *[Coffee Liqueur, p.208]*, also spotted in **Frangelico** *[Nut Liqueur, p.254]*, **Rwandan Coffee** *[Coffee, p.207]*, **Eggnog** *[Bourbon, p.249]* and **Baileys Irish Cream** *[Whisky, p.243]* with their mocha-adjacent and white chocolate credentials.

If you like . . . **Sweet**, *you'll love . . .*

Spicy Sweet

Dried Fruit

These sugary treats are 'to dry for' – get it? Dehydrating via the sun, desiccator or microwave modifies the molecular properties of fruit, swapping out their fresh-fruity compounds for roasted odours and a chewy texture. We've all popped a dried pineapple into our gobs at some point or nibbled a desiccated apricot, coming across enough crystallised sugar to comfortably put our dentists' kids through college. Whether it's dates, figs, apricots, pineapple or raisins, dried-fruit notes loom large in rich and concentrated beverages like **Port** *[p.168]*, **Dessert Wine** *[p.162]* and **Sherry** *[p.171]*.

Date & Walnut They're the *Love Island* pairing that actually lasted, finally. For starters, dates and walnuts share a grassy-fruity compound that can bring bitterness to walnuts that aren't in the first flush of youth. Fresh walnuts are sweet and buttery, covered by a sharp, astringent papery outer skin or pellicle *[Glossary, p.18]*. This bittersweet combo takes a shine to sweet, brown flavours, especially dates, which share the nutty mannerisms of a **Bual Madeira** or a **Pedro Ximenez Sherry** *[Fortified Wine, pp.167, 174]*, which tastes like liquidised dates and walnuts on steroids, then drizzled over your vanilla ice cream for dessert.

Dried Apricot & Candied Orange Peel Dried apricots look like orange earlobes to me. Anyone else? They work hard flavour-wise, bringing sweet, sour and savoury to the party, all in one wrinkled amber nugget. Neither their tang nor tint would be possible without sulphur dioxide, which is used to prevent them from spoiling. Dried apricots match joyfully with glazed shards of glassy candied orange peel and their saccharine-citrus notes, that soft jab of resin and apricot aromas reminiscent of **Southern Comfort** *[Whisky, p.249]*, a fireside slurp of **Crusted Port** *[Port, p.169]*, **Vin Santo**, **Rivesaltes Ambré**, **Rutherglen Muscat** *[Dessert Wine, pp.166, 164, 162]* or a more savoury serving of **Palo Cortado Sherry** *[Fortified Wine, p.173]*.

Dried Fig & Plum I've always thought 'bring us some figgy pudding and bring it right here' were annoyingly bossy lyrics. I'd rather bring a bottle of dried-fig-like, plummy **Sweet Marsala Superiore Riserva** *[Fortified Wine, p.168]*, frankly, the figgy flavours of a Puglian **Primitivo** *[Red Wine, p.155]*, an intense **Recioto della Valpolicella** or **Mavrodaphne de Patras** *[Dessert Wine, pp.166, 165]*. A key compound behind dried figs' aroma is also found in wine grapes, delivering flavours ranging from honey, tea, stewed apple and caramel to – most importantly here – plum. Dried figs share a bittersweet flavour compound with plums for a creamy pop of cherry and bitter almond.

Dried Pineapple & Cooked Ginger Nature's confectionery doesn't come much sweeter than dried pineapple, which even has a chewy texture for goodness' sake. In its raw form pineapple's sweet-shop aromas of caramel, candyfloss, honey and burnt caramel are tweaked by the drying process, unlocking roasted, caramel-drizzled tropical notes. Ginger releases a mild-mannered compound when it's cooked, expressing burnt vanilla notes that prove an absolute belter with aromas of dried pineapple, sampled in a sumptuous bottle of **Vidal Ice Wine** *[Dessert Wine, p.163]*, **Pineapple Rum** *[Rum, p.197]* or a **White Rioja Reserva** as a drier alternative *[White Wine, p.138]*.

Sultana & Hazelnut Describing wine as 'grapey' is a cop-out, so opt for 'raisiny' instead, or drop in 'sultanas' to sound savvy, aka golden currants. Sultanas are regular raisins treated with sulphur, giving them a sun-kissed hue and a juicier bite. It's no accident that sultanas and hazelnuts play together in breakfast cereal; hazelnuts have the sweet, roasted, earthy, beany, chocolatey aromas also found in coffee, while sultanas have a raisin-like, fruity odour. Creamy hazelnuts and sultanas unite to form the intoxicating notes of a **Pedro Ximenez Sherry** *[Fortified Wine, p.174]*, an **Aged Tawny Port** *[Fortified Wine, p.168]*, a **Pineau de Charentes**, **Rutherglen Muscat** and a **Vin Santo** *[Dessert Wine, pp.163, 162, 166]*.

Flavours

Floral

Herbaceous

Fruity

Sweet

Creamy

Baked

Smoky

Savoury

Minerally

Spicy

If you like . . . **Creamy**, *you'll love . . .*

Buttery Creamy

Butter

Butter's all around us, or is that love? Either way, buttery aroma compounds have been bringing smooth and creamy notes to beverages for yonks, from ***Whisky*** *[Whisky, p.243]*, ***White Wine*** *[White Wine, p.123]*, ***Rum*** *[Rum, p.195]*, ***Cognac*** *[Brandy, p.175]* and even ***Tea*** *[Tea, p.200]*. Diacetyl *[Glossary, p.16]* is the hardest-working compound in buttery-flavoured beverages, and is released via the fermentation process, though we can't ignore the peachy aromas brought in by lactones *[Glossary, p.17]*. Don't get me started on cooked butter, which invites in caramel and a touch of nuttiness.

Black Butter & Muscovado Sugar You caught me; it's basically brown butter, only cooked for longer. In the case of *beurre noire*, as we call it in the biz, a squirt of lemon juice before it turns dark provides a welcome pop of citrus. Butter's nearly burnt notes are mimicked by the molasses in muscovado sugar, adding to its roster of dried-fruity, floral and toffee flavours. Burnt-treacle flavour in molasses is mainly down to a compound that smacks of maple syrup and which mingles with the black butter notes in aged ***Vintage Rum*** *[Rum, p.198]* and ***Añejo Tequila*** *[Tequila, p.190]*.

Brown Butter & Nutmeg A knob of butter tends to take on toffee notes with enough searing, when heat breaks down proteins into nutty-smelling roasted and caramelised compounds. Fatty flavours vibe with nutmeg's pine-like, balsamic, citrus, floral, peppery and woody warmth; think ***Eggnog*** *[Bourbon, p.249]* and you're in the right aroma ballpark. Nutmeg's flavour back catalogue is largely down to peppery woody compounds, one of which is hallucinogenic in high doses, with barrel-aged ***VSOP Calvados***, ***XO Cognac*** and ***VS Cognac*** *[Brandy, pp.177, 178, 177]* mimicking brown butter and nutmeg aromas, without the mind-altering superpowers. *[Cocktail Recipe, p.250]*

Cultured Butter & Fudge Who doesn't love butter with a bit of culture? To clarify, we're talking about adding a live culture to buttercream, resulting in tangy flavours of buttermilk and hazelnuts. Lactose *[Glossary, p.17]* converted into lactic acid, carves yoghurt-like edges into cultured butter and amplifies its buttery compound, diacetyl *[Glossary, p.16]*. Thankfully, once upon a time someone messed up a batch of caramel to create fudge, letting it crystallise, and with less sucrose content than toffee it weaves itself into drinks flavours, notably among the buttery tones of a ***Japanese Single Malt Whisky*** *[Whisky p.245]*.

Foaming Butter & Green Tea *Matcha's* where it's at with the online influencer crowd *[Tea, p.203]*. The ceremonial green tea powder is an eye-catching staple in social media 'wellness' snaps; we've all seen them, often accompanied by avocado on toast, the praying hands emoji and the #blessed. Aroma-wise, there's a melee of compounds scrapping for supremacy in Matcha, delivering 'green' aromas of asparagus, beans, Brussels sprouts, celery, parsley and spinach with the consistency and creaminess of foaming butter. A major compound in **Green Tea**'s grassy, herbaceous profile *[Tea, p.200]* contains an umami amino acid that beckons in savoury nori notes. Pyrazines *[Glossary, p.18]* in butter and green tea tie things up in a nutty bow, bringing in roasted aromas verging on the buttery.

Melted Butter & Lemon Curd Melted butter and lemon curd are what the kids might call 'savage flavour goals', which is apparently a good thing. Melting butter, and I'm talking sweet-creamy butter with salt here, wakes up the foaming compounds that lie low in the solid stuff. They interact with the nutty flavours brought on by cooking, pumping out aromas associated with buttery baked goods. Add in the rich, creamy, tart, fresh flavours of lemon curd, a paradox in a pan, and witness this flavour partnership play out in a bottle of buttery-citrusy **Australian Chardonnay** *[White Wine, p.124]*.

If you like . . . **Creamy**, *you'll love . . .*

Decadent Creamy

Cream

Cheers to milk fat, the tent pole holding up our favourite forms of cream, from clotted and whipped to patisserie. Flavours depend on factors from the animal's diet, the production method and fat content, but all share the sweet and floral aromas of lactic acid compounds along with varying degrees of sour tang. Creamy notes in booze can either be whipped up by yeast interaction in **English Blanc de Blancs** *[Sparkling Wine, p.116]* and **Prosecco** *[Sparkling Wine, p.122]*, or actually added in the case of **Baileys Irish Cream** *[Whisky, p.243]*.

Clotted Cream & Scones Short of pairing Beefeater bearskins to corgi aromas, pairings don't come more English than clotted cream and scones. Seamlessly, cream and baked goods have a flavour alliance found in **English Blanc de Blancs** *[Sparkling Wine, p.116]*, a hub of tearoom odours with only the tea and strawberry jam left out. Clotted is one of cream's richest iterations, with subtly baked, nutty notes that come from gentle heating. It's a similar story for scones, which echo clotted cream's buttery profile, replicating all the light caramel, toasted flour-like and lactic notes found in the finest fizz from our green and pleasant land.

Cream Soda & Williams Pear No shade intended, but a half-decent **Prosecco** *[Sparkling Wine, p.122]* smacks of pears and cream soda. For the uninitiated, **Cream**

Soda *[Mixers, p.261]* is a sweet pop with vanilla flavouring, hints of marshmallow and a toasted honey and caramel finish. Pears are a heat map of cooked apple, floral, grassy, honeyed, malty and nutty notes that are pumped out of their skin via ester compounds *[Glossary, p.16]*. Fresh pear flavours in wine fit into cream soda's uncouth, buttery, sugared vanilla notes, as released by the pop of a **Prosecco** cork or in a frothy **Bellini** *[Sparkling Wine, pp.122, 120]*.

Crème Pâtissière & Praline That yellow filling oozing over our eager chops when we bite down on a high-end patisserie is crème pâtissière. A dense custard or Chantilly cream, where the addition of vanilla does the heavy lifting is replicated flavour-wise in unctuous beverages like **Eggnog** *[Bourbon, p.249]* and **Advocaat** *[Brandy, p.179]*. Praline is a choco-nutty confection that shares crème pât's vanilla, ushering in a hazelnut and caramel angle of its own. Together with hazelnut's fatty compound, they form the familiar notes of butter, nuts, chocolate and vanilla we relish in **Baileys Irish Cream** *[Whisky, p.243]* or the hazelnut-laden whites of **Meursault** and **White Rioja Reserva** *[White Wine, pp.127, 138]*.

Vanilla Custard & Rhubarb Who remembers rhubarb-and-custard penny sweets that tasted nothing like rhubarb or custard? At least they gave us an inkling into how these opposingly sour, sweet, creamy, floral and fruity flavours can interact so well. Rhubarb is a heady contradiction of highly aromatic, floral and red-berry-like flavours with candied strawberry notes over a grassy infrastructure. Super-tart and herbaceous, rhubarb demands an obnoxiously sweet pairing to counter the sour, and just happens to be creamy vanilla's flavour bestie. The custard-drizzled, tingly rhubarb flavours of **Tavel Rosé** *[Rosé Wine, p.141]*, **Rosé Champagne** and **English Blanc de Noirs** *[Sparkling Wine, pp.118, 116]* are the boozy proof of the pudding.

Whipped Cream & Lemon Soda Creaminess is a sensation: fatty without being greasy, courtesy of tiny fat globules suspended in liquid for that luxuriant, silken mouthfeel. Whipped cream is full of lipid compounds that are destabilised through the whipping process. The lipids cling to air bubbles, creating a frothy house of cards, which is only achieved with a minimum thirty per cent of fat. Lemon soda provides a welcome pop of saccharine citrus to slice through all that richness, with a balancing brightness you'll find in a German **Riesling Sekt**, **Champagne Demi-Sec** *[Sparkling Wine, pp.120, 117]*, **Peach Martini** *[Vodka, p.234]*, a **Tom Collins** *[Gin, p.230]* or an agitated **Tequila Slammer** *[Tequila, p.192]*.

Tropical Creamy

Coconut

Think we've figured out coconut's flavours? Think again. From the delicate fragrance of its water, the dense intensity of its creamed flesh, the muted sweetness of its pulp and the rich nutty notes of the toasting process to its boiled-down smoked-caramel-like sap. Even in its raw form, coconut's flavour Rolodex referneces everything from fruity, milky and buttery to green and woody notes largely brought in by fatty lactone compounds *[Glossary, p.17]*. We connect with coconut's nuances in drinks like the **Pina Colada** *[Rum, p.199]*, **Zinfandel** *[Red Wine, p.161]* and aged **Añejo Tequila** *[Tequila, p.190]*.

Coconut Cream & Pineapple Puerto Rico's national drink must surely have come back around into fashion by now? The **Pina Colada** cocktail *[Rum, p.199]* defines the ritzy 'Club Tropicana' vibe of the eighties with its tried and tested coconut cream and pineapple combo, both card-carrying members of the tropical fruit family that are jam-packed with complementary ester and lactone compounds *[Glossary, pp.16, 17]*. You only have to slice a pineapple down the middle, breathe in and you'll get a lungful of coconut, courtesy of their shared flavour compound, with both flavours apparent in **Aged Japanese Single Malt** *[Whisky, p.245]* and **Coconut Rum** *[Rum, p.196]*. *[Cocktail Recipe, p.200]*

Coconut Pulp & Blueberry They couldn't be more opposed, right? Blueberries, with their floral-fruity-sour flavour profile and coconut meat's openly tropical-creamy-lactic mannerisms, surely that's just a flavour brawl waiting to happen? Not so. Coconuts see something other than sour in blueberries and work hard to draw out their fruitier side. Blueberries' fresh, leafy, fruity, sweetly pungent notes with inflections of eucalyptus are tied up in a flowery-smelling bow thanks to a floral compound that teams up with coconut's buttery, green and woody side in American **Old-Vine Zinfandel** *[Red Wine, p.161]*.

Coconut Sugar & Pink Peppercorn There's a shedload of volatile aromas involved in coconut sugar's pan-heating process: from nutty, sweet, roasty notes to smoky, burnt, bready, caramel-like candyfloss aromas to full-on burnt sugar, not unlike the nuances in **White Rum** *[Rum, p.197]*. Pink peppercorns lack the pungent piperine compound of black pepper, which is also found in other coloured peppercorns, punctuating coconut sugar's caramel and smoked-nut profile with a freshening pop of pine, citrus and herbaceous notes, as per the flavours in an **Añejo Tequila** *[Tequila, p.190]*.

CREAMY

Coconut Water & White Chocolate I would have gone with vanilla over white chocolate, but there's a whisper of cocoa in **Coconut Rum** *[Rum, p.196]* that resides in white chocolate, which was once called 'the white lie' for its lack of chocolatey cocoa solids, poor thing. Fresh coconut water, also known by the deliciously technical name 'coconut liquid endosperm', keeps its coconut-like essence thanks to the fatty acid compounds responsible for that sweet, vanilla-creamy mouthfeel we relish in **Cream Soda** *[Mixers, p.261]* and **Champagne Demi-Sec** *[Sparkling Wine, p.117]*.

Toasted Coconut & Dried Spearmint In a reverse Sampson's hair situation, the drying process ramps up spearmint's superpower compound that's responsible for its characteristic minty-liquorice flavour. Depending on the drying method, spearmint ditches those docile floral and herbaceous aromas present in its raw state, further intensifying its minty impact. Similarly, coconut's mild aromas are concentrated by toasting, with an injection of cooked odours for a nutty, roasty muscle flex. Dried mint and roasted coconut aromas are among the central players in the aromatic profile of an **American Wheat Whisky** *[Whisky, p.249]* and the **Mint Julep** cocktail *[Bourbon, p.252]*.

Flavours

Floral

Herbaceous

Fruity

Sweet

Creamy

Baked

Smoky

Savoury

Minerally

Spicy

If you like . . . **Baked**, *you'll love . . .*

Malty Baked

Malt

Malt is the heart and soul of **Beer** *[Beer, p.237]* and **Whisky** *[Whisky, p.243]* production, the nuts and bolts to their figurative flatpack furniture, if you get the Ikea-based metaphor. Depending on the intensity of cereal malting, malt's breadth of aromas ranges from nuts to biscuits, caramel to sourdough, and raisins to cocoa. Maltol *[Glossary, p.18]* is malt's key compound, with a bittersweet aroma identity that can bring in everything from light honey nuances through to semi-burnt, bitter dark notes via intense roasting, unleashing coffee-odorous compounds.

Barley Malt Syrup & Roast Plantain Mixologists love a funky alternative to, well, everything really. Barley malt syrup is made in the same way as beer, then the roasted grains are boiled to extract their sugars. Whereas simple syrup relies on sugary sucrose, barley syrup is mainly maltose, a compound also known as 'malt sugar', giving it half the sweetness of regular sugar, with malty and earthy undertones that excel in an **Old-Fashioned** cocktail or **Kentucky Straight** *[Bourbon, pp.252, 251]*. Barley syrup is also a primary ingredient in beer, so you'll notice nuances of cooked plantain, banana's savoury, starchy, sweet-potato-adjacent cousin, in **Australian Pale Ale** *[Beer, p.237]*. *[Cocktail Recipe, p.253]*

Malt Biscuit & Heather Honey Allegedly the Rat Pack's preferred poison, the **Rusty Nail** cocktail *[Whisky, p.247]* gives us layers of Scotch whisky over **Drambuie**'s honied, medicinal notes *[Whisky, p.246]*. Malting barley coaxes out the compound, maltol *[Glossary, p.18]*, with biscuity, roasty, caramelly, nutty, earthy aromas and a creamy richness found in **Irish Whiskey** and **Japanese Single Malt** *[Whisky, pp.244, 245]*. I would have gone with malted tea biscuit as a flavour comparison, but malted barley's roasty notes are more akin to coffee's. Heather honey, a key ingredient in Drambuie, itself houses a malty compound among a pantryful of warm woody, floral and sweetly smoky aromas reminiscent of **Rooibos** *[Tea, p.203]*. *[Cocktail Recipe, p.248]*

Malt Loaf & Peanut Butter Not unlike the tanning process, there are different grades of malting, with the highest setting beckoning in the greatest number of brown, caramel and nutty flavours. There's a raft of aroma compounds in a malt loaf, expressing honey, buttery, earthy, vanilla and potato-like odours, with malty inflections also coming through from maltol *[Glossary, p.18]*, a compound brought about by the cooking process. **Brazilian Coffee** *[Coffee, p.204]* is known for its mildly sweet, roasty and nutty nuances, showing aroma traits of the popcorn-flavoured compound found in both peanut butter, malted bread and even **Frangelico** *[Nut Liqueur, p.254]*.

Malted Breakfast Cereal & Marmalade We get it: everything's bad for us, though surely not when it comes to breakfast cereal? Nothing with aromas of spun sugar, cocoa and toasted candyfloss can possibly be naughty. Maltol *[Glossary, p.18]* is the compound behind the caramel-butterscotch aroma of malted cereal, which is brought about by the caramelisation process of degrading sugar via cooking. With enough heat maltol takes a burnt, bittersweet turn, with a flavour not a million miles from marmalade's pine-like, resinous intensity. Both have a caramelised fruitiness offset by bitterness, faithfully replicated by an **Irish Whiskey** *[Whisky, p.244]*.

Malted Honeycomb & Molasses Maltesers may be the only confectionery with milk chocolate over malted honeycomb, aside from Crunchie bars. Balsa-wood-light, there's a drying pinch as the salted honeycomb docks on to your tongue with its powdery toffee craters. Caramelised cereal notes are the mainstay flavours of beer and whisky production, delivered by drying and toasting cereal grain. Browned flavours also abound in molasses, that inky, unctuous, tar-like residue formed by refining sugarcane. Malt, toffee, chocolate and molasses aromas orbit tightly around **Brown Ale** *[Beer, p.238]*, **Irish Coffee** *[Whisky, p.244]* and sticky **Rutherglen Muscat** *[Dessert Wine, p.162]*.

If you like . . . **Baked**, *you'll love . . .*

Nutty Baked

Nuts

True, some nuts are actually seeds or drupes *[Glossary, p.16]*, but this book is no place for nut-based bickering. Flavour-wise, nuts are the missing link between sweet and savoury, with somewhat muted aromas when they're raw. Roasting endows nuts with their flavour superpowers by fully unleashing their volatile odours and introducing new compounds from the cooking process. From the herbal-nutty walnut, the creamy-sweet hazelnut, the rich and buttery macadamia, the potato-powdery chestnut to the pine and citrus powers of the pistachio, we feel their flavours in **Sherry** *[Sherry, p.171]*, **White Wine** *[Wine, p.123]* and **Nut Liqueur** *[Nut Liqueur, p.253]*.

Macadamia Nut & Citrus Honey Is 'soggy' better than 'flabby'? I wouldn't be happy being called either, though macadamias are cruelly referred to as the former in their raw state. True, macadamias have an oleaginous factor that's more about texture than flavour, though they are 'big-boned' with nearly eighty per cent fat, bless them. It's precisely this buttery, lightly nutty creaminess that describes the sublime flavours of **Alsace Pinot Gris**, **Puligny Montrachet**, **Meursault**, **Fiano di Avellino** *[White Wine, pp. 126, 129, 127, 133]*, a **Marsala Sweet Superiore Riserva** *[Fortified Wine, p.168]* or an **English Heritage Cider** *[Cider, p.187]*, which all have the floral powdery nuances and orange-like flavours of citrus honey.

Pistachio Nut & Lime It's an acquired taste all right, with pine resin, citrus notes and nuts as some of the most common flavour descriptors for *Vin Jaune* from France's Jura region, or Greek *Retsina* [*White Wine, pp.131, 133*]. Believe it or not, pistachio nuts are close to lime in flavour, with aromas of pine resin and citrusy, pea-like, woody, peppery, minty, fresh, herbaceous and balsamic notes taking up the rear. Lime, the citrus-family renegade, further amplifies pistachio's pine and cedar notes with a tannoy system of resinous compounds, sewing up the partnership with a pump of citrus and herb, also picked out in the lean and lime-like style of *Gavi di Gavi* [*White Wine, p.134*].

Roast Chestnut & Bruised Apple Press a *Georgian Orange Wine* [*Orange Wine, p.139*] to your lips and feel that chestnut-like powdery, tannic texture, while breathing in aromas so eclectic it's like a fevered flavour dream. It's not to everyone's tastes, and neither is this chestnut and bruised apple combo, *Vin Jaune* from Jura [*White Wine, p.131*] or a *Rhum Agricole Blanc* from Martinique [*Rum, p.199*]. Chestnut has a semi-sweetness that becomes caramel-like thanks to compounds brought on by roasting. Chestnut has a unique earthiness that connects with the nutty notes and bitter flavours brought into apples by bruising, also witnessed in the bone-dry profile of a *Fino Sherry* [*Fortified Wine, p.172*], *Sweet Potato Shōchū* [*Grain Spirits, p.256*] or a heritage *Cask-Aged Cider* [*Cider, p.186*].

Toasted Hazelnut & Digestive Biscuit The loyal digestive biscuit is the flavour version of chunky knitwear, containing homely aromas of wheat flour, butter, cream and malt. Baked nuances loom large in the digestive biscuit, those nutty, buttery flavours that peak when it's dunked into hot tea. Hazelnuts naturally house a bean pyrazine compound [*Glossary, p.18*], giving them an earthy, beany, chocolatey nuttiness also found in coffee. This roasty, fatty and sweet pairing replicates the creamy, buttery, hazelnut and digestive biscuit notes found in *Frangelico* [*Nut Liqueur, p.254*], *Mature* and *Vintage Champagne*, *Franciacorta Riserva* [*Sparkling Wine, pp.117, 118, 121*], *Brown Porter* [*Beer, p.238*] and *VSOP Cognac* [*Brandy, p.177*].

Walnut & Orange Zest I need to namecheck *Nocino* [*Nut Liqueur, p.254*], a liqueur made from walnuts soaked in *Vodka* [*Vodka, p.232*] along with sugar, vanilla and orange zest. The very same flavours can be found in a *Palo Cortado Sherry* [*Sherry, p.173*], with its whip of salinity, or the marmalade-like *Malmsey Madeira* [*Fortified Wine, p.167*]. Walnuts and orange zest share green and pine-like aromas that consummate their partnership, with the nut contingent continuing the green theme with potent lactone compounds [*Glossary, p.17*] that are sweet, herbal, grassy and, bizarrely, shared with celery leaves and lovage.

If you like . . . **Baked**, *you'll love . . .*

Roasty Baked

Coffee

Our morning cup of joe contains almost a thousand aroma compounds. It's staggering, though I won't deep-dive into how the roasting process brings in those spicy, chocolatey, fruity, nutty aromas. I won't mention how certain compounds draw in candied, caramel-like odours, or that others bring about those freshly roasted coffee aromas. Don't get me started on how location affects the coffee beans' aroma profile, from caramel-like *Nicaraguan*, fruity-herbal **Peruvian**, wine-like **Kenyan**, the sweetly floral **Rwandan** or the delicate earthiness of **Mexican Coffee** *[Coffee, p.206]*. Okay, fine, I will if you insist . . .

Kenyan Coffee & Blueberry Ever found a coffee to be wine-like? Just me then. **Kenyan** beans *[Coffee, p.205]* are known for their vibrant fruitiness, which verges on the vinous, and their zesty mouth-gushing qualities that are not unlike those of apples, with which they share malic acid *[Glossary, p.18]*. Kenyan beans tend to twin with blueberries in the flavour stakes, both rocking citrus notes that are brought into blueberries by ascorbic acid, aka vitamin C. The **Primitivo** grape *[Red Wine, p.155]* is famed for its zesty blueberry and spicy coffee flavours, with Kenya's big, bold beans proving the closest flavour match.

Mexican Coffee & White Pepper We don't necessarily think of coffee when we picture Mexico; tequila or burritos would more stereotypically spring to mind. Well, fancy that, **Coffee Tequila** *[Tequila, p.190]* ticks two of Mexico's boxes as I refuse to try burrito-flavoured tequila, if it even exists. **Mexican Coffee** *[Coffee, p.206]* has earthy notes of roasted hazelnuts, dark chocolate and demerara sugar with a decent snap of tang to it, not unlike **Hermitage** *[Red Wine, p.150]* and **Nocino** *[Nut Liqueur, p.254]*. White pepper's compounds give it **Sambuca**-like *[Anise Liqueur, p.219]* woody, herbal, spicy aromas with perceptible camphor notes, which were formerly muted under black pepper's essential oil-blaring shell.

Nicaraguan Coffee & Dark Caramel Picking a coffee bean is enough to get our Nicaraguans in a twist. As a rule of thumb, **Nicaraguan** beans *[Coffee, p.206]* herald flavours of caramel, chocolate and citrus fruit with a sprinkling of vanilla and nuts. Mellower than most South American beans, they're grown at one of the highest elevations, leading to a milder acidity and a medium-level strength. It's the compounds in roasted coffee that we find in well-done caramel, which pump out the same deep butterscotch, burnt-sugar notes and bitterness we crave in an **Espresso Martini** *[Coffee Liqueur, p.208]* or a **Coffee Stout** *[Beer, p.239]*. *[Cocktail Recipe p.209]*

BAKED

Peruvian Coffee & Malted Milk The kick of an *Irish Coffee* [Whisky, p.244] is largely down to how much of a lush we're feeling in the moment. Fighting fiery flavours with further fire isn't a fun way forward, so we want our coffee component to be on the milder side. Hey presto, *Peruvian* beans [Coffee, p.207], known for their herbal, sweet-fruity aromas of plum and orange. Mild mannered with malty notes, they're often chosen as a foundation for coffee-based drinks, delivering a whiff of smoke and honey over malted milk, a combo that's a dead ringer for *Irish Whiskey* over creamy coffee [Whisky, p.244] or *Dry*, *Coffee* and *Chocolate Stouts* [Beer, pp.241, 239]. [Drink Recipe, p.244].

Rwandan Coffee & Popcorn 'In what world does *Vintage Champagne* [Sparkling Wine, p.118] have coffee flavours?', I hear you ask. Pop open a bottle if you don't believe me, for research purposes of course. It's down to a group of compounds from the fermentation process that also makes coffee smell of, well, roast coffee. *Rwandan* beans [Coffee, p.207] are a flavour match for champers: floral-fruity with notes of cherry, grape, lime, white chocolate, cantaloupe, mandarin orange, nectarine and plum. The same compound can be found in popcorn, merging roasted coffee with fatty, fried, buttery aromas all housed neatly under a Champagne cork, in a plunger of *Brazilian Coffee* [Coffee, p.204] or a tumbler full of *White Russian* [Coffee Liqueur, p.208]. [Cocktail Recipe, p.208]

If you like . . . **Baked**, *you'll love . . .*

Toasty Baked

Toast

I love a Venn diagram, and if there was an aroma-based one, toast's circle would overlap nutty, spicy, creamy, baked, roasty and a roster of other odour categories to the point of engulfing them. Like it or not, toast is a major player in boozy aromas, largely brought on by barrel-ageing. Whether it's **Wine** [White Wine, p.123, Red Wine, p.143], **Cognac** [Brandy, p.175], **Whisky** [Whisky, p.243], **Sherry** [Sherry, p.171] or anything that spends any downtime in wood, it's the heat-induced notes of toasted barrel wood that seep into grown-up drinks, creating complex aromas of nuts, spices, vanilla, cream, cereal and fried bread.

Cinnamon Toast & Candied Tarragon What do you mean candied tarragon isn't a thing? Well, tell that to *White Rioja Reserva* [White Wine, p.138] which picks up warming sweet anise-like tones when it's been languishing in barrels. Real tarragon contains estragole, a close relative of anethole [Glossary, pp.16, 15] – star anise and liquorice's major compound. Tarragon may be grassy, but it's also clove-like from a warm and woody compound shared by cinnamon. This is a floral, peppery, warming, woody and grassy aroma combo with savoury notes of our morning toast. Oh, and don't forget the candied-coating.

French Toast & Lemon Balm Like a rescued Golden Retriever puppy, we don't choose French toast, it chooses us. With its fluffed-up toasty notes, figuratively topped with golden syrup, served with butter and powdered sugar, French toast aptly describes the nuances of *Crémant de Loire*, *Crémant D'Alsace* and *Pétillant Naturel Sec Chenin Blanc* [*Sparkling Wine, p.119*] down to a dry, sparkling T. There's nothing major lemon balm shares aromatically with those odours, yet it brings in a lemony top note, a pop of floral and a medicinal, pine-like, woody subwoofer.

Fried Croutons & Apple Pie This isn't a cookery lesson, though the best apple pie is a sacred conglomeration of sweet apple aroma compounds cooked together with cloves, cinnamon and at times even cardamom, collectively framed by browned, baked notes. Croutons bring in oily-creamy, toasty, malty, fatty, deep-fried notes, not to mention roasted popcorn, butter, baked potato and curls of woodsmoke aromas. If that's your aroma bag, seek out similar sweet-savoury flavours in a chilled glass of *Cava de Paraje* or *Vintage Champagne* [*Sparkling Wine, pp.123, 118*].

Melba Toast & Cereal Milk Ah, the flavours of breakfast, without the French *Wheat Vodka* [*Vodka, p.233*] that they're here to describe, of course. Or maybe that is breakfast. I'm not here to judge. With our taste buds on high alert first thing in the morning, milk, steeped in our favourite cereal, is the Goldilocks flavour zone that needs to be chugged straight from the bowl quite frankly. Milk's floral-lactic flavours layered over with sucrose and cereal's gentle grainy, malty, flour-like fragrance, lean into Melba toast's crustless lightly toasty aromas, giving us the basis for the nuanced complexity of *Wheat Whisky* [*Whisky, p.249*].

Toasted Oats & Caramelised Peach Not unlike a good night out on the town, oats come into their own when they're slightly baked. Reticent and hay-like in their raw state, they only give a glimmer of nutty sweetness. Toasting ramps up their aroma game, giving them a flex of earthy, roasted odours that seek out the nutty, creamy, caramel-like notes of peach's pan-fried profile. *VSOP Cognac* [*Brandy, p.177*] captures this partnership with an almost malted sweetness, toasted aromas and peachy, caramel tones thanks to its time spent in charred oak barrels.

If you like . . . **Baked**, *you'll love . . .*

Yeasty Baked

Baked Goods

We're suckers for baked goods; our obsession with *Bake Off* is proof of that particular pudding. Scientific studies show that bakery aromas actually make us kinder, so there's our excuse right there. There's a world of bread aromas, from gingerbread's spiced-honey high notes, strudel's cinnamon-butter fragrance, the caramel-yeasty combo of a brioche bun, focaccia's rich savoury apple flavour to soda bread's lactic tang. Baked aromas are infused into booze during fermentation, where we find their influence in drinks ranging from ***Japanese Whisky*** *[Whisky, p.245]* to ***Sparkling Wine*** *[Sparkling Wine, p.116]*.

Apricot Strudel & Greengage Sabre open a bottle of super-dry ***Cava Brut Nature*** *[Sparkling Wine, p.122]* with a sword, as one does, and you'll go through a checklist of stone fruits, nuts and baked, yeasty aroma descriptors swinging squarely towards greengages and apricot strudel. Greengage plums are small yellowy-green orbs that fill the air with perfume from their treetop vantage point, cracking easily to release their honied essences. Apricots and greengages are a playground of peachy notes and almond-rich compounds, beautifully expressed on their play date with strudel's toy box of buttery, baked, cinnamon and vanilla aromas.

Brioche & Bramley Apple Sauce I'm no fashion guru, but wearing floral prints in spring isn't groundbreaking, nor is pairing apples with baked goods. Unless we're talking the home-cooked, knobbly, rustic apple sauce, not the suspiciously smooth baby-food-like purée. Cooking apples collapses their cell walls, releasing gloopy pectin, which cuddles up to caramelised sucrose and a parchment-light coil of warming cinnamon. Baking brioche buns cranks up their cracker-like malty compounds and blasts out buttery, caramelly, yeasty base notes that do an uncanny impersonation of a lees-aged ***Crémant d'Alsace*** *[Sparkling Wine, p.119]*, a ***Pétillant Naturel Sec Chenin Blanc***, ***Cava de Paraje*** *[Sparkling Wine, pp.119, 123]*, an apple-crisp ***Breton Brut Cidre*** *[Cider, p.187]* and a savoury ***Manzanilla Sherry*** *[Fortified Wine, p.172]*.

Focaccia & Pear Skin We don't use 'bready' to describe baked notes in wine – not on my watch. Given that bread differs wildly according to its preparation, it would be like describing something as tasting 'foody'. Focaccia is a flatbread with a rich oily profile, thanks to the generous input of olive oil. Like wine, olive oil has an almost infinite aromatic variety, but it's the salted-apple note present in many that ties it to the grassy, piney, floral, lime-like pear skin with a teasing bitter-anise note, as seen in a 'bready' bottle of ***Franciacorta Riserva*** *[Sparkling Wine, p.121]*, ***Vintage Perry*** *[Perry, p.188]* and ***Georgian Orange Wine*** *[Orange Wine, p.139]*.

Gingerbread & Smoked Vanilla Talk about the 'six degrees of Kevin Bacon', which is now a board game by the way. Manufactured vanilla shares compounds with wood smoke, giving them interchangeable sweet, woody, caramel, smoky, vanilla-like aroma profiles. When ginger is cooked, its zingy compound morphs into a less pungent, warmly spiced vanilla-adjacent version, also found in a **Châteauneuf-du-Pape** *[Red Wine, p.147]*. Gingerbread also gives us cinnamon, clove, nutmeg, cardamom, anise and honey notes, which tag-team smoked vanilla in an **Aged Japanese Single Malt Whisky** *[Whisky, p.245]*, **Mature Champagne** *[Sparkling Wine, p.117]* and **Sweet Potato Shōchū** *[Grain Spirits, p.256]*.

Soda Bread & Lemon Salt Lean into the zesty, yeasty, citrus and mineral notes of a **Pétillant Naturel Sec Chenin Blanc** *[Sparkling Wine, p.119]*, or 'Pét-Nat' in the biz, and you'll be glad you did. Soda bread's tang is triggered by lactic acid in the buttermilk, which reacts with sodium bicarbonate, aka baking soda. Yes, lemon salt's a thing, ask Gordon Ramsay; just crush up Meyer lemon zest and Malden Salt in a pestle and mortar to make it. It's the jab of the rind's pine-like notes, its spicy-citrus and sodium-based minerality over soda bread that reminds us of Pét-Nat's fermented aromas or the yeasty, citrus scent of a **Crémant d'Alsace** *[Sparkling Wine, p.119]* or **Muscadet Sèvre-et-Mains Sur Lie** *[White Wine, p.128]*.

BAKED

Flavours

Floral

Herbaceous

Fruity

Sweet

Creamy

Baked

Smoky

Savoury

Minerally

Spicy

If you like . . . **Smoky**, *you'll love . . .*

Earthy Smoky

Deep Earth

We're not going to see flavours of peat, graphite, lava rock, wet earth and kerosene on an ice-cream menu any time soon. Believe it or not though, these are common features in booze flavours, whether it's the wild sea kelp and creosote notes of an **Islay Malt** *[Whisky, p.246]*, the graphite and berry flavours of a Spanish **Priorat** *[Red Wine, p.158]*, the igneous minerality of a Sicilian **Nerello Mascalese** *[Red Wine, p.155]*, the earth and honey tones of a Mexican **Mezcal Joven** *[Mezcal, p.193]* or the petrol and stone-fruit notes of an aged German **Riesling** *[White Wine, pp.131, 132]*, we don't have to dig deep to appreciate them.

Graphite & Sloe Berry Licking pencil lead and sucking sloe berries doesn't bring us joy; I learned that the hard way. Sloes are the fruit of the blackthorn bush, bejewelling the autumn landscape before being made into **Sloe Gin** *[Gin, p.181]*. They pack a mouth-puckering wallop without the first frost of the year dialling down their astringency enough for us to savour their plum-like flavours. Together with the notes of a newly sharpened graphite pencil, with its cedar and metallic notes, they mimic the unique slate and black-fruit flavours of the famed reds of **Pauillac** and the Spanish wines of **Priorat** *[Red Wine, pp.146, 158]*.

Kerosine & Nectarine Who secretly loves the smell of a freshy filled tank of petrol? I know I do. It's bizarre that a chemical cocktail of de-icer, lubricant, anti-rust agents and hydrocarbon compounds could get us all fired up. In booze, though? Petrol aromas are famously sought after in aged **Spätlese Riesling** *[White Wine, p.132]*, and are down to a particular compound that can be triggered by sun exposure on grape skins. These kerosine notes are often bundled up with nectarine's creamy, lactic-rich flesh, dripping in honeyed sweetness and offset by a resinous underbelly.

Lava Rock & Pomegranate There are no puns about eruptions of flavour here, though I will say that the **Nerello Mascalese** and **Aglianico del Vulture** *[Red Wine, pp.155, 151]* were lava at first sight. Volcanic regions are said to inject smoky flavours into wine, with an earthy, savoury, herbal character and a dab of salinity. I'm talking basalt, pumice and tufa soils, with volcanic ash beckoning in mouth-watering acidity and pleasing bitterness from minerals like potassium, magnesium and calcium. Pomegranate layers on sweet and sour grenadine notes and balsamic, floral and vegetal aromas from terpene compounds with sweet, wine-like woody flavours.

Peat & Seashore Fans of beach barbecue flavours in booze will lose their minds over **Islay Malt Whisky** *[Whisky, p.246]*. Coastal nuances are rife in island whiskies, with rugged notes of ocean spray, sea kelp, brine, rock pools, barnacles and general seashore-funk. These flavours are often paired with the burnt, tarry, sooty, ashy, first-aid-kit nuances brought in by drying barley via peat, with its distinctive marine aromas. Peat-dried barley malt gives us notes of iodine-rich seaweed, intensely penetrating woodsmoke and creosote-lacquered fishing boats found in **Coastal Whisky** [Whisky, p.246].

Wet Earth & Eucalyptus Honey We're not going mad – that smell of rain on dry soil is scientifically a thing. It's from a compound called geosmin, which is generated by soil-dwelling bacteria, agitated by the rain to release aromas human noses are finely tuned to pick up. Interestingly, the same compound gives beetroot an earthiness not dissimilar to the soaked-earth notes found in a **Mezcal Joven**, **Reposado** or **Añejo** [Mezcal, pp.193, 194, 193]. Mezcal also houses an earthy sweetness comparable to eucalyptus honey, with undertones of menthol and butterscotch and its liquorice-like, bitter-medicinal component, as sipped in honeyed **Traditional Mead** [Herb Liqueur, p.212] or **Suze** [Amaro, p.222].

If you like . . . **Smoky**, *you'll love . . .*

Spicy Smoky

Tobacco

We're not talking cigarette butts in our booze; it's the aroma of tobacco leaves that works its way into our favourite beverages, from aged red wines to port. Aside from its herbaceous fresh leaves, many of tobacco's aromatic mannerisms come courtesy of the process of drying, curing and heating. Massively important are compounds with floral, apple, plum, raisin, tea, rose and tobacco aromas and others with violet, woody and raspberry-like notes. There's hundreds more tobacco-adjacent notes that are brought into the likes of aged **Pauillac** [Red Wine, p.146] and **Vintage Port** [Port, p.170] via barrel-ageing.

Bright Tobacco & Blueberry What's bright tobacco when it's at home? It's flue-cured, meaning dried out in a smoke-free curing barn, which retains tobacco leaf's natural tannins and sugars for a mildly sweet-spicy flavour. **South African Pinotage** [Red Wine, p.157] is a hub of sweetly smoked aromas, juxtaposed against the creamy, herbaceous, woody and citrusy profile that blueberry nuances bring to the blend. Latent pine notes in blueberries are thanks to terpene compounds, which also gift them their earthy, clove-like flavours. Together, flue-cured tobacco and blueberry notes are a taste worth acquiring in this unique South African red or in the familiar flavours of a **Montepulciano D'Abruzzo** or **Ribera del Duero** [Red Wine, pp.154, 159].

Cigar Box & Parma Violets Next time you inspect your Montecristo cigar collection, dip your nose deep into the box and inhale its resinous cedar and ashy, charred, smoky tobacco-leaf notes. Cigar boxes are largely made of Spanish cedar, which is prized for its aromatic wood that mimics the terpene-like resiny aromas in an aged *Vintage Port* [Port, p.170] and *Bordeaux Pauillac* [Red Wine, p.146]. We often see 'cigar box' referenced side by side with violets in vintage port tasting notes, specifically Parma Violet, with its gamut of shrill high notes and deep, orris-root, powdery base tones, also captured in *Amarone della Valpolicella* and *Chianti Classico Riserva* [Red Wine, pp.151, 153].

Dark-Fire Tobacco & Black Olive *Crozes-Hermitage* [Red Wine, p.149] is a swarthy red with aromas of black fruit, tobacco and black olives, and it's a similar story for *Washington State Syrah* [Red Wine, p.162]. Dark-Fire cured tobacco has matching savoury, woody and smoky aromas, containing almost zero sucrose for a super-intense, almost cigar-like flavour experience a lot like *Lapsang Souchong* [Tea, p.201]. Smoky-smelling compounds are introduced through drying over hickory, oak and pine wood, mirroring the flavours of black olives and their nutty, bittersweet, woody, floral, herbaceous, spicy, earthy tobacco nuances brought in by fermentation and roasting.

Pipe Tobacco & Crème de Cassis Most of us are probably sitting in a leather wing chair right now in a wood-panelled drawing room, pulling on a pipe in front of a roaring fire. Spot on? There should be an aromatic combination of sweet hay, moss, autumn leaves, tea, honey, caramel, leather, nuts and woodsmoke filling the air. Pair this with Crème de Cassis's concentrated notes of dark plum and sandalwood with musty aromas of cat litter tray, courtesy of a fermentation-triggered compound, and bingo: *Pauillac*, *South African Cabernet Sauvignon* and *Priorat* [Red Wine, pp.146, 157, 158] with their spirity cassis depth and spicy, herbaceous undertones of dried pipe tobacco.

Turkish Tobacco & Wild Raspberry These two flavours are like peas in a pod – not literally, although anything's possible in the world of flavours. Turkish tobacco is gently sun-cured, bringing out pronounced aromas of lavender-like, woody and raspberry-adjacent notes, with sweet hay, saffron and medicinal nuances. Wild raspberries contain three times the bosky, red-fruit intensity of regular berries, thanks to an abundance of a compound called raspberry ketone. *Aglianico del Vulture* [Red Wine, p.152] majors on wild raspberry and Turkish tobacco flavours, so much so that it's been dubbed the *Barolo* [Red Wine, p.152] of southern Italy, sharing notes with its sticky sidekick *Recioto della Valpolicella* [Dessert Wine, p.166].

If you like . . . **Smoky,** *you'll love . . .*

Woody Smoky

Woody

Immature wood jokes aside, the barky, smoked notes we pick up in booze are largely courtesy of barrel-ageing, making us question whether some wines are made by winemakers or carpenters. From **Spanish Reds** *[Red Wine, p.158]* to **Mezcal** *[Mezcal, p.193]*, used cleverly, flavours veer from light, sweet and spicy with a whiff of smoke to deeply charred, bitter and medicinal. Much of this is down to the cooper who beat the barrel, and, depending on the char intensity, woody aromas vary from the smoked bakery notes of hickory, the perfumed fragrance of sandalwood, mesquite's baritone minty notes to cedar's earthy, alpine forest adjacency and pine's peaty, resinous aromas.

Cedar & Saffron This pairing shouldn't work, as saffron has a fair whack of bitterness from a medicinal-tasting compound that dries to form an essential oil that's usually twinned with sweeter flavours to offset its medicinal mannerisms. Not here – cedar is stuffed full of compounds with fresh, pine-like, woody, earthy and sandalwood aromas; I mean, jet fuel is even known to contain one of its compounds for goodness' sake. In no way linked to the aeronautical industry, **Fernet-Branca** *[Amaro, p.224]* owes its bitterness, iridescent glow and medicinal notes to saffron and finishes on a pine and cedar-like base note.

Hickory Campfire & Loganberry Ah, camping, those golden sparks, crackles of wood, curls of smoke and bad ghost stories – in that order. Hickory is commonly used for campfires, giving off robust smoky aromas when its lignin compounds *[Glossary, p.17]* are broken down by heat. Fibres found in wood are essentially sucrose, so heating them releases aromas as varied as caramelised, fruity, floral and fresh bread. Paired alongside sweet-sour loganberries, with their herbal, thyme-like, woody edges, and we start to see the aroma outline of a **Ribera del Duero** or a muscle-bound **Madiran** *[Red Wine, pp.159, 150]*.

Mesquite & Cardamom Talk about intense, mesquite wood gives off deeply pungent, earthy-smelling smoke that's threaded through with a cadence of perfumed aromatics. Cardamom is the lifeblood of our favourite Indian dishes, prized for its exotically floral-citrus fragrance, which is offset by its eucalyptus and cooling minty notes. One of cardamom's major compounds is found in eucalyptus, while another is spotted in lavender and citrus fruit. It also shares a compound with basil, bringing in sweet mint and herbs, collectively matching the smoky, citrus and floral aromas of a **Mezcal Reposado** *[Mezcal, p.194]*, **Zucca Rabarbaro** *[Amaro, p.225]*, **Coastal** and **Islay Malt Whisky** *[Whisky, p.246]* or a cup of **Lapsang Souchong** *[Tea, p.201]*.

SMOKY

Pine Resin & Smoked Paprika *Lapsang Souchong [Tea, p.201]* allows me to bust out the word 'empyreumatic', aka flavours that come from fire – smoky, scorched, grilled, burnt, you get it. Drying via pine smoke infuses the leaves with resinous aroma compounds that aren't found in other teas, with smoky, turpentine-like compounds delivering aromas of pine, peat, smoked paprika, sawdust, pencil, pepper and vanilla. Likewise, smoking brings in cooking-related aromas to the dried chilli pepper notes of paprika, conjuring odours of smoked earth, hints of chocolate, caramel, citrus and even grilled lardons, which are all aroma components of ***Mezcal Reposado*** *[Mezcal, p.194]*.

Sandalwood & Raspberry Chin up. Sandalwood is a mood enhancer, and its signature aromas are mainly down to incense-rich, woody odours we'd recognise from New Age gift shops in Camden Market. Raspberry shares a woody aroma, releasing violet, barky and red-fruit notes not disimilar to those you'd find when you nuzzle a nose of ***LBV Port*** *[Fortified Wine, p.169]*. There's also a smoke-dried element to sandalwood thanks to a clove-like compound, which is also responsible for its soft floral and balsamic notes. Collectively, these are key aromas found in a hauntingly brawny Uruguayan ***Tannat*** *[Red Wine, p.160]*.

Flavours

Floral

Herbaceous

Fruity

Sweet

Creamy

Baked

Smoky

Savoury

Minerally

Spicy

If you like . . . **Savoury**, *you'll love . . .*

Brothy Savoury

Umami

Umami is a Marmite taste, quite literally; it is the recently accepted fifth taste with a rich, meaty flavour that unlocks depth in accompanying ingredients. Well, it translates as 'delicious taste' in Japanese, so the clue's in the name. The Romans first fermented fish into a condiment called liquamen, a funky version of ketchup, forming the savoury blueprint for sauces like Worcestershire. Cue the brothy fruitiness of a **Bloody Mary** *[Vodka, p.235]*, the miso-floral aromas of **Shōchū** *[Grain Spirit, p.256]*, the honeyed soy flavours in **Koshu Sake** *[Sake, p.243]*, the nutty brine notes found in **Amontillado Sherry** *[Sherry, p.171]* and the tofu and sesame aromas of a **Junmai-Shu Sake** *[Sake, p.242]*.

Olive Brine & Walnut Brittle An umami section with no sherry would be like a party without cake: just disappointing. **Amontillado**, **Palo Cortado Sherry** *[Fortified Wine, pp.171, 173]* and **Koshu Sake** *[Sake, p.243]* bust out hefty notes of olive brine and walnut brittle, perfect for savoury junkies feeding a flavour craving. Olives are a conglomerate of fatty, floral, fruity, honeyed, tea-like and citrus notes, prized for their briny flavours from the salting process to banish their naturally bitter notes. Walnuts share olives' green, earthy mannerisms with an added blast of astringency from their papery membrane, which is offset by the sweetness of its caramelised outer casing, flavours that collectively conjure **Baijiu Sesame Aroma** *[Grain Spirits, p.255]*.

Red Miso & Pretzel Crust Koji-kin *[Glossary, p.17]* is the hardest-working mould in Japan – just ask soy sauce or miso. It kick-starts the fermentation of soya beans into miso and soy sauce, creating compounds that form the aroma of roasted foodstuffs. Caramel, fruity, nutty and cheesy are notes we find in miso, along with an umami component from monosodium glutamate. Red miso is aged for longer, bringing in complex aromas not unlike a mature wine. Pretzel has been treated with a diluted lye solution to bring about its chewy super-baked crust, with intense notes of butter, malt, mushroom, cooked potato, burnt caramel and cheese, which meets with miso in the spirity notes of a Japanese **Sweet Potato Shōchū** or **Baijiu Sauce Aroma** *[Grain Spirits, pp.256, 255]*.

Soy Sauce & Dry-Roasted Peanut Soy sauce is such a flavour saviour, its influence should be in everything, including beverages. Cue **Koshu Sake** *[Sake, p.243]*, with savoury soy sauce and dry-roasted peanut notes brought in by refrigerated ageing. Koji-Kin mould *[Glossary, p.17]* takes centre stage in fermenting soy sauce and sake, coaxing out umami, salty, caramel, malty, cooked potato, fruit, maple syrup and smoky notes. Likewise, dry-roasting conjures complex compounds in peanuts, ramping up their raw beany, woody, pine-like flavours to full-on scorched caramel and earth, putting the 'mmm' in umami and the 'ooh' in **Baijiu Sauce Aroma** [Grain Spirits, p.255] and the **Bloody Mary** [Vodka, p.235].

Tofu & Toasted Sesame Seed Anyone who's suspicious of tofu, just think of it as cheese. It's not, but it acts like it, with a similar texture and mild, creamy, beany, chalky, cooked-pasta aromas, becoming super-stinky when fermented. A green, leafy compound is a major part of tofu's subtler aromas, which has the potential to turn lightly earthy during the production process. **Junmai-Shu** [Sake, p.242] is the purest form of Sake, with its savoury tofu tones, and sesame seeds, with their umami, sulphurous, meaty, nutty, fruity, grain-like and earthy compounds developed through toasting, can also be sipped in **Baijiu Sesame** and **Sauce Aroma** [Grain Spirits, p.255].

Worcestershire Sauce & Tomato Seed Flushing out a hangover with a **Bloody Mary** [Vodka, p.235] is one thing, but I'd be anxious about the addition of pungent clam juice in a **Bloody Caesar** [Vodka, p.232]. Tomato's seeds are rich in glutamic acids; think of those gelatinous tadpoles as tomato's collective placental sac, like a rich umami jelly. Anchovy fermentation is key to freeing umami in Worcestershire sauce, releasing a compound that tastes distinctly savoury. Throw in vinegar, molasses, salt, garlic with its sulphurous compounds, sweet-sour tamarind, warming clove, chilli and super-savoury asafoetida spices and we've just pieced together Worcestershire sauce. All we need now is vodka and a celery stirrer. [Cocktail Recipes, pp.235, 232]

If you like . . . **Savoury**, *you'll love . . .*

Earthy Savoury

Mushroom

This section is a forager's happy place, with all those odours of fungi over the heavy, damp woodiness we inhale on a forest walk. Barky, earthy, forest-floor aromas are largely thanks to a compound called 'mushroom alcohol', with some fungi even whiffing of almonds, shellfish, garlic and anise. Fresh mushroom flavours in wine tie in with game, leather and damp earth, with grape skins actually harbouring the same compound given off by soil after a rainstorm. Just look at black truffle's musty sweetness, which is found in **Mature Champagne** [Sparkling Wine, p.117], or the brothy nuttiness of dried porcini mushrooms in **Chinon** [Red Wine, p.148].

Black Truffle & Mocha Coffee This paragraph smells of rich people's problems, so Gucci-strap yourself in. Black truffle fungus and mocha notes appear in **Mature Champagne** [Sparkling Wine, p.117]; see what I mean? To some, truffles reek of locker room and sweaty socks, while others find their musty odours sensual, seductive and unique. It's all down to our personal feelings for truffle's sulphurous, cabbagey and garlicky compound. There's a redeeming chocolate note to cooked black truffle, echoed in earthy, gamey mocha coffee from the Yemen, with its raisin, cassia bark and cardamom aromas, not to be confused with the chocolate 'mocha' monstrosity served in coffee shops.

Chanterelle & Apricot This is the greatest flavour match you've never heard of. Chanterelles are those golden trumpet-shaped mushrooms, also known as girolles, prized by chefs for the fruity, peppery, grassy notes they bring to the plate. They're known for their apricot-like flavours, with a side hustle in pumpkin, cooked carrot and butternut squash characteristics. Chanterelles and apricots share compounds, with peach and woodland aromas layered over with green grassy notes. **Rhum Agricole Blanc** [Rum, p. 199] is super-rustic in style and ripe with earthy, herbaceous chanterelle and creamy apricot notes.

Dried Shiitake & Caramel Stinkier than a wheel of Camembert in a mosh pit, **Baijiu Sauce Aroma** [Grain Spirits, p. 255] is a notch beyond an acquired taste. With flavours ranging from shiitake mushrooms, soy sauce and bitter herbs, Baijiu is savoury central, with a redeeming glimmer of caramel for those with a sweet tooth. Shiitake mushrooms major on a smelly, sulphurous compound that's intensified by drying and rehydration. Aromas of malt, butter, grass, rubber, popcorn, earth and cooked potato come through in shiitakes, offset by caramel's sugar crystals, which, bizarrely, share earthy compounds found in fungi.

Forest Floor & Black Raspberry 'Bosky' is slang for forest floor, or if we're feeling fancy, 'sous bois'. These are terms for woodland aromas – think damp earth, fungi and fallen branches. Without running our tongues along a forest walking trail, we can find these deliciously damp, decomposing, nostalgic aromas in **Central Otago Pinot Noir**, Sicilian **Nerello Mascalese**, **Beaujolais**, **Aged Red Burgundy**, **Côte-Rôtie** or a **Châteauneuf-du-Pape** [Red Wine, pp. 156, 155, 146, 145, 148, 147]. Earthy notes of new dawn and ploughed field are down to volatile sulphur compounds brought in by fermentation. Black raspberries, hailed as 'homegrown Haribo', bring in those raspberry-cordial-meets-blackberry-jam flavours, along with a bosky, minty component.

Porcini & Lavender It should really be cep over porcini, given **Chinon** [Red Wine, p. 148] is from the Loire. Oh, well, there's a rich nutty, brothy character to porcinis, over and above the usual moss, nut and soil aromas ushered in by fungi's formative compound, mushroom alcohol. It's no wonder porcinis are coined the 'tsars of mushrooms', as their aromas survive drying, picking up additional complexity in the process. Their earthy-sweet flavours connect with the fragrant woodiness of lavender's major ionone compound [Glossary, p. 17], with its evergreen notes of camphor, which ushers in dried-spice aromas through its ties to rosemary.

If you like . . . **Savoury**, *you'll love . . .*

Meaty Savoury

Meat

Just to be clear, if you find meat in your favourite tipple, send it back. The theme of this segment refers to meaty flavours found in beverages. Whether it's roast beef's brothy caramel aromas that are prized in northern **Rhône Reds** *[Red Wine, p.145]*, smoky bacon's sweet-earthy flavours we savour in **Washington State Syrah** *[Red Wine, p.162]*, wild game's fragrantly pronounced notes as spotted in **Aged Red Burgundy** *[Red Wine, p.145]*, salami's cured-spiced odours that come through in a **Chianti Classico Riserva** *[Red Wine, p.153]* or the richly tannic leather notes that emanate from a glass of **Rioja Gran Reserva** *[Red Wine, p.159]*.

Full-Grain Leather & Tobacco Leaf Replace any thoughts of John Wayne, muddy boots, damp dog lead and horse blanket with new saddle, expensive gloves, first-edition books and Birkin bags. There's around fifty chemicals that go into processing leather, from chrome and dyes through to oils, which collectively give off rich earthy aromas that remind us of prairies, clean chaps and riding crops. These flavours find themselves in wine, particularly in reds like **Rioja Gran Reserva** and **Aged Rhône Grenache** and **Ribera del Duero** *[Red Wine, pp.159, 145, 159]* via tannins, which are actually used by tanning houses to preserve hides. Tobacco leaf aromas freshen things up with notes of saffron, grassy, hay-like hints and a woody, violet edge.

Italian Salami & Espresso Salami spins a lot of plates aroma-wise – for a start there's the influence of lactic acid bacteria on fatty meat during dry-curing, then there's the herbs and spices to factor in. Aromas range from meat, fruit, pine, mushroom and pepper to citrus, flowers, camphor, spice, wood and potting soil. Anise odours loom large courtesy of absinthe-like compounds derived from fennel seeds in the salami mix. Espresso coffee has its own buttery caramel notes from roasting, along with an earthy nuttiness and fruity-musty aromas that converge with salami notes in a cheeky glass of **Chianti Classico Riserva** *[Red Wine, p.153]*.

Roast Beef & Black Tea Lady Gaga's meat dress is now in my head, just as beef and black tea flavours are lodged in **Hermitage** and **Washington State Syrah** *[Red Wine, pp.150, 162]*, where meaty, brothy and beefy meet floral, honeyed and earthy. Beef's intensity depends on the breed of cow, its diet and fat content, with a particular compound responsible for making it smell, well, beefy, with caramelised, fatty and buttery aromas brought in by cooking. Black tea shares savoury aromas with beef, majoring on woody, floral and cooked apple notes with sweet tea and caramel-covered popcorn nuances from drying and fermentation.

Smoky Bacon & Clove It's the cooked-breakfast aroma that makes us zombie-walk to the kitchen of a morning. Bacon's smoky, sweet-fatty aromas are down to lipids breaking down in the cured, smoked pork belly, releasing compounds with buttery, nutty, caramelly aromas. Smoking injects sweet bonfire notes into pork, with a compound called maple lactone *[Glossary, p.17]* giving bacon its uniquely fatty-savoury odour. Pork enjoys an earthy partnership with clove's formative chemical compound, with warming camphor aromas that pique the sweet, smoky, earthy notes in bacon, masterfully impersonating the flavours of a ***Washington State Syrah*** *[Red Wine, p.162]* or aged ***Koshu Sake*** *[Sake, p.243]*.

Wild Game & Cola 'A brace of pheasants hanging in the pantry', describes the meaty aromas in booze that are lighter and more fragrant than beef's. Although game's aromatic compounds lack appeal when they're raw, cue the mothball aromas, heating causes the fatty acids to break down into volatile compounds that include fruity-scented esters *[Glossary, p.16]*, floral alcohols, cheesy-lactic notes and caramel odours. Cola brings in a spicy-woody element, with the minty-eucalyptus compound, earthy-soapy aromas and smoked vanilla component, making all the aromatic gestures of a gamey spiced ***Aged Red Burgundy*** *[Red Wine, p.145]*.

Flavours

Floral

Herbaceous

Fruity

Sweet

Creamy

Baked

Smoky

Savoury

Minerally

Spicy

If you like . . . **Minerally**, *you'll love . . .*

Marine Minerally

The Coast

Louis Armstrong summed up jazz music by saying, 'Man, if you have to ask, you'll never know'. He may as well have been talking about minerality in drinks, which is equally elusive and open to interpretation – half poetry, half science. Although defining minerality is like punching smoke, there's something about saline flavours that are easier to prove than, say, geological flavours, like rocks. That said, from the beach-pebble mannerisms of **Muscadet** *[White Wine, p.128]* to the sea spray intensity of a **Fino Sherry** *[Fortified Wine, p.172]*, call them salty, sapid or seasoned, but seashore-adjacent flavours can be some of the most sublime, if you like that sort of thing.

Beach Pebble & Thyme I prefer sand for lying on, though I'll take a beach pebble to describe my drink. It's that smooth, cool, pebble-like, saline experience you get from sipping a **Muscadet Sèvre-et-Mains Sur Lie**, **Chablis**, **Assyrtiko**, **Greco di Tufo** *[White Wine, pp.128, 126, 133, 134]* or a herbal-umami **Nerello Mascalese** *[Red Wine, p.155]*. Salty acids, triggered by grape fermentation, are thought to be partly responsible for salinity in wine, with sulphurous compounds bringing in whispers of sea life. Thyme's cooling compound complements salty notes with an appealingly bitter, herbal murmur on the finish, mirroring the grassy-saline notes of **Matcha** *[Tea, p.203]*.

Iodine & Garrigue Forget the aromas of hospitals, blood and metal, it's iodine's sea-briny, coastal persona we want for this exercise. Iodine is a natural element found in seawater that's created by compounds produced by marine worms and algae for those briny sea-life flavours. Sicilian **Grillo** *[White Wine, p.135]* fits the profile, with an accompanying aroma of garrigue, the low-lying shrub you'll have kicked while out hiking in the Mediterranean hills. Flavours of rosemary, lemon verbena, lavender, marjoram, juniper and thyme meet earthy, salty and appropriately, rocky, given garrigue comes from *carra*, the Provençal word for rock.

Pacific Oyster & Meyer Lemon Oysters are basically the ocean in fishy form, and if you've ever shucked one, you'll know its dense, calcified casing is used in wine lingo to depict chalky, saline notes. Pacific oyster flesh is sweet, creamy, buttery, nutty and melon-like through to coppery, briny and marine. It's a product of its surroundings and the influences in its bay: the ocean, its habitat, phytoplankton, marsh vegetation and minerals in the mud. Cue the marine style of a **Bloody Caesar** *[Vodka, p.232]* or **Reuilly Sauvignon Blanc** *[White Wine, p.130]*, which share the sweet-tart flavours of Meyer lemon and balancing bergamot notes.

Rock Pool & Quince Cheese Bear with me on the rock-pool analogy, as these complex ecosystems are a blend of brine, fresh water, shrimps, crabs, small fish and sea herbs. I'm not saying we'll find a hermit crab in a coastal *South African Chenin Blanc* *[White Wine, p.137]*, though there's a marked marine component to both Chenin and rock pools, a suggestion of sea life, a herbaceous element and, in the case of the wine, long flavour fronds of perfumed quince cheese. When it's cooked in sugar, quince becomes lusciously sweet with a bitter nuance and a perfumed flourish, flavours often picked up in this South African white.

Sea Spray & Bread Dough You've got to admire the moxie of a *Manzanilla*, *Amontillado* or a *Fino Sherry* *[Fortified Wine, pp.172, 171, 172]*, that unapologetically saline style with accents of raw bread dough. Sea spray has a whole network of aromas, with sulphurous compounds from algae and seaweed woven in with airborne salt for a marine-tinged whip of saline. Bring in bread dough at the proving stage, the action of yeast munching on maltose as it ferments, and it delivers those intensely yeasty, malty, umami notes we associate with bone-dry Sherry, *Reuilly Sauvignon Blanc* *[White Wine, p.130]* and the umami style of *Junmai-Shu* *[Sake, p.242]*.

If you like . . . **Minerally**, you'll love . . .

Rocky Minerally

Minerals

Debbie Downers of science reckon that the chances of sensing actual minerals in beverages is slim; talk about a buzzkill. Well, if minerals are virtually tasteless, how are we getting sensations of 'flint', 'slate' or 'gravel' in our glass, never mind 'sucking on wet stones'? Turns out, we're not going bonkers, compounds in the liquid mimic the characteristics of gunmetal in *Gavi* *[White Wine, p.134]*, crushed gravel in *Mencia* reds *[Red Wine, p.158]*, slatey sensations in *Mosel Kabinett Riesling Trocken*, flintiness in *Chablis* *[White Wine, pp.132, 126]* and wet stones in *Mineral Water*. Our mental associations piece together the rest.

Crushed Gravel & Pomegranate Who hasn't shoved dirty gravel into their mouth at some point? Spoiler alert: it doesn't end well. That aside, the combination of earth, stone, rubber tyre and a pinch of salinity from trace elements of calcium and magnesium in the soil is not dissimilar to what we pick up in a red wine from *Mencia* *[Red Wine, p.158]*. Cue the word 'sapid', meaning a savoury, salt-seasoned taste that makes you salivate, which is very different to zesty acidity. Pomegranates have an earthiness, punctuating the wine's sapidity with herbaceous aromas of anise and mint housed in their sweet-tangy ruby seeds.

Flint & Lemon Balm Here's a brain-teaser: *Chablis [White Wine, p.126]* tastes of flint, a variety of silicon dioxide, the compound that produced the wine glass we're sipping from. In a further plot twist Chablis's soil is made up of fossilised seashells, not flint, with the mineral-flinty note brought in by fermentation. Lemon balm lends a lift of citrus, stuffed with floaty florals that collectively mimic Chablis's citrus, flowery, flinty inflections, as tasted in *Sancerre*, *Pouilly Fumé*, the taut, mineral lines of *Puligny Montrachet* and *Gavi di Gavi [White Wine, pp.131, 129, 129, 134]* and the super-minerally *Vichy Catalan [Mixers, p.259]*.

Gunmetal & Grapefruit Please let's not run our tongues over the barrel of a firearm. Deal? Gunmetal refers to the struck steel frizzen, or hammer, on an antique musket, which kicks up filings of burning steel particles as it connects with the gunpowder. Unoaked whites are particularly susceptible to taking on smoky, metallic, mineral-adjacent characteristics, largely from a sulphurous compound generated by yeast metabolism during fermentation. Grapefruit tag-teams the gunmetal in Italian *Gavi di Gavi* and Loire *Pouilly Fumé [White Wine, pp.134, 129]*, adding its own musky aromas and warm citrusy, woody notes from its deliciously bitter blast.

River Stone & Alka-Seltzer 'Smooth', 'slick', 'cool' and 'rocky' are the best terms I can muster to describe a river stone. It's that freshwater stony purity that evokes the flavours of mineral water, which sounds like the marketing blurb on the back of a bottle. Unlike wine, groundwater completely dissolves minerals, giving it an undeniably minerally, sapid and salty taste. *Vichy Catalan [Mixers, p.259]* is high in dissolved minerals, bicarbonates, sulphates, halides, sodium and potassium, making it taste psychedelically refreshing. Similarly, Alka-Seltzer majors on sodium bicarbonate for a closely matched flavour experience, even delivering a twist of citrus for authenticity.

Slate Tile & Granny Smith You don't have to be a roofer to recognise the smell of hot slate tiles after a downpour: iron, earth, clay and smoke. I'm sure we'd get a tongueful of mineral salts if we gave one a lick, though I can't say I've given it a go. Slate is also used metaphorically to describe white wines with clean minimal lines and edgy acidity. Bingo, *Mosel Kabinett Riesling Trocken* or a sweet-saline *Spätlese Riesling [White Wine, p.132]* to which the term is frequently twinned. With the tangy outline of a lean green Granny Smith apple, its cell walls bulging with malic acid *[Glossary, p.18]* and herbaceous-tasting compounds, the wine is beautifully offset by a slate-like salinity.

If you like . . . **Minerally**, *you'll love . . .*

Vegetal Minerally

Sea Greens

Terms like 'salty' and 'saline' don't do coastal aromas justice – those iodine, crustacean, vegetal, sulphurous odours kicked up by the breakdown of seaweed and algae. Sea greens act like amped-up versions of our favourite vegetables, bringing inimitable spice, umami notes and an inbuilt seasoning from their maritime ties. Cue the lemon-saline *Picpoul de Pinet*, *Greco di Tufo*'s spice-rack sapidity, the citrus-grassy tones of *Vinho Verde* [*White Wine, pp.129, 134, 136*], *Coastal Whisky*'s peppery-truffle intensity [*Whisky, p.246*] or the bitter-green profile of *Grillo* from Sicily [*White Wine, p.135*].

Dried Wakame & Preserved Eureka Lemon Admittedly, 'lip-stinger' doesn't sound great, though it does in the context of its direct translation, *Picpoul de Pinet* [*White Wine, p.129*]. Lean, marine and lightly floral, Picpoul's style is well represented by the saline-citrusy profile of dried wakame and preserved lemon. Wakame is a brown seaweed with mildly maritime, oyster-like aromatics majoring on a lynchpin compound in marine odours that's intensified by drying. Eureka lemons, preserved in salt, bring in umami and fermented notes, their thicker skin withstanding the 'pickling' process and further concentrating their floral aromas.

Pepper Dulse & Burnt Orange *Coastal Whiskies* [*Whisky, p.246*] take style tips from the rugged, wave-tormented, barnacle-suckered Davy Jones's locker-like seascapes that surround them. Kelp, iodine, salt, smoke and iron are common aromatic markers, with the similarly flavoured pepper dulse seaweed coined 'the truffle of the sea' for its intense, peppery, garlicky, umami, anchovy, black-olive and saline flavours. There's a mushroom-like sulphur compound at play, with others providing pepper and light smoke nuances. Likewise waving a blowtorch over orange peel promotes scorched-marmalade notes, pungent pine-like odours from the expressed essential oils and a smoky nuance, all reminiscent of a coastal single malt.

Rock Samphire & Asian Pear Let's go easy on the Asian pear; it's having an identity crisis. Apple-like in texture and aesthetics, it shares sulphurous aroma compounds with pineapples, a floral component with roses and gets its woody, herbaceous note from, well, being a pear. Likewise *Greco di Tufo* [*White Wine, p.134*] has delicate aromas of pome fruit, with citrus, florals, a crisp texture and a thwack of something salty. Samphire sums up the savoury framework for which this wine is famed, with saline succulence, a minty-citrusy moment and a green, fennel-come-dill aroma.

Sea Grapes & Kiwi *Vinho Verde* *[White Wine, p.136]* is the white wine equivalent of bubble tea. Similar to sea grapes, it's light, crisp, citrusy and saline with herbal notes of **Green Tea** *[Tea, p.200]*. Biting down on those marine micro-orbs produces a popping sound, which the Japanese call 'punchi punchi', squirting out a sweet, briny substance with a hint of herbaceous. That grassy compound is shared by the kiwi, a hairy swollen ball that's actually a berry, continuing the green, salty theme with the vegetal, herbaceous and citrus flavours found in **Picpoul de Pinet** *[White Wine, p.129]*.

Sea Spaghetti & Lemon Blossom Sea spaghetti's other name is 'sea thong'. I know which I'd prefer to be called. Brown fronds up to a metre long deliver a mildly saline, cucumber, grassy, nutty flavour not a million miles from a saline-citrusy **Assyrtiko** from Santorini *[White Wine, p.133]*. Brown seaweeds major on grassy, leafy aromas with herbal, floral, nutty, fruity and fatty mannerisms, as opposed to the mushroom and earthy tones of red wrack seaweed. Lemon blossom provides the sweet and floral top note, with woody, herbaceous aromas wrapping up Assyrtiko's saline, lemony flavour package.

Flavours

Floral

Herbaceous

Fruity

Sweet

Creamy

Baked

Smoky

Savoury

Minerally

Spicy

If you like . . . **Spicy,** *you'll love . . .*

Bitter Spicy

Bitters

You know that back-of-the-tongue thwack you get from sipping something bitter? It seems that sensation has evolved as a defence mechanism, saving our primitive ancestors from poisons and toxins. Interestingly, when this happens the body steps up its saliva and digestive juice production to get rid of the threat, and, voila, the non-toxic aperitif was invented. Everything from quinine's citrus influence on **Tonic Water** *[Mixers, p.259]*, gentian's earthy-bitterness in **Suze** *[Amaro, p.222]*, the bittersweet medicinal notes of **Cynar** *[Amaro, p.224]* to **Campari**'s line of fruit and bitter herbs *[Amaro, p.223]* to the floral bitterness of **Cocchi Americano** *[Vermouth, p.175]*.

Blood Orange & Rocket Putting aside the meaning of the emoji, eggplants get their dark pigment from anthocyanins *[Glossary, p.15]*, compounds that are also responsible for the sanguine appearance of blood orange flesh. Flavour-wise, blood oranges pump out unique raspberry, cranberry and fruit-punch flavours that make them stand out from their orange siblings. Their light, red-fruit bitterness leans into the similarly flavoured profile of a **Paloma** cocktail *[Tequila, p.191]* or **Campari** *[Amaro, p.223]*, with a secret blend of rocket-adjacent bitter herbs that provide a similarly sulphurous, pungently peppery component.

Gentian Root & Pomelo Peel Face-planting on to the dirt in a field full of yellow flowers while sucking a bittersweet liquorice stick, crushing the pomelo in your pocket; that's what **Suze** tastes like *[Amaro, p.222]*. Its main ingredient is gentian root, which majors on compounds with stridently earthy, bitter tones, florals and anise. Given its ties to grapefruit and bitter oranges, pomelo peel leans into orange-zest aromas with a spicy, woody, lime-like, green, grapefruity, floral and resinous skill set that bounces off gentian's botanical bitterness in a bag of **Earl Grey** *[Tea, p.202]*, an **Indian Tonic Water** *[Mixers, p.259]* a **White Negroni** *[Gin, p.227]* or a bottle of **Cocchi Americano** *[Vermouth, p.175]*.

Globe Artichoke & Saffron Another foodstuff resembling a petrified pangolin, globe artichokes aren't noted for their connection to booze, aside from forming the key ingredient in Italian amaro **Cynar** *[Amaro, p.224]*. Globes mess with our minds via a compound called cynarin *[Glossary, p.16]*, which disables our sweet flavour receptors, bestowing the next thing we put in our mouths with a false saccharine taste. Artichoke's bitter, green nuttiness comes through with medicinal, hay-like tones that are similar to saffron, a spendy spice with notes of sea air, sweet-dried grass and a hint of rusting metal. Saffron's major compound expresses bitter-herbaceous notes, tempered by honeyed and super-floral nuances.

<u>**Quinine & Lemon Oil**</u> Lemons don't stop at sour; they also have a bitter appeal. Get it? Their peel is bitter, with citrusy, spicy, pine-like terpene compounds in their essential oils playing matchy-matchy with quinine, a compound drawn from the bark of the cinchona tree and found in lemony ***Indian Tonic Water*** *[Mixers, p.259]*. A naturally white, crystalline, colourless, odourless but nose-wrinklingly bitter-tasting compound, quinine is best known for its pivotal role as gin's main carbonated mixer in a ***Gin & Tonic*** *[Gin, p.226]*. For added visuals, give tonic water a UV backlight and you'll actually see the agitated quinine alkaloid glowing phosphorescent blue.

<u>**Wormwood & Elderflower**</u> There'll be no ear severing today, it's wormwood's aromatic mannerisms we're interested in. Saying that, going cuckoo is down to wormwood's infamous neurotoxin compound, thujone *[Glossary, p.19]*, which enabled artistry back in the golden-age via ***Absinthe*** overindulgence *[Anise Liqueur, p.216]*. It had more to do with the sky-high alcohol content in reality, though nowadays liquors are thujone-free and the bitter component stems from non-toxic compounds with floral, herbaceous and woody undertones. ***Dry White Vermouth*** and ***Cocchi Americano*** *[Vermouth, pp.174, 175]* have wormwood-style herbaceous bitterness, which is offset by the floral, creamy, musky, green, bittersweet, herb and honey notes of elderflower.

If you like . . . **Spicy**, *you'll love . . .*

Fragrant Spicy

Asian Spices

Asian spices make up a broad brief, it has to be said. Location-wise, we're talking north, south, east, west, central – you name it, we only cover a small snapshot of spices in this section. From the sweetly fragrant to the downright earthy, Asian spices appear in booze in anything from ***Ricard***'s reliance on star anise *[Anise Liqueur, p.218]*, ***Sauternes***' treacly fenugreek flavours *[Dessert Wine, p.164]*, ***Sangiovese***'s earthy cumin adjacency *[Red Wine, p.142]*, the lime-vegetal nature of a ***Caipirinha*** *[Cachaça, p.194]* or the lean-lemongrass lines of a ***Pessac-Leognan*** *[White Wine, p.128]*.

<u>**Cumin & Watermelon**</u> Call cumin the savoury alternative to cinnamon – it doesn't mind. 'Rich', 'hearty', 'earthy', 'warm', 'citrusy', 'pungent', 'sweet-spicy' and 'bitter' are regular descriptors, but don't forget its nutty nuances. Cuminaldehyde *[Glossary, p.16]* is its key compound, with a green-herbaceous aroma and uniquely meaty notes, given it's also a chemical constituent of roast beef. Likewise ***Sangiovese*** and ***Syrah Rosé*** *[Rosé Wine, pp.142, 141]* have savoury, green, earthy, brothy aromas, overlaid by the vibrant red-fruit notes of watermelon and its herbaceous, cucumber-like undercarriage. Watermelon has a red-fruity, melon-herbaceous flavour identity, with grassy notes following closely behind.

Dried Lime & Tomatillo Put Brazil in your *boca* by trying a **Caipirinha** *[Cachaça, p.194]*, the tangier, earthier, more vegetal version of a **Mojito** *[Rum, p.197]*, mirroring the citrus, bitter, floral, earthy, green and herbal flavours of dried limes and tomatillos. Boiling in brine and sun-drying dials down limes' angular zing, coaxing out earthy, bittersweet, smoky notes and funky fermentation flavours. Tomatillos are like green cherry tomatoes, their flavours dominated by citric acid and a leafy, green-apple tang that mirrors the notes of **Mosel Kabinett Riesling Trocken** *[White Wine, p.132]*, **Green Tea Kombucha** *[Tea, p.200]*, **Kenyan Coffee** *[Coffee, p.205]*, the **Bloody Mary** *[Vodka, p.235]* and **Sangiovese Rosé** *[Rosé Wine, p.142]*. *[Cocktail Recipes, pp.195, 198, 235]*

Fenugreek & Saffron Sweeter than a baby otter licking a lollipop, the indecently syrupy **Sauternes** and **Tokaji Aszú** *[Dessert Wine, pp.164, 165]* are liquid proof of fenugreek and saffron's compatibility. Fenugreek, Latin for 'Greek hay', is dominated by sotolon *[Glossary, p.19]*, a sweet compound with a distinctive flavour of maple syrup-drizzled pancakes, brown sugar and caramel. Saffron can relate to fenugreek's treacly tendencies, with some honied, hay-like, floral tricks of its own, though it also contains compounds that bring a lingeringly bitter foil to all that sweetness, with a medicinal lick on the finish.

Lemongrass & Papaya We should be reclining beachside in a Thai hammock with descriptors like these, and . . . we're back in the room. Believe it or not, these exotic flavours are typical of high-end Bordeaux white blends, specifically those of **Pessac-Leognan**, also capturing the herbal-tropical dichotomy of a New Zealand **Marlborough Sauvignon Blanc** and **English Bacchus** *[White Wine, pp.128, 136, 125]*. Lemongrass lacks lemon's citric-acid kick, majoring instead on more herbaceous, citrusy, floral and minty compounds. Here we have lemongrass's clean grassy, delicately lemony lines converging with the perfumed, sweet, musty flavours pumping out of papaya's bright ochre flesh.

Star Anise & Lemon Verbena Star anise looks like a hand-carved wooden gift-shop trinket you'd pay a fortune for in Goa. It majors on a warm and woody compound shared with other anise-led ingredients like fennel and liquorice. **Ricard** *[Anise Liqueur, p.218]* is anise-central, aside from the citrusy influence of lemon verbena's flavour compound, citral *[Glossary, p.15]*, as sipped in **Yellow Chartreuse**, **Strega** *[Herb Liqueur, pp.214, 215]* and **Limoncello** *[Fruit Liqueur, p.184]*. Bright notes break through the cloudy liquorice louche, or haze, itself a neat display of boozy alchemy, conjured up by aquaphobic oil forming an emulsion in water that scatters waves of light. Try having **The Last Word** *[Herb Liqueur, p.216]*, a **Sazerac** cocktail *[Whisky, p.248]* or a **Pimm's** *[Fruit Liqueur, p.181]* for the reverse thwack of lemon verbena with teasing notes of star anise.

If you like . . . **Spicy**, *you'll love . . .*

Fruity Spicy

Christmas Spices

It's the most wonderful time of the year all right, belting out aromas of brandy, dried fruit, oranges and spice-rack whiffs of cinnamon, ginger, clove and anise. These nuances are found year-round in our favourite drinks, whether it's the woody warmth of aniseed notes in Spanish **Pacharán** *[Fruit Liqueur, p.186]*, clove's sweet perfume in **Frappato** *[Red Wine, p.154]*, inflections of navel orange peel in **Metaxa** *[Brandy, p.178]*, Christmas tree's pine-like influence in **Retsina** *[White Wine, p.133]* or the full-on festive flavours of Christmas cake, caught in a bottle of a **Colheita** *[Port, p.169]*.

Aniseed & Sloe Berry **Pacharán** *[Fruit Liqueur, p.186]* may not scream Christmas, but its flavour descriptors certainly do. It's a liqueur produced from soaking sloe berries in anise-infused spirit for Pete's sake, with aniseed aromas smacking squarely of Santa. Centred around anethole *[Glossary, p.15]*, a compound thirteen times sweeter than sugar, which is tempered by the woody warmth of a doppelganger compound and another with cherry, vanilla and chocolate mannerisms. Soaking subdues sloe berries' boisterous bitterness, which basks in aniseed's sweetness and channel their inner **Jägermeister** *[Herb Liqueur, p.214]*.

Christmas Cake & Chocolate Orange I love the thought of a Christmas cake wearing an almond weave, describing its lid-like marzipan covering. Big hair, don't care, as they say. Port is the boozy boss-beverage for the festive period, overflowing with cinnamon, orange, clove, ginger, star anise, dried fruit, nuts and nutmeg, comprehensively captured in a **Colheita** *[Port, p.169]*. It's an unruly creche of flavour compounds, though brandy-soaked dried fruit in Christmas cake marvellously mimics **Rivesaltes Ambré** *[Dessert Wine, p.164]* and **Aged Tawny Port**'s *[Fortified Wine, p.168]* fortified mannerisms, often with orange-infused chocolate notes for a level of decadence we can only get away with at Christmas.

Christmas Tree & Preserved Lime Unless we're picking pine needles out of our teeth, let's not knock Christmas-tree notes in tipples. Modern **Retsina** *[White Wine, p.133]* boasts balanced resinous, citrusy, saline and floral flavours far removed from the tree-sappy monstrosities produced in the old days. Pine aromas are powered by pinene *[Glossary, p.18]*, a compound found in fir trees' sticky resin that smacks of turpentine, and which can form a blue haze over pine-covered mountains by shortening waves of light. Limes are bitter-tart with a more bracingly resinous profile than their lemony siblings, while preserving them in salt tempers their pugnacious flavours, sweetening the piney pill as captured in a **Last Word** cocktail, **Crème de Menthe** *[Herb Liqueur, pp.216, 213]* or a foamy **Pisco Sour** *[Brandy, p.180]*.

Clove & White Strawberry I'm not a qualified doctor, but surely strawberry-allergy sufferers could chomp a white one given it lacks the offending ripening protein? Probably not, though these albino berries are also lower in tang than the red sort and packed with a berry-like compound that smacks of Concord grapes and neroli oil, not to mention their caramel-like flavour chops reflected in **Pineapple Rum** [Rum, p.197]. Sicilian **Frappato** [Red Wine, p.154] is rife with white strawberry and spiced-herbaceous flavours, specifically the sweetly perfumed, woody notes of cloves and their minty nuances.

Navel Orange Peel & Violet Somewhere between straddling the spice rack and looking like a Christmas ornament is dried orange peel. Whereas navel orange pulp is all about super-sweet, fatty, floral, woody and citrusy aromas, its peel promotes pine-like odours that pump out of its aptly named outer flavedo [Glossary, p.16]. Drying orange peel dials down the fresh essential oils, bringing in aromatic turpentine-like, woody and rye-adjacent aromas. Violet's bittersweet profile accentuates those bosky tones, flexing its powdery-floral flavours, collectively found in **Metaxa 12-Star** [Brandy, p.178] and the citrusy-floral reds of **Touriga Nacional** [Red Wine, p.156].

If you like . . . **Spicy**, *you'll love . . .*

Herbal Spicy

Herbes de Provence

It's exactly what it says on the jar, a blend of herbs from the paysan paradise of Provence – those heady, garrigue-like Mediterranean herbs that waft through the windows of our *deux chevaux* while we're driving around southern French dirt tracks. We know the aromas: rosemary's minty-medicinal mannerisms in **Corbières** [Red Wine, p.148], **Mourvèdre Rosé**'s thyme-like bittersweet moment [Rosé Wine, p.140], bay leaf's sweetly herbal influence in the wines of **Pomerol** [Red Wine, p.147], oregano's earthily herbal notes in **Montepulciano d'Abruzzo** [Red Wine, p.154] and marjoram's sweet-woody swagger, shown in **Soave Classico** [White Wine, p.135].

Bay Leaf & Black Raspberry Call me Mr Picky, but the best bay leaves are plucked in June when they're higher in eucalyptol. Bay's waxy, minty, camphoraceous [Glossary, p.15], cooling, lightly medicinal leaves are dead ringers for the herbal flavours we savour in a Bordeaux **Pomerol**, a **South African Cabernet Sauvignon** or an **Australian Cabernet Sauvignon** [Red Wine, pp.147, 157, 143]. Bay's clove-like compound provides a warm, woody and sweetly herbal foil to penetrating eucalyptus, beckoning in woody, minty aromas from black raspberry. A one-stop shop for black and red fruit, there's a complex flavour network in black raspberries with citrusy, camphor and rosy notes stuffed into those blacked-out drupelets.

Oregano & Boysenberry Here's the good news: describing *Montepulciano d'Abruzzo* *[Red Wine, p.154]* as having notes of oregano means it pairs well with pizza. Heck, it even tastes like one. Oregano majors on compounds that give it an earthy, musty, green, hay-adjacent flavour with minty notes and a balancing bitterness. Bring a boysenberry into the flavour equation, the fruit of a fumble between a raspberry and a blackberry, and there's a juicy, almost wine-like intensity, sweet-florals and citric-acid tang that's a smidge more pronounced than either of its parents, which comes through in the pinks of *Tavel* and *Bandol [Rosé Wine, pp.141, 140]* and the reds of **Chianti Classico** *[Red Wine, p.153]*.

Rosemary & English Lavender I get the irony: English lavender in the *herbes de Provence* section, but French lavender smells more of rosemary, which would be overkill. The two twin freely in the wild – rosemary's needled, camo-green leaves pushing into English lavender's smoky-lilac-hued petals. Rosemary delivers eucalyptus and minty tones, courtesy of a compound it shares with bay leaf and cardamom. Lavender takes it in a more floral direction, thanks to rosy aroma compounds, but it shares eucalyptus and camphor notes with rosemary, reuniting them in a liquorice and lightly medicinal embrace, witnessed in the wildly herbal reds of **Corbières** and **Mencia** *[Red Wine, pp.148, 158]* and **Echinacea Tea** *[Tea, p.204]*.

Sweet Marjoram & White Peach Mispronouncing *Soave Classico [White Wine, p.135]* is probably as shameful as calling Versace, *Ver-say-se* during Fashion Week. *Swah-vay* has sweet marjoram and white peach as its major flavour markers, with a saline nod to its volcanic Italian origins. Marjoram is a mild-mannered version of oregano and thyme in flavour terms, with additional sweetness and a warm woody spiciness. White peach builds on marjoram's floral notes via soft, creamy, floral lactone compounds *[Glossary, p.17]*, delivering a milder flavour experience, dialled-up sweetness and lower acid than their yellow-fleshed siblings.

Wild Thyme & Pomegranate Nothing beats a Mediterranean scrubland scene for romance, with patchy sprigs of wild thyme poking out of arid earth. Thyme is the backbone of *herbes de Provence*, with a pungent bittersweet, feral, piney, smoky and medicinal flavour thanks to the compound, thymol. *Bandol Rosé's* grapes *[Rosé Wine, p.140]* grow along the Mediterranean coast, harbouring flavours of pomegranate and thyme with a distinctive meaty moment, not unlike **Averna** *[Amaro, p.223]*, **Chilean Carménère** or a rustic **Corbières** *[Red Wine, pp.144, 148]*. Fittingly, thymol is also found in lamb meat, and here it is punctuated by pomegranate's green, herbal undertones of mint and anise with woody, earthy, musty, bittersweet red-fruit notes and a twist of citrus.

SPICY

If you like . . . **Spicy**, *you'll love . . .*

Medicinal Spicy

Botanical Spices

We've reached the rhizome 'n' booze section *[Glossary, p.17]*. You're welcome for the botanical pun, by the way. Anything that's herby, rooty, berry-like, barky, floral or seedy counts, especially their essential oils, or 'absolute' in the perfume business. Dandelion and burdock conjure the complexity of **Root Beer** *[Mixers, p.262]*, **Jägermeister** *[Herb Liqueur, p.214]* counts liquorice root as a major flavour marker, candied angelica sums up the herbaceous sweetness of **Green Chartreuse** *[Herb Liqueur, p.213]*, orris root has a floral influence in **Strega** *[Herb Liqueur, p.215]* while caraway contends with a carvone *[Glossary, p.15]* conundrum in **Aquavit** *[Herb Liqueur, p.215]*, more on that story later.

Candied Angelica & Thai Basil Angelica is big on the booze scene, like a spunky compere at a kitschy disco. A key ingredient in herb liqueurs, from **Green Chartreuse** to **Bénédictine** *[Herb Liqueur, p.213, 212]*, when angelica's stems are boiled in heavy syrup, then dried and rolled in caster sugar, they smack convincingly of the candied, herbaceous tones of Green Chartreuse. Blasting out peppery, minty, citrusy notes from a chorus of aromatic compounds, candied angelica harmonises with Thai basil's sweet anise notes, along with the nuances of cinnamon and mint flavours found in **Peppermint Tea** *[Tea, p.202]*.

Caraway & Dill Weed Here's a geeky flavour conundrum: caraway and dill share a compound with spearmint, but they act in reverse. Spearmint's sweet-minty R-carvone *[Glossary, p.15]* is the mirror image of caraway and dill's S-carvone, which expresses rye aromas, verging on anise. In drinks, Scandinavia's signature spirit, **Aquavit** *[Herb Liqueur, p.215]*, is centred around caraway, with a complex, warming flavour and rye-like, woody, herby, citrus notes. Dill's brightening, green, clean, citrusy, anise notes shine forth with an 'is it sweet, is it tart?' moment, like a bag of Sour Patch sweets or a bottle of **High-Rye Bourbon** *[Bourbon, p.250]*.

Dandelion & Burdock Dandelion and burdock are more British than complaining about the weather in the queue for M&S. Blighty's double-act answer to **Root Beer** or **Dr Pepper** *[Mixers, p.262]* are essentially weeds, though bundled together they have a fruity character with a botanical, rooty, barky blend of liquorice and anise. Whereas Root Beer majors on sassafras, produced artificially nowadays due to health concerns around a compound called safrole, dandelion has a similar earthy, minty, cooling, bitter profile to a **White Negroni** *[Amaro, p.227]*. Burdock echoes dandelion's light bitterness, delivering sweet, earthy, mushroom-like, nutty nuances not unlike a Jerusalem artichoke.

Liquorice Root & Black Cardamom *Jägermeister* [Herb Liqueur, p.214] smells like peer pressure and Red Bull. Well, in my mind's nose it does anyway. The recipe is sworn to more secrecy than a Masonic handshake, though liquorice and black cardamom flavours loom large, as they do in **Fernet-Branca** [Amaro, p.224], **Black Spiced Rum** [Rum, p.196] and **Root Beer** [Mixers, p.262]. Liquorice root and cardamom major on the sinus-clearing compound eucalyptol, and another with a super-sweet anise note offset by a balancing bitterness and underlying flavours of Vicks VapoRub, or **Ouzo** [Anise Liqueur, p.218]. Black cardamom shares green's citrus characteristics, replacing floral fragrances for camphoraceous [Glossary, p.15], resinous aromas and smoky notes from drying over fire, and are found in the opaque Uruguayan **Tannat**, **Old-Vine Zinfandel** and **Graciano** [Red Wine, pp.160, 161, 158].

Orris Butter & Hyssop Time is money with orris, the fussy root of the iris flower that demands years of drying for its aromas to develop. Made into a butter to extract its essential oil, unique compounds give orris those soft, powdery, woody, Parma Violet flavours. Orris is also a 'fixer' in booze and perfumes, keeping in place adjoining aromas that would otherwise disappear. Good job it fixes hyssop, a headily smelling mint-family member resembling a peppermint-like stalk of lavender, which injects a medicinal, herbaceous bitterness into **Dry White Vermouth** [Fortified Wine, p.174], **Bénédictine** or canary-yellow **Strega** [Herb Liqueur, pp.212, 215] via camphor-adjacent compounds.

If you like . . . **Spicy**, *you'll love . . .*

Peppery Spicy

Peppercorn

Here's a fun fact: 'pepper-chasers' are people who actively seek out peppery flavours in drinks. If that's you, then this section is your wheelhouse. Piperine is the active chemical compound in peppercorns, either added to booze in botanicals or mimicked with similar molecules. We're looking for beverages like the cracked-black-peppery, meaty **Côte-Rôtie** [Red Wine, p.148], the herbaceous, green-peppery kick of a **Chilean Carménère** [Red Wine, p.144], **Pisco Sour**'s white pepper and grapey tones [Brandy, p.180], **Pink Gin**'s red-berry piquancy [Gin, p.226] and **Root Beer**'s medicinal markers [Mixers, p.262].

Black Peppercorn & Smoky Bacon Like an Italian waiter twisting an oversized grinder, **Côte-Rôtie** [Red Wine, p.148] is the 'peppicentre' of the black pepper wine style. Piperine in black peppercorns is the chemical compound responsible for their warm spicy, terpy, herbaceous flavours. Similar nuances wind up in wine via a black-peppery compound in the grapes' skin, producing flavours prized by pepper-chasers. Bring in nuances of smoky bacon and we're not necessarily going in a breakfast direction, that's because compounds brought on by the breakdown of bacon's fat molecules are mirrored in wine, shown in the majestically meaty flavours of **Bandol** *[Red Wine, p.145]*.

Grains of Paradise & Wintergreen They may look and act like peppercorns, but grains of Paradise are actually ginger's cousin. Unsurprisingly, ginger's major compound gingerol *[Glossary, p.17]* makes an appearance, as does another with a flavour similar to black pepper. Grains of Paradise harbour bitter, hoppy, earthy, woody, root-beer-like tones we'd be able to identify in **Dr Pepper** *[Mixers, p.262]*. Wintergreen herbs major on sweet, minty, medicinal flavours from a star-studded supporting cast of compounds with fresh, clean, woody, thyme-like, peppery characteristics, as replicated in **Arak** *[Anise Liqueur, p.219]* and **Tequila Reposado** *[Tequila, p.192]*.

Green Peppercorn & Raspberry 'Born to be mild' is a dubious strapline for green peppercorns, but it works. With fragrant, fruity, brine-preserved, herbaceous edges kept fresh by a lack of sun-drying, green peppercorns make a jackpot flavour comparison for **Chilean Carménère** *[Red Wine, p.144]*. Green bell peppers are Carménère's usual flavour double, but I always think green peppercorns' bright grassy aromas bordering on pine needles could be a closer match. Raspberries add the required sweet-tart, red-berry component, doubling down on barky tones with woody-violet base notes, found alongside green peppercorn in the reds of **Mencia** and **Chinon** *[Red Wine, pp.158, 148]*.

Pink Peppercorn & Juniper Pink peppercorns are actually berries, forming part of the edgier cashew, mango and poison ivy crew. Who knew? They bring heat, not fire, sourced from a compound with a peppery, fresh minty, citrusy profile. They also harbour woody, resinous, pine-like flavour tendencies, giving them something in common with juniper, their bottle mate in **Pink Gin** *[Gin, p.226]*. Juniper blasts out herbal, woody, spicy, lemony, eucalyptus and like-minded camphoraceous notes *[Glossary, p.15]*, softened by pink peppers' pop of red-berry sweetness, just like **Rosso Vermouth** *[Fortified Wine, p.175]* and **Campari** in a **Negroni** cocktail *[Amaro, pp.223, 224]*.

White Peppercorn & Starfruit What's shaped like a star and tastes of grape, apple, lemon, pear, pineapple and apricot? Starfruit, of course, whose unique sweet-sour flavours are found in a **Pisco Sour** *[Brandy, p.180]* or with a pinch of ground white pepper and salt in a classic **Margarita** *[Tequila, p.190]*. Starfruit majors on ester compounds *[Glossary, p.16]* that are dead ringers for the aroma of grapes, with accompanying notes of green apple. White pepper delivers floral, citrusy, earthy, turmeric-like, herbaceous, pine-like and woody flourishes, all flavour characteristics of the South American Pisco in the sour cocktail. *[Cocktail Recipe, p.180]*

Warm Spicy

Cinnamon

When did cinnamon spring cassia on us? Close cousins, one comes in elegant parchment-like furls, is warmly sweet-tasting and fragrantly woody, the other is cassia. More pronounced, with bitter, earthy tones, cassia has rougher edges and none of cinnamon's floral-fruity nuances. Cinnamon's aromatic influence is found in beverages ranging from the 'Costa del citrusy' **Sangria** *[Red Wine, p.160]*, the spiced-apple sparkles of **Breton Brut Cidre** *[Cider, p.187]*, **Sazerac** cocktail's light liquorice tones *[Whisky, p.248]* and the sappy richness of a **Manhattan** *[Bourbon, p.251]*, while cassia co-creates **Coca-Cola**'s bitter-sweet, citric blueprint *[Mixers, p.260]*.

Cassia & Lime Promise to act surprised when I break the world's worst-kept trade secret? Cassia and lime are major flavours in **Coca-Cola** *[Mixers, p.260]*, which comes as brand-new information, wink. Cassia bark is less refined than cinnamon, with earthy, barky, resinous tones that lack its floral, citrusy flourishes. It pairs well with lime's angular, cedary, pine-like, bitter profile, as tasted in **Sangria** *[Red Wine, p.160]*, a **Moscow Mule** *[Vodka, p.236]* and **Angostura Bitters** *[Mixers, p.258]*. Milder flavour compounds sand down cassia's edges and offer up sweetness, with the help of a boatload of sugar in **Cherry Coke** *[Mixers, p.260]*.

Cinnamon & Blood Orange Admit it, we've all sat Med-side glugging a jug of **Sangria** *[Red Wine, p.160]*. There's no aroma more evocative of summer, apart from tanning lotion, which isn't nearly as appetising. Try licking a cinnamon scroll instead; it won't taste sweet, but it ramps up perceived sweetness in accompanying flavours. Cue the raspberry tang, pine-resin woodiness and burst of grapefruit-like citrus in a blood orange, sweetened by cinnamon's warm woody, medicinal flavours in this Latin punch, as well as in **Mulled Wine/Glühwein** *[Red Wine, p.150]*, **Campari** *[Amaro, p.223]* and **Cranberry Juice** *[Mixers, p.261]*. The rustic pinks of **Bandol** *[Rosé Wine, p.140]* share a minty mannerism, mirrored by a compound in blood orange. *[Drink Recipe, p.160]*

Cinnamon & Candied Rosemary **Wheated Bourbon** *[Bourbon, p.253]* and **Whisky** *[Whisky, p.243]* are internalising a cinnamon note from the charring of their wooden casks, and just need to let it all out. The addition of sweet Vermouth and Angostura Bitters in a **Manhattan** *[Bourbon, p.251]* brings in rosemary notes which taste like they're coated in sugar. Chew a fresh rosemary leaf for an instant hit of herbal, packed with minty, liquorice, pepper, camphor, citrus and balsamic components. Cinnamon's woody warmth is cooled by rosemary's bitter evergreen flavours with a punctuating pop of pine resin that resides in **Black Spiced Rum** *[Rum, p.196]* and **High-Rye Bourbon** *[Bourbon, p.250]*. *[Cocktail Recipe, p.251]*

SPICY

Cinnamon & Fennel Pollen Star anise is so yesterday; it's all about fennel pollen among today's spicearati, also known as 'sweet cumin'. For starters it's more fennel-tasting than the bulb, with a citrus-minty profile, camphor notes, a honied mellowness and a grassy component; well, it is from the Latin word meaning 'fragrant hay'. The *Sazerac* cocktail *[Whisky, p.248]* owes its light anise notes to an absinthe glass rinse, accented by cinnamon's sweetening superpower, with its smoked vanilla aromas and woody-spicy notes all present and correct in **High-Rye Bourbon** *[Bourbon, p.250]*. *[Cocktail Recipe, p.248]*

Cinnamon & Heirloom Apple Like biting into an acidic dehumidifier, the apples that go into **Breton Brut Cidre** *[Cider, p.187]* are so tart and tannic we'd struggle to munch them fresh. The finished cider smacks squarely of heirloom apples, those forgotten orchard varieties with names like Ellison's Orange, D'Arcy Spice and Fenouillet Gris, each with complex flavours of anise and clove from compounds in their skin. These yesteryear pommes house a network of flavours also found in herbs and spices, from star anise to fennel, complementing cinnamon's barky, clove-like warmth and peppery bite.

If you like . . . **Spicy**, *you'll love . . .*

Zingy Spicy

Ginger

Don't call ginger a root – it's a rhizome *[Glossary, p.18]*, basically a stalk like turmeric and lotus. It majors on gingerol *[Glossary, p.17]*, a chemical compound which is related to capsaicin *[Glossary, p.15]* from chilli peppers and piperine from peppercorns, though it's not as rambunctiously spicy as either. Ginger's flavours depend on where it's grown, its stage of life and preparation, from Australian ginger's lemony leanings in **Ginger Beer** *[Mixers, p.259]*, baby ginger's floral-spice in **King's Ginger** *[Herb Liqueur, p.212]*, the dried-ginger fury of a **Moscow Mule** *[Vodka, p.236]*, the vanilla and perfumed bordello flavours in an **Australian Viognier** *[White Wine, p.124]* to the baked-goods and bacon-fat profile of an **Alsace Pinot Gris** *[White Wine, p.126]*.

Australian Ginger & Cardamom *Ginger Beer [Mixers, p.259]* and **King's Ginger** *[Herb Liqueur, p.212]* garner scores of 'lemony' descriptions in tasting notes, sometimes even cardamom, ginger's cousin. Australian ginger contains high levels of citral *[Glossary, p.15]*, the compound that defines the flavour of lemon pulp, as well as a score of floral aromas. Gingerol *[Glossary, p.17]* is ginger's hitman compound, delivering the peppery blow that makes a pincushion out of our tongues in a **Dark 'n' Stormy** *[Rum, p.195]* or a **Moscow Mule** *[Vodka, p.236]*. Cardamom has a flicker of warmth, betraying its family ties by bringing in floral flourishes and a bright, citrus pop with sweet mint and camphoraceous *[Glossary, p.15]*, eucalyptus tones courtesy of eucalyptol.

Baby Ginger & Linden Honey Just remember, where there's a hide, there's heat. Baby ginger hasn't grown that gnarled, corky skin yet, hence it harbours fewer pungent compounds than the older, wizened knobs. Baby ginger is mild, creamy, radish-like, camphoraceous *[Glossary, p.15]*, lightly spicy, balsamic, floral and fruity, thanks to compounds that give it myrrh-like, orange-flower-water notes. ***King's Ginger*** *[Herb Liqueur, p.212]* radiates baby ginger to the backdrop of linden honey's lusciously sweet, fresh-woody, minty, balsamic, mentholated hay-like notes, with thyme-like green and floral aromas reminiscent of super-sweet ***Spätlese Riesling***, ***Auslese Riesling*** *[White Wine, pp.132, 131]* and ***Sauternes*** *[Dessert Wine, p.164]*.

Cooked Ginger & Quince Cooking ginger puts the fiery beast back in the box, releasing a mild-mannered, vanilla-like compound for a less tongue-punishing experience. There's a floral component to ginger: a woody, camphoraceous *[Glossary, p.15]*, fruity flutter that takes wing when it comes into contact with quince's concentrated perfumed notes. We're not talking eau de toilette-style perfume, though quince is fragrant and shares a wisp of vanilla with ginger, a citrus streak and more than a flicker of floral. Violet and vanilla compounds form the markings of the quince and ginger-infused notes of ***Australian Viognier*** or ***South African Chenin Blanc*** *[White Wine, pp.124, 137]*.

Dried Ginger & Lime Ginger is a shape-shifter, going all rampaging Godzilla on us at the click of a dehumidifier switch. Gingerol *[Glossary, p.17]*, ginger's mouth-stinging compound, intensifies via desiccation, transforming into a chemical packing double the wallop. ***Moscow Mules*** *[Vodka, p.236]*, ***Ginger Beer*** *[Mixers, p.259]* and ***Dark 'n' Stormies*** *[Rum, p.195]* show ginger on full peppery form, with a citrusy swagger coming through from flavour compounds that accurately match lime's bitter-citrus flavours in ***King's Ginger*** *[Herb Liqueur, p.212]*. Resinous, cedar and pine-like flavours in lime connect with ginger's camphor and eucalyptus leanings, thanks to an anise-flavoured compound that's also found in fennel. *[Cocktail Recipes, pp.237, 196]*

Gingerbread & Bacon Fat ***Alsace Pinot Gris*** *[White Wine, p.126]* is big-boned, boozy and lightly smoky, as if it's just got back from last orders at the pub. Flavour-wise, it's better than it sounds, with a festive gingerbread thread that brings in a raft of spice-rack flavours from warming cinnamon, creamy clove, citrusy cardamom, woody nutmeg, sweet anise and the floral foundation of honey. The syrupy-tasting maple lactone *[Glossary, p.17]* is infused into bacon via the smoking process, bringing in a bittersweet balance with nutty, buttery, caramelised nuances formed during the heating process.

Drinks

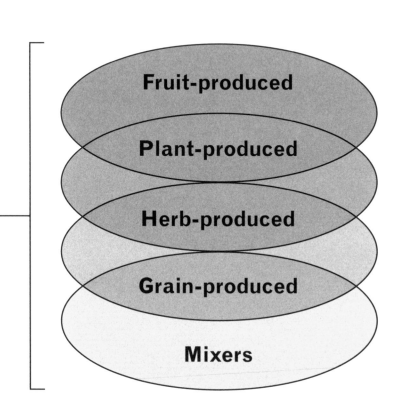

.

Drinks

Fruit-produced

Plant-produced

Herb-produced

Grain-produced

Mixers

Sparkling Wine

England

Blanc de Blancs Tastier than an episode of *Bake Off* during scone week, Blanc de Blancs is bubbly made from white grapes that delivers showstopping creamy, buttery, baked, stone-fruit flavours, usually based around Chardonnay. Bridget Jones's favourite grape harbours a complex network of compounds that cook up floral-citrus, raisiny and woody-violet nuances to name a few. Heady flavours of clotted cream dolloped over toasty, bakery notes come courtesy of yeast-derived, fermentation-triggered compounds that are dragged to the surface by playful bubbles of CO_2 towards Paul's golden handshake.

If you like:
Clotted Cream & Scones
[See 'Decadent Creamy', Creamy, p.67]
Flat Peach & Honeysuckle
[See 'Creamy Fruity', Fruity, p.43]

Try:
Dessert Wine: Tokaji Aszú [p.165]
White Wine: Albariño [p.137], Australian Viognier [p.124], Sonoma Coast Chardonnay [p.139]

Blanc de Noirs Pale fizz made of black grapes – now we've heard everything. Cue Pinot Noir, aka the heartbreak grape as it's a pain to grow, and its underrated partner, Pinot Meunier. There's no astringent, tannic pucker factor or red pigmentation here; we don't do skin contact with white sparkling. English Blanc de Noirs are all red-apple bubbles and creamy, floral, berry-like notes over buttery brioche. Ester compounds *[Glossary, p.16]* mimic the red-apple aroma, as does a major compound found in Pinot Noir, with its fruity, perfumed notes, hints of rose and honey with buttery-smelling compounds formed through yeast fermentation.

If you like:
Royal Gala & Brioche
[See 'Crisp Fruity', Fruity, p.46]
Strawberry & Whipped Cream
[See 'Sweet Fruity', Fruity, p.50]
Vanilla Custard & Rhubarb
[See 'Decadent Creamy', Creamy, p.68]

Try:
Amaro: Zucca Rabarbaro [p.225]
Rosé Wine: New Zealand Pinot Noir Rosé [p.142], Tavel Rosé [p.141]
Sparkling Wine: Rosé Champagne [p.118]

Non-Vintage Blend Like a less pricey Banksy, non-vintage is the stylistic 'tag' of a sparkling wine producer. Blending wines together from different years is fair game,

If you like:
Fennel & Green Apple
[See 'Veggie Herbaceous', Herbaceous, p.40]

though it makes the resulting fizz less high-end than a blend from one particular year. The two fermentations required for a traditional-method bubbly, the first in tank, the second in bottle, bring in ester and terpene compounds *[Glossary, pp.16, 19]* with vibrant fruit and veg flavours, including green apple and bitter-creamy fennel notes. Blighty's cool climate ramps up grapes' acidity, giving them clean, lean, green, herbaceous flavours that become more complex with age.

France

Champagne Demi-Sec Here goes nothing: 'demi-sec' and 'sec' are sweeter than 'brut', then there's 'extra brut' and 'zero dosage', the super-dry styles. And breathe. Dosage *[Glossary, p.16]* is the sugary liquid added to sparkling wine before the cork goes in, and Demi-Secs have more of it, giving them an intense white peach and vanilla creaminess. Natural sugars compete for water in wine, forcing aroma compounds squarely up our noses when we pop the cork. The more sugar you add, the more of a nostrilful we get, with Demi-Sec giving us dialled-up fruit and a luxe vanilla-like crème brûlée mouth coating.

Mature Champagne Mint-condition, 170-year-old bubbly found knocking around at the bottom of the Baltic Sea doesn't bode well for the stuff ageing in our temperature-fluctuating garages. Black truffle and mocha coffee are well-known aromas of mature fine fizz, so are toast, woodsmoke, baked bread, quince, smoky vanilla and gingerbread. Fermentation and ageing on yeast can eventually nudge fresh fungi flavours into bubbly, which verge

Granny Smith & Lemon
[See 'Crisp Fruity', Fruity, p.46]

Try:
Cachaça: Caipirinha [p.194]
Fortified Wine: Fino Sherry [p.172]
Vodka: Appletini [p.234]
White Wine: Clare Valley Riesling [p.124], Picpoul de Pinet [p.129], Rueda Verdejo [p.138], Vinho Verde [p.136]

If you like:
Coconut Water & White Chocolate
[See 'Tropical Creamy', Creamy, p.70]
Whipped Cream & Lemon Soda
[See 'Decadent Creamy', Creamy, p.68]
White Peach & Crème Brûlée
[See 'Creamy Fruity', Fruity, p.44]

Try:
Mixer: Cream Soda [p.261]
Rum: Coconut [p.196]
Sparkling Wine: Riesling Sekt [p.120]
Tequila: Slammer [p.192]
Vodka: Peach Martini [p.234]

If you like:
Black Truffle & Mocha Coffee
[See 'Earthy Savoury', Savoury, p.89]
Gingerbread & Smoked Vanilla
[See 'Yeasty Baked', Baked, p.79]
Toasted Hazelnut & Digestive Biscuit
[See 'Nutty Baked', Baked, p.74]

Try:
Beer: Brown Porter [p.238]
Brandy: VSOP Cognac [p.177]

on savoury, earthy and umami. Complex reactions oxidise the sugars, conjuring up sulphur-containing compounds, giving the wine a whiff of roast coffee, chocolate and black truffle.

Rosé Champagne Any self-respecting Rosé Champagne will have a higher price tag than the regular sort. There's an extra process involved, see; you're pumping in pink pigment housed in the grapes' skin. Pinot Noir leaves its flavour fingerprints all over Rosé Champagne, with fermentation drawing out fruity ester compounds *[Glossary, p.16]* and another called strawberry furanone, a chemical found in Pinot Noir grapes. Dairy aromas are down to lactone compounds *[Glossary, p.17]* from the yeast contact, then there's malolactic fermentation *[Glossary, p.18]*, which converts the wine's green-appley malic acid *[Glossary, p.18]* into whipped-creamy, yoghurty-tasting lactic acid.

Vintage Champagne When Martha and the Vandellas sang 'Nowhere To Run', they were clearly singing about Vintage Champagne. I'd almost put money on it. A high percentage of Vintage Champagne grapes must be harvested in the year on the label, so there's no hiding behind berries from better-performing vintages. Whereas non-vintage fizz produces a consistent 'house style', Vintage is typically more complex, with characteristics such as cherry, grape, lime, white chocolate-stashed Rwandan coffee beans and popcorn's buttery, fried aromas, which are brought in by fermentation-triggered compounds and occasionally from contact with the oak barrel staves.

Grain Spirit: Sweet Potato Shōchū [p.256]
Nut Liqueur: Frangelico [p.254]
Red Wine: Châteauneuf-du-Pape [p.147]
Sparkling Wine: Vintage Champagne [p.118]
Whisky: Aged Japanese Single Malt [p.245]

If you like:
Ruby Chocolate & Violet
[See 'Roasty Sweet', Sweet, p.63]
Strawberry & Whipped Cream
[See 'Sweet Fruity', Fruity, p.50]
Vanilla Custard & Rhubarb
[See 'Decadent Creamy', Creamy, p.68]

Try:
Amaro: Zucca Rabarbaro [p.225]
Red Wine: Amarone [p.151], Graciano [p.158]
Rosé Wine: New Zealand Pinot Noir Rosé [p.142], Tavel Rosé [p.141]
Sparkling Wine: English Blanc de Noirs [p.116]

If you like:
Fried Croutons & Apple Pie
[See 'Toasty Baked', Baked, p.77]
Rwandan Coffee & Popcorn
[See 'Roasty Baked', Baked, p.76]
Toasted Hazelnut & Digestive Biscuit
[See 'Nutty Baked', Baked, p.74]

Try:
Beer: Brown Porter [p.238]
Brandy: VSOP Cognac [p.177]
Coffee: Brazilian [p.204], Rwandan [p.207]
Nut Liqueur: Frangelico [p.254]
Sparkling Wine: Cava de Paraje [p.123], Mature Champagne [p.117]

Crémant d'Alsace Tightly blindfolded, I bet apple would be your go-to description of Crémant d'Alsace, a fizz that makes up half France's crémant production and which majors on the Pinot Blanc grape. More specifically Bramley apple sauce, with its citrusy, buttery side and a suggestion of cinnamon with its implied soupçon of sweetness to offset that tart malic bite. Crémant's early-picked Pinot Blanc grapes go large on ester compounds *[Glossary, p.16]* for those spicy apple notes with a good level of lip-smack, while lees ageing *[Glossary, p.19]* on yeast packs crémant's flavour rucksack full of creamy, toasty, brioche-adjacent flavours.

If you like:
Brioche & Bramley Apple Sauce
[See 'Yeasty Baked', Baked, p.78]
French Toast & Lemon Balm
[See 'Toasty Baked', Baked, p.77]
Soda Bread & Lemon Salt
[See 'Yeasty Baked', Baked, p.79]

Try:
Cider: Breton Brut [p.187]
Fortified Wine: Manzanilla Sherry [p.172]
Sparkling Wine: Crémant de Loire [p.119], Pétillant Naturel Sec Chenin Blanc [p.119]
White Wine: Muscadet Sèvre-et-Mains Sur Lie [p.128]

Crémant de Loire Shocker alert: there's more to the Loire Valley than *Sancerre [White Wine, p.131]*. Crémant de Loire is carving its own path into the region's chalky tuffeau stone, trumping Prosecco on quality and Champagne on price. Chenin Blanc is the headliner here, which is considered a blank-canvas grape just waiting to be lathered up like a foaming bar of lemon balm-scented soap, figuratively speaking, by its second fermentation in bottle. A lemony compound is coaxed out of Chenin Blanc's berries via yeast action, and is layered over creamy proteins for a thoroughly toasty, creamy, honeyed take on lemon.

If you like:
French Toast & Lemon Balm
[See 'Toasty Baked', Baked, p.77]
Lemon & Fresh Pear
[See 'Zingy Fruity', Fruity, p.52]

Try:
Brandy: Peruvian/Chilean Pisco [p.179]
Coffee: Nicaraguan [p.206]
Sparkling Wine: Crémant d'Alsace [p.119]
White Wine: South African Chenin Blanc [p.137], Vermentino [p.135]

Pétillant Naturel Sec Chenin Blanc
I love a Pétillant Naturel, but its zeitgeisty, woke image is the drink version of wearing glasses when you have twenty-twenty vision. Even worse, it's shortened to Pét-Nat, pronounced 'Pet-naa', which now just sounds like I'm being judgy. This edgy newcomer is based on

If you like:
Brioche & Bramley Apple Sauce
[See 'Yeasty Baked', Baked, p.78]
French Toast & Lemon Balm
[See 'Toasty Baked', Baked, p.77]
Soda Bread & Lemon Salt
[See 'Yeasty Baked', Baked, p.79]

natural fermentation, an ancient sparkling winemaking technique that's also called the *méthode ancestrale*, delivering sparkling wines with cider-adjacent, rustic, off-dry prickles. Pét-Sec is the drier version, which appeals to my palate and illustrates this flavour combo better. Based around a single fermentation by natural yeast halted before it's finished, Pét-Nat Sec Chenin delivers lean lines of salted lemon and soda bread with lighter alcohol.

Try:

Cider: Breton Brut [p.187]

Fortified Wine: Manzanilla Sherry [p.172]

Sparkling Wine: Crémant d'Alsace [p.119], Crémant de Loire [p.119]

White Wine: Muscadet Sèvre-et-Mains Sur Lie [p.128]

Germany

Riesling Sekt You've got to be careful offering someone 'some Sekt'; maybe just call it 'German sparkling'. Just in case you do, Riesling Sekt is the good kind, not the basic, rent-a-grape bubbles generally guzzled over in Deutschland. Everyone bangs on about the kerosene aromas in Riesling that come from a compound triggered by sun contact and fermentation, but get the ripeness right and you lure out its lemon, apple and peachy side. Given Riesling is higher in aromatic compounds than Chardonnay or Pinot Noir, bottle fermentation swaps out the biscuity characteristics for a lemony cream soda froth.

If you like:

Granny Smith & Lemon
[See 'Crisp Fruity', Fruity, p.46]

Whipped Cream & Lemon Soda
[See 'Decadent Creamy', Creamy, p.68]

Try:

Cachaça: Caipirinha [p.194]

Sparkling Wine: English Non-Vintage [p.116]

Tequila: Slammer [p.192]

Vodka: Appletini [p.234], Peach Martini [p.234]

White Wine: Clare Valley Riesling [p.124], Picpoul de Pinet [p.129], Vinho Verde [p.136]

Italy

Bellini As I always say, if it's good enough for Ernest Hemingway, it's good enough for me. While it's more likely that Papa Hemingway was knocking back manly Martinis over Bellinis at Harry's Bar in Venice where the Bellini was created, or both, we know he was a regular there. Flavour-wise, the classic Bellini cocktail is based around flowery peachy-creamy

If you like:

Chantilly Cream & Yellow Peach
[See 'Creamy Sweet', Sweet, p.59]

Cream Soda & Williams Pear
[See 'Decadent Creamy', Creamy, p.67]

Elderflower & Yellow Peach
[See 'Fruity Floral', Floral, p.25]

Peach Blossom & Cream Soda
[See 'Soft Floral', Floral, p.29]

bubbles, combining Prosecco's naturally floral fragrance with the honeyed, creamy, nutty perfume of puréed peach's mainstay lactone compound *[Glossary, p.17]*, gamma-decalactone *[Glossary, p.16]*, all wrapped up in a vanilla-flavoured, cream-soda bow.

Try:
Fruit Liqueur: Peach Schnapps [p.183]
Mixer: Cream Soda [p.261]
Sparkling Wine: Prosecco [p.122]
Vodka: Peach Martini [p.234]
Whisky: Southern Comfort [p.249]

Cocktail recipe

BELLINI [Fruit-Produced Drinks, Sparkling Wine, Prosecco]

60ml Peach Purée
10ml Peach Schnapps
5ml Lemon Juice
Prosecco (to serve)

Shake peach purée (we're not making it ourselves!), peach schnapps and lemon juice together with ice, then strain into a Champagne flute half filled with Prosecco. Simples.

Franciacorta Riserva I'm not being ageist, but Italy's answer to Champagne requires serious mileage on the clock to be called a Riserva. We're talking sixty months in bottle with the yeast inside, minimum – a lifetime in fizz-years. That's where Franciacorta's Chardonnay-based juice picks up baked focaccia, green-olive, salted-apple and spicy pear-skin flavours. Bottle fermentation strips out the fresh-fruit aromas over time, replacing them with savoury notes that intensify with continued wine-on-yeast contact. Proteins and amino acids emerge from dead yeast cells, making Franciacorta smell of an artisan Italian bakery.

If you like:
Focaccia & Pear Skin
[See 'Yeasty Baked', Baked, p.78]
Toasted Hazelnut & Digestive Biscuit
[See 'Nutty Baked', Baked, p.74]

Try:
Beer: Brown Porter [p.238]
Brandy: VSOP Cognac [p.177]
Nut Liqueur: Frangelico [p.254]
Orange Wine: Georgian [p.139]
Perry: Vintage [p.188]
Sparkling Wine: Mature Champagne [p.117], Vintage Champagne [p.118]

Moscato d'Asti You've officially arrived when Jay-Z, Kanye and Drake are spitting rhymes about you. Not me, but Moscato d'Asti, not to be confused with the sparkling wine formerly known as 'spumante'. Lightly frizzante and honeyed, with a strong tropical-fruit game and florist-shop notes, Moscato Bianco contains more perfumed terpene compounds than any other grape, and, like papaya, linalool *[Glossary, p.18]* is the chemical compound that drives its signature musky, citrus

If you like:
Orange Blossom & Honey
[See 'Soft Floral', Floral, p.29]
Papaya & Lavender Honey
[See 'Tropical Fruity', Fruity, p.51]

Try:
Coffee: Peruvian [p.207]
Fruit Liqueur: Curaçao [p.182]
Gin: Sakura Bee's Knees [p.228]
Mixer: Coca-Cola [p.260]
Whisky: Drambuie [p.246]

and lavender aromas. The 'metodo asti' involves a single fermentation in a closed tank, pumping out fresh papaya, grape and lavender honey notes on full blast.

Prosecco Glera, Prosecco's headline grape, always sounds like the good witch out of *Wicked* to me. Fun, fresh and sparkly, Prosecco is more bish-bash-bosh than pricier bottles, as aside from the occasional sip of 'Superiore DOCG', we're largely glugging the basic stuff. Prosecco's fruity Insta-froth is made via the 'tank' or 'cuve-close' method *[Glossary, p.16]*, with a second fermentation in a closed pressurised tank, not a bottle. This method is well suited to keeping Glera's aromatic compounds intact, giving it drink-me-quick, off-dry, Williams pear and cream soda pop notes and shorter-lived, gravity-defying bubbles, without getting bogged down with yeast-aged complexity.

If you like:
Citrus Honey & Charentais Melon
[See 'Floral Sweet', Sweet, p.60]
Cream Soda & Williams Pear
[See 'Decadent Creamy', Creamy, p.67]
White Peach & Crème Brûlée
[See 'Fruity Creamy', Fruity, p.44]

Try:
Fruit Liqueur: Midori [p.185]
Mixer: Cream Soda [p.261]
Sparkling Wine: Champagne Demi-Sec [p.117]
White Wine: Auslese Riesling [p.131], Condrieu [p.127], South African Chenin Blanc [p.137]

Spain

Cava Brut Nature If you've ever posted a photo without a filter, that's what Brut Nature does for sparkling. Without the soft-focus sugary solution, aka dosage *[Glossary, p.16]*, which is normally popped into the bottle before the cork goes in, Cava has bone-dry bubbles that smack of baked pastry, apricots and greengages. Refermentation in bottle rustles up those baked-strudel flavours, thanks to buttery, bakery-adjacent compounds. Doughy aromas creep in from yeast-on-sugar action, releasing sweet bready notes that vibe with the creamy, soft-cheesy, apricot and greengage notes introduced through lees contact *[Glossary, p.19]*.

If you like:
Apricot Strudel & Greengage
[See 'Yeasty Baked', Baked, p.78]
Fennel & Green Apple
[See 'Veggie Herbaceous', Herbaceous, p.40]
Granny Smith & Lemon
[See 'Crisp Fruity', Fruity, p.46]

Try:
Cachaça: Caipirinha [p.194]
Fortified Wine: Fino Sherry [p.172]
Sparkling Wine: English Non-Vintage [p.116], Riesling Sekt [p.120]
Vodka: Appletini [p.234]
White Wine: Clare Valley Riesling [p.124], Picpoul de Pinet [p.129], Rueda Verdejo [p.138], Vinho Verde [p.136]

Cava de Paraje Cava de what now? *Paraje* basically translates as 'crème de la crème', 'platinum standard' or, more specifically 'Cava of place'. Without going too granular, Paraje Cavas are aged for longer, the vines are older, the wines are vintage – you get the gist. It's a flavour game changer, given that the longer a sparkling is laid down 'sur lie' *[Glossary, p.19]*, on the dead yeast cells, the more complexity it collects. Fresh, appley ester compounds *[Glossary, p.16]* are switched out for cooked, spicy notes, delivering stewed apple and anise with a whisper of eucalyptus and deep-fried crouton notes.

If you like:
Brioche & Bramley Apple Sauce
[See 'Yeasty Baked', Baked, p.78]
Dried Croutons & Apple Pie
[See 'Toasty Baked', Baked, p.77]

Try:
Cider: Breton Brut [p.187]
Fortified Wine: Manzanilla Sherry [p.172]
Sparkling Wine: Crémant d'Alsace [p.119], Pétillant Naturel Sec Chenin Blanc [p.119], Vintage Champagne [p.118]

White Wine

Argentina

Torrontés Wine warriors need to relax and run a bath, as I've also referenced Torrontés under floral. Does this aromatic grape major on flowery styles of wine? Absolutely. It's powered by perfumed compounds like rose oxide for that rose petal and jasmine calling card. Juniper also contains a floral component thanks to geraniol *[Glossary, p.16]*, a pop of citrus and a pine-like quality that mirrors a resinous compound found in Torrontés. High-altitude Torrontés takes on a distinctive cooling, minty, herbaceous quality with flickers of woody-citrusy lemon zest.

If you like:
Lemon Zest & Apricot
[See 'Zingy Fruity', Fruity, p.53]
Rose & Violet
[See 'Intense Floral', Floral, p.26]
Spearmint & Juniper
[See 'Minty Herbaceous', Herbaceous, p.37]

Try:
Flower Liqueur: Crème de Violette [p.209]
Fortified Wine: LBV Port [p.169], White Port & Tonic [p.171]
Herb Liqueur: Strega [p.215]
Red Wine: Nero D'Avola [p.155]
Tea: Echinacea [p.204]
White Wine: Grüner Veltliner [p.125]

Australia

Chardonnay I remember the 'ABC Club', anything but Chardonnay. Ah, nineties cancel culture. We joined in our droves, tired of the toasty butter bombs made by shovelling oak chips into giant mesh bags, infused into monstrous Frankenwine. How things have changed; used judiciously, spicy, smoky, vanilla notes are brought into Chardonnay via oak barrels, whereas melted-butter notes are thanks to malolactic fermentation *[Glossary, p.18]*, a process that breaks down tart malic acid *[Glossary, p.18]* into milky lactic acid. A compound is produced that happens to form the basis of actual butter, softening those citric edges to creamy peaks of lemon curd.

If you like:
Flat Peach & Honeysuckle
[See 'Creamy Fruity', Fruity, p.43]
Melted Butter & Lemon Curd
[See 'Buttery Creamy', Creamy, p.67]

Try:
Dessert Wine: Tokaji Aszú [p.165]
Sparkling Wine: English Blanc de Blancs [p.116]
White Wine: Albariño [p.137], Alsace Gewürztraminer [p.126], Australian Viognier [p.124], Sonoma Coast Chardonnay [p.139]

Clare Valley Riesling Cool-climate wines are smoking hot. Does that make sense? Not that Australia is exactly cold, but high-altitude areas like Clare Valley nurture Riesling's exquisite acidity. Riesling has it all flavour-wise: purity, minerality, mouth-watering acidity, floral perfume, citrus and green apple in a young wine, with honey, toast, smoke and petrol notes with ageing. Younger wines tend to be on the Granny Smith apple, lemon and fennel flavour markers, thanks to a combo of yeast-introduced compounds, grape-derived esters and terpenes *[Glossary, pp.16, 19]* for citrusy, green-apple, grassy, herbaceous notes.

If you like:
Fennel & Green Apple
[See 'Veggie Herbaceous', Herbaceous, p.40]
Granny Smith & Lemon
[See 'Fruity Crisp', Fruity, p.46]

Try:
Cachaça: Caipirinha [p.194]
Fortified Wine: Fino Sherry [p.172]
Sparkling Wine: Cava Brut Nature [p.122], English Non-Vintage [p.116], Riesling Sekt [p.120]
Vodka Martini: Appletini [p.234]
White Wine: Picpoul de Pinet [p.129], Rueda Verdejo [p.138], Vinho Verde [p.136]

Viognier Think *James and the Giant Peach* and we're getting into the flavour mindset of Viognier. It's a massively peachy wine that's a hedonist's happy place, all stone fruit, perfumed quince, honeysuckle and ginger. Full disclosure: science hasn't

If you like:
Cooked Ginger & Quince
[See 'Zingy Spicy', Spicy, p.111]
Flat Peach & Honeysuckle
[See 'Creamy Fruity', Fruity, p.43]

fully nailed the complex network of compounds responsible for the stone-fruit component, but it's thought to be a heady combination of creamy lactones *[Glossary, p.17]* brought in by yeast contact, which vibe with Viognier's floral-fruity aromatic terpenes *[Glossary, p.19]* that are found in the grape skins themselves.

Try:
Dessert Wine: Tokaji Aszú [p.165]
Sparkling Wine: English Blanc de Blancs [p.116]
White Wine: Albariño [p.137], Alsace Gewürztraminer [p.126], Australian Viognier [p.124], Chardonnay [p.124], Sonoma Coast Chardonnay [p.139]

Austria

Grüner Veltliner Some Grüner Veltliner fans shorten it to Grü-Vee, though I am a fan who doesn't, just to be clear. It's the spicier version of Sauvignon Blanc, with naturally high levels of a compound called rotundone *[Glossary, p.19]* giving it that infamous thwack of white pepper. Rotundone is one of the most potent odorant compounds in wine, and it's found in grape skins, the essential oils of peppercorns and herbs like rosemary, thyme and basil. Grüner's departing ping of acidity reminds me of the soft malic bite of a Golden Delicious apple, which is swiftly atoned for by its creamy, honeyed manners.

If you like:
Golden Delicious & White Pepper [See 'Crisp Fruity', Fruity, p.45]
Golden Russet & Pear [See 'Crisp Fruity', Fruity, p.45]
Lemon Zest & Apricot [See 'Zingy Fruity', Fruity, p.53]

Try:
Cider: English Heritage [p.187]
Fortified Wine: White Port & Tonic [p.171]
White Wine: Soave Classico [p.135], Sonoma Coast Chardonnay [p.139], Torrontés [p.123]

England

Bacchus Deconstructing Britain's poster grape is like taking a picture of a hologram of an impressionist painting. Show me the Monet and I'll do it, though . . . Sorry, terrible joke. Back to Bacchus, often touted as the closest England has to Marlborough Sauvignon Blanc, which is a good shout given both are rich in aromatic compounds that are preserved by cooler climates and ramped up by fermentation. These compounds form flavours ranging from elderflower and gooseberry to cantaloupe melon, with

If you like:
Elderflower & Cantaloupe Melon [See 'Fruity Floral', Floral, p.24]
Lemongrass & Papaya [See 'Fragrant Spicy', Spicy, p.102]

Try:
Fruit Liqueur: Melon Ball Drop [p.184], Midori [p.185]
Mixer: Elderflower Cordial [p.258]
Sake: Junmai Ginjo [p.242]
White Wine: Marlborough Sauvignon Blanc [p.136], Pessac-Leognan [p.128]

factors like yeast strain playing a role in
the notes that are formed.

France

Alsace Gewürztraminer
Gewürztraminer's flavours read like a
checklist of Liberace's dressing-room rider
demands. Rose petals strewn over lychees,
served with Turkish delight, smouldering
incense, honeysuckle, citrus, peach,
mango, potpourri and sweet spices. Yes,
you know when you've been 'Gewürzed',
you'll have the Chelsea Flower Show up
your nose and everyone's invited. Rose
oxide is the culprit compound in both
roses and lychees, wrapping them in a
sensual feather boa of bordello aromas.
Linalool *[Glossary, p.18]* balances out
the rosy overkill with a woody note
over a lightly smoky, spicy, nutty, citrusy
bitterness.

If you like:
Flat Peach & Honeysuckle
[See 'Creamy Fruity', Fruity, p.43]
Honeycomb Toffee & Turkish Delight
[See 'Burnt Sweet', Sweet, p.58]
Rose
[See 'Intense Floral', Floral, p.26]

Try:
Dessert Wine: Rutherglen Muscat [p.162],
Tokaji Aszú [p.165]
Sparkling Wine: English Blanc de Blancs
[p.116]
White Wine: Albariño [p.137], Australian
Viognier [p.124], Sonoma Coast Chardonnay
[p.139]

Alsace Pinot Gris
Like a minor royal
gone rogue, Pinot Gris is a mutant clone
of a noble family. Problematic, prone to
bitterness and a bit 'meh' in the wrong
hands, plus it can get weighty, boozy and
smoky, which sounds like Snow White's
less Disney-friendly dwarfs. Alsace brings
out the potential in this black sheep, with a
cool climate that dials down the pugnacious
tones, expressing warming clove-laden,
cinnamon-sprinkled gingerbread notes
from this semi-aromatic grape variety.
Pinot Gris's macadamia nut-like richness
and smoky mannerism mirror the acrid-
sweet phenol compounds *[Glossary, p.18]*
blasted out by sizzling bacon fat.

If you like:
Gingerbread & Bacon Fat
[See 'Zingy Spicy', Spicy, p.111]
Macadamia Nut & Citrus Honey
[See 'Nutty Baked', Baked, p.73]

Try:
Cider: English Heritage [p.187]
Fortified Wine: Marsala Sweet Superiore
Riserva [p.168]
White Wine: Fiano di Avellino [p.133],
Puligny-Montrachet [p.129]

Chablis
The oxymoron 'I hate
Chardonnay, but I love Chablis' almost
makes sense, given Chablis is Chardonnay

If you like:
Beach Pebble & Thyme
[See 'Marine Minerally', Minerally, p.94]

in its purest form. Without oaky interference, cool-climate Chardonnay is an alpine lake of cut-glass citrus and white flowers with a whisper of struck flint. Descriptors include 'lean', 'racy', 'austere' and 'flinty', all pointing to the illusive conundrum of minerality. Left Bank Chablis' fresh, zingy, flinty, stony, chalky, smoky, sapid, sea-life sensation is suspected to be partly down to the sulphurous compounds activated by yeast-on-grape interaction.

Condrieu The road to hell is paved with Viognier, apparently. Who knew? Chris Rea did when he released 'The Road to Hell', *via Gehennae* in Latin, which I assume was written about Viognier being a nightmare to grow. Condrieu is Viognier's most swanky format; from the eponymous Rhône appellation it's the finest white required to be drunk young, given its low-acid, high-alcohol model unravels after around three years. Honey and melon flavours come from terpene compounds in the grapes, enhanced by ageing on dead yeast cells with an oily texture from phenol compounds *[Glossary, p.18]* in Viognier's skin.

Meursault Remember Top Trumps? With names like Puligny and Pommard under its belt, Burgundy's Côte de Beaune district beats every Chardonnay-producing region in the pack. Meursault is considered a zenith of the White Burgundy style, an aroma concertina in a bottle, pumping out jasmine high notes against a fatty, creamy, praline harmony. Hazelnut flavours are produced by amino acids reacting with compounds generated by oak contact. One in particular is also a key compound in

Flint & Lemon Balm
[See 'Rocky Minerally', Minerally, p.96]

Try:
Mixer: Vichy Catalan [p.259]
Red Wine: Nerello Mascalese [p.155]
Tea: Matcha [p.203]
White Wine: Assyrtiko [p.133], Gavi di Gavi [p.134], Muscadet Sèvre-et-Mains Sur Lie [p.128], Pouilly Fumé [p.129], Puligny Montrachet [p.129], Sancerre [p.131]

If you like:
Citrus Honey & Charentais Melon
[See 'Floral Sweet', Sweet, p.60]
Orange Blossom & Honey
[See 'Soft Floral', Floral, p.29]

Try:
Coffee: Peruvian [p.207]
Fruit Liqueur: Curaçao [p.182], Midori [p.185]
Gin: Sakura Bee's Knees [p.228]
Sparkling Wine: Moscato d'Asti [p.121], Prosecco DOCG [p.122]
Whisky Liqueur: Drambuie [p.246]
White Wine: Auslese Riesling [p.131], South African Chenin Blanc [p.137]

If you like:
Crème Pâtissière & Praline
[See 'Decadent Creamy', Creamy, p.68]
Jasmine & Hazelnut
[See 'Sweet Floral', Floral, p.30]
Macadamia Nut & Citrus Honey
[See 'Nutty Baked', Baked, p.73]

Try:
Bourbon: Eggnog [p.249]
Cider: English Heritage [p.187]
Fortified Wine: Marsala Sweet Superiore Riserva [p.168]

praline, conjured up in the conching process *[Glossary, p.15]*.

Muscadet Sèvre-et-Mains Sur Lie

Mindful that 'neutral' isn't code for 'boring', Muscadets are made from Melon de Bourgogne, which is confusingly a grape with no ties to melons. We'll have spotted 'Sèvre-et-Mains' on labels, those rivulets snaking through the Muscadet region, but it's really the 'sur lie' we want. Lees *[Glossary, p.19]* are mission-completed yeast cells suspended in the tank, along with random fragments of grape skin and pulp. Lees contact builds up creamy complexity in wine via proteins and fatty acids released during yeast breakdown, plus a citrus-saline, pebbly prickle of pétillance in an otherwise neutral-tasting vino.

Pessac-Leognan

When a famous white Bordeaux producer compared himself to a dog that 'when it bites your arse, it doesn't let go', he could have been describing white wines from the Graves region in general. Sauvignon Blanc and Semillon grapes are white Bordeaux's super twosome, whipping up wines on the fuller, food-friendlier scale, with their formative flavour compounds displaying papaya-like, sweet, tropical, musky nuances, activated by fermentation and preserved by Burgundian-style ageing on dead yeast cells, aka the lees *[Glossary, p.19]*. Lemongrass's citrus notes and herbaceous mannerisms are replicated in the grapes' flavour chemistry and are ramped up by yeast during fermentation.

Whisky: Baileys Irish Cream [p.243]
White Wine: Alsace Pinot Gris [p.126], Fiano di Avellino [p.133], Puligny Montrachet [p.129]

If you like:
Beach Pebble & Thyme
[See 'Marine Minerally', Minerally, p.94]
Soda Bread & Lemon Salt
[See 'Yeasty Baked', Baked, p.79]

Try:
Red Wine: Nerello Mascalese [p.155]
Sparkling Wine: Crémant d'Alsace [p.119], Pétillant Naturel Sec Chenin Blanc [p.119]
Tea: Matcha [p.203]
White Wine: Assyrtiko [p.133]

If you like:
Lemon Blossom & Sea Mist
[See 'Soft Floral', Floral, p.28]
Lemongrass & Papaya
[See 'Fragrant Spicy', Spicy, p.102]

Try:
White Wine: Albariño [p.137], Bacchus [p.125], Grillo [p.135], New Zealand Marlborough Sauvignon Blanc [p.136], Soave Classico [p.135], Vinho Verde [p.136]

Picpoul de Pinet Picpoul is the new Muscadet, which is now the new Sancerre that was once the new Chablis, replaced by Grüner Veltliner, the ex-new Albariño. Did I get that right? It's easier to keep track of the lip-smacking green apple, citrus and iodine-saline flavours inside a glass of Picpoul, translated as 'stings the lips'. Well, we can't say they didn't warn us. The cunning Picpouliers use canny tricks like cool night-time harvesting to retain the lightly bitter, preserved-lemon-like, briny-vegetal wakame and sea grape intensity from the Picpoul berry's marine-saline flavour compounds.

If you like:
Dried Wakame & Preserved Eureka Lemon
[See 'Vegetal Minerally', Minerally, p.97]
Granny Smith & Lemon
[See 'Crisp Fruity', Fruity, p.46]
Sea Grapes & Kiwi
[See 'Vegetal Minerally', Minerally, p.98]

Try:
Cachaça: Caipirinha [p.194]
Sparkling Wine: Cava Brut Nature [p.122], English Non-Vintage [p.116], Riesling Sekt [p.120]
Tea: Green [p.200]
Vodka: Appletini [p.234]
White Wine: Clare Valley Riesling [p.124], Vinho Verde [p.136]

Pouilly Fumé We'd easily sniff out Sauvignon Blanc in a *Usual Suspects*-style line-up, or, should I say, wine-up, there's just something comfortingly textbook about this reliable berry. While most grape varieties mimic familiar flavours via a cocktail of chemical compounds, which individually bear zero resemblance to the finished product, Sauvignon Blanc actually shares green bell pepper's unmistakable compound, bell pepper pyrazine *[Glossary, p.18]*. Grapefruit, clipped grass and smoky gunmetal are other classic aromas of a Loire Pouilly Fumé, brought in by compounds in the grapes' skins, which react with yeast cells to make the magic flavours happen.

If you like:
Flint & Lemon Balm
[See 'Rocky Minerally', Minerally, p.96]
Green Bell Pepper & Cut Grass
[See 'Sweet Herbaceous', Herbaceous, p.36]
Gunmetal & Grapefruit
[See 'Rocky Minerally, Minerally, p.96]

Try:
Mixer: Vichy Catalan [p.259]
Red Wine: Gaillac Rouge [p.149]
White Wine: Chablis [p.126], Gavi di Gavi [p.134], Puligny Montrachet [p.129], Sancerre [p.131]

Puligny Montrachet In a *Real Housewives* franchise, Côte de Beaune is Beverly Hills and Puligny Montrachet is too dignified for drama. Well, with a reputation as the planet's best expression of Chardonnay, we would be too. Flavour-wise, there's honeyed, citrusy,

If you like:
Flint & Lemon Balm
[See 'Rocky Minerally', Minerally, p.96]
Macadamia Nut & Citrus Honey
[See 'Nutty Baked', Baked, p.73]

fatty macadamia-nut girth to Puligny, less about fruit opulence, more a dichotomy between richness and mineral, puppy-like energy. The flinty minerality is brought in from sulphurous compounds during fermentation, while others bring in rosy lemon-balm notes. Aged Puligny also develops a compound that gives it honey-drizzled, macadamia-nut muscles to flex.

Reuilly Sauvignon Blanc Hear me out. I'm not comparing Reuilly Sauvignon Blanc to a bowl of shellfish ramen, it's the light oyster notes I'm fishing for. Reuilly's vines are parked in the same Kimmeridgian clay as Chablis and Sancerre, soil basically made of smushed-up oyster-shell fossils. Is it a coincidence there's a thread of citrus-briny, creamy oyster flesh and chalky seashell sewn through the wines? Most likely, as it's got all the hallmarks of a savoury, salty-tasting compound kicked up from fermentation by certain yeast strains that smack of shellfish. We'll go with the more romantic version, though . . .

Roussanne Sting might have been on to something had he sung, 'Roussanne, put on the red light', given it comes from the French word *roux* for red, after the grapes' rusty colouring. It feels like we've taken Sting away from the Police, though, given Roussanne often performs with Marsanne and Viognier. Going solo gives us the chance to appreciate Roussanne's jasmine, apricot and clove-like profile uninterrupted. Speaking of Viognier, it's often mistaken for Roussanne, though I'm not sure which is more flattered by the comparison, given that Roussanne resides on the earthier, more uncouth side of the flavour spectrum.

Try:
Cider: English Heritage [p.187]
Fortified Wine: Marsala Sweet Superiore Riserva [p.168]
Mixer: Vichy Catalan [p.259]
White Wine: Alsace Pinot Gris [p.126], Chablis [p.126], Fiano di Avellino [p.133], Gavi di Gavi [p.134], Meursault [p.127], Pouilly Fumé [p.129], Sancerre [p.131]

If you like:
Cut Grass & Quince
[See 'Grassy Herbaceous', Herbaceous, p.35]
Pacific Oyster & Meyer Lemon
[See 'Marine Minerally', Minerally, p.94]
Sea Spray & Bread Dough
[See 'Marine Minerally', Minerally, p.95]

Try:
Sake: Junmai-Shu [p.242]
Sherry: Fino [p.172], Manzanilla [p.172]
Vodka: Bloody Caesar [p.232]
White Wine: Sancerre [p.131]

If you like:
Golden Russet & Pear
[See 'Crisp Fruity', Fruity, p.30]
Jasmine & Clove
[See 'Sweet Floral', Floral, p.28]
Jasmine & Apricot
[See 'Sweet Floral', Floral, p.30]

Try:
Cider: English Heritage [p.187]
Rosé Wine: Provence Rosé [p.141]
White Wine: Grüner Veltliner [p.125], Soave Classico [p.135], Sonoma Coast Chardonnay [p.139]

Sancerre Sancerre is basically Lourdes for Sauvignon Blanc pilgrims, seen by devotees as its spiritual homeland. Given the Loire's flagship wine district whips up flavours ranging from grass, quince, anise, honeysuckle to lime, grapefruit and lemon curd, I've picked out the most impactful so we're not here all day. The Loire's cool climate brings forth green, grassy flavours from compounds in the grapes' skins and quince notes from another chemical compound that morphs into asparagus at higher concentrations. Chablis, Sancerre's neighbouring soil-sister, shares a struck-flint aroma connection, with the help of a smoky odour formed during fermentation.

If you like:
Cut Grass & Quince
[See 'Grassy Herbaceous', Herbaceous, p.35]
Flint & Lemon Balm
[See 'Rocky Minerally', Minerally, p.96]
Jasmine & Apricot
[See 'Sweet Floral', Floral, p.30]

Try:
Mixer: Vichy Catalan [p.259]
Pisco: Peruvian [p.179]
White Wine: Chablis [p.126], Gavi di Gavi [p.134], Pouilly Fumé [p.129], Puligny Montrachet [p.129]

Vin Jaune Vin Jaune is France's answer to the durian, the whiffy 'king of fruit' that tastes of chives and icing sugar. A fair analogy, given the messy flavour messageing going on inside Vin Jaune's squat clavelin bottle *[Glossary, p.15]*. Made in a similar way to sherry, from late-picked Savagnin grapes, emerging after six years' ageing under a sherry-like veil of yeast as a contradiction of pistachio nuts, pine, lime, candyfloss, bone-broth, bread and even seaweed notes. Flavours are shaped around apple-vinegar flavoured compounds and nutty, caramelly-flavoured lactones produced through oxidative ageing.

If you like:
Pistachio Nut & Lime
[See 'Nutty Baked', Baked, p.74]
Roast Chestnut & Bruised Apple
[See 'Nutty Baked', Baked, p.74]

Try:
Fortified Wine: Fino Sherry [p.172]
Orange Wine: Georgian [p.139]
White Wine: Gavi di Gavi [p.134]
Cider: Cask-Aged [p.186]
Grain Spirit: Sweet Potato Shōchū [p.256]
Rum: Rhum Agricole Blanc [p.199]

Germany

Auslese Riesling Riesling ages like a fine wine, which makes sense, as it is one. In fact, its naturally high acidity and sugar content give it the best ageing potential of all white grapes. *Ows-lay-zuh*, or Auslese if we want to be bogged down with accuracy, is one of its sweeter styles thanks to mould called 'noble rot'.

If you like:
Baby Ginger & Linden Honey
[See 'Zingy Spicy', Spicy, p.111]
Citrus Honey & Charentais Melon
[See 'Floral Sweet', Sweet, p.60]
Thyme Honey & Granny Smith
[See 'Floral Sweet', Sweet, p.61]

The deliberately overripened grapes are prime candidates for the humidity-loving botrytis fungus, sucking them dry into withered sugar bombs. Without getting all *New Scientist*, botrytis rearranges the grapes' flavour chemistry, introducing exciting new compounds for honey, tropical melon and sweet ginger.

Mosel Kabinett Riesling Trocken

Just to conclusively settle the nature–nurture argument, Riesling is famous for chanelling its surroundings in the wines it produces but also retains its unique flavour characteristics. Isn't that nature and nurture? The light, dry Kabinett wines made from grapes grown in the cooler Mosel region tend to taste of slate. A sulphurous, fermentation-formed compound could be partly responsible for the smoky, flinty, wet-stony, earthy nuances, but I'm going with my explanation that the grapes have hoovered them up from the soil. Tangy malic acid *[Glossary, p.18]* in the grapes is nurtured by the cooler climate, bringing forth the clean, green, precise, mouth-squirting flavours of Granny Smith apples.

Spätlese Riesling

Getting to grips with German wine can feel like death by umlauts, but it's worth it. Spätlese is the Goldilocks Riesling style for anyone who mixes sweet and salted popcorn at the cinema, me included. The name Spätlese is tied to grape ripeness and these bunches are picked later than normal, hence the 'late-harvest' translation. Kerosine aromas, though? We're not talking full-on petrol sniffing, but a specific Riesling-related compound powers up the paraffin aromas, which are brought in by grape degradation through the ageing process, balanced out by a nectarine-like acidity.

Try:

Dessert Wine: Sauternes [p.164]
Fruit Liqueur: Midori [p.185]
Herb Liqueur: King's Ginger [p.212]
Sparkling Wine: Prosecco DOCG [p.122]
White Wine: Condrieu [p.127], South African Chenin Blanc [p.137]

If you like:

Dried Lime & Tomatillo
[See 'Fragrant Spicy', Spicy, p.102]
Lemon Zest & Apricot
[See 'Zingy Fruity', Fruity, p.53]
Slate Tile & Granny Smith
[See 'Rocky Minerally', Minerally, p.96]

Try:

Cachaça: Caipirinha [p.194]
Coffee: Kenyan [p.205]
Fortified Wine: White Port & Tonic [p.171]
Rosé Wine: Sangiovese Rosé [p.142]
Tea: Green Tea Kombucha [p.200]
White Wine: Grüner Veltliner [p.125], Spätlese Riesling [p.132], Torrontés [p.123]

If you like:

Baby Ginger & Linden Honey
[See 'Zingy Spicy', Spicy, p.111]
Kerosine & Nectarine
[See 'Earthy Smoky', Smoky, p.82]
Slate Tile & Granny Smith
[See 'Rocky Minerally', Minerally, p.96]

Try:

Dessert Wine: Sauternes [p.164]
Herb Liqueur: King's Ginger [p.212]
White Wine: Auslese Riesling [p.131], Mosel Kabinett Riesling Trocken [p.132]

Greece

Assyrtiko Picture *Jurassic World*, replacing Isla Nublar with the island of Santorini and dinosaurs with ancient vines. Smaller jaw-to-claw ratio, but the wines have a saline bite and we've just pictured Assyrtiko's growing landscape. Ferocious winds, desiccating summer heat and zero summer rain provide suitably stressful conditions for the intensifying citrusy flavours of lemon blossom and orange. It's romantic to imagine that volcanic stone transmits notes of smoke, salt, herbs, seaweed and rocky earthiness from vine stem to glass stemware, though in reality high acid and fermented, reductive sulphurous compounds are the probable chemical culprits.

If you like:
Beach Pebble & Thyme
[See 'Marine Minerally', Minerally, p.94]
Sea Spaghetti & Lemon Blossom
[See 'Vegetal Minerally', Minerally, p.98]
Valencia Orange & Cooked Ginger
[See 'Juicy Fruity', Fruity, p.48]

Try:
Red Wine: Nerello Mascalese [p.155]
Tea: Matcha [p.203]
White Wine: Chablis [p.126], Muscadet Sèvre-et-Mains Sur Lie [p.128]

Retsina Ditch the mass-produced vinegary apple juice hybrid that smacks of pine-scented shampoo, we're talking craft Retsina here. The choicest versions are made with the indigenous Savatianó, Roditis and Assyrtiko grape triumvirate, plus an infusion of resin from the Aleppo pine tree, with its unctuous flavours of menthol, incense, blossom, lime, apple and bittersweet piquancy. A resin-filled perforated bag is suspended in the barrel, unleashing piney, limey, camphoraceous terpene compounds *[Glossary, pp.15, 19]* into the wine, adding a warming kick of peppery spice to Assyrtiko's mineral salinity.

If you like:
Christmas Tree & Preserved Lime
[See 'Fruity Spicy', Spicy, p.103]
Pistachio Nut & Lime
[See 'Nutty Baked', Baked, p.74]

Try:
Brandy: Pisco Sour [p.180]
Herb Liqueur: Crème de Menthe [p.213], The Last Word [p.216]
White Wine: Gavi di Gavi [p.134], Vin Jaune [p.131]

Italy

Fiano di Avellino Drop enough cash and Fiano can be whatever you want it to be: big and sweet, lean and highly strung, but always a bit nutty. Dry styles of Fiano di

If you like:
Jasmine & Mint
[See 'Sweet Floral', Floral, p.30]

Avellino have rich jasmine, citrus flavours accented by a minty, mineral moment. It's fuller in aromatic compounds than some of its peers, which cheerlead its citrus-floral game alongside an unctuous macadamia and honey component found in richer styles. Well, Fiano isn't nicknamed 'the vine beloved of bees' for nothing, I suppose.

Gavi di Gavi Gavi di Gavi di Gavi – is that too many 'di Gavi's? It's hard to know when to stop with Gavi, which really should be its strapline. Confusingly Gavi is the regional denomination, the grape is Cortese, 'di Gavi' means from the premium growing area of the region. Flavour-wise, I'd venture to suggest that it's Piedmont's version of Chablis or Sancerre, with a similarly lean citrus-saline style, though with a value-added nutty nuance and a herbaceous burst of lime. Grape-based terpene compounds activate Cortese's resident pine-resinous aromas, which are also found in lime zest and pistachio nuts.

Greco di Tufo Pavarotti quaffed it to relax his vocal cords before performances, so does that mean Greco di Tufo can be sipped medicinally? Asking for a friend. Made from the Greco di Tufo grape in the eponymous DOCG region of southern Campania, the wines are characterised by their savoury, smoky-saline, herbal, warmly spiced, citrusy and roasted-almond characteristics. These flavour mannerisms stem from a citrusy compound and a smoky phenolic molecule *[Glossary, p.18]* that mimics its volcanic ashen 'tuff' soil, with a clove-like nuttiness and a salty kick of rock samphire to soothe our singing voices.

Macadamia Nut & Citrus Honey
[See 'Nutty Baked', Baked, p.73]

Try:
Cider: English Heritage [p.187]
Fortified Wine: Marsala Sweet Superiore Riserva [p.168]
Fruit Liqueur: Cointreau [p.182]
White Wine: Alsace Pinot Gris [p.126], Meursault [p.127], Puligny Montrachet [p.129]

If you like:
Gunmetal & Grapefruit
[See 'Rocky Minerally', Minerally, p.96]
Flint & Lemon Balm
[See 'Rocky Minerally', Minerally, p.96]
Pistachio Nut & Lime
[See 'Nutty Baked', Baked, p.74]

Try:
Mixer: Vichy Catalan [p.259]
White Wine: Chablis [p.126], Pouilly Fumé [p.129], Puligny Montrachet [p.129], Retsina [p.133], Sancerre [p.131], Vin Jaune [p.131]

If you like:
Beach Pebble & Thyme
[See 'Marine Minerally', Minerally, p.94]
Cut Grass & Salt-Roasted Almonds
[See 'Grassy Herbaceous', Herbaceous, p.35]
Rock Samphire & Asian Pear
[See 'Vegetal Minerally', Minerally, p.97]

Try:
Red Wine: Nerello Mascalese [p.155]
Sherry: Manzanilla [p.172]
Tea: Matcha [p.203]
White Wine: Assyrtiko [p.133], Chablis [p.126], Muscadet Sèvre-et-Mains Sur Lie [p.128], South African Chenin Blanc [p.137]

Grillo I'm no psychiatrist, but I've diagnosed the Grillo grape with dual-personality disorder. Early-picked Grillo grapes produce Sauvignon Blanc-alikes with fruity flavours and a racy grapefruit and orange-peel profile. Picked later and grape-based compounds take over, whipping up wines with a chunkier texture and a meatier, muskier vibe, verging on rustic. The fresher styles are produced in an air-starved environment to preserve the high-maintenance fruity traits that would degrade through oxygen contact. This winemaking technique is also linked to floral-herbal garrigue, iodine, saline and lightly smoky flavours, checking off Grillo's more savoury flavour boxes.

If you like:
Iodine & Garrigue
[See 'Marine Minerally', Minerally, p.94]
Lemon Blossom & Sea Mist
[See 'Soft Floral', Floral, p.28]
Seville Orange Marmalade & Grapefruit
[See 'Juicy Fruity', Fruity, p.48]

Try:
Aperitivo Cocktail: Negroni [p.224]
Dessert Wine: Vin de Paille [p.164]
White Wine: Albariño [p.137], Pessac-Leognan [p.128], Soave Classico [p.135], Vinho Verde [p.136]

Soave Classico Allegedly a favourite of Romeo and Juliet, though if it was the same sub-par Soave the world was mainlining in the seventies, that really would be a tragedy. Premium Soave majors on the Garganega grape with vines parked on pumice stone, though I must have missed the memo that Veneto once had volcanoes. Who knew? Garganega flaunts its florals thanks to aromatic compounds, with fresh pear, russet apple, white peach and lemon notes and sweet almond, sandalwood and marjoram nuances stemming from aromatic esters *[Glossary, p.16]* kicked up during fermentation.

If you like:
Golden Russet & Pear
[See 'Crisp Fruity', Fruity, p.45]
Lemon & Marzipan
[See 'Zingy Fruity', Fruity, p.53]
Lemon Blossom & Sea Mist
[See 'Soft Floral', Floral, p.28]
Sweet Marjoram & White Peach
[See 'Herbal Spicy', Spicy, p.105]

Try:
Cider: English Heritage [p.187]
Nut Liqueur: Amaretto [p.253]
Sake: Daiginjo [p.242]
White Wine: Albariño [p.137], Grillo [p.135], Grüner Veltliner [p.125], Pessac-Leognan [p.128], Roussanne [p.130], Sonoma Coast Chardonnay [p.139], Vinho Verde [p.136]

Vermentino Safe to say, we're not thinking of vermin when we sip a Vermentino, thank goodness. The grape naming committee feared the vermin association might be a problem, but we're far too busy getting our heads

If you like:
Lemon & Fresh Pear
[See 'Zingy Fruity', Fruity, p.52]
Yellow Grapefruit & Sea Air
[See 'Bitter Fruity', Fruity, p.43]

around its intense flavours of fresh pear and lemon with a light grapefruit bitterness, partially subdued by sea-air salinity. Oily textured, sapid and citrusy, the Sardinian Vermentino grape is high in bitter-aromatic phenol compounds *[Glossary, p.18]* that are housed in its skin, nudging in a pine-resinous nuance that leans into pithy yellow-grapefruit aromas pumped out by fermentation-activated compounds.

Try:
Brandy: Peruvian/Chilean Pisco [p.179]
Coffee: Nicaraguan [p.206]
Gin: Salty Dog [p.227]
Mixer: Elderflower Cordial [p.258]
Sparkling Wine: Crémant de Loire [p.119]
Tequila: Paloma [p.191]
White Wine: Rueda Verdejo [p.138],
South African Chenin Blanc [p.137]

New Zealand

Marlborough Sauvignon Blanc If you haven't met a New Zealand Sauvignon Blanc yet, you need to get out more. Introducing Marlborough, the region responsible for the benchmark Kiwi Sauvignon style, a dry dichotomy of cut grass, yellow pepper and a tropical-beach breakfast of passion fruit and papaya. At a molecular level, bell pepper pyrazine *[Glossary, p.18]* harnesses the grass and, well, green bell pepper notes, while fermentation-triggered compounds deliver the fruity fanfare. New Zealand's high-UV environment ramps up compounds called thiols *[Glossary, p.19]*, to which humans are sensitive, pumping out passion fruit, papaya and nuances of human sweat.

If you like:
Cut Grass & Quince
[See 'Grassy Herbaceous', Herbaceous, p.35]
Lemongrass & Papaya
[See 'Fragrant Spicy', Spicy, p.102]
Yellow Bell Pepper & Passion Fruit
[See 'Sweet Herbaceous', Herbaceous, p.39]

Try:
Vodka: Pornstar Martini [p.232]
White Wine: Bacchus [p.125], Pessac-Leognan [p.128], Reuilly Sauvignon Blanc [p.130], Sancerre [p.131]

Portugal

Vinho Verde When Tom Jones sang about the 'green, green glass of Vin-ho', I'm almost certain he was referring to the youthful green-tinged Portuguese wine Vinho Verde. It's actually pronounced *veen-yo vairdh*, but we'll let Tom off this time. A blend of tough-to-pronounce indigenous grapes, including Loureiro,

If you like:
Granny Smith & Lemon
[See 'Crisp Fruity', Fruity, p.46]
Lemon Blossom & Sea Mist
[See 'Soft Floral', Floral, p.28]
Sea Grapes & Kiwi
[See 'Vegetal Minerally', Minerally, p.98]

Arinto and Alvarinho, produces lean, floral, tingly whites that smack of green apple, citrus blossom and kiwi with a vibrant prickle of marine salinity. Linalool *[Glossary, p.18]* is the leading flavour compound with its citrus-floral influence, which is punctuated by a lick of Granny Smith apple spritz on the finish.

Try:
Cachaça: Caipirinha [p.194]
Sparkling Wine: Cava Brut Nature [p.122], Riesling Sekt [p.120]
Tea: Green [p.200]
Vodka: Appletini [p.234]
White Wine: Albariño [p.137], Clare Valley Riesling [p.124], Grillo [p.135], Picpoul de Pinet [p.129]

South Africa

South African Chenin Blanc I'm not sure why Natasha Bedingfield's 'Pocketful of Sunshine' track springs to mind when I think of Cape Chenin Blanc. Probably because South Africa provides sunshine in a way the Loire can't, rocking a Mediterranean climate that brings out a grape's fruitier side. Chenin Blanc is a blank canvas, waiting to be Jackson-Pollocked with splurges of fermentation-derived shades of flavour. Ester compounds *[Glossary, p.16]* colour in the flavour outline, with others providing strokes of perfumed quince, signature rosy-honeyed tones and sea-life notes into unoaked Chenin Blanc.

If you like:
Citrus Honey & Charentais Melon
[See 'Floral Sweet', Sweet, p.60]
Lemon & Fresh Pear
[See 'Zingy Fruity', Fruity, p.52]
Rock Pool & Quince Cheese
[See 'Marine Minerally', Minerally, p.95]

Try:
Brandy: Peruvian/Chilean Pisco [p.179]
Coffee: Nicaraguan [p.206]
Fruit Liqueur: Midori [p.185]
Sparkling Wine: Crémant de Loire [p.119], Prosecco DOCG [p.122]
White Wine: Auslese Riesling [p.131], Condrieu [p.127], Vermentino [p.135]

Spain

Albariño On paper, Albariño should taste like quaffing Covent Garden Flower Market. It doesn't, though there is a high floral intensity to this super-aromatic variety, from citrus-blossomy through to intensely rosy. So flowery is this grape that it's considered a close genetic match to German Rhine Riesling, though without the penchant for petrol-pump aromas. Ester compounds *[Glossary, p.16]* formed during fermentation bring forth

If you like:
Flat Peach & Honeysuckle
[See 'Creamy Fruity', Fruity, p.43]
Lemon Blossom & Sea Mist
[See 'Soft Floral', Floral, p.28]

Try:
Dessert Wine: Tokaji Aszú [p.165]
Sparkling Wine: English Blanc de Blancs [p.116]
White Wine: Australian Viognier [p.124], Alsace Gewürztraminer [p.126], Grillo [p.135],

Albariño's fruity side to balance out the botanical, herbaceous flavours, with a honeyed component that, dare I say, verges on the flowery.

Rueda Verdejo I'm a sucker for anything Spanish. Heck, I thought I was a little Iberian until I took the ancestry test. The dramatic Latin flourish extends to Verdejo, Spain's flagship white grape that smacks of wild fennel, green apple, star anise and yellow citrus. It may come off like a Sauvignon Blanc, but its flavours veer from anise-spiced, green-apple, peach notes to grassy, vegetal and floral with a farewell thwack of grapefruit bitterness from fermentation-derived compounds and malic acid *[Glossary, p.18]*.

White Rioja Reserva We all know people who improve with age; well, meet Viura, White Rioja's headline grape. Though appealing as a citrusy bright young thing, wood maturation puts distinguished flavour rings round its trunk, so to speak. Spelling it out, Viura is a neutral variety, lacking the aromatic charms of a grape like Albariño. High in tangy malic acid *[Glossary, p.18]*, the required two-year wood-ageing softens Viura's edges, bringing in a flavour network of lactone-toasty, warming cinnamon, candied tarragon, dried pineapple and vanilla-adjacent cooked ginger notes.

Pessac-Leognan [p.128], Soave Classico [p.135], Sonoma Coast Chardonnay [p.139], Vinho Verde [p.136]

If you like:
Fennel & Green Apple
[See 'Veggie Herbaceous', Herbaceous, p.40]
Yellow Grapefruit & Sea Air
[See 'Bitter Fruity', Fruity, p.43]
Yellow Peach & Star Anise
[See 'Creamy Fruity', Fruity, p.44]

Try:
Fortified Wine: Fino Sherry [p.172]
Gin: Salty Dog [p.227]
Sake: Junmai Ginjo [p.242]
Sparkling Wine: Cava Brut Nature [p.122], English Non-Vintage [p.116]
Tequila: Paloma [p.191]
White Wine: Clare Valley Riesling [p.124], Vermentino [p.135]

If you like:
Cinnamon Toast & Candied Tarragon
[See 'Toasty Baked', Baked, p.76]
Crème Pâtissière & Praline
[See 'Decadent Creamy', Creamy, p.68]
Dried Pineapple & Cooked Ginger
[See 'Spicy Sweet', Sweet, p.64]

Try:
Bourbon: Eggnog [p.249]
Dessert Wine: Vidal Ice Wine [p.163]
Rum: Pineapple [p.197]
Whisky Liqueur: Baileys Irish Cream [p.243]
White Wine: Meursault [p.127]

USA

Sonoma Coast Chardonnay Taking
Taylor Swift's advice, Chardonnay should
shake it off, because haters gonna hate,
hate, hate. In fact, I think I've missed out
a 'hate'. Sonoma Coast Chardonnay bucks
the buttery trend that brought about the
backlash, benefitting from the cool Pacific
breeze that lengthens the ripening time,
nurturing its lean lemony lip-smacking
acidity. Aromatic compounds linalool
[Glossary, p.18], geraniol *[Glossary, p.16]*
and nerol are the chemical triumvirate
that make Chardonnay's apricot aroma
possible, bringing about a peachy, yellow–
apple, pear-flavoured, floral, honeyed
complexity, with a lactic creaminess from
lees-activated protein compounds.

If you like:
Flat Peach & Honeysuckle
[See 'Creamy Fruity', Fruity, p.43]
Golden Russet & Pear
[See 'Crisp Fruity', Fruity, p.45]
Lemon Zest & Apricot
[See 'Zingy Fruity', Fruity, p.53]

Try:
Cider: English Heritage [p.187]
Dessert Wine: Tokaji Aszú [p.165]
Fortified Wine: White Port & Tonic [p.171]
Sparkling Wine: English Blanc de Blancs
[p.116]
White Wine: Alsace Gewürztraminer [p.126],
Australian Chardonnay [p.124], Australian
Viognier [p.124], Grüner Veltliner [p.125],
Roussanne [p.130], Torrontés [p.123]

Orange Wine

Georgia

Amber Wine When Doris Day sang
'Quevri Será, Será', I like to think she was
referencing the earthenware 'quevri' pots
used to ferment and mature the wines of
Georgia back in the day. The Georgia in
Europe, not America. Like many things in
life, it's all about skin contact and oxygen,
which gives the wine a carotene colouring
and a boatload of flavour complexity.
Notes of roast chestnut, bruised apple,
focaccia bread and pear skin are thanks to
wild yeast working on unpronounceable
local grapes that house high levels of
aromatic compounds in their skin.

If you like:
Focaccia & Pear Skin
[See 'Yeasty Baked', Baked, p.78]
Roast Chestnut & Bruised Apple
[See 'Nutty Baked', Baked, p.74]

Try:
Cider: Cask-Aged [p.186]
Fortified Wine: Fino Sherry [p.172]
Grain Spirit: Sweet Potato Shōchū [p.256]
Perry: Vintage [p.188]
Sparkling Wine: Franciacorta Riserva [p.121]
White Wine: Vin Jaune [p.131]

South Africa

Chenin Blanc Orange wine is like discovering a new room in your house, though some prefer to keep that door securely bolted. Not me – I'm down with the mismatched flavour messageing and semi-astringent texture that straddles white, rosé and red wine in style. Skin-steeping rearranges flavour molecules, switching out fresh, tropical-fruity compounds for more mature stone-fruity, grassy, shrubland-aromatic, herbal alcohols. Chenin keeps some of its signature honey notes, and a saline, roast-nutty note from oxygen contact.

If you like:
Cooked Ginger & Quince
[See 'Zingy Spicy', Spicy, p.111]
Cut Grass & Salt-Roasted Almonds
[See 'Grassy Herbaceous', Herbaceous, p.35]
Manuka Honey & Custard Apple
[See 'Floral Sweet', Sweet, p.61]
Nectarine & Oolong Tea
[See 'Creamy Fruity', Fruity, p.44]

Try:
Mead: Traditional [p.212]
Sherry: Manzanilla [p.172]
Tea: Oolong [p.201]
White Wine: Australian Viognier [p.124],
Greco di Tufo [p.134]

Rosé Wine

France

Bandol Nothing sounds as sexy as it does in French. Take *vin de fourchette*, meaning food-friendly wine, which directly translates as 'fork wine'. See? Bandol rosé has earned a place at the dinner table as a bona fide *rosé d'assiette*, or 'plate rosé', which sounds just as naff anglicised. Although Bandol rosé is officially Provençal, its headlining Mourvèdre grape comes equipped with brawny scrubland-style tannins, perfectly evolved for its epicurean agenda. Like sun-ripening a buffalo, Mourvèdre takes its time, ultimately resulting in the *fourchette*-friendly flavours of Mediterranean herbs, blood orange, pomegranate, aniseed cinnamon and roses.

If you like:
Cinnamon & Blood Orange
[See 'Warm Spicy', Spicy, p.109]
Oregano & Boysenberry
[See 'Herbal Spicy', Spicy, p.105]
Rose & Liquorice
[See 'Intense Floral', Floral, p.26]
Wild Thyme & Pomegranate
[See 'Herbal Spicy', Spicy, p.105]

Try:
Amaro: Campari [p.223]
Fortified Wine: Vintage Port [p.170]
Mixer: Cranberry Juice [p.261]
Red Wine: Aged Red Burgundy [p.145],
Barbaresco [p.152], Barolo [p.152], Corbières
[p.148], Montepulciano d'Abruzzo [p.154],
Sangria [p.160]
Rosé Wine: Tavel Rosé [p.141]

Provence You couldn't pay a reality star to look 'pale and interesting', though Provence rosé has made a career out of it. Aesthetics play a massive part in Provence's rosy success, which it partially owes to that trademark shade of ballet-slipper-pink. Flavours err squarely on the citrusy, stone-fruity and fresh, florally side, thanks to a high ester [Glossary, p.16] count, strawberry, candyfloss and caramel notes from the compound, strawberry furanone, and a pink grapefruit profile. Lighter skin contact means fewer harsh-tasting compounds, a paler pigment and lower concentrations of a particular chemical that supresses red-fruit notes.

If you like:
Jasmine & Apricot
[See 'Sweet Floral', Floral, p.30]
Pink Grapefruit & Strawberry
[See 'Bitter Fruity', Fruity, p.42]
Strawberry & Whipped Cream
[See 'Sweet Fruity', Fruity, p.50]

Try:
Gin: Pink [p.226]
Rosé Wine: New Zealand Pinot Noir Rosé [p.142]
Sparkling Wine: English Blanc de Noirs [p.116], Rosé Champagne [p.118]
White Wine: Roussanne [p.130]

Syrah A grape's junk is all in its trunk, so to speak. Pop the bonnet on a berry and you'll find flavour and colour-impacting compounds housed in its skin, or exocarp, to get geeky. One way of nailing a lighter hue is by cutting short the grape-on-skin contact time, which inputs less pigment. Side effects include less flavour complexity, which in the case of Syrah dials down its peppery-flavoured compound, replacing cracked black pepper with a milder white form and an echo of cherry via fermentation-derived esters [Glossary, p.16].

If you like:
Cumin & Watermelon
[See 'Fragrant Spicy', Spicy, p.101]
Red Cherry & White Pepper
[See 'Floral Fruity', Fruity, p.47]

Try:
Amaro: Campari [p.223]
Red Wine: Crozes-Hermitage [p.149], Frappato [p.154], Gaillac Rouge [p.149]
Rosé Wine: Sangiovese Rosé [p.142]

Tavel 'Deep Watermelon' and 'African Sunset' aren't the names of home hair dyes, they're the colour palettes of Tavel. The antidote to 'powder-puff' Provence pink, Tavel is drier, darker, spicier, beefier; heck, even 'man's man' Ernest Hemingway was a fan. A rosé officially, though we can drop the term, as Tavel's wines legally have to be of the pink persuasion. Located next to Châteauneuf-du-Pape, the Avignon popes, aka *papes*, loved Tavel's almost light red, aka 'clairet', plonk, which was created

If you like:
Oregano & Boysenberry
[See 'Herbal Spicy', Spicy, p.105]
Vanilla Custard & Rhubarb
[See 'Decadent Creamy', Creamy, p.68]
Wild Thyme & Pomegranate
[See 'Herbal Spicy', Spicy, p.105]

Try:
Amaro: Zucca Rabarbaro [p.225]
Red Wine: Montepulciano d'Abruzzo [p.154]
Rosé Wine: Bandol Rosé [p.140]

by a short skin soak so as not to take up too much colour. Aromatic compounds nudge in red-fruit notes with herbal, spicy, creamy credentials.

Sparkling Wine: English Blanc de Noirs [p.116], Rosé Champagne [p.118]

Italy

<u>Sangiovese</u> When your name is derived from *sanguis Jovis*, Latin for 'the blood of Jove', the pressure's on to bring pigment to the party. Slightly awkward then that Sangiovese grapes run low on colour-creating compounds, producing rosé wines that could benefit from a prescription of iron tablets. Flavour-wise, Sangiovese rosé brings its A-positive game, with an echo of cumin and dried lime-style earthiness, a morello-cherry astringency, a thwack of savoury tomatillo-adjacent acidity and a watermelon-like dichotomy of red-fruit and vegetal, herbaceous flavours.

If you like:
Cumin & Watermelon
[See 'Fragrant Spicy', Spicy, p.101]
Dried Lime & Tomatillo
[See 'Fragrant Spicy', Spicy, p.102]
Morello Cherry & Almond
[See 'Floral Fruity', Fruity, p.47]

Try:
Brandy: Armagnac [p.175]
Cachaça: Caipirinha [p.194]
Coffee: Kenyan [p.205]
Fruit Liqueur: Kirsch [p.183], Maraschino [p.180]
Mixer: Cherry Coke [p.260]
Nut Liqueur: Amaretto [p.253]
Red Wine: Amarone [p.151]
Rosé Wine: Syrah Rosé [p.141]
Vodka: Bloody Mary [p.235]

New Zealand

<u>Pinot Noir</u> Remember *Minority Report*, with Tom Cruise stopping crimes before they happened via premonitions from the sinister-looking 'Precogs'? Great movie and a tenuous connection, but grapes house odourless compounds called 'precursors' that are programmed to morph into predetermined flavours during fermentation. New Zealand's UV-rich environment is the perfect forum for building the pathways for those flavour-carrying compounds, with sun exposure a major nurturing factor. Pinot Noir rosé

If you like:
Pink Grapefruit & Strawberry
[See 'Bitter Fruity', Fruity, p.42]
Strawberry & Whipped Cream
[See 'Sweet Fruity', Fruity, p.50]
Violet & Raspberry
[See 'Rich Floral', Floral, p.27]

Try:
Gin: Pink [p.226]
Red Wine: Argentinian Malbec [p.143], Beaujolais [p.146], Côte-Rôtie [p.148]
Rosé Wine: Provence Rosé [p.141]

expresses pink-grapefruit notes during fermentation, plus violets, raspberries and fruity esters *[Glossary, p.16]* for unstoppable strawberries.

Sparkling Wine: English Blanc de Noirs [p.116], Rosé Champagne [p.118]
Rum: White [p.197]

Red Wine

Argentina

<u>Malbec</u> What happened before Argentinian Malbec came on the scene? I need a Nurofen from trying to picture the second bottle down on a wine list before Argentinian Malbec, or BAM. Life without that ubiquitous liquorice, prune, dark-chocolate, powdery, floral, clove and eucalyptus profile doesn't bear thinking about. Luckily we don't have to, as Argentina's viticultural engine room, Mendoza, has a high-altitude location in the Andean foothills that's perfect for pumping out those ester-rich *[Glossary, p.16]*, red-fruity wines punctuated by anise low notes and powdery Parma Violet and raspberry flavours.

If you like:
Dark Chocolate Mousse & Plum
[See 'Roasty Sweet', Sweet, p.62]
Liquorice & Prune
[See 'Spicy Sweet', Sweet, p.57]
Violet & Raspberry
[See 'Rich Floral', Floral, p.27]

Try:
Anise Liqueur: Sambuca [p.219]
Beer: Brown Ale [p.238]
Coffee: Peruvian [p.207]
Dessert Wine: Mavrodaphne de Patras [p.165]
Red Wine: Amarone della Valpolicella [p.151], Côte-Rôtie [p.148], Madiran [p.150], Pomerol [p.147], Uruguayan Tannat [p.160]
Rum: White [p.197]

Australia

<u>Cabernet Sauvignon</u> I'm surprised we don't see more koala bears chugging Aussie Cabernet Sauvignon, so eucalyptus-based are its flavours. It's actually a real thing, and the culprit is a compound called eucalyptol, which is brought in by the vapour from neighboring eucalyptus tree leaves coating the vines and some finding their way into the grape press. They're called MOG, material other than grapes, and you couldn't make it up. A compound related

If you like:
Bay Leaf & Black Raspberry
[See 'Herbal Spicy', Spicy, p.104]
Violet & Eucalyptus
[See 'Rich Floral', Floral, p.25]

Try:
Brandy: XO Cognac [p.178]
Fortified Wine: Crusted Port [p.169]
Red Wine: Gaillac Rouge [p.149], Pomerol [p.147]

to eucalyptol is found in bay leaves and Aussie Cabernet Sauvignon, ushering in lightly camphoraceous notes *[Glossary, p.15]* over the classic flavours of black raspberries and violets.

Chile

Carménère In a Lord Lucan-style drama scenario, Bordeaux native grape Carménère was assumed dead until it was spotted in Chile of all places. It got there as a stowaway, living under the assumed identity of Merlot until an eagle-eyed expert noticed the leaf shape and, oh, that it produces completely different wines. Carménère has herbaceous edges and uniquely angular bell pepper and green peppercorn corners thanks to an aromatic compound also found in Sauvignon Blanc. No wonder Carménère's part of the Cabernet Sauvignon family tree for goodness' sake, with a raspy raspberry, pomegranate, wild-herb and woody-floral flavour profile.

If you like:
Green Bell Pepper & Cut Grass
[See 'Sweet Herbaceous', Herbaceous, p.38]
Green Peppercorn & Raspberry
[See 'Peppery Spicy', Spicy, p.108]
Wild Thyme & Pomegranate
[See 'Herbal Spicy', Spicy, p.105]

Try:
Red Wine: Chinon [p.148], Corbières [p.148], Gaillac Rouge [p.149], Mencia [p.158]
Rosé Wine: Bandol Rosé [p.140]
White Wine: Pouilly Fumé [p.129]

France

Aged Bordeaux Cabernet Sauvignon
Mint isn't always menthol, and it's certainly not eucalyptus, which in turn isn't anise or pine. Spearmint is the major minty marker in wine, it's mint in a less intense format to menthol-driven peppermint thanks to its mellower compound, carvone. Aged Cabernet Sauvignon-dominated blends from Bordeaux's Left Bank develop distinguished spearmint notes, thanks to a chemical called piperitone, also found in mint plants. You'll find that blackcurrant flavours form a package deal

If you like:
Liquorice & Black Cherry
[See 'Bittersweet', Sweet, p.56]
Mint & Blackcurrant
[See 'Minty Herbaceous', Herbaceous, p.36]

Try:
Fruit Liqueur: Pacharán [p.186]
Red Wine: Madiran [p.150], Nero D'Avola [p.155], South African Cabernet Sauvignon [p.157]

with spearmint in Cabernet Sauvignon, thanks to a compound activated during fermentation that smells of them both.

Aged Red Burgundy Purists would slap me in the village stocks for this generic subheading, though in my defence, Burgundy's côtes are more complex than the Hadron Collider and its wines are about as costly. If pushed, I'd go with the super-spendy Vosne-Romanée in the Côte de Nuits, specifically Domaine de la Romanée-Conti, or DRC as I call it. As Pinot Noir ages, esterification *[Glossary, p.16]* of acids and phenol compounds *[Glossary, p.18]* takes place, replacing its bright fruity notes with more complex savoury flavours with base notes of wild game, liquorice, rose, cloves, cola and smoked vanilla.

If you like:
Forest Floor & Black Raspberry
[See 'Earthy Savoury', Savoury, p.90]
Rose & Liquorice
[See 'Intense Floral', Floral, p.26]
Wild Game & Cola
[See 'Meaty Savoury', Savoury, p.92]

Try:
Fortified Wine: Vintage Port [p.170]
Red Wine: Barbaresco [p.152], Barolo [p.152], Central Otago Pinot Noir [p.156], Châteauneuf-du-Pape [p.147]
Rosé Wine: Bandol Rosé [p.140]

Aged Rhône Grenache Noir I mean it, aged Grenache tastes of black truffles; just ask the flavour maestros at the legendary El Bulli restaurant. Actually you can't as it closed down, but they'd have told you that aged Grenache and black truffles share the same sulphur compound, dimethyl sulphide *[Glossary, p.16]*. Without getting all Heston Blumenthal, 'DS' is formed via the breakdown of a sulphur-containing amino acid during the wine maturation process, which at low concentrations contributes a black-truffle, vegetal, fruity aroma to ageing Grenache. It also enhances the level of raspberry-flavoured compounds for an earthy-fruity flavour-fest.

If you like:
Full-Grain Leather & Tobacco Leaf
[See 'Meaty Savoury', Savoury, p.91]
Liquorice & Prune
[See 'Spicy Sweet', Sweet, p.57]
Raspberry & Black Truffle
[See 'Sweet Fruity', Fruity, p.50]

Try:
Anise Liqueur: Sambuca [p.219]
Red Wine: Argentinian Malbec [p.143], Amarone della Valpolicella [p.151], Barolo [p.152], Ribera del Duero [p.159], Rioja Gran Reserva [p.159]

Bandol Horsebox is an acquired taste; I learned that the hard way. Smoky bacon, however, is a mainstay flavour of brawny Bandol from the French Riviera, majoring on the meaty Mourvèdre grape. Bandol

If you like:
Black Peppercorn & Smoky Bacon
[See 'Peppery Spicy', Spicy, p.107]
Liquorice & Smoked Bacon
[See 'Spicy Sweet', Sweet, p.57]

pumps out black pepper and garrigue aromas from a compound called rotundone *[Glossary, p.19]*, while phenol compounds *[Glossary, p.18]* spark notes of smoked bacon, cloves, first-aid kit and liquorice. These are caused by a rogue yeast strain called Brettanomyces *[Glossary, p.15]*, which creeps into Mourvèdre endowing it with meaty, spicy mannerisms seen as 'desirable faults' by some, or unwelcome horsebox and bandage aromas by others.

Beaujolais Remember when mad-dashing over to France for Nouveau November was a thing? It doesn't really happen any more, not while the young stuff still tastes of bubblegum, candyfloss and bananas. These confectionary flavours come from a process called carbonic maceration, or *carbo* if you're French, fermenting grapes intracellularly, aka in their own skins, in a closed carbon dioxide-filled vessel until they're bursting with cherry-flavoured Hubba Bubba notes and purple pigmentation. The best Beaujolais areas or 'crus' swap out Willy Wonka flavours for ripe cherry, raspberry, elderflower and Parma Violet notes for a more serious sipping experience.

Bordeaux Pauillac Megastigmatrienone *[Glossary, p.18]* sounds like it could do some damage in a scrap against Godzilla, possibly sporting multiple heads. It's a key compound component of tobacco and is also cited as a major contributor to tobacco aromas in certain bottle-matured red wines, including Cabernet-dominated Pauillac. The ageing process gives a smoke-odorous compound a molecular shake-up, rearranging it into woody-whiffing, pipe tobacco-mimicking megastigmatrienone, which

Oregano & Boysenberry
[See 'Herbal Spicy', Spicy, p.105]

Try:
Red Wine: Corbières [p.148], Côte-Rôtie [p.148], Montepulciano d'Abruzzo [p.154], Pinotage [p.157]
Rosé Wine: Tavel Rosé [p.141]

If you like:
Elderflower & Red Cherry
[See 'Fruity Floral', Floral, p.25]
Forest Floor & Black Raspberry
[See 'Earthy Savoury', Savoury, p.90]
Violet & Raspberry
[See 'Rich Floral', Floral, p.27]

Try:
Red Wine: Aged Red Burgundy [p.145], Argentinian Malbec [p.143], Central Otago Pinot Noir [p.156], Châteauneuf-du-Pape [p.147], Côte-Rôtie [p.148]
Rosé Wine: New Zealand Pinot Noir Rosé [p.142]
Rum: White [p.197]

If you like:
Cigar Box & Parma Violets
[See 'Spicy Smoky', Smoky, p.84]
Graphite & Sloe Berry
[See 'Earthy Smoky', Smoky, p.82]
Pipe Tobacco & Crème de Cassis
[See 'Spicy Smoky', Smoky, p.84]

Try:
Fortified Wine: Vintage Port [p.170]
Fruit Liqueur: Sloe Gin [p.181]
Red Wine: Amarone della Valpolicella [p.151], Priorat [p.158]

is further intensified by barrel contact. A sulphurous compound, which is formed during fermentation, also brings with it Cabernet's calling-card crème de cassis flavour characteristics.

Bordeaux Pomerol This is unsubstantiated, but I believe Leonard Bernstein based *West Side Story* on Bordeaux. There's a similar rivalry going on between Cabernet Sauvignons on the Left Bank, which I have pegged as the Jets, while right-bank Merlots are the Sharks. That's literally all I've got. But in a plot twist both come from the same Cabernet family and the Bordeaux region, so it's nothing like *West Side Story* but I'm sticking with it. Pomerol is the clay-soiled village that produces Chateau Pétrus, Merlot-based wines that contain the fermentation-activated 'strawberry furanone', a sweet-fruity compound that also tastes caramelly, and brings in an entire orchestra of sensual red fruit, black raspberry and dark chocolate.

If you like:
Bay Leaf & Black Raspberry
[See 'Herbal Spicy', Spicy, p.104]
Dark Chocolate Mousse & Plum
[See 'Roasty Sweet', Sweet, p.62]

Try:
Beer: Brown Ale [p.238]
Coffee: Peruvian [p.207]
Dessert Wine: Mavrodaphne de Patras [p.165]
Red Wine: Argentinian Malbec [p.143],
Australian Cabernet Sauvignon [p.143],
Uruguayan Tannat [p.160]

Châteauneuf-du-Pape It sounds surrealist, but if Monet were sipping a southern Rhône red while painting its sun-soaked scenery, his artwork would have looked more like Picasso's. Forget the heavy embossed bottles of Grenache-dominated Châteauneuf-du-Pape, it's the high alcohol that's a more effective bludgeon to the skull. There's a flash mob of flavours in a Châteauneuf-du-Pape, from ripe plums to earthy, bosky notes, through to warm and smoky spices, thanks to grape-skin-based compounds that bring in notes of smoke, vanilla and ginger.

If you like:
Forest Floor & Black Raspberry
[See 'Earthy Savoury', Savoury, p.90]
Gingerbread & Smoked Vanilla
[See 'Yeasty Baked', Baked, p.79]
Rose & Plum
[See 'Intense Floral', Floral, p.26]

Try:
Fortified Wine: Ruby Port [p.170]
Grain Spirit: Sweet Potato Shōchū [p.256]
Red Wine: Aged Red Burgundy [p.145],
Beaujolais [p.146], Californian Pinot Noir
[p.161], Central Otago Pinot Noir [p.156]
Sparkling Wine: Mature Champagne [p.117]
Whisky: Aged Japanese Single Malt [p.245]

Chinon We've all mimicked Marlon Brando with a mouthful of marshmallows, doing the chubby bunny challenge as Don Corleone in *The Godfather*. Well, Marlon is like Cabernet Franc, godfather to the house of Carmenet, the family name for grapes including Cabernet Sauvignon, Sauvignon Blanc, Carménère and Merlot. Cabernet Franc rules Loire *rouges* with flavours of red fruit, purple flowers, earthy fungi, leafy greens and aromatic herbs, which is my kind of boss. Cabernet Franc is known for having the same 'green gene' as Sauvignon Blanc, meaning it hangs on to bell pepper pyrazine, a compound *[Glossary, p.18]* that gives it a grassy, jalapeño-adjacent vibe.

Corbières Not to milk the horse theme, but you could have thrown a saddle over Carignan back in the day, such a workhorse grape was it. Old-vine Carignan is a different beast and is featured as the backbone grape in Corbières blends against a noisy old-fashioned telephone exchange of flavours from blending buddies Syrah, Grenache and Mourvèdre. Linalool *[Glossary, p.18]* in the grape's skin brings the lavender notes, which multitasks with the offbeat tones of chewy black liquorice, while other compounds smash out a floral-herbal, peppery, piney, rosemary hum and a meaty, smoky bacon-flavoured Frazzles moment.

Côte-Rôtie As Jennifer Aniston once said in a shampoo ad, 'Here comes the science', or, in this case, quantum wine chemistry. Viogner and Syrah are co-fermented in Côte-Rôtie, with Viognier's tannin molecules stabilising red pigment in Syrah's berries. Reactions take place

If you like:
Green Bell Pepper & Cut Grass [See 'Sweet Herbaceous', Herbaceous, p.38]
Green Peppercorn & Raspberry [See 'Peppery Spicy', Spicy, p.108]
Porcini & Lavender [See 'Earthy Savoury', Savoury, p.90]

Try:
Red Wine: Chilean Carménère [p.144], Gaillac Rouge [p.149], Mencia [p.158]
White Wine: Pouilly Fumé [p.129]

If you like:
Liquorice & Smoked Bacon [See 'Spicy Sweet', Sweet, p.57]
Rosemary & English Lavender [See 'Herbal Spicy', Spicy, p.105]
Wild Thyme & Pomegranate [See 'Herbal Spicy', Spicy, p.105]

Try:
Red Wine: Bandol [p.145], Chilean Carménère [p.144], Corbières [p.148], Mencia [p.158], Pinotage [p.157]
Rosé Wine: Bandol Rosé [p.140]
Tea: Echinacea [p.204]

If you like:
Black Peppercorn & Smoky Bacon [See 'Peppery Spicy', Spicy, p.107]
Forest Floor & Black Raspberry [See 'Earthy Savoury', Savoury, p.90]
Violet & Raspberry [See 'Rich Floral', Floral, p.25]

between Viognier's flavanols and Syrah's red-pigmented anthocyanin compounds *[Glossary, p.15]*, resulting in an overall darker wine. Pepper, Syrah's major nuance, is brought in by a compound also found in black pepper's essential oil. Finally, a clove-like compound is infused from the barrel wood and converted into breakfast-like whiffs of smoky bacon.

Try:
Red Wine: Aged Red Burgundy [p.145], Argentinian Malbec [p.143], Bandol [p.145], Beaujolais [p.146], Central Otago Pinot Noir [p.156], Châteauneuf-du-Pape [p.147]

Crozes-Hermitage When Kim shouted at Kourtney 'You're the least exciting to look at', that must have been tough for Crozes-Hermitage to hear. Sandwiched between the two northern Rhône jewels, Côte-Rôtie and Hermitage, Crozes-Hermitage is the relatable one. As the largest wine-producing zone in the northern Rhône, it's less consistent and put-together than the other two, but 'baby's first northern Rhône' can save us some serious coin. Stylistically Crozes downplays acidity via its potassium-rich soil with a higher pH, which beckons in black-olive notes during ageing along with whiffs of smouldering tobacco.

If you like:
Dark-Fire Tobacco & Black Olive
[See 'Spicy Smoky', Smoky, p.84]
Red Cherry & White Pepper
[See 'Floral Fruity', Fruity, p.47]

Try:
Amaro: Campari [p.223]
Red Wine: Frappato [p.154], Gaillac Rouge [p.149], Washington State Syrah [p.162]
Rosé Wine: Syrah Rosé [p.141]
Tea: Lapsang Souchong [p.201]

Gaillac Rouge Attention all pepper-chasers, it's time to grab your grinders. The cracking provincial reds of Gaillac, an inch north of Toulouse on a map, could easily be slugged over an entrecôte steak and called pepper sauce. Local grape Duras is high in peppercorn mothership compound rotundone *[Glossary, p.19]*, while its blending buddy grape, Fer Servadou, contains the sweet-spicy compound, eucalyptol, for a menthol moment not a million miles away from Left Bank Cabernet Sauvignon. Distantly related to Carménère, Fer Servadou is rich

If you like:
Green Bell Pepper & Cut Grass
[See 'Sweet Herbaceous', Herbaceous, p.38]
Red Cherry & White Pepper
[See 'Floral Fruity', Fruity, p.47]
Violet & Eucalyptus
[See 'Rich Floral', Floral, p.27]

Try:
Amaro: Campari [p.223]
Brandy: XO Cognac [p.178]
Red Wine: Australian Cabernet Sauvignon [p.143], Chilean Carménère [p.144], Chinon [p.148], Crozes-Hermitage [p.149], Frappato [p.154]

in bell pepper pyrazine *[Glossary, p.18]* for a flash of green pepper and a grassy freshen-up.

Hermitage You know when you get back from work and need five minutes to decompress? The reds of Hermitage need five years, minimum, by which time the dinner's been in the dog a thousand times over. This southern sun-baked fine wine micro-Mecca is the acknowledged birthplace of Syrah, producing reds that can feel like chewing a Spartan warrior: meaty, macho, brooding, fruity, reeking of black tea and dark-roast coffee. Well, I guess he needs the caffeine. Pepper is a flavour staple of Syrah's spiritual avatar, brought in by a compound actually found in peppercorns.

Madiran Go hard or go home with Madiran, the big-boned, Tannat-based red so stuffed with antioxidants that it's touted as a health elixir, which I'm taking to mean that we count it as some of our five a day. It's built like a brawny French farmhand chain-toking on a filterless Gitanes while wolfing down a duck cassoulet, which is ironic given Madiran's cardio-curating properties. No wonder it's nicknamed 'The Heart of Darkness'. Madiran is cited as the key to the 'French Paradox', explaining why a high-fat southern-French diet yields super-low cases of heart disease. I'll drink to that.

Germany

Mulled Wine/Glühwein Mulled wine stops us from being driven into a Christmas coma by Mariah Carey, Cliff Richard and Michael Bublé, therefore it's medicinal. A festive comfort blanket of aromatic

Fortified Wine: Crusted Port [p.169]
Rosé Wine: Syrah Rosé [p.141]
White Wine: Pouilly Fumé [p.129]

If you like:
Mexican Coffee & White Pepper
[See 'Roasty Baked', Baked, p.75]
Roast Beef & Black Tea
[See 'Meaty Savoury', Savoury, p.91]

Try:
Anise Liqueur: Sambuca [p.219]
Coffee: Mexican [p.206]
Nut Liqueur: Nocino [p.254]
Tequila: Coffee [p.190]

If you like:
Hickory Campfire & Loganberry
[See 'Woody Smoky', Smoky, p.85]
Liquorice & Black Cherry
[See 'Spicy Sweet', Sweet, p.56]

Try:
Fruit Liqueur: Pacharán [p.186]
Red Wine: Aged Bordeaux Cabernet Sauvignon [p.144], Nero D'Avola [p.155], Ribera del Duero [p.159]

If you like:
Cinnamon & Blood Orange
[See 'Warm Spicy', Spicy, p.109]
Sweet Orange & Cinnamon
[See 'Juicy Fruity', Fruity, p.48]

compounds based around red wine of some astringent description, orange rind's bright citrusy compounds and the mouth-puckering citric acid, offset by spoonfuls of sucrose. On the spicy side, lip-numbing cloves release their medicinal jab tempered by cinnamon's saccharine warmth, with a woody baritone flavour from nutmeg, all to ward off yuletide crooners.

Try:

Amaro: Campari [p.223]
Fruit Liqueur: Pimm's [p.181]
Herb Liqueur: Harvey Wallbanger [p.220]
Mixer: Cranberry Juice [p.261]
Red Wine: Sangria [p.160]
Rosé Wine: Bandol Rosé [p.140]

Cocktail recipe

MULLED WINE/GLÜHWEIN [Fruit-Produced Drinks, Red Wine]

Juice of 2 Oranges
2 bottles of Red Wine (preferably unoaked)
Zest of 1 Lemon
150g Caster Sugar
Cardamom Pods, bruised
1 Cinnamon Stick
Cloves
Grated Nutmeg

Add the orange juice to a saucepan with most of the red wine, lemon zest, caster sugar, cardamom pods, cinnamon stick, cloves and nutmeg. Heat slowly until it's boiling, stirring occasionally, then add in the rest of the wine if it's too thick, or even if it's not, and serve.

Italy

Aglianico del Vulture What's the deal with autosuggestion *[Glossary, p.15]*? In my mind, volcanic wines taste like cooled-down liquid lava with basalt base notes and a pop of pyroclastic on the palate. Aglianico is yet more delectable knowing that Monte Vulture in Naples was one of Italy's most brutal volcanos, giving its farewell lid flip thousands of years ago and petrifying the surrounding landscape. Aglianico del Vulture is the edgier version of Barolo, building on its lavender aromas with saline, mineral, smouldering flavours from its links to lava and woody, tobacco, herbal, wild-raspberry notes from a compound in the grape berries.

If you like:

Lava Rock & Pomegranate
[See 'Earthy Smoky', Smoky, p.82]

Sweet Cherry & Milk Chocolate
[See 'Floral Fruity', Fruity, p.47]

Turkish Tobacco & Wild Raspberry
[See 'Spicy Smoky', Smoky, p.84]

Try:

Dessert Wine: Recioto della Valpolicella [p.166]
Fortified Wine: Ruby Port [p.170]
Red Wine: Barolo [p.152], Central Otago Pinot Noir [p.156], Montepulciano d'Abruzzo [p.154], Nerello Mascalese [p.155]

Amarone della Valpolicella You know what they say, 'Red sky at night, Amarone delight'. No one says that actually, and I'm

If you like:

Cigar Box & Parma Violets
[See 'Spicy Smoky', Smoky, p.84]

not even sure who 'they' are, but Amarone is a delight. Made around Verona by air-drying Corvina and Rondinella grapes in ventilated lofts where they shed a third of their water content, winding up like shrivelled raisins. Withered grapes double down on dried-fruit, spice, violet and tobacco notes, with ramped-up levels of smoky and age-triggered tobacco-odorous compounds. Balsamic notes of liquorice and camphor are courtesy of eucalyptol and are brought in by grape desiccation.

Liquorice & Prune
[See 'Spicy Sweet', Sweet, p.57]
Morello Cherry & Almond
[See 'Floral Fruity', Fruity, p.47]
Ruby Chocolate & Violet
[See 'Roasty Sweet', Sweet, p.63]

Try:
Anise Liqueur: Sambuca [p.219]
Brandy: Armagnac [p.175]
Fortified Wine: Vintage Port [p.170]
Fruit Liqueur: Kirsch [p.183], Maraschino [p.180]
Herb Liqueur: The Last Word [p.216]
Mixer: Cherry Coke [p.260]
Nut Liqueur: Amaretto [p.253]
Red Wine: Aged Rhône Grenache [p.145], Argentinian Malbec [p.143], Graciano [p.158], Pauillac [p.146]
Rosé Wine: Sangiovese Rosé [p.142]

Barbaresco 'Always the bridesmaid, never the bride' is something we lovingly say about Barbaresco. Behind its back obviously; we weren't born in a barn. Once a less desirable substitute for Barolo, which is bizarre given they're made in a similar way from the same Nebbiolo grape and grown down the road from each other. Sibling rivalry aside, Barbaresco's warmer conditions and shorter ageing makes its tannins less brawny, giving it a more floral flavour-silhouette. Rose oxide and geraniol *[Glossary, p.16]* are the compound culprits for Nebbiolo's rosy aroma, along with deep, woody, violet notes.

If you like:
Cigar Box & Parma Violets
[See 'Spicy Smoky', Smoky, p.84]
Rose & Liquorice
[See 'Intense Floral', Floral, p.24]

Try:
Fortified Wine: Vintage Port [p.170]
Red Wine: Aged Red Burgundy [p.145], Amarone della Valpolicella [p.151], Barolo [p.152], Pauillac [p.146]
Rosé Wine: Bandol Rosé [p.140]

Barolo 'The wine of kings, the king of wines' isn't the strapline to a movie starring Dwayne 'The Rock' Johnson with a low Rotten Tomatoes score; it describes Barolo. A force of nature with powerful flavours of cherry, rose,

If you like:
Black Cherry & Raspberry Jam
[See 'Floral Fruity', Fruity, p.46]
Raspberry & Black Truffle
[See 'Sweet Fruity', Fruity, p.50]

liquorice, raspberry, tobacco and black truffle, Barolo's renowned cherry chops are partly down to the Nebbiolo grapes' high phenol content *[Glossary, p.18]*, which requires softening by long maceration and ageing. A bacteria can creep into Nebbiolo, spawning airborne volatile acids, which, though technically flaws, at low levels give one-dimensional fruit flavours a complex vibrancy, like applying an HD filter.

Chianti Classico Remember those 'authentic' Italian *enotecas*, all chequered tablecloths and bottles of Chianti squatting in straw baskets? What a fiasco, literally, as that's the name of the straw-covered bottle. Modern Tuscan Chianti has ditched the *Mamma Mia* packageing, instead concentrating on the black cherry, raspberry and woody-herbal liquid inside. Descriptors like 'tart', 'sour', 'astringent' and 'raspy' are all sought-after search terms for Chianti's protagonist grape, Sangiovese. A naturally neutral-flavoured variety, it leans on fruity fermentation-derived compounds for its black cherry calling-card notes.

Chianti Classico Riserva A *Silence of the Lambs* reference in the Chianti section is way too predictable. Instead I'll mention the black rooster, which is stickered on bottles to mark the superior Chianti Classico region. Riserva is all about longer barrel-ageing, a minimum of two years, which yields savoury flavours of hung Italian sausage and bitter espresso coffee in a porcelain *tazza*. Roasty, meaty notes are nudged in via a specific age-activated

Rose & Liquorice
[See 'Intense Floral', Floral, p.26]
Turkish Tobacco & Wild Raspberry
[See 'Spicy Smoky', Smoky, p.84]

Try:
Coffee: Ethiopian [p.205]
Dessert Wine: Recioto della Valpolicella [p.166]
Fortified Wine: Vintage Port [p.170]
Red Wine: Aged Red Burgundy [p.145], Aged Rhône Grenache Noir [p.145], Aglianico del Vulture [p.151], Barbaresco [p.152], Californian Pinot Noir [p.161], Chianti [p.153], Primitivo [p.155]
Rosé Wine: Bandol Rosé [p.140]

If you like:
Black Cherry & Raspberry Jam
[See 'Floral Fruity', Fruity, p.46]
Oregano & Boysenberry
[See 'Herbal Spicy', Spicy, p.105]

Try:
Coffee: Ethiopian [p.205]
Red Wine: Barolo [p.152], Californian Pinot Noir [p.161], Montepulciano d'Abruzzo [p.154], Primitivo [p.155]
Rosé Wine: Bandol Rosé [p.140], Tavel Rosé [p.141]

If you like:
Cigar Box & Parma Violets
[See 'Spicy Smoky', Spicy, p.84]
Italian Salami & Espresso
[See 'Meaty Savoury', Savoury, p.91]

Try:
Fortified Wine: Vintage Port [p.170]
Red Wine: Amarone della Valpolicella [p.151], Barbaresco [p.152], Pauillac [p.146]

compound, with savoury whiffs of cured meat and roasted coffee. Extended wood contact infuses smoky, spicy volatile phenols [Glossary, p.18] into Chianti Classico Riserva, which goes well with fava beans . . . Just saying.

Frappato Beaujolais diehards will lose it for Frappato, the Sicilian Gamay-alike with a dialled-up floral intensity that screams 'Don't compare me to Beaujolais'. The Frappato grape is the spawn of Sangiovese after some naughty time with a local berry, though DNA aside, they're really nothing alike flavour-wise. Frappato is focused on forthright floral and fruity flavours, with its aromatic compounds coming through right out of the gate, bringing glad tidings of white strawberry and red cherry with a pinch of white pepper and clove.

If you like:
Clove & White Strawberry
[See 'Fruity Spicy', Spicy, p.104]
Red Cherry & White Pepper
[See 'Floral Fruity', Fruity, p.47]

Try:
Amaro: Campari [p.223]
Red Wine: Crozes-Hermitage [p.149], Gaillac Rouge [p.149]
Rosé Wine: Syrah Rosé [p.141]
Rum: Pineapple [p.197]

Montepulciano d'Abruzzo You know that moment when you start resembling your pet? Maybe it's a hairstyle, a mannerism or buying yourself a matching chew toy. Budget Montepulciano d'Abruzzo is such a staple pairing with pizza, it's taken on the traits of a fruity, savoury, herbal topping. Putting aside the sweatshop-produced simpletons we mainline in mid-range pizza chains, fancier Montepulciano curates more complex notes of boysenberries, blueberries, cherries, tobacco, chocolate and dried oregano. Fermentation-created ester compounds [Glossary, p.16] are mainstays of the Montepulciano grape's fruit-based flavours, while oak contact introduces smoky, woody notes of bosky bright tobacco.

If you like:
Bright Tobacco & Blueberry
[See 'Spicy Smoky', Smoky, p.83]
Oregano & Boysenberry
[See 'Herbal Spicy', Spicy, p.105]
Sweet Cherry & Milk Chocolate
[See 'Floral Fruity', Fruity, p.47]

Try:
Fortified Wine: Ruby Port [p.170]
Red Wine: Aglianico del Vulture [p.151], Central Otago Pinot Noir [p.156], Chianti Classico [p.153], South African Pinotage [p.157]
Rosé Wine: Bandol Rosé [p.140], Tavel Rosé [p.141]

Nerello Mascalese Whoever thought of growing grapes on an active volcano wasn't right in the head. Thank Dante's Peak they did though, otherwise we wouldn't have the red-fruity, smoky, spicy, saline nuances of Nerello in our lives. Perched on the smouldering shoulders of Mount Etna, the top vines are rooted in lava flows, with a unique microclimate and a high mineral content. Whether we're actually sipping pumice is hotly debated; the mineral, herbal and saline traits could be partly thanks to smoky compounds and salty acids brought in from reductive, oxygen-starved winemaking.

If you like:
Beach Pebble & Thyme
[See 'Marine Minerally', Minerally, p.94]
Forest Floor & Black Raspberry
[See 'Earthy Savoury', Savoury, p.90]
Lava Rock & Pomegranate
[See 'Earthy Smoky', Smoky, p.82]

Try:
Red Wine: Aged Red Burgundy [p.145], Aglianico del Vulture [p.151], Beaujolais [p.146], Central Otago Pinot Noir [p.156], Châteauneuf-du-Pape [p.147], Côte-Rôtie [p.148]
Tea: Matcha [p.203]
White Wine: Assyrtiko [p.133], Chablis [p.126], Greco di Tufo [p.134], Muscadet Sèvre-et-Mains Sur Lie [p.128]

Nero D'Avola I'm not a qualified genealogist, but it's almost as though the Nero D'Avola grape was Syrah's sister from another mister. Super similar in biological profile and wine style, and both from muddled backgrounds with hints of black pepper. Coincidence? Frustratingly yes. I thought I was on to something. Nero D'Avola has higher acidity and intense aromatics, delivering blackberry and black cherry versus Syrah's blackcurrant and plum. Floral-fruity terpene compounds give Nero a rose, violet, black-fruit fragrance on the scale of a department-store beauty counter, while balsamic, liquorice base notes are shoehorned in via warming peppery compounds.

If you like:
Blackberry & Fig
[See 'Sweet Fruity', Fruity, p.49]
Liquorice & Black Cherry
[See 'Spicy Sweet', Sweet, p.56]
Rose & Violet
[See 'Intense Floral', Floral, p.26]

Try:
Fortified Wine: LBV Port [p.169]
Fruit Liqueur: Pacharán [p.186]
Red Wine: Aged Bordeaux Cabernet Sauvignon [p.144], Madiran [p.150], Old-Vine Zinfandel [p.161]
White Wine: Torrontés [p.123]

Primitivo In some sort of grape-based *Ancestry.com* revelation, Italian Primitivo DNA-matches perfectly to Zinfandel from the USA and an unpronounceable Croatian grape. It's all too Netflix's *Three Identical Strangers* for words. It seems Zinfandel stowed away stateside, leaving

If you like:
Black Cherry & Raspberry Jam
[See 'Floral Fruity', Fruity, p.46]
Dried Fig & Plum
[See 'Spicy Sweet', Sweet, p.64]
Kenyan Coffee & Blueberry
[See 'Roasty Baked', Baked, p.75]

Primitivo to do its thing in Puglia on the heel of Italy's boot. A naturally non-aromatic grape variety, fermentation-derived compounds are flagbearers for the plentiful fruit flavours in Primitivo, which is generally lighter in alcohol than Zinfandel, with spicier balsamic dark fruit, fresh coffee beans and low-key nuances of dried figs.

Try:

Coffee: Ethiopian [p.205], Kenyan [p.205]
Dessert Wine: Mavrodaphne de Patras [p.165], Recioto della Valpolicella [p.166]
Fortified Wine: Sweet Superiore Marsala [p.168]
Red Wine: Barolo [p.152], Californian Pinot Noir [p.161], Chianti Classico [p.153], Old-Vine Zinfandel [p.161]

New Zealand

Central Otago Pinot Noir Pinot Noir grown in Middle Earth – now I've heard everything. With Central Otago's erratic day, night and seasonal temperatures, Earth's most southerly winemaking region teeters on a sword edge. Technically Pinot Noir 'shall not pass' in Otago. I mean, how's a grape known for its royally demanding tendencies going to survive the hottest, coldest, highest, driest, Mordor-style conditions? In a plot twist, Otago's climactic mood swings ripen Pinot Noir's grape-housed compounds beautifully, nudging in raspberry, plum, chocolate, violet, earthy, spicy and intense cherry jam notes.

If you like:
Forest Floor & Black Raspberry
[See 'Earthy Savoury', Savoury, p.90]
Sweet Cherry & Milk Chocolate
[See 'Floral Fruity', Fruity, p.47]

Try:
Red Wine: Aged Red Burgundy [p.145], Aglianico del Vulture [p.151], Beaujolais [p.146], Châteauneuf-du-Pape [p.147], Côte-Rôtie [p.148], Montepulciano d'Abruzzo [p.154], Nerello Mascalese [p.155]

Portugal

Touriga Nacional Spike any red wine with an Earl Grey teabag, mandarin skin and violet petals and you'll have yourself a glass of Touriga Nacional, more or less. I'm not even joking – flavour scientists have done experiments on it and everything. With its pungent floral-citrusy profile, bergamot is the big aroma descriptor for high-quality Touriga Nacional, Portugal's principal red grape, which is used predominantly in Port

If you like:
Blueberry & Spearmint
[See 'Sweet Fruity', Fruity, p.49]
Earl Grey & Blueberry
[See 'Dried Herbaceous', Herbaceous, p.33]
Naval Orange Peel & Violet
[See 'Fruity Spicy', Spicy, p.104]
Rose & Plum
[See 'Intense Floral', Floral, p.26]

production. It's no wonder really, when it shares the formative flavour compounds in bergamot orange rind's essential oil. Cue the mic drop – my work here is done.

Try:
Brandy: Metaxa 12-Star [p.178]
Coffee: Ethiopian [p.205]
Fortified Wine: Ruby Port [p.170]
Red Wine: Californian Pinot Noir [p.161], Châteauneuf-du-Pape [p.147], Rioja Gran Reserva [p.159]
Tea: Earl Grey [p.202]

South Africa

Cabernet Sauvignon Ironically, my attempt at a South African accent sounds like I'm speaking French, while South African winemakers love using French grapes. I know: full circle. From Bordeaux blends and Loire-alikes through to their 'Capes du Rhône', it's no shocker that Cabernet Sauvignon is their most planted red grape. Stylistically, Cape Cabernet Sauvignon straddles fruity and herbaceous, the warmer climate dialling down its natural compounds, banishing the bell pepper but leaving a murmur of mint, while fermentation produces a sulphurous compound that belts out notes of blackcurrant.

If you like:
Bay Leaf & Black Raspberry
[See 'Herbal Spicy', Spicy, p.104]
Mint & Blackcurrant
[See 'Minty Herbaceous', Herbaceous, p.36]
Pipe Tobacco & Crème de Cassis
[See 'Spicy Smoky', Smoky, p.84]

Try:
Red Wine: Aged Bordeaux Cabernet Sauvignon [p.144], Australian Cabernet Sauvignon [p.143], Pauillac [p.146], Pomerol [p.147], Priorat [p.158]

Pinotage Someone needs to address the springbok in the room, that budget Pinotage can reek of rubber, rusty nails and burnt hair. There, I said it. Given its volatility, Pinotage requires expert oenological handling so as not to develop tarmac-whiffing 'volatile acidity' *[Glossary, p.19]*. A lab-created labradoodle-style crossing of Pinot Noir and Cinsault, aka Hermitage, hence the catchy name Pinotage. Premium examples are a sweet-savoury oxymoron, with dark, spiced fruit, purple florals, balsamic liquorice, savoury smoked meat and roasty coffee notes from charred-barrel-infused compounds.

If you like:
Bright Tobacco & Blueberry
[See 'Spicy Smoky', Smoky, p.83]
Liquorice & Smoked Bacon
[See 'Spicy Sweet', Sweet, p.57]
Violet & Coffee
[See 'Rich Floral', Floral, p.27]

Try:
Cognac: Armagnac [p.175]
Red Wine: Bandol [p.145], Corbières [p.148], Montepulciano d'Abruzzo [p.154]

Spain

Graciano I can't relate to Graciano; it's a grape that stands back and lets others shine. Yawn. Being a bit player in Rioja blends makes it tricky to appreciate Graciano's white-pepper, liquorice, cherry, ruby-chocolate, violet and menthol prowess, especially over Tempranillo's tobacco-odorous clatter. Rotundone [Glossary, p.19] provides a pinch of pepper; as it should, it is one of the most potent compounds found in wine and is also present in certain herbs. Brooding violet nuances come through, with a spicy lick of black cardamom and liquorice.

If you like:
Liquorice Root & Black Cardamom
[See 'Medicinal Spicy', Spicy, p.107]
Red Cherry & White Pepper
[See 'Floral Fruity', Fruity, p.47]
Ruby Chocolate & Violet
[See 'Roasty Sweet', Sweet, p.63]

Try:
Amaro: Campari [p.223]
Anise Liqueur: Ouzo [p.218]
Herb Liqueur: Jägermeister [p.214]
Red Wine: Amarone [p.151], Crozes-Hermitage [p.149], Frappato [p.154], Gaillac Rouge [p.149], Old-Vine Zinfandel [p.161], Uruguayan Tannat [p.160]
Rosé Wine: Syrah Rosé [p.141]
Rum: Black Spiced [p.196]

Mencia Mencia tastes like a piece of schist, by which I mean it smacks of the minerals and smashed-slate soil of the north-western Bierzo region of Spain. Why, what did you think I meant? Speaking of rocky ground, mentioning the geological flavours of Mencia risks a nerdy showdown over the volatile aromatic properties of boulders, and trust me, no one wants that. Instead, let's appreciate Mencia's pomegranate and raspberry fruit basket of flavours, its lavender florals, those rosemary herbal notes and the sweet-herbaceous pique of green peppercorns.

If you like:
Crushed Gravel & Pomegranate
[See 'Rocky Minerally', Minerally, p.95]
Green Peppercorn & Raspberry
[See 'Peppery Spicy', Spicy, p.108]
Rosemary & English Lavender
[See 'Herbal Spicy', Spicy, p.105]

Try:
Red Wine: Chilean Carménère [p.144], Chinon [p.148], Corbières [p.148]
Tea: Echinacea [p.204]

Priorat You've got to admire monks, blending beverages around their busy prayer schedule; now that's multitasking. The Carthusian brothers were thrown some Catalan land back in the day, which they called Priorat, the priory, planting

If you like:
Graphite & Sloe Berry
[See 'Earthy Smoky', Smoky, p.82]
Pipe Tobacco & Crème de Cassis
[See 'Spicy Smoky', Smoky, p.84]

Garnacha and Cariñena grapes at altitude. As one of the world's 'vertical' wine regions, the vineyards here are so steep you practically have to abseil down them. The wines yield flavours of sloe berries, cassis and tobacco with Priorat's unique volcanic 'llicorella' slate soil, edging in deep-earth, sharpened-pencil and smoky notes.

Try:
Fruit Liqueur: Sloe Gin [p.181]
Red Wine: Pauillac [p.146], South African Cabernet Sauvignon [p.157]

Ribera del Duero It wouldn't feature in the Rightmove ad, but if you're moving to Ribera del Duero, their strapline is 'Ten months of winter, two months of hell'. Deal-breaker? It's a region of extremes: a barren elevated plateau with scorching summers and bitter winters, and let's not go there with the day-to-night temperature differences. Actually let's, as these bring out the best in Ribera's headline grape, Tempranillo, or Tinto Fino, leaving its berries swelling with ripeness, super-pigmented compounds and vivid acidity, while oak interaction yields phenol compounds *[Glossary, p.18]* for smoky-leather aromas.

If you like:
Bright Tobacco & Blueberry
[See 'Spicy Smoky', Smoky, p.83]
Full-Grain Leather & Tobacco Leaf
[See 'Meaty Savoury', Savoury, p.91]
Hickory Campfire & Loganberry
[See 'Woody Smoky', Smoky, p.85]

Try:
Red Wine: Aged Rhône Grenache [p.145], Madiran [p.150], Montepulciano d'Abruzzo [p.154], Rioja Gran Reserva [p.159], South African Pinotage [p.157]

Rioja Gran Reserva Pass me a pack of Nytol, curl me up in an oak barrel and set my alarm for five years' time. Well, it works for Tempranillo grapes in a Rioja Gran Reserva, which emerge from their oak-barrel chrysalis a dark-fruity, sappy, minty-herbaceous, spicy, leather-trimmed sought-after sipper. Forget ageism, it's age envy that lives loud and proud in Rioja, a region where maturity turns heads. Ageing gives Tempranillo a lighter brick-red hue, compounds with minty and tobacco notes and a molecular cabinet reshuffle that rearranges formerly one-dimensional flavours into complex age-enhanced savoury layers.

If you like:
Blueberry & Spearmint
[See 'Sweet Fruity', Fruity, p.49]
Full-Grain Leather & Tobacco Leaf
[See 'Meaty Savoury', Savoury, p.91]
Vanilla Pod & Roasted Pecan
[See 'Creamy Sweet', Sweet, p.60]

Try:
Fortified Wine: Malmsey Madeira [p.167]
Red Wine: Aged Rhône Grenache [p.145], Ribera del Duero [p.159], Touriga Nacional [p.156]
Sherry: Oloroso [p.173]

Sangria Sangria smells of email out-of-office, knock-off sunglasses and inflatable lilos – in that order. It's down to 'smell image' in the forebrain of the olfactory bulb, where odours bypass the brain's mainframe thalamus, hooking up with associated emotions, like summery mown grass or takeaway for one on Valentine's Day. Sangria's red base wine contains compounds ranging fruity, woody, floral flavours from its natural sugars and alcohols. Add in a warming scroll of cinnamaldehyde-rich *[Glossary, p.15]* cinnamon with a pop of pine and citrus from limes and oranges and we're practically on our holidays.

If you like:
Cassia & Lime
[See 'Warm Spicy', Spicy, p.109]
Cinnamon & Blood Orange
[See 'Warm Spicy', Spicy, p.109]

Try:
Amaro: Campari [p.223]
Mixer: Angostura Bitters [p.258], Cherry Coke [p.260], Coca-Cola [p.260], Cranberry Juice [p.261]
Red Wine: Mulled Wine/Glühwein [p.150]
Rosé Wine: Bandol Rosé [p.140]

SANGRIA [Fruit-Produced Drinks, Fruit Liqueur/Drinks]

Cocktail recipe

15ml Spanish Brandy
15ml Cointreau or Peach Schnapps
Bottle of Tempranillo
30ml Orange Juice
10ml Lemon Juice, freshly squeezed or Lemonade
5ml Sugar Syrup
Orange slices and chopped Strawberries
Mint sprig

Combine Brandy, Cointreau or Peach Schnapps, Tempranillo, orange juice, lemon juice or lemonade and sugar syrup in a hefty jug, stir in sliced oranges and chopped strawberries, then garnish with mint.

Uruguay

Tannat The clue's in the name with Tannat, which is tipped as the healthiest grape on the planet by anyone cardiovascular. Tannat is a tannin factory, those heart-curating compounds that hang out in grape skins, pips and stems giving the wine structure and longevity while leaving imbibers' lips looking like desiccated special effects from the movie *Cocoon*. With five pips compared to two to three in regular grapes, Tannat

If you like:
Dark Chocolate Mousse & Plum
[See 'Roasty Sweet', Sweet, p.62]
Liquorice Root & Black Cardamom
[See 'Medicinal Spicy', Spicy, p.107]
Sandalwood & Raspberry
[See 'Woody Smoky', Smoky, p.86]

Try:
Anise Liqueur: Ouzo [p.218]
Beer: Brown Ale [p.238]

delivers twice the tannin of Cabernet Sauvignon, while its balsamic, smoky, medicinal notes are conjured by the compound limonene *[Glossary, p.17]*, molecularly rearranged into eucalyptus's main compound, eucalyptol.

Coffee: Peruvian [p.207]
Dessert Wine: Mavrodaphne de Patras [p.165]
Fortified Wine: LBV Port [p.169]
Herb Liqueur: Jägermeister [p.214]
Red Wine: Argentinian Malbec [p.143], Graciano [p.158], Old-Vine Zinfandel [p.161], Pomerol [p.147]
Rum: Black Spiced [p.196]

USA

Californian Pinot Noir Not to ruin the mood, but the Pinot Noir highway is littered with the roadkill of winemakers who nearly nailed it, where RIP means 'Rest in Pinot'. Why? It's a finicky Goldilocks grape that done right expresses its location like no other, something the French call *terroir* and they should know. California's cooler sites convey tempering Pacific breezes and morning fogs that roll over the vines to offset the solar intensity, offering Pinot the bandwidth to showboat rich notes of cherries, plums and raspberries, together with newly-bloomed rose aromas.

If you like:
Black Cherry & Raspberry Jam
[See 'Floral Fruity', Fruity, p.46]
Rose & Plum
[See 'Intense Floral', Floral, p.26]
Vanilla & Clove-Spiced Toffee Apple
[See 'Creamy Sweet', Sweet, p.60]

Try:
Brandy: VSOP Calvados [p.177]
Cider: Cask-Aged [p.186]
Coffee: Ethiopian [p.205]
Fortified Wine: Ruby Port [p.170], White Port & Tonic [p.171]
Red Wine: Barolo [p.152], Châteauneuf-du-Pape [p.147], Chianti Classico [p.153], Primitivo [p.155], Touriga Nacional [p.156]
Tea: Rooibos [p.203]
Whisky: Speyside Single Malt [p.247]

Old-Vine Zinfandel OAP vineyards are where it's at; only varicose vines can create the world's most complex iterations of Zimmerfandel. At fifty-plus years, the unofficial definition in the States, old-vine trunks resemble the twisted stumps that most likely line Tim Burton's driveway. As veteran vines lose branches and their leaves thin out, there's more sun exposure for fewer bunches and deep roots with less competition for nutrients, therefore a greater concentration of

If you like:
Black Cherry & Raspberry Jam
[See 'Floral Fruity', Fruity, p.46]
Blackberry & Fig
[See 'Sweet Fruity', Fruity, p.49]
Coconut Pulp & Blueberry
[See 'Tropical Creamy', Creamy, p.69]
Liquorice Root & Black Cardamom
[See 'Medicinal Spicy', Spicy, p.107]

Try:
Anise Liqueur: Ouzo [p.218]

flavour, jacked-up complexity, lower yields and higher prices. Lodi, California's Mecca of Old-Vine Zinfandel, supercharges spicy compounds over notes of deep blackberry, blueberry, fig, liquorice and smoked cardamom.

Washington State Syrah No wonder Syrah gets around – it's a light packer. Ditching the figurative kitchen sink gets Syrah through security and fast-tracks adapting to its new surroundings. Take note, Tempranillo. Case in point: the Pacific Northwest is home to Jeff Bazos, Bill Gates and now this Rhône ranger grape, so they must be doing something right over there. Washington State's sheltered, near-desert conditions offer Syrah grapes prolonged hang time on the vine, with fermentation and ageing developing savoury flavours of smoky bacon, black olives, tobacco and warming spices so prized in northern Rhône reds.

Coffee: Ethiopian [p.205]
Herb Liqueur: Jägermeister [p.214]
Red Wine: Barolo [p.152], Californian Pinot Noir [p.161], Chianti Classico [p.153], Graciano [p.158], Nero D'Avola [p.155], Primitivo [p.155], Uruguayan Tannat [p.160]
Rum: Black Spiced [p.196]

If you like:
Dark-Fire Tobacco & Black Olive
[See 'Spicy Smoky', Smoky, p.84]
Roast Beef & Black Tea
[See 'Meaty Savoury', Savoury, p.91]
Smoky Bacon & Clove
[See 'Meaty Savoury', Savoury, p.92]

Try:
Red Wine: Crozes-Hermitage [p.149], Hermitage [p.150]
Sake: Koshu [p.243]
Tea: Lapsang Souchong [p.201]

Dessert Wine

Australia

Rutherglen Muscat Who needs teeth anyway? All that brushing is so exhausting. It pays to be dentally indifferent with a sugar content that would give Tate & Lyle sucrose-envy; Australia's flagship sticky wine is basically a dessert in a dinky bottle. It's made from brown Muscat grapes with a super-high sugar content, which are pressed, fortified with grape spirit and barrel-aged in furnace-like sheds. Zero fermentation maintains Muscat's perfumed, floral terpene compounds, while heating-induced

If you like:
Honeycomb Toffee & Turkish Delight
[See 'Burnt Sweet', Sweet, p.58]
Malted Honeycomb & Molasses
[See 'Malty Baked', Baked, p.73]
Sultana & Hazelnut
[See 'Spicy Sweet', Sweet, p.64]

Try:
Beer: Brown Ale [p.238]
Dessert Wine: Pineau de Charentes [p.163], Vin Santo [p.166]
Fortified Wine: Aged Tawny Port [p.168],

chemicals from sugar decomposition bring home tip-top notes of molasses and toffee.

Pedro Ximenez Sherry [p.174]
Whisky: Irish Coffee [p.244]
White Wine: Alsace Gewürztraminer [p.126]

Canada

Vidal Ice Wine Canadian dentists must be snowed under. Teeth and cold-weather references in one sentence – nailed it. Ice Wines are made from grapes that have frozen on the vine, yielding treacly juice that's twice the sweetness of full-fat Coca-Cola *[Mixers, p.260]*, for goodness' sake. It's frankly a nightmare to produce, with machinery occasionally breaking in the process of pressing rock-solid berries. The freeze–thaw cycle endured by the Vidal Blanc grapes rearranges their compounds, ushering in ester-rich *[Glossary, p.16]* aromas of dried pineapple, while the sweet-heat of cooked ginger comes from fermentation.

If you like:
Dried Apricot & Candied Orange Peel
[See 'Spicy Sweet', Sweet, p.64]
Dried Pineapple & Cooked Ginger
[See 'Spicy Sweet', Sweet, p.64]

Try:
Dessert Wine: Rivesaltes Ambré [p.164], Vin Santo [p.166]
Fortified Wine: Crusted Port [p.169], Palo Cortado Sherry [p.173]
Rum: Pineapple [p.197]
Whisky: Southern Comfort [p.249]
White Wine: White Rioja Reserva [p.138]

France

Pineau de Charentes Some of the best things in life were created by accident; just look at the Post-it note and Teflon. Neither tastes as good as Pineau de Charentes, though, which was conceived by a cellar-hand tossing unfermented grape juice into an 'empty' barrel of eau-de-vie. He was fired and the world got a serendipitous drink, the end. This mistaken libation is called a *mistelle*, made when strong spirits block fruit fermentation, retaining the fresh flavour compounds. It's all about sweetness and crisp acidity, with nutty sultana notes coming through from compounds formed via barrel-ageing.

If you like:
Mexican Vanilla & Cinnamon
[See 'Creamy Sweet', Sweet, p.59]
Sultana & Hazelnut
[See 'Spicy Sweet', Sweet, p.64]

Try:
Coffee: Mexican [p.206]
Dessert Wine: Rutherglen Muscat [p.162], Vin Santo [p.166]
Fortified Wine: Aged Tawny Port [p.168], Bual Madeira [p.167], Pedro Ximenez Sherry [p.174]
Fruit Liqueur: Pacharán [p.186]
Tequila: Reposado [p.192]

Rivesaltes Ambré Rivesaltes reminds me of those tear-jerking videos showing abandoned puppies finding forever homes. Left outside in glass demijohn containers for a year, this studiously neglected *Vin Doux Naturel* takes on the elements, undergoing temperature swings, humidity changes, direct sunlight and darkness, which collectively conspire to contort its fresh-fruity flavours into complex notes of dried apricots, salted caramel, candied orange zest and Christmas spices. Rivesaltes Ambré is maderised *[Glossary, p.18]*, heated and oxidised in a way you wouldn't ordinarily wish on a wine, which weaves in prematurely developed dried-fruit notes from age-triggered compounds.

Sauternes Knowing the world's most expensive dessert wine is formed from a fungus makes me reassess the furry artefacts lurking in my fridge. In a classic 'when life hands you mouldy grapes' scenario, Bordeaux Sauvignon Blanc and Semillon bunches are attacked by the rot-triggering *botrytis* fungus, draining them of moisture like Bella begged Edward to do to her in *Twilight*. Now for the upside: the infected berries become desiccated sugar bullets with newly acquired aroma compounds like sotolon *[Glossary, p.19]* for fenugreek notes, honeyed baby ginger and hay-adjacent saffron.

Vin de Paille It seems the scarecrow finally found his brain, when you consider the chemical complexity of straw wine or Vin de Paille. Ironically, the wine, made from drying Chenin Blanc grapes on straw mats isn't cut and dried. Working to the opposite principal of a fruit bowl, where moisture is trapped at the bottom, straw

If you like:
Christmas Cake & Chocolate Orange
[See 'Fruity Spicy', Spicy, p.103]
Dried Apricot & Candied Orange Peel
[See 'Spicy Sweet', Sweet, p.64]
Salted Caramel & Lychee
[See 'Burnt Sweet', Sweet, p.58]

Try:
Dessert Wine: Vidal Ice Wine [p.163], Vin Santo [p.166]
Flower Liqueur: St Germain [p.209]
Fortified Wine: Aged Tawny Port [p.168], Crusted Port [p.169], Palo Cortado Sherry [p.173]
Port: Colheita [p.169]
Whisky: Southern Comfort [p.249]

If you like:
Baby Ginger & Linden Honey
[See 'Zingy Spicy', Spicy, p.111]
Fenugreek & Saffron
[See 'Fragrant Spicy', Spicy, p.102]

Try:
Dessert Wine: Tokaji Aszú [p.165]
Herb Liqueur: King's Ginger [p.212]
White Wine: Auslese Riesling [p.131], Spätlese Riesling [p.132]

If you like:
Blonde Caramel & Dried Fig
[See 'Burnt Sweet', Sweet, p.57]
Clover Honey & Gingerbread
[See 'Floral Sweet', Sweet, p.61]
Seville Orange Marmalade & Grapefruit
[See 'Juicy Fruity', Fruity, p.48]

allows air circulation while the grapes dry, crucially ensuring a rot-free zone. Slow dehydration prevents the berries from raisining, maintains moisture and acidity, creating flavours majoring on the heat-induced notes of cooked fruit, marmalade, honey, baked gingerbread and citrus.

Try:
Aperitivo Cocktail: Negroni [p.224]
Brandy: VSOP Cognac [p.177]
Fortified Wine: Aged Tawny Port [p.168], Colheita Port [p.169], Cream Sherry [p.171]
Whisky: Irish Whiskey [p.244]
White Wine: Grillo [p.135]

Greece

Mavrodaphne de Patras More Greek than Zeus sipping a shot of Ouzo on Mount Olympus. Now that's something I'd pay to see. This famously opaque fortified dessert wine from the Peloponnese region of southern Greece is a port-sherry-madeira hybrid that finds its flavour chakra slap bang in the middle of all three beverages. Dusky Mavrodaphne grapes are dried in sun-exposed vats and aged in a solera system of wine barrels of various vintages, which are stacked on top of one another, the booze trickling down to refill the barrels below. Spicy oak lactones *[Glossary, p.17]*, heat-formed caramel and age-induced compounds bring chocolate, plum and marzipan notes to the meze platter.

If you like:
Dark Chocolate Mousse & Plum
[See 'Roasty Sweet', Sweet, p.62]
Dried Fig & Plum
[See 'Spicy Sweet', Sweet, p.64]

Try:
Beer: Brown Ale [p.238]
Coffee: Peruvian [p.207]
Dessert Wine: Recioto della Valpolicella [p.166]
Fortified Wine: Sweet Superiore Marsala [p.168]
Red Wine: Argentinian Malbec [p.143], Pomerol [p.147], Primitivo [p.155], Uruguayan Tannat [p.160]

Hungary

Tokaji I'd take the name Noble Rot over Grey Mould any day. Both are aliases of the famous fungi that creates Tokaji Aszú, the world's noblest dessert wine. Does Tokaji sound Japanese? Yes, though it's actually Hungarian and comes in a version that's so sweet it's teaspoon-sipped and still turns our eyes into pinwheels. Production-wise, Furmint grapes are mauled by mould and plucked from the vine in a state of advanced shrivelling, aka Aszú. The fungi rewires Furmint's

If you like:
Fenugreek & Saffron
[See 'Fragrant Spicy', Spicy, p.102]
Flat Peach & Honeysuckle
[See 'Creamy Fruity', Fruity, p.43]
Mint & Dates
[See 'Minty Herbaceous', Herbaceous, p.37]

Try:
Dessert Wine: Sauternes [p.164]
Sparkling Wine: English Blanc de Blancs [p.116]

molecular hard-drive, ramping up glycerol *[Glossary, p.17]*, injecting complex flavour compounds with treacly, spiced, minty, floral, dried-fruity influence.

White Wine: Albariño [p.137], Alsace Gewürztraminer [p.126], Australian Chardonnay [p.124], Australian Viognier [p.124], Sonoma Coast Chardonnay [p.139]

Italy

Recioto della Valpolicella Remember the movie *Sliding Doors*, where Gwyneth Paltrow's life forked off depending on whether she caught the train? There's a similar story arc for Recioto della Valpolicella, which could have been Amarone if more sugars had fermented into alcohol. Both involve *apassimiento*, the process of desiccating Corvina grapes on ropes dangling from wooden beams like aromatic shower curtains, in a *fruttaio*, a low-humidity drying room to ward off opportunistic rot. Age-related flavours are brought in by tobacco-smelling compounds, while liquorice and eucalyptus notes intensify through oak contact, simultaneously dialling up the wild raspberry and plum.

If you like:
Dried Fig & Plum
[See 'Spicy Sweet', Sweet, p.64]
Liquorice & Dark Chocolate
[See 'Spicy Sweet', Sweet, p.56]
Turkish Tobacco & Wild Raspberry
[See 'Spicy Smoky', Smoky, p.84]

Try:
Dessert Wine: Mavrodaphne de Patras [p.165]
Fortified Wine: Sweet Superiore Marsala [p.168]
Red Wine: Aglianico del Vulture [p.151], Barolo [p.152], Primitivo [p.155]

Vin Santo All good things come to those who wait . . . and wait. Vin Santo's fermentation can take a whopping four years, by which time it's developed the nutty, dried-fruity middle-aged spread characteristics of a wine that's been around the block. Still, it's the holy grail of dessert wines. Literally, as Vin Santo translates as 'saintly wine'. Trebbiano grapes are semi-raisined and naturally fermented, a glacially paced process that rises and falls with the seasonal temperatures and maintains more tropical-fruity notes than the similarly made Madeira, with barrel- and bottle-aged compounds edging in caramel, candied fruit and hazelnut nuances.

If you like:
Dried Apricot & Candied Orange Peel
[See 'Spicy Sweet', Sweet, p.64]
Dulce de Leche & Mango
[See 'Burnt Sweet', Sweet, p.58]
Sultana & Hazelnut
[See 'Spicy Sweet', Sweet, p.64]

Try:
Dessert Wine: Pineau de Charentes [p.163], Rivesaltes Ambré [p.164], Rutherglen Muscat [p.162], Vidal Ice Wine [p.163]
Fortified Wine: Aged Tawny Port [p.168], Crusted Port [p.169], Palo Cortado Sherry [p.173], Pedro Ximenez Sherry [p.174]
Whisky: Southern Comfort [p.249]

Fortified Wine

Madeira

Madeira

<u>Bual</u> Alanis Morissette was bang on when she asked, 'Isn't it ironic?' It's unclear if she was asking about Madeira, a fortified wine we use for cooking even though it's already been cooked during the production process. I know – we could almost taste the irony if it wasn't hidden under Bual's intense flavours. Made by the estufagem system of accelerated ageing, Bual is 'baked' in wine casks for three months under forty-five-degree-centigrade heat. Extended baking degrades Bual's high fructose *[Glossary, p.16]* content, forming cooking-related compounds that mimic the flavour of nuts, spice, dried fruit and butterscotch.

If you like:
Bitter Orange & Butterscotch
[See 'Juicy Fruity', Fruity, p.48]
Date & Walnut
[See 'Spicy Sweet', Sweet, p.63]
Mexican Vanilla & Cinnamon
[See 'Creamy Sweet', Sweet, p.59]

Try:
Amaro: Aperol Spritz [p.222]
Coffee: Mexican [p.206]
Dessert Wine: Pineau de Charentes [p.163]
Fortified Wine: Pedro Ximenez Sherry [p.174]
Fruit Liqueur: Cointreau [p.182], Curaçao [p.182], Grand Marnier [p.182], Pacharán [p.186]
Tequila: Reposado [p.192]

<u>Malmsey</u> Malmsey must have a portrait in an attic somewhere, to taste so fresh after everything it's been through. Fermentation, fortification, cooking, oxidation and barrel-ageing would have destroyed a lesser wine, but Malmsey has emerged indestructible. The richest Madeira style is made from the Malvasia grape, with Malmsey's high residual sugar *[Glossary, p.18]* a result of fermentation that's stopped early. The Canteiro system works by 'cooking' top Madeiras in rooms via the subtropical heat of the sun, inputting slow-cooked flavours of burnt caramel, nuts, spice, vanilla pod and marmalade.

If you like:
Scorched Caramel & Cayenne Pepper
[See 'Burnt Sweet', Sweet, p.58]
Vanilla Pod & Roasted Pecan
[See 'Creamy Sweet', Sweet, p.60]
Walnut & Orange Zest
[See 'Nutty Baked', Baked, p.74]

Try:
Nut Liqueur: Nocino [p.254]
Red Wine: Rioja Gran Reserva [p.159]
Sherry: Oloroso [p.173], Palo Cortado [p.173]

Marsala

Italy

Sweet Superiore Riserva Chicken tikka springs to mind when someone mentions Marsala, that, or the bottle-shaped dust magnet at the back of the drinks cabinet. With concentrated flavours of dried figs, plums, scorched toffee and bitter chocolate, the 'cook's share' comes before, during and after we've slugged Marsala into our sauce *au poivre*. It's produced from a base wine, stopped by fortification and sweetened by cooked grape juice or 'mosto cotto'. Four years' barrel-ageing provides the flavour forum for Marsala's notes of dried fruit, macadamia nuts, burnt toffee, plum and citrus honey.

If you like:
Bitter Chocolate & Burnt Toffee
[See 'Roasty Sweet', Sweet, p.62]
Dried Fig & Plum
[See 'Spicy Sweet', Sweet, p.64]
Macadamia Nut & Citrus Honey
[See 'Nutty Baked', Baked, p.73]

Try:
Beer: Brown Porter [p.238], Stout [p.239]
Cider: English Heritage [p.187]
Dessert Wine: Mavrodaphne de Patras [p.165], Recioto della Valicella [p.166]
Red Wine: Primitivo [p.155]
Tequila: Coffee [p.190]
White Wine: Alsace Pinot Gris [p.126], Fiano di Avellino [p.133], Meursault [p.127], Puligny Montrachet [p.129]

Port

Portugal

Aged Tawny Port If you're offered a glass of 'mouthwash' after a meal, here's hoping it's a Tawny Port as Colgate Plax just isn't as tasty. I'm always up for swishing a mouthful of caramel, honey, spices, dried fruit and hazelnuts. Heck, I'd even give it a gargle. Aged Tawny majors on oxidation flavours, and is matured in dinky barrels for an amber hue and the complex flavour compounds that come through controlled aeration. Ageing summons in a compound that nails the nuts and spices brief, while others dish out notes of dried figs and caramel.

If you like:
Blonde Caramel & Dried Fig
[See 'Burnt Sweet', Sweet, p.57]
Christmas Cake & Chocolate Orange
[See 'Fruity Spicy', Spicy, p.103]
Sultana & Hazelnut
[See 'Spicy Sweet', Sweet, p.64]

Try:
Brandy: VSOP Cognac [p.177]
Dessert Wine: Pineau de Charentes [p.163], Rivesaltes Ambré [p.164], Rutherglen Muscat [p.162], Vin Santo [p.166]
Fortified Wine: Colheita Port [p.169], Cream Sherry [p.171], Pedro Ximenez Sherry [p.174]
Madeira: Malmsey [p.167]

Colheita Port Tawny comes off as 'yawny' compared to a Colheita – the port, not the brown-tinted owl. Pronounced *col-yate-ah*, meaning 'harvest', it's the limited-edition vintage version of tawny port, serving a seven-year-minimum sentence in barrel. Sotolon *[Glossary, p.19]* is a major influence in Colheita's flavour Rolodex, a compound that creeps into oxidising barrel-maturing Port, possibly through the degradation of grape sugars. It increases with barrel time, stepping up the complex notes of grilled nuts, dried fruit and spice, with compounds from the fortification process bringing in roasty 'rancio' flavours *[Glossary, p.18]* and scorched caramel.

If you like:
Blonde Caramel & Dried Fig
[See 'Burnt Sweet', Sweet, p.57]
Christmas Cake & Chocolate Orange
[See 'Fruity Spicy', Spicy, p.103]

Try:
Brandy: VSOP Cognac [p.177]
Dessert Wine: Rivesaltes Ambré [p.164]
Fortified Wine: Aged Tawny Port [p.168],
Cream Sherry [p.171]
Madeira: Malmsey [p.167]

Crusted Port I'm crushing on Crusted Port and if loving it is wrong, I don't want to be right. Who cares if it's nicknamed the 'poor man's port' or 'the crusty charlatan' when it's a safe place of plum, liquorice, eucalyptus, violets and candied orange rind? Whipped up by British Port shippers as a knock-off version of Vintage, it's essentially a fine Non-Vintage, unfiltered Ruby Port that *throws* a sediment called a crust. From this, heady notes of violet emerge while camphoraceous *[Glossary, p.15]* eucalyptus aromas escalate via age-triggered flavour molecules.

If you like:
Dried Apricot & Candied Orange Peel
[See 'Spicy Sweet', Sweet, p.64]
Violet & Eucalyptus
[See 'Rich Floral', Floral, p.27]

Try:
Brandy: XO Cognac [p.178]
Dessert Wine: Rivesaltes Ambré [p.164], Vidal Ice Wine [p.163], Vin Santo [p.166]
Fortified Wine: Palo Cortado Sherry [p.173]
Red Wine: Australian Cabernet Sauvignon [p.143], Gaillac Rouge [p.149]
Whisky: Southern Comfort [p.249]

LBV Port LBV isn't the wine version of LBW, or Leg Before Wicket; it stands for Late Bottled Vintage. I don't usually 'do' cricket unless it's a reference to port's jolly British influence, with names like Cockburn's and Taylor's frequently branded across bottles. A mash-up of zhuzhed-up Ruby and poor-man's Vintage, LBV is produced from a single year with longer ageing in big old 'tonel'

If you like:
Rose & Dark Chocolate
[See 'Intense Floral', Floral, p.25]
Rose & Violet
[See 'Intense Floral', Floral, p.26]
Sandalwood & Raspberry
[See 'Woody Smoky', Smoky, p.86]

Try:
Brandy: Metaxa 12-Star [p.178]

barrels, named after their tunnel-like shape. Bottle-ageing brings in roses, violets and raspberries, while oak-infused compounds deliver roasty-rich notes of caramel and chocolate.

Ruby Port Ah, the exuberance of youth. Nope, can't relate. Ruby is the baby of the fortified family, all intense pigment, restless red fruit and shrill alcohol, leaping out of the glass when our backs are turned and practically drinking itself for us. A three-year stint in Port production's biggest barrel, the 'balseiro', doesn't provide enough wood-contact to change anything stylistically, so do the right thing and drink it immediately. The ruby hue is down to pigment-forming compounds in the grape skins, with sweet-cherry and floral aroma compounds preserved by a short fermentation that is abruptly stopped by adding in a fortifying wine spirit.

Vintage Port Pass the port on the left-hand side, or is it the dutchie? I always get them confused. Either works, as you must always keep your sword arm free, apparently. Well, you know what those port drinkers are like. We're talking Vintage, the most spendy Port that's only made, or declared, in exceptional years and builds flavours via bottle-ageing. It has no less than ten to fifty years languishing under glass, a reductive form of ageing that triggers complex compounds with Parma Violet, rosy, woody, cigar-box notes and another that pumps out eucalyptus and liquorice.

Flower Liqueur: Crème de Violette [p.209]
Red Wine: Nero D'Avola [p.155], Uruguayan Tannat [p.160]
White Wine: Torrontés [p.123]

If you like:
Rose & Plum
[See 'Intense Floral', Floral, p.26]
Sweet Cherry & Milk Chocolate
[See 'Floral Fruity', Fruity, p.47]

Try:
Red Wine: Aglianico del Vulture [p.151], Californian Pinot Noir [p.161], Central Otago Pinot Noir [p.156], Châteauneuf-du-Pape [p.147], Montepulciano d'Abruzzo [p.154], Touriga Nacional [p.156]

If you like:
Cigar Box & Parma Violets
[See 'Spicy Smoky', Smoky, p.84]
Rose & Liquorice
[See 'Intense Floral', Floral, p.26]

Try:
Red Wine: Aged Red Burgundy [p.145], Amarone della Valpolicella [p.151], Barbaresco [p.152], Barolo [p.152], Chianti Classico Riserva [p.153], Pauillac [p.146]
Rosé Wine: Bandol Rosé [p.140]

White Port Anyone remember Crystal Pepsi or Tab Clear? Exactly, me neither. Tab ditched caramel from Coca-Cola's formula, decolouring it to create a clear version. It didn't sell and goes to show how certain drinks are linked to pigment. This is a case in point with Port, a wine associated with specific shades of red, when making it from white grapes could have gone either way. Thankfully, oxidative ageing hones its toffee-apple, apricot and lemon-zest notes, while oak delivers cloves and vanilla, and while purists pretend White Port doesn't exist, we're pouring it into tumblers full of ice topped up with tonic.

If you like:
Lemon Zest & Apricot
[See 'Zingy Fruity', Fruity, p.52]
Vanilla & Clove-Spiced Toffee Apple
[See 'Creamy Sweet', Sweet, p.60]

Try:
Brandy: VSOP Calvados [p.177]
Cider: Cask-Aged [p.186]
Red Wine: Californian Pinot Noir [p.161]
Tea: Rooibos [p.203]
Whisky: Speyside Single Malt [p.247]
White Wine: Grüner Veltliner [p.125], Mosel Kabinett Riesling Trocken [p.132], Torrontés [p.123]

Sherry

Spain

Amontillado Like the forgotten bandmember of One Direction, whose name escapes me, Amontillado is often neglected for its stablemates. Shame, given sherry's most under-represented style is also the most representative of the drink, a halfway house of fruity-saline and nutty-savoury styles. Yeast-aged sherries, Fino and Manzanilla have whip-fresh flavours, whereas oxidative, cask-aged Oloroso and Palo Cortado nurture nut-fest notes. Amontillado is the only sherry with both, straddling the flavour camps with the fresh, fruity saline notes of Fino and nutty, toasty, savoury tones of an Oloroso without veering too far in, well, one direction.

If you like:
Olive Brine & Walnut Brittle
[See 'Brothy Savoury', Savoury, p.88]
Sea Spray & Bread Dough
[See 'Marine Minerally', Minerally, p.95]

Try:
Fortified Wine: Fino Sherry [p.172], Manzanilla Sherry [p.172], Palo Cortado Sherry [p.173]
Sake: Junmai-Shu [p.242], Koshu [p.243]
White Wine: Reuilly Sauvignon Blanc [p.130]

Cream Smooth, sweet, nutty and great with grannies, but enough about me – this is Cream Sherry's segment. Confusingly,

If you like:
Blonde Caramel & Dried Fig
[See 'Burnt Sweet', Sweet, p.57]

Cream Sherry has never been near a Friesian's udder, with a golden-amber hue from the melanoid pigment produced by heating the sweetening juice in low-rent versions. Quality Creams are built around Oloroso sherry, blended with Pedro Ximenez for their trademark caramel, nuts and spices rubbing up against raisiny dried fruit. Barrel-ageing allows flavours to integrate slowly, infusing violet, clove, vanilla, brown sugar, brandy, caramel and dried-fig notes from oak-infused compounds.

Violet & Christmas Cake
[See 'Rich Floral', Floral, p.27]

Try:
Brandy: VSOP Cognac [p.177]
Fortified Wine: Aged Tawny Port [p.168], Colheita Port [p.169]
Madeira: Malmsey [p.167]

Fino Fino needs a decent estate agent, as it's all about location, location, location, darling. While Fino ages inland, Manzanilla matures on the Atlantic coast, nurturing cooler conditions for a meatier blanket of flor covering its sherry. What's flor again? The Gaudi of biofilm yeast that's present in the Andalusian air and which moulds Fino's famous flavours, working on the wine and metabolising alcohol into sherry-like compounds, carving out bone-dry notes of fennel, bitter chicory, briny olive, bread dough and bruised apple. Temperature fluctuations and lower humidity weaken Fino's flor, playing peekaboo with oxygen for light nutty nuances.

If you like:
Chicory & Green Olive
[See 'Bitter Herbaceous', Herbaceous, p.32]
Fennel & Green Apple
[See 'Veggie Herbaceous', Herbaceous, p.40]
Roast Chestnut & Bruised Apple
[See 'Nutty Baked', Baked, p.74]
Sea Spray & Bread Dough
[See 'Marine Minerally', Minerally, p.95]

Try:
Cider: Cask-Aged [p.186]
Fortified Wine: Amontillado Sherry [p.171], Manzanilla Sherry [p.172]
Gin: Dirty Martini [p.229]
Grain Spirit: Sweet Potato Shōchū [p.256]
Orange Wine: Georgian [p.139]
Sake: Junmai-Shu [p.242]
Sparkling Wine: Cava Brut Nature [p.122], English Non-Vintage [p.116]
White Wine: Clare Valley Riesling [p.124], Reuilly Sauvignon Blanc [p.130], Rueda Verdejo [p.138], Vin Jaune [p.131]

Manzanilla You can't unsee an ageing Manzanilla, that layer of gunk floating on top like a giant dollop of cottage cheese. Put another way, it's the alchemistic vale of flor yeast converting Palomino

If you like:
Brioche & Bramley Apple Sauce
[See 'Yeasty Baked', Baked, p.78]
Cut Grass & Salt-Roasted Almonds
[See 'Grassy Herbaceous', Herbaceous, p.35]

base wine into Manzanilla, the most delicately saline style of sherry. Flor yeast is fundamental, and assisted by southern-Spanish Sanlúcar's humid sea air it switches ethanol into a cooked-apple-like compound, a major reason for Manzanilla's appley mannerisms, with another compound responsible for almonds. Flor yeast also goes through a complex process that beckons in bread-dough aromas from yeasty protein compounds.

Oloroso Oloroso bursts out of the butt like *The Legend of Zorro*, all swarthy flavours and pungent aromas. Well, it does translate as 'smelly'. Fortified sufficiently to kill the natural yeast, sherry casks, or butts, are then piled high, youngest on top, oldest down below in cathedral-like bodegas, refilling one another as the wine is drawn off. Exposure to oxygen ushers in a kaleidoscopic array of flavours, with older liquid bringing in fruity nuances, smoky notes with spiced caramel and vanilla from compounds triggered by wood-ageing.

Palo Cortado They seek him here, they seek him there – Palo Cortado's enigmatic origin story smacks of the Scarlet Pimpernel's. This shady sherry style started out as a deviated Fino, not actively produced but triggered by certain conditions like an offbeat barrell or rogue yeast activity. These irregular casks were marked by a diagonal 'Cortado' line, crossing out the Fino's vertical 'Palo' line, aka 'cut stick', then fortified to kill the protective flor yeast and aged oxidatively. Style-wise, it has Oloroso's nutty, savoury caramel notes, retaining

Sea Spray & Bread Dough
[See 'Marine Minerally', Minerally, p.95]

Try:
Cider: Breton Brut [p.187]
Fortified Wine: Amontillado Sherry [p.171], Fino Sherry [p.172]
Orange Wine: South African Chenin Blanc [p.137]
Sake: Junmai-Shu [p.242]
Sparkling Wine: Cava de Paraje [p.123], Crémant d'Alsace [p.119], Pétillant Naturel Sec Chenin Blanc [p.119]
White Wine: Greco di Tufo [p.134], Reuilly Sauvignon Blanc [p.130]

If you like:
Date & Walnut
[See 'Spicy Sweet', Sweet, p.63]
Vanilla Pod & Roasted Pecan
[See 'Creamy Sweet', Sweet, p.60]

Try:
Fortified Wine: Amontillado Sherry [p.171], Bual Madeira [p.167], Malmsey Madeira [p.167], Palo Cortado Sherry [p.173]
Red Wine: Rioja Gran Reserva [p.159]

If you like:
Dried Apricot & Candied Orange Peel
[See 'Spicy Sweet', Sweet, p.64]
Olive Brine & Walnut Brittle
[See 'Brothy Savoury', Savoury, p.88]
Walnut & Orange Zest
[See 'Nutty Baked', Baked, p.74]

Try:
Dessert Wine: Rivesaltes Ambré [p.164], Vidal Ice Wine [p.163], Vin Santo [p.166]
Fortified Wine: Amontillado Sherry [p.171], Crusted Port [p.169], Malmsey Madeira [p.167], Oloroso Sherry [p.173]

Amontillado's briny bite from flor yeast-aged compounds.

Nut Liqueur: Nocino [p.254]
Sake: Koshu [p.243]
Whisky: Southern Comfort [p.249]

Pedro Ximenez It's tricky to describe Pedro Ximenez without quoting 'Sweet Dreams (Are Made of This)' by the Eurythmics. I won't as there's a copyright fee. Pedro Ximenez is a beverage so treacly, opaque and unctuous that it tastes more like a squirty dessert topping than a sherry. Overripe Pedro Ximenez grapes are withered in the sun to concentrate their sugars and dial up their molecular complexity, particularly the raisin and honey-like compounds. The combination of drying, fortification and oxidative barrel-ageing brings home sultanas, dates, walnuts, hazelnuts, bitter chocolate and toffee.

If you like:
Bitter Chocolate & Burnt Toffee
[See 'Roasty Sweet', Sweet, p.62]
Date & Walnut
[See 'Spicy Sweet', Sweet, p.63]
Sultana & Hazelnut
[See 'Spicy Sweet', Sweet, p.64]

Try:
Beer: Brown Porter [p.238], Stout [p.239]
Dessert Wine: Pineau de Charentes [p.163], Rutherglen Muscat [p.162], Vin Santo [p.166]
Fortified Wine: Aged Tawny Port [p.168], Bual Madeira [p.167], Marsala Sweet Superiore [p.168]
Tequila: Coffee [p.190]

Vermouth

England

Dry White If today's medicine came in the shape of an aromatised wine, my GP wouldn't be able to get rid of me. Botanical-led beverages like vermouth started out as a health drink to cure just about anything stomach-related. The deliberately bland-tasting base wine is fortified and infused with aromatic botany-based ingredients like citrus peel, herbs, spices and a bittering agent. *Vermouth* means 'wormwood' or 'manhood' in German, which is a plant with bitter elderflower-like flavours and psychoactive side effects from a compound called thujone *[Glossary, p.19]*, with vermouth's grapefruit-woody notes from the spicy compounds in juniper berries and citrus peel.

If you like:
Cut Grass & Yuzu
[See 'Grassy Herbaceous', Herbaceous, p.36]
Orris Butter & Hyssop
[See 'Medicinal Spicy', Spicy, p.107]
Wormwood & Elderflower
[See 'Bitter Spicy', Spicy, p.101]
Yellow Grapefruit & Juniper
[See 'Bitter Fruity', Fruity, p.42]

Try:
Anise Liqueur: Absinthe [p.216]
Gin: Salty Dog [p.227]
Herb Liqueur: Strega [p.215]
Vermouth: Cocchi Americano [p.175]

Italy

Cocchi Americano Talk about a cocktail condiment, mixologists would have a bottle of Cocchi Americano grafted to their pouring hand if that was an option. Cocchi cultivated its cult image by refusing to go down the route of Lillet, a rival aromatised wine that banished the bitter from the recipe to sell out. Gentian root is a major taste in Cocchi, doubling down with fellow bitter buddies wormwood and quinine, providing a foil to sweet floral flavours of its Moscato d'Asti base wine, which has been cold-infused with citrus peel and elderflowers.

If you like:
Gentian Root & Pomelo Peel
[See 'Bitter Spicy', Spicy, p.100]
Wormwood & Elderflower
[See 'Bitter Spicy', Spicy, p.101]

Try:
Amaro: Suze [p.222]
Anise Liqueur: Absinthe [p.216]
Mixer: Indian Tonic Water [p.259]
Tea: Earl Grey [p.202]
Vermouth: Dry White Vermouth [p.174]

Rosso 'Just popping to the shops to grab some clammy sage and lungwort,' said no one, ever. Anyway, you'd have to say that in Italian if you were making Rosso Vermouth, with its dark amber colour and sweet nutty, peppery, liquorice and herbal-bitter profile. There's an amplified sugar content and an abundance of herbs in Italian-style vermouth. Well, I guess they like things a little more 'extra' over there. Caramel can be added to provide pigment, either that or by cooking the base wine, which brings in brown notes over maraschino cherries and minty liquorice from wormwood's artemisia ketone compound.

If you like:
Chicory & Liquorice
[See 'Bitter Herbaceous', Herbaceous, p.32]
Maraschino Cherry & Damson Skin
[See 'Floral Fruity', Fruity, p.47]
Pink Peppercorn & Juniper
[See 'Peppery Spicy', Spicy, p.108]

Try:
Amaro: Negroni [p.224], Zucca Rabarbaro [p.225]
Anise Liqueur: Pastis [p.217], Ricard [p.218]
Fruit Liqueur: Cherry Brandy [p.185], Maraschino [p.180], Sloe Gin [p.181]
Gin: Pink [p.226]

Brandy

France

Armagnac I like it rough – like velvet versus silk, or like gritty Glastonbury with its undone and imperfect style over

If you like:
Morello Cherry & Almond
[See 'Floral Fruity', Fruity, p.47]

prissy Coachella. Armagnac tastes like Cognac's regional cousin, whose rustic magic emerges in production and, when compared to Cognac, isn't all clean minimal lines and brutalist structural design. Its single distillation in a Heath Robinson-style column still *[Glossary, p.15]* preserves the unfiltered flavour compounds that multiple processing and higher alcohol would knock out. Folle Blanche grapes bring in floral notes from aromatic terpenes *[Glossary, p.19]* in their skin, which are roughed up by coffee, cherry and almond notes from wood-infused compounds.

Sidecar Not to get all Charles Dickens, but cocktails are storytelling in a glass. No one cares how big the fabled fish actually was; we've been enjoying half-true stories from way back in early man's cave-era campfire gatherings to modern-day binge-stream docuseries. Let's go with Sidecar's colourful origin story: first whipped up at the Ritz, Paris, on the behest of an American sergeant major riding a motorcycle sidecar. Flavours balance around Cognac's spirity-fruity esters *[Glossary, p.16]* and alcohols, Cointreau's pine-like orange-peel references, citrus juice and a sucrose trim round the rim to dial down the sour.

Violet & Coffee
[See 'Rich Floral', Floral, p.27]

Try:
Brandy: VSOP Cognac [p.177]
Fruit Liqueur: Kirsch [p.183], Maraschino [p.180]
Herb Liqueur: The Last Word [p.216]
Mixer: Cherry Coke [p.260]
Nut Liqueur: Amaretto [p.253]
Red Wine: Amarone [p.151], Pinotage [p.157]
Rosé Wine: Sangiovese Rosé [p.142]

If you like:
Bitter Orange & Butterscotch
[See 'Juicy Fruity', Fruity, p.47]
Mandarin Orange & Lemon
[See 'Juicy Fruity', Fruity, p.48]

Try:
Amaro: Aperol Spritz [p.222]
Beer: Belgian Wheat [p.237]
Fortified Wine: Bual Madeira [p.167]
Fruit Liqueur: Cointreau [p.182], Curaçao [p.182], Grand Marnier [p.182]

Cocktail recipe

SIDECAR [Fruit-Produced Drinks, Brandy]

40ml Cognac
20ml Cointreau
20ml Lemon Juice
Ice
Sugar (optional)

Shake Cognac, Cointreau and lemon juice with ice, then strain into a chilled cocktail glass. Play around with the Cognac/Cointreau levels until you find your sweet spot.

VS Cognac There's been an a-salted caramel, so spread 'em – someone's going behind bars. Seriously though, it's not uncommon practice for distillers to infuse caramel into Cognac to deepen its amber pigment and fluff up its toffee flavours. To be fair, the youngest style of Cognac has already had an injection of diacetyl *[Glossary, p.16]*, a compound produced via fermentation with a butterscotch flavour profile. 'Very Special' Cognac has a mandatory two-year stint in barrel, which coupled with a double distillation draws out heat-related notes smacking of caramel, with a herbaceous undercurrent from grape-derived flavour compounds.

If you like:
Brown Butter & Nutmeg
[See 'Buttery Creamy', Creamy, p.66]
Cut Grass & Toffee
[See 'Grassy Herbaceous', Floral, p.36]

Try:
Amaro: Cynar [p.224]
Bourbon: Eggnog [p.249]
Brandy: XO Cognac [p.178]
Herb Liqueur: Green Chartreuse [p.213]
Rum: Mojito [p.197], Rhum Agricole Blanc [p.199]
Tequila: Reposado [p.192]

VSOP Calvados I'm outraged that my school careers adviser never suggested 'pomologist' as a profession, probably because drinking fermented apples appealed to me more than studying the trees. *Calva*, to the French, is produced in Normandy from slow-ripened apples, late-picked once the frosts have killed the natural bacteria responsible for run-away fermentation, then double-distilled and barrel-aged. Young apple eau-de-vie is all about gawky fruit and fire flavours, with ageing-induced clove-spiced toffee-apple and vanilla flavours drawn in via the oxidative interplay between the apple spirit and those roasty compounds housed in the oak barrel.

If you like:
Baked Braeburn & Cinnamon
[See 'Crisp Fruity', Fruity, p.45]
Brown Butter & Nutmeg
[See 'Buttery Creamy', Creamy, p.66]
Vanilla & Clove-Spiced Toffee Apple
[See 'Creamy Sweet', Sweet, p.60]

Try:
Bourbon: Eggnog [p.249]
Brandy: VS Cognac [p.177], XO Cognac [p.178]
Cider: Cask-Aged [p.186]
Fortified Wine: White Port [p.171]
Red Wine: Californian Pinot Noir [p.161]
Tea: Rooibos [p.203]
Whisky: Speyside Single Malt [p.247]

VSOP Cognac Some of us can relate to the name 'Very Superior Old Pale', especially over the winter months. VSOP Cognac has been sentenced to four years in barrel, or at least the youngest component of the blend has. Confusingly, it's released looking, well, anything but pale, with a compound infused into the

If you like:
Blonde Caramel & Dried Fig
[See 'Burnt Sweet', Sweet, p.57]
Toasted Hazelnut & Digestive Biscuit
[See 'Nutty Baked', Baked, p.74]
Toasted Oats & Caramelised Peach
[See 'Toasty Baked', Baked, p.77]

distilled spirit via barrel-ageing, which injects flavours of toasted oats, digestive biscuits and hazelnuts. 'Pale' means no added caramel, though the brandy barrel infuses compounds that give the spirit caramelised peach tones and the flavour of dried figs.

Try:
Beer: Brown Porter [p.238]
Brandy: Armagnac [p.175]
Fortified Wine: Aged Tawny Port [p.168], Colheita Port [p.169], Cream Sherry [p.171], Malmsey [p.167]
Nut Liqueur: Frangelico [p.254]
Sparkling Wine: Franciacorta Riserva [p.121], Mature Champagne [p.117], Vintage Champagne [p.118]

XO Cognac Forget stemware, it's more like stem war; who knew Cognac glasses could garner so much drama? There are calls to 'smash the snifter' and 'banish the brandy balloon' in favour of the flavour-funnelling tulip glass. People really need to relax and have another drink, using whichever shape glass works best to siphon up those spicy, nutty, buttery, aka *Rancio Charentais* flavours in mature XO Cognac. Extreme ageing has welcomed in highly odorous compounds like eucalyptol from the oxidative degradation of oak-barrel lignans *[Glossary, p.17]* that collectively smell of eucalyptus, nutmeg and violets, with brown-butter notes from roasty-odorous compounds.

If you like:
Brown Butter & Nutmeg
[See 'Buttery Creamy', Creamy, p.66]
Violet & Eucalyptus
[See 'Rich Floral', Floral, p.27]

Try:
Bourbon: Eggnog [p.249]
Brandy: VS Cognac [p.177]
Fortified Wine: Crusted Port [p.169]
Red Wine: Australian Cabernet Sauvignon [p.143], Gaillac Rouge [p.149]

Greece

Metaxa 12-Star 'Boozistas' know that if a brandy tastes suspiciously smooth, we could be looking at a brandy-based liqueur. Bingo Metaxa, a beverage loosely centred around brandy without being bogged down by all those regulations. The base spirit is mellowed out by luscious Muscat wines, sweetened and pigmented by caramel, before it's beautified by an infusion of Mediterranean botanicals, which they keep tight-lipped about but

If you like:
Navel Orange Peel & Violet
[See 'Fruity Spicy', Spicy, p.104]
Orange Blossom & Honey
[See 'Soft Floral', Floral, p.29]
Rose & Dark Chocolate
[See 'Intense Floral', Floral, p.25]

Try:
Coffee: Peruvian [p.207]
Fortified Wine: LBV Port [p.169]
Fruit Liqueur: Curaçao [p.182]

absolutely includes rose petals and anise. Barrel-maturation infuses dark-chocolate roasty compounds into the flavour equation, with violet notes emerging from its lengthy twelve-year ageing.

Gin: Sakura Bee's Knees [p.228]
Mixer: Coca-Cola [p.260]
Red Wine: Touriga Nacional [p.156]
Sparkling Wine: Moscato d'Asti [p.121]
Whisky Liqueur: Drambuie [p.246]
White Wine: Condrieu [p.127]

The Netherlands

Advocaat Does Advocaat look like liquidised Big Bird from Sesame Street and taste like boozy custard? Yes, but it's made from egg yolks, vanilla, sugar, cream and Cognac, so what do we expect? Though it may appear like an eggnog knock-off, Advocaat is a fancy beverage emulsion that translates as 'lawyer's drink' in Dutch and comes with a bit of chemistry. It's held in a colloid dispersion, which sounds painful but involves large hydrophobic *[Glossary, p.17]*, undissolvable molecules of cream and egg yolk suspended in liquid, that scatter light particles, making the beverage look opaque.

If you like:
Crème Pâtissière & Praline
[See 'Decadent Creamy', Creamy, p.68]
Orange Pepper & Vanilla
[See 'Sweet Herbaceous', Herbaceous, p.38]

Try:
Bourbon: Eggnog [p.249]
Whisky Liqueur: Baileys Irish Cream [p.243]
White Wine: Meursault [p.127], White Rioja Reserva [p.138]

Peru/Chile

Pisco I'd have to sleep with one eye open if I credited Pisco to either Peru or Chile, so ferocious is the tug of war over its ownership. We'll call it a tie, even though it's named after the Peruvian port of Pisco. Style-wise, there's no escape from grapes, with Pisco's flavour Rolodex down to the fragrant flower power of the Muscat and Italia varieties. This single-distilled grape brandy with minimal barrel-ageing houses highly aromatic compounds diffusing lavender, rose and citrus notes with honey and jasmine and grassy nuances.

If you like:
Cut Grass & Acacia Honey
[See 'Grassy Herbaceous', Herbaceous, p.35]
Jasmine & Mint
[See 'Sweet Floral', Floral, p.30]
Lemon & Fresh Pear
[See 'Zingy Fruity', Fruity, p.52]

Try:
Coffee: Nicaraguan [p.206]
Fruit Liqueur: Cointreau [p.182]
Herb Liqueur: Yellow Chartreuse [p.214]
Sparkling Wine: Crémant de Loire [p.119]
Tea: Oolong [p.201]

Fiano di Avellino [p.133],
South African Chenin Blanc [p.137],
Vermentino [p.135]

Pisco Sour Who doesn't love a mouthful of sour fluff, though getting the egg-white foam on a Pisco Sour just right is as tricky as playing Jenga in an earthquake. While whisking folds air into egg whites to supposedly create soft peaks, whipping them in a copper vessel frees up the metal ions [Glossary, p.17] that combine with the sulphur in eggs. This unravels and firms up their amino acids, making the whisked egg whites stand tall like the mountains Shakira was on about. Citric acid in lime stabilises the eggy froth, while punctuating it with a punch of pine and white pepper.

If you like:
Christmas Tree & Preserved Lime
[See 'Fruity Spicy', Spicy, p.103]
White Peppercorn & Starfruit
[See 'Peppery Spicy', Spicy, p.108]

Try:
Herb Liqueur: Crème de Menthe [p.213],
The Last Word [p.216]
Tequila: Margarita [p.190]
White Wine: Retsina [p.133]

Cocktail recipe

PISCO SOUR [Fruit-Produced Drinks, Brandy]

50ml Pisco
25ml fresh Lime Juice
25ml Sugar Syrup
1 Egg White
3 drops Angostura Bitters

Add Pisco, lime juice, sugar syrup and the whisked egg white into your shaker. Shake without ice to aerate the ingredients, then again with ice, then strain into a big coupe glass and garnish with Angostura Bitters.

Fruit Liqueur

Croatia

Maraschino For some reason that cherry-stone scene in *The Witches of Eastwick* springs to mind when I sip Maraschino. It's made from crushed sour marasca cherries, fermented with their leaves, stalks and stones – the whole kit and caboodle. What basically starts out as boozy cherry soup, steeped in neutral spirit, is redistilled to produce an eau-de-vie spirit that is blended with a water-

If you like:
Maraschino Cherry & Damson Skin
[See 'Floral Fruity', Fruity, p.47]
Morello Cherry & Almond
[See 'Floral Fruity', Fruity, p.47]
Rose & Black Cherry
[See 'Intense Floral', Floral, p.25]

Try:
Brandy: Armagnac [p.175]

based sucrose solution and aged in Finnish ashwood vats. Benzaldehyde *[Glossary, p.15]* is a key compound in cherries and damson skin that whiffs of almonds, bringing in tipsy nuances of Bakewell tart.

Fortified Wine: Rosso Vermouth [p.175]
Fruit Liqueur: Cherry Brandy [p.185], Kirsch [p.183], Sloe Gin [p.181]
Herb Liqueur: The Last Word [p.216]
Mixer: Cherry Coke [p.260]
Nut Liqueur: Amaretto [p.253]
Red Wine: Amarone [p.151]
Rosé Wine: Sangiovese Rosé [p.142]

England

Pimm's If the sun never set on the British Empire, how was it ever 'Pimm's o'clock'? Maybe it always was; now that's a clever slogan. As ever, medicine was more fun in Victorian times, when this gin-based herb-infused 'fruit cup' concoction was originally road-tested as a health tonic. Said to be a colonial inheritance of New Orleans, the high commission of cocktails, though I can't readily imagine Mardi Gras revellers sipping Pimm's with their pinkies out. Pimm's is a flavour conglomeration of unspecified herbal botanicals, spices and caramelised orange, further influenced by its cut strawberry, cucumber and mint leaves over lemonade.

If you like:
Star Anise & Lemon Verbena
[See 'Fragrant Spicy', Spicy, p.102]
Sweet Orange & Cinnamon
[See 'Juicy Fruity', Fruity, p.48]

Try:
Anise Liqueur: Ricard [p.218]
Fruit Liqueur: Limoncello [p.184]
Herb Liqueur: Harvey Wallbanger [p.220], The Last Word [p.216], Yellow Chartreuse [p.214]
Red Wine: Mulled Wine/Glühwein [p.150]

Sloe Gin Sloe berries are bitter and vicious. Just ask anyone who's fallen into a sloe bush – I'm speaking for a friend. They taste better in Kilner clip-top jars, where they belong under the mellowing influence of sugar and gin. This diminutive wild plum packs serious phenolic compounds *[Glossary, p.18]* and a brutally sour astringency, crying out for a gin-infused flavour makeover. Gin's botanically enhanced DNA is already jammed with barky-spicy compounds delivering pepper, woody-herbaceous and piney notes from juniper, with cherry and almond notes brought on by a compound released by the degrading sloe stones.

If you like:
Graphite & Sloe Berry
[See 'Earthy Smoky', Smoky, p.82]
Maraschino Cherry & Damson Skin
[See 'Floral Fruity', Fruity, p.47]

Try:
Fortified Wine: Rosso Vermouth [p.175]
Fruit Liqueur: Cherry Brandy [p.185], Maraschino [p.180]
Red Wine: Bordeaux Pauillac [p.146], Priorat [p.158]

France

Cointreau It's the classic Hoover conundrum, where the brand name becomes the category. Triple Sec is a style of orange liqueur, while Cointreau is its best-known brand. Glad we cleared that up. Macerating dried, fresh, bitter and sweet orange peel together in sugar-beet alcohol oxidises its orangey-smelling compound into a spectrum of pine, floral and spearmint notes. Sweet orange rind provides a citrusy-woody aroma, while bitter oranges bring lemon-adjacent acidity and florals from linalool *[Glossary, p.18]* with an added pop of butterscotch from the sugar-beet distillation.

If you like:
Bitter Orange & Butterscotch
[See 'Juicy Fruity', Fruity, p.48]
Jasmine & Mint
[See 'Sweet Floral', Floral, p.30]
Mandarin Orange & Lemon
[See 'Juicy Fruity', Fruity, p.48]

Try:
Amaro: Aperol Spritz [p.222]
Beer: Belgian Wheat [p.237]
Brandy: Sidecar [p.176]
Fortified Wine: Bual Madeira [p.167]
Fruit Liqueur: Curaçao [p.182], Grand Marnier [p.182]
Pisco: Peruvian [p.179]
White Wine: Fiano di Avellino [p.133]

Curaçao The Dutch are my collective spirit animal, not just for inventing orange liqueur, though that's a major factor. Curaçao is the original style of orange liqueur, concocted by Dutch colonists on the eponymous Caribbean island from unpalatably bitter Laraha oranges. Curaçao is now made all over the place, some artificially coloured and flavoured with a secret infusion of spices said to include cinnamon, nutmeg, cloves and coriander. Peel steeping and distillation lock in bitter orange's desirable pine-like, minty, woody, spicy, floral and citrus-odorous compounds, removing its unwanted notes of plastic, metal and fat.

If you like:
Bitter Orange & Butterscotch
[See 'Juicy Fruity', Fruity, p.48]
Orange Blossom & Honey
[See 'Soft Floral', Floral, p.29]

Try:
Amaro: Aperol Spritz [p.222]
Brandy: Metaxa [p.178], Sidecar [p.176]
Coffee: Peruvian [p.207]
Fortified Wine: Bual Madeira [p.167]
Fruit Liqueur: Cointreau [p.182], Grand Marnier [p.182]
Gin: Sakura Bee's Knees [p.228]
Mixer: Coca-Cola [p.260]
Sparkling Wine: Moscato d'Asti [p.121]
Whisky: Drambuie [p.246]
White Wine: Condrieu [p.127]

Grand Marnier We'd have a face like a grieving pug if we chowed down on a raw bitter orange, that's why they're generally used in booze. Oranges, not dogs. Bitter

If you like:
Bitter Orange & Butterscotch
[See 'Juicy Fruity', Fruity, p.48]

orange peel is literally the essence of Grand Marnier, and is prized by distillers and perfumiers for its persistent, freshly floral bergamot-infused aromas, which are less synthetic than sweet orange's. Grand Marnier is a hybrid of the Triple Sec and Curaçao styles, based around Cognac, sun-dried bitter orange peel and sugar, with wood-induced vanilla and butterscotch nuances brought in by brief barrel-ageing.

Vanilla & Bitter Orange
[See 'Creamy Sweet', Sweet, p.59]

Try:
Amaro: Aperol Spritz [p.222]
Bourbon: Manhattan [p.251],
Old-Fashioned [p.252]
Brandy: Sidecar [p.176]
Coffee: Rwandan [p.207]
Fortified Wine: Bual Madeira [p.167]
Fruit Liqueur: Cointreau [p.182],
Curaçao [p.182]
Mixer: Coca-Cola [p.260]

Germany

Kirsch Kirsch isn't water, like it's full name 'Kirschwasser' would suggest. I learned that the hard way. It's a cherry eau-de-vie, served neat in its native Germany where they clearly no longer have functioning mouth roofs. Benzaldehyde [Glossary, p.15] is a biggie flavour-wise, a cherry-come-almond-smelling compound conjured by the breakdown of the cherry stones. Cherries are crushed, the mash is left to ferment and then distilled into a see-through spirit with zero sweetening or ageing. Flowery and fruity notes from compounds are ramped up by cherry-dwelling floral compounds.

If you like:
Elderflower & Red Cherry
[See 'Fruity Floral', Floral, p.25]
Morello Cherry & Almond
[See 'Floral Fruity', Fruity, p.47]

Try:
Brandy: Armagnac [p.175]
Fruit Liqueur: Maraschino [p.180]
Herb Liqueur: The Last Word [p.216]
Mixer: Cherry Coke [p.260]
Nut Liqueur: Amaretto [p.253]
Red Wine: Amarone [p.151], Beaujolais [p.146]
Rosé Wine: Sangiovese Rosé [p.142]

Peach Schnapps When you are name-checked by Tom Cruise, your work on this planet is done. Peach Schnapps had a shout-out in *Cocktail* as part of the tacky tipple, Sex on the Beach. Ah, the eighties. Although not exactly classy in its sugary liqueur form, Peach Schnapps can do better than the Fuzzy Navel and the Woo Woo cocktails, let's be honest. Proper Schnapps is an unsweetened, fruit-distilled

If you like:
Elderflower & Yellow Peach
[See 'Fruity Floral', Floral, p.25]
Flat Peach & Honeysuckle
[See 'Creamy Fruity', Fruity, p.43]

Try:
Dessert Wine: Tokaji Aszú [p.165]
Sparkling Wine: Bellini [p.120], English Blanc de Blancs [p.116]

eau-de-vie from the Norse word *Snappen*, meaning 'to snatch a gulp'. The liqueur version sees peaches steeped in neutral alcohol for a free pour of peachy lactone compounds *[Glossary, p.17]*, sugar and glycerine *[Glossary, p.17]*.

White Wine: Albariño [p.137], Alsace Gewürztraminer [p.126], Australian Chardonnay [p.124], Australian Viognier [p.124], Sonoma Coast Chardonnay [p.139]

Italy

Limoncello Attempting to leave a trattoria without being accosted by a complementary bottle of Limoncello is almost mission impossible. I'm not complaining, they can give me a bottle of that chilled canary-coloured, hazy colloidal system *[Glossary, p.15]* of citrus-floral essential oils any day. Alcohol's chemical structure allows it to fully extract lemon's hydrophobic flavour molecules *[Glossary, p.17]* from its super-rich rind during soaking, cue Limoncello's citrus blossom and pine-like mannerisms. Bittersweet star anise flavours are brought in by lemon's essential oils and subdued via dilution by the sugar-syrup solution.

If you like:
Elderflower & Lemon Sherbet
[See 'Fruity Floral', Floral, p.24]
Star Anise & Lemon Verbena
[See 'Fragrant Spicy', Spicy, p.102]

Try:
Anise Liqueur: Necromancer [p.221], Ricard [p.218]
Flower Liqueur: St Germain [p.209]
Fruit Liqueur: Melon Ball Drop [p.184], Pimm's [p.181]
Herb Liqueur: The Last Word [p.216], Yellow Chartreuse [p.214]

Japan

Melon Ball Drop Aside from aliens, money, Harrods, the environment and my eye colour, which is technically hazel, what's the real meaning of green? The Melon Ball Drop cocktail symbolises none of these things, but who knew this Kermit-coloured concoction could make us so existential? *Midori* means 'green' in Japanese, representing the lime-coloured rind of the super-spendy Japanese Yubari melons they're part made from. It's a green-hued tag team of flavours, from the saccharine-herbaceous musk melon, a shared compound found in the elderfloral

If you like:
Elderflower & Cantaloupe Melon
[See 'Fruity Floral', Floral, p.24]
Elderflower & Lemon Sherbet
[See 'Fruity Floral', Floral, p.24]

Try:
Anise Liqueur: Necromancer [p.221]
Flower Liqueur: St Germain [p.209]
Fruit Liqueur: Limoncello [p.184], Midori [p.185]
Mixer: Elderflower Cordial [p.258]
Sake: Junmai Ginjo [p.242]
White Wine: Bacchus [p.125]

St Germain *[Flower Liqueur, p.209]* and a necessary lift of lemon vodka.

MELON BALL DROP [Fruit-Produced Drinks, Fruit Liqueur]

40ml Midori
30ml Vodka
15ml St Germain
15ml Lemon Juice, freshly squeezed
Melon Balls to garnish

Shake Midori with Vodka, St Germain, lemon and ice, then strain into a chilled Martini glass with a sugared rim and garnish with melon balls.

Midori Disclaimer, Midori gives you a fever, a Saturday-night fever, considering its launch was celebrated at Studio 54 with John Travolta. An Elphaba-green liqueur in a bottle with the texture of musk-melon skin, how could anyone resist? Somehow we managed to, but our interest in the provenance of drinks got us curious over Midori's secret ingredients, which aren't secret any more. Made from high-end volcanic-soil-grown Japanese Yubari and musk melons with all their herbaceous, floral, honeyed and tropical-fruity compounds, pulped, distilled with neutral spirit, blended with Cognac and cane sugar and pigmented with lurid green food colouring.

If you like:
Citrus Honey & Charentais Melon
[See 'Floral Sweet', Sweet, p.60]
Elderflower & Cantaloupe Melon
[See 'Fruity Floral', Floral, p.24]

Try:
Fruit Liqueur: Melon Ball Drop [p.184]
Mixer: Elderflower Cordial [p.258]
Sake: Junmai Ginjo [p.242]
Sparkling Wine: Prosecco DOCG [p.122]
White Wine: Auslese Riesling [p.131], Bacchus [p.125], Condrieu [p.127], South African Chenin Blanc [p.137]

The Netherlands

Cherry Brandy I'm probably being dramatic, but thinking about hydrogen cyanide gives me anxiety. It's rife in cherry stones; just ask Agatha Christie who used it to dispatch a fair few of her characters. You'd need to drink a lot of Cherry Brandy, though, but what a delicious way to go, given its concentrated flavours of black and red cherries, roses, damsons, vanilla and cinnamon. Copper stills take out the toxins, allowing complex

If you like:
Black Cherry & Raspberry Jam
[See 'Floral Fruity', Fruity, p.46]
Maraschino Cherry & Damson Skin
[See 'Floral Fruity', Fruity, p.47]
Rose & Black Cherry
[See 'Intense Floral', Floral, p.25]

Try:
Coffee: Ethiopian [p.205]
Fortified Wine: Rosso Vermouth [p.175]

compounds to come forward with notes of cherry, warmly spiced cloves, cinnamon, roses and pomace syrup *[Glossary, p.18]* as the, well, cherry on top.

Fruit Liqueur: Maraschino [p.180], Sloe Gin [p.181]
Red Wine: Barolo [p.152], Californian Pinot Noir [p.161], Chianti Classico [p.153], Old-Vine Zinfandel [p.161], Primitivo [p.155]

Spain

<u>Pacharán</u> Attempting to pronounce the Basque word *Patxaran* makes me sound like I'm having a funny turn. It's essentially Spanish sloe gin, made by steeping sloe berries, coffee beans and vanilla in a distilled anise liqueur with added sugar. Anise's formative compounds jive sweetly with sloe's black-cherry and plummy flavour traits, courtesy of a cherry-and-almond-odorous compound that is summoned by berry maceration in anisette, aka anise liqueur. Sloes' naturally plucky, mouth-puckering tannins are tempered by ethanol, sweet anise, balmy vanilla and warming cinnamon.

If you like:
Aniseed & Sloe Berry
[See 'Fruity Spicy', Spicy, p.103]
Liquorice & Black Cherry
[See 'Spicy Sweet', Sweet, p.56]
Mexican Vanilla & Cinnamon
[See 'Creamy Sweet', Sweet, p.59]

Try:
Coffee: Mexican [p.206]
Dessert Wine: Pineau de Charentes [p.163]
Fortified Wine: Bual Madeira [p.167]
Herb Liqueur: Jägermeister [p.214]
Red Wine: Aged Bordeaux Cabernet Sauvignon [p.144], Madiran [p.150], Nero D'Avola [p.155]
Tequila: Reposado [p.192]

Cider

England

<u>Cask-Aged</u> Vinegar, maple syrup, Worcestershire sauce, Tabasco – we'll whack anything into barrels these days. A cidery, which sounds made up, ages cider via gentle oxidation to smooth out any angular edges. The wood-ageing process dials down vibrant, rich, whip-fresh fruit flavours, substituting them for complex notes of bruised apple, spices, nuts, vanilla and toffee. Only certain apples are suited to languishing in oak lignans *[Glossary, p.17]*, with 'bittersweet' and 'bittersharp' heirloom varieties showing the right

If you like:
Roast Chestnut & Bruised Apple
[See 'Nutty Baked', Baked, p.74]
Vanilla & Clove-Spiced Toffee Apple
[See 'Creamy Sweet', Sweet, p.60]

Try:
Brandy: VSOP Calvados [p.177]
Fortified Wine: Fino Sherry [p.172], White Port [p.171]
Grain Spirit: Sweet Potato Shōchū [p.256]
Orange Wine: Georgian [p.139]
Red Wine: Californian Pinot Noir [p.161]

malic-acid-to-tannin balance, beckoning in clove and vanilla nuances via oak-infused compounds.

Heritage Why do English cider apples sound like they've been invented by J. K. Rowling? With names like Brown Snout, Somerset Redstreak, Wickson Crab, Harry Master's Jersey, Foxwhelp and Ashmead's Kernel they should either be Hagrid's illegal beasts or newly employed Dark Arts teachers. As a rule of thumb, if it's good enough to eat, it'll work for commercial cider styles but won't cut it as a crafty heritage. Golden Russets are a hub of honey and nuts in their cider guise, with the russeting process ramifying their flavours via oxidation, bringing in an earthier, spicier profile and bitter-fruity intensity.

France

Breton Brut Cidre Nothing can stop me referring to it as *cidre* in this section, not even spellcheck. Breton Brut Cidre is known for its rich floral, fruity, full-bodied, spicy and rustic flavour profile, or, perhaps I should say, *rustique*. Breton majors on 'bittersweet', 'acidic' and 'bitter' apple varieties, bringing a balance of astringent tannins, dry acidity and bittersweetness under its cork, made in a *bouché* style of bottle fermentation that's similar to Champagne. A preference for wild over cultured yeast nurtures rustic baked-bread and cooked-apple flavours, while bottling *cidre* before fermentation finishes creates fizz à la Champagne.

Tea: Rooibos [p.203]
Whisky: Speyside Single Malt [p.247]
White Wine: Vin Jaune [p.131]

If you like:
Golden Russet & Pear
[See 'Crisp Fruity', Fruity, p.45]
Macadamia Nut & Citrus Honey
[See 'Nutty Baked', Baked, p.73]

Try:
Fortified Wine: Marsala Sweet Superiore Riserva [p.168]
White Wine: Alsace Pinot Gris [p.126], Fiano di Avellino [p.133], Grüner Veltliner [p.125], Meursault [p.127], Puligny Montrachet [p.129], Roussanne [p.130], Soave Classico [p.135], Sonoma Coast Chardonnay [p.139]

If you like:
Brioche & Bramley Apple Sauce
[See 'Yeasty Baked', Baked, p.78]
Cinnamon & Heirloom Apple
[See 'Warm Spicy', Spicy, p.110]

Try:
Fortified Wine: Manzanilla Sherry [p.172]
Sparkling Wine: Cava de Paraje [p.123], Crémant d'Alsace [p.119], Pétillant Naturel Sec Chenin Blanc [p.119]

Perry

England

Vintage If we thought cider apples belonged at Hogwarts, get the Sorting Hat ready for perry pears named Butt, Harley Gum, Merrylegs, Mumblehead, Brown Bess, Trumper, Nailer, Snake Pole, Tettenhall Dick, Water Lugg and Zealous Wick. Perry is produced in the same way as cider, though perry pears have naturally lower aromatics but higher tannins, acids, bitter-savoury compounds and astringency than apples, complete with their own pear-specific compounds. Their toppy sorbitol content, a sugar that isn't readily fermented by yeast, rounds off perry's astringency with a residual sugary *[Glossary, p.18]* softness.

If you like:

Focaccia & Pear Skin
[See 'Yeasty Baked', Baked, p.78]
Golden Russet & Pear
[See 'Crisp Fruity', Fruity, p.45]
Radicchio & Pear
[See 'Bitter Herbaceous', Herbaceous, p.33]

Try:

Cider: English Heritage [p.187]
Orange Wine: Georgian [p.139]
Sparkling Wine: Franciacorta Riserva [p.121]
White Wine: Grüner Veltliner [p.125], Roussanne [p.130], Soave Classico [p.135], Sonoma Coast Chardonnay [p.139]

Drinks

Fruit-produced

Plant-produced

Herb-produced

Grain-produced

Mixers

Tequila

Mexico

Añejo Moth-buster alert: there's no such thing as a tequila worm. It's the Comadia moth larva that's found in Mezcal. More on that story later. Tequila-wise, the heart of the Blue Weber agave succulent plant, or piña as it's known, is steam-roasted in an autoclave oven *[Glossary, p.15]*, shredded by rollers, fermented, double-distilled and matured in oak for one to three years. Bingo, añejo, an oldie but goldie, soaker-upper of spicy compounds from barrel staves that add herbaceous vanilla, nutty and spiced notes to its peppery terpenic profile, intensifying the caramelised notes from roasting-introduced compounds that make it sip like an aged whisky.

If you like:
Black Butter & Muscovado Sugar
[See 'Buttery Creamy', Creamy, p.66]
Coconut Sugar & Pink Peppercorn
[See 'Tropical Creamy', Creamy, p.69]
Cut Grass & Toffee
[See 'Grassy Herbaceous', Herbaceous, p.36]

Try:
Amaro: Cynar [p.224]
Brandy: VS Cognac [p.177]
Herb Liqueur: Green Chartreuse [p.213]
Rum: Mojito [p.197], Rhum Agricole Blanc [p.199], Vintage [p.198]
Tequila: Reposado [p.192]

Coffee Tequila Who knew booze and beans jived? The Irish did when they slugged whisky into their steaming cuppa, and hey presto, Irish coffee became a thing, part of the 'hard coffee' stable, separate even from coffee liqueur. Now we can have our morning reviver the night before, wide awake, while still seeing double. Tequila and coffee are both uppers, and coffee's roasted, earthy, floral, caramelised flavour portfolio counts on hundreds of aromatic compounds from bean processing. Cooked agave syrup has burnt-toffee and bitter-chocolate intensity that is slathered over tequila's white-pepper notes from the peppery compound, rotundone *[Glossary, p.19]*.

If you like:
Bitter Chocolate & Burnt Toffee
[See 'Roasty Sweet', Sweet, p.62]
Mexican Coffee & White Pepper
[See 'Roasty Baked', Baked, p.75]

Try:
Anise Liqueur: Sambuca [p.219]
Beer: Brown Porter [p.238], Coffee Stout [p.239]
Coffee: Mexican [p.206]
Fortified Wine: Marsala Sweet Superiore [p.168], Pedro Ximenez Sherry [p.174]
Nut Liqueur: Nocino [p.254]
Red Wine: Hermitage [p.150]

Margarita Here's a health hack: salt-rimming a cocktail glass is a smart way of sneaking sodium into our diet, if you're ever dehydrated in Mexico. As a cocktail component, salt increases the ionic strength of water-based solutions, allowing volatile molecules to separate from their liquid source and stray up our noses, where they belong. The margarita's blend of sweet agave syrup and tequila's bitter-peppery flavours are neutralised by the sourness of lemon and the salt-dusted rim, nailing the four flavour pillars of bitter, sour, sweet and salty, which basically equals a balanced diet.

If you like:
Lemon & Salt
[See 'Zingy Fruity', Fruity, p.53]
Lemon Blossom & Sea Mist
[See 'Soft Floral', Floral, p.28]
White Peppercorn & Starfruit
[See 'Peppery Spicy', Spicy, p.108]

Try:
Brandy: Pisco Sour [p.180]
Tequila: Slammer [p.192]
White Wine: Albariño [p.137], Grillo [p.135], Pessac-Leognan [p.128], Soave Classico [p.135], Vinho Verde [p.136]

Cocktail recipe

MARGARITA [Plant-Produced Drinks, Tequila]

Lime Wedges
Salt (optional)
50ml Tequila Blanco
25ml Lime Juice, freshly squeezed
15ml Cointreau
1 teaspoon Agave Syrup

Run the lime wedge round the rim of a small cocktail glass and dip in salt (optional). Fill a shaker with ice then add Tequila Blanco, lime juice and Cointreau, then shake and pour into the prepped glass with a lime wedge as garnish and agave syrup for sweetness.

Paloma '*Una paloma blanca . . .* I'm just a bird in the sky', are lyrics from a track released way before my time. As a strapline, though, it wouldn't work for this pink-hued beverage anyway, though it has to be said that Mexico's most popular cocktail is certainly uplifting. Who needs a strapline anyway, when you're more refreshing than a Margarita, with the bubbly, bitter, sour-spicy tones of tequila, ruby-grapefruit, soda, lime and salt? Ruby is less of a bitter-Betty than yellow, sweetened by the salt's bitterness-blocking properties while leaning into lime's woody, green, citrusy acidity.

If you like:
Blood Orange & Rocket
[See 'Bitter Spicy', Spicy, p.100]
Ruby Grapefruit & Persian Lime
[See 'Bitter Fruity', Fruity, p.42]
Yellow Grapefruit & Sea Air
[See 'Bitter Fruity', Fruity, p.42]

Try:
Amaro: Campari [p.223]
Gin: Salty Dog [p.227]
Vodka: Cosmopolitan [p.236]
White Wine: Rueda Verdejo [p.138], Vermentino [p.135]

Cocktail recipe

PALOMA [Plant-Produced Drinks, Tequila]

Salt (optional)
50ml Tequila Blanco
15ml Sugar Syrup
10ml Lime Juice
40ml Ruby Grapefruit Juice
Pink Grapefruit Wedge to garnish
Soda or Prosecco

Salt the rim (optional) of a highball glass.
Fill a cocktail shaker with ice and mix Tequila
Blanco, sugar syrup, lime juice and ruby
grapefruit juice, strain into the prepped glass,
garnish with a wedge of pink grapefruit and
top with soda or, even better, Prosecco.

Reposado Calling tequila 'rested'
suggests it's been bundled into an assisted-
living home on the down-low. It hasn't.
Reposado means it's had a few months'
downtime in barrel, turning the see-
through *blanco* spirit a honey-amber
colour and dousing it with complex notes
of toffee and spices. The reposado style
sits in between the herbaceous blanco and
caramelised añejo styles, retaining distilled
agave syrup's tongue-pricking piquancy
and earthy, grassy flavours from peppery
compounds, mellowing them out with
barrel-leached molecules that bring in
flavours of vanilla and cinnamon.

If you like:
Cut Grass & Toffee
[See 'Grassy Herbaceous', Herbaceous, p.36]
Grains of Paradise & Wintergreen
[See 'Peppery Spicy', Spicy, p.108]
Mexican Vanilla & Cinnamon
[See 'Creamy Sweet', Sweet, p.59]
Pineapple & Brown Sugar
[See 'Tropical Fruity', Fruity, p.51]

Try:
Amaro: Cynar [p.224]
Anise Liqueur: Arak [p.219]
Brandy: VS Cognac [p.177]
Coffee: Mexican [p.206]
Dessert Wine: Pineau de Charentes [p.163]
Fortified Wine: Bual Madeira [p.167]
Fruit Liqueur: Pacharán [p.186]
Herb Liqueur: Green Chartreuse [p.213]
Mezcal: Joven [p.193]
Mixer: Dr Pepper [p.262]
Rum: Mojito [p.197], Pina Colada [p.199],
Pineapple [p.197], Rhum Agricole Blanc [p.199]
Whisky: Aged Japanese Single Malt [p.245]

Slammer The slammer: you mean the
place we would wake up in if we'd had
too many? They should have called it
the 'Jailhouse Shot' given Elvis was a fan.
We're not talking the lick-salt-suck-lemon
shooter, but the bubbly tequila training-
wheels tipple called a 'muppet' in Mexico.

If you like:
Lemon & Salt
[See 'Zingy Fruity', Fruity, p.53]
Whipped Cream & Lemon Soda
[See 'Decadent Creamy', Creamy, p.68]

Tequila layered over with sparkling wine, covered with our hand-palm, slammed against a surface and downed in one. The frenzied, fruity foam fills our stomach, forcing alcohol into our bloodstream, triggering fast-tracked intoxication. Don't waste good barrel-matured añejo and Champagne, mind; Blanco and bargain bubbles will do the job.

Try:

Sparkling Wine: Champagne Demi-Sec [p.117], Riesling Sekt [p.120]
Tequila: Margarita [p.190]
Vodka: Peach Martini [p.234]

Cocktail recipe

TEQUILA SLAMMER [Plant-Produced Drinks, Tequila]

Tequila Blanco
Sparkling Wine

Two-thirds fill a shot glass with Tequila Blanco, then carefully layer over with sparkling wine. Hold the top of the glass, gripping tight, then slam it down on a surface, but not hard enough to smash the shot glass, and shoot.

Mezcal

Mexico

Añejo Echoing Dean Martin's wisecrack about Frank Sinatra: it's mezcal's world – tequila just lives in it. Well, *mezcal* does translate as 'cooked agave', so no wonder all tequila is mezcal but not vice versa. While we're spouting clichéd adages, reworking 'manners maketh the man' into 'smoke maketh the mezcal, as do floral, fruity, earthy and roasted notes' isn't as catchy. Mezcalistas know what I mean; añejo is a flavour fusion of agave's spicy, fruity, honeyed, smoky compounds, delivering scorched earth, toasted timber and oaky smoked vanilla.

If you like:

Rooibos & Smoked Vanilla
[See 'Dried Herbaceous', Herbaceous, p.34]
Wet Earth & Eucalyptus Honey
[See 'Earthy Smoky', Smoky, p.83]

Try:

Amaro: Suze [p.222]
Herb Liqueur: Traditional Mead [p.212]
Mezcal: Joven [p.193], Reposado [p.194]
Tea: Rooibos [p.203]
Whisky: Rusty Nail [p.247]

Joven Mezcal is more than just wood char and worms, lit lignans *[Glossary, p. 17]* and larvae, coke smoke and caterpillars.

If you like:

Fennel & Vanilla
[See 'Veggie Herbaceous', Herbaceous, p.40]

That said, bonfire and pickled pupae are formative flavours in Mezcal; heck, it's even been coined 'the worm's beverage'. Mezcal's moth larvae, languishing at the bottom of bottles, contributes a compound called leaf alcohol, found in insects and foliage. It delivers herbaceous anise nuances that vibe with agave and its vegetal and vanilla-flavoured compounds, with cooked brown sugar, honey and pineapple tepache notes *[Glossary, p.19]* from roasting and fermentation, and its earthy smokiness from firewood-infused flavour molecules.

Reposado Who wouldn't want to be the Cheech and Chong of drinks? Mezcal and Tequila take that title, with Mezcal in the role of Cheech Marin, only because he's a real-life fan, if he's still around. It's the smokier association, see, from the smouldering wood used to heat the cooking stones that line the underground agave roasting pits. Furan compounds released during the slow combustion of over forty agave varieties are expressed as the earthy-spicy-smoky notes of paprika, mesquite and cardamom, further developing as the Mezcal kicks back in barrel for up to a year for the mellow resinous Reposado style.

Cachaça

Brazil

Caipirinha Cachaça puts the 'um?' in 'rum', as technically it isn't one. Well, that's inconvenient; now it can't go in the rum section. Both spirits derive from sugarcane; rum from molasses and cachaça from freshly pressed cane juice,

Pineapple & Brown Sugar
[See 'Tropical Fruity', Fruity, p.52]
Wet Earth & Eucalyptus Honey
[See 'Earthy Smoky', Smoky, p.83]

Try:
Amaro: Suze [p.222]
Anise Liqueur: Galliano [p.219], Harvey Wallbanger [p.220]
Herb Liqueur: Traditional Mead [p.212]
Mezcal: Añejo [p.193]
Rum: Pina Colada [p.199], Pineapple [p.197]
Tequila: Reposado [p.192]
Whisky: Aged Japanese Single Malt [p.245]

If you like:
Mesquite & Cardamom
[See 'Woody Smoky', Smoky, p.85]
Pine Resin & Smoked Paprika
[See 'Woody Smoky', Smoky, p.86]
Wet Earth & Eucalyptus Honey
[See 'Earthy Smoky', Smoky, p.83]

Try:
Amaro: Suze [p.222], Zucca Rabarbaro [p.225]
Herb Liqueur: Traditional Mead [p.212]
Mezcal: Añejo [p.193], Joven [p.193]
Tea: Lapsang Souchong [p.201]

If you like:
Dried Lime & Tomatillo
[See 'Fragrant Spicy', Spicy, p.102]
Granny Smith & Lemon
[See 'Crisp Fruity', Fruity, p.46]

hence its greener, more angular, vegetal, grassy edges that come through in Brazil's national cocktail. The caipirinha is basically a mojito, with cachaça on base spirit duties, but hold the mint. *Caipira* means country bumpkin, after the creators of this raw, floral, citrusy, grassy, vegetal cocktail with a pop of pine-citric lime and apple florals.

Try:
Coffee: Kenyan [p.205]
Rosé Wine: Sangiovese Rosé [p.142]
Sparkling Wine: Cava Brut Nature [p.122], English Non-Vintage [p.116], Riesling Sekt [p.120]
Tea: Green Tea Kombucha [p.200]
Vodka: Appletini [p.234], Bloody Mary [p.235]
White Wine: Clare Valley Riesling [p.124], Mosel Kabinett Riesling Trocken [p.132], Picpoul de Pinet [p.129], Vinho Verde [p.136]

Cocktail recipe

CAIPIRINHA [Plant-Produced Drinks, Cachaça]

1 Lime
60ml Cachaça
20ml Sugar Syrup
Ice Cubes
Sugar Cube (optional)

Cut lime into segments, lay them in a tumbler and lightly bash them with something resembling a muddler. Add cachaça and sugar syrup with ice cubes, then swizzle the mix with a spoon and strain it over the lime in the glass. Garnish with another lime segment and a sugar cube for those with a sweet tooth.

Rum

Bermuda

Dark 'n' Stormy Cocktails and law courts don't usually cross, unless it's over a crime involving dark rum, ginger ale and lime. Talk about tempestuous, the Dark 'n' Stormy has been coined the 'world's most litigious cocktail' and is protected by five trademarks that are fiercer than the stinging compounds in its ginger ale mixer. Pouring Gosling's Black Seal Rum prevents a visit from the cocktail police, an English-style spirit with heavily charred barrel-ageing for smoky phenolic *[Glossary, p.18]* spice and deep pigmentation. Lime's resinous rind and spicy-citrus flavour profile twins well with ginger's green-citrus notes in the famously peppery cocktail.

If you like:
Australian Ginger & Cardamom
[See 'Zingy Spicy', Spicy, p.110]
Dried Ginger & Lime
[See 'Zingy Spicy', Spicy, p.111]
Fennel & Ginger
[See 'Veggie Herbaceous', Herbaceous, p.39]

Try:
Herb Liqueur: King's Ginger [p.212]
Mixer: Ginger Beer [p.259]
Rum: Black Spiced [p.196]
Vodka: Moscow Mule [p.236]

DARK 'N' STORMY [Plant-Produced Drinks, Rum]

50ml Gosling's Black Seal Rum
20ml fresh Lime Juice
10ml Sugar Syrup
2 dashes of Angostura Bitters
Ginger Beer

Shake up Gosling's Black Seal Rum (as I'm not cut out for jail time), lime juice, sugar syrup and Angostura Bitters, then strain into an ice-filled highball glass, top with ginger beer and stir.

Caribbean

Black Spiced I love a repurposed item, especially when it's upcycled as a drink that tastes caramelised, fruity and spicy over ice. Something distilled from molasses perhaps – you know, that sweet and sludgy by-product of sugarcane refinement with zero nutritional value? In a sow's ear/silk purse scenario, or at least satin, Caribbean spiced rum has light barrel-ageing and draws flavour from an infusion of botanicals and spices in the form of warming cinnamon and cloves, lip-stinging ginger, citrus–balsamic notes from cardamom, sweet anise and cooling camphor over rum's rich fruity, butterscotch baseline flavours.

If you like:
Cinnamon & Candied Rosemary
[See 'Warm Spicy', Spicy, p.109]
Fennel & Ginger
[See 'Veggie Herbaceous', Herbaceous, p.39]
Liquorice Root & Black Cardamom
[See 'Medicinal Spicy', Spicy, p.107]

Try:
Anise Liqueur: Ouzo [p.218]
Bourbon: Manhattan [p.251], Wheated [p.253]
Herb Liqueur: Jägermeister [p.214]
Red Wine: Graciano [p.158], Old-Vine Zinfandel [p.161], Uruguayan Tannat [p.160]

Coconut Rum Diehard rum purists, look away; there's nothing for you in this segment. Coconut is already part of barrel-aged rum's flavour roll call, via whisky lactone [Glossary, p.16] in charred American oak barrel staves, so adding actual coconut is a natural-ish next step. Generally a reunion of rums from various locations, coconut is infused and blended into the mix with a longer fermentation, resulting in a heavier rum style. Meanwhile, vanilla flavour is jacked up by caramelised oak wood over a buttery fermentation-produced compound, which

If you like:
Coconut Cream & Pineapple
[See 'Tropical Creamy', Creamy, p.69]
Coconut Water & White Chocolate
[See 'Tropical Creamy', Creamy, p.70]

Try:
Mixer: Cream Soda [p.261]
Rum: Pina Colada [p.199]
Sparkling Wine: Champagne Demi-Sec [p.117]
Whisky: Aged Japanese Single Malt [p.245]

is basically a recipe for cocoa butter we didn't see coming.

Pineapple Rum *Pineapples of the Caribbean* sounds like a sequel too far, though I'd go to see it, as Captain Jack would still be teetering around with his flagon of rum, bless him. Like the Jack Sparrow in spirit, pineapples play up to the brown sugar, white strawberry and cooked-ginger flavours already present in rum from fruity compounds at its core. Steeping fresh fruit flesh in aged rum, distilling its rind with white rum and blending the two, leaves you with the prickle and spicy snap of pineapple and brown sugar tepache *[Glossary, p.19]*.

If you like:
Clove & White Strawberry
[See 'Fruity Spicy', Spicy, p.104]
Dried Pineapple & Cooked Ginger
[See 'Spicy Sweet', Sweet, p.64]
Pineapple & Brown Sugar
[See 'Tropical Fruity', Fruity, p.52]

Try:
Dessert Wine: Vidal Ice Wine [p.163]
Mezcal: Joven [p.193]
Red Wine: Frappato [p.154]
Rum: Pina Colada [p.199]
Tequila: Reposado [p.192]
Whisky: Aged Japanese Single Malt [p.245]
White Wine: White Rioja Reserva [p.138]

White Rum I don't do *Star Trek*, but surely a tie-in with a rum brand is on the cards, now ethyl formate, one of the spirit's molecules has been found in our galaxy? They could use it as an ingredient for their blue drink and call it Rumulan ale. You're welcome. Seamlessly, ethyl formate is also a building block of raspberries, giving them a rum-like component I've personally never noticed. Yeast-derived compounds abound in Spanish-style white rum, an unaged, purer, charcoal-filtered, fruity-floral format without the external flavour influences of barrel-infused compounds like the coconut and vanilla-like whisky lactone *[Glossary, p.17]*.

If you like:
Coconut Sugar & Pink Peppercorn
[See 'Tropical Creamy', Creamy, p.69]
Violet & Raspberry
[See 'Rich Floral', Floral, p.27]

Try:
Red Wine: Argentinian Malbec [p.143], Beaujolais [p.146], Côte-Rôtie [p.148]
Rosé Wine: New Zealand Pinot Noir Rosé [p.142]
Tequila: Añejo [p.190]

Cuba

Mojito Given how picky he is with his Martini order, here's hoping the mixologist got Bond's mojito ratios right

If you like:
Cut Grass & Toffee
[See 'Grassy Herbaceous', Herbaceous, p.36]

in *Die Another Day*. In the wrong hands this herbaceous cocktail can be the Cuban mojito crisis: unbalanced and harsh, quickly veering from Aristotle's golden mean of measures to a fumbled science experiment. White rum lacks the full suite of aged rum's complex compounds, providing the neutral forum to balance mint's mouth-cooling menthol, with lime's pine-like citric-acid sting, and brown sugar's sweet caramel molasses; muddled, not stirred.

Dried Lime & Tomatillo
[See 'Fragrant Spicy', Spicy, p.102]
Mint & Lime
[See 'Minty Herbaceous', Herbaceous, p.37]

Try:
Amaro: Cynar [p.224]
Brandy: VS Cognac [p.177]
Cachaça: Caipirinha [p.194]
Coffee: Kenyan [p.205]
Herb Liqueur: Green Chartreuse [p.213]
Rosé Wine: Sangiovese Rosé [p.142]
Rum: Rhum Agricole Blanc [p.199]
Tea: Green Tea Kombucha [p.200]
Tequila: Añejo [p.190], Reposado [p.192]
Vodka: Bloody Mary [p.235]
White Wine: Mosel Kabinett Riesling Trocken [p.132]

Cocktail recipe

MOJITO [Plant-Produced Drinks, Rum]

1 Mint Sprig
50ml White Rum
20ml Lime Juice
20ml Sugar Syrup
Soda

Arrange mint leaves at the bottom of a highball glass, then add white rum, lime juice and sugar syrup. Stir hard with a long spoon, then fill the glass with crushed ice. Top with a dash of soda, stir and serve.

Jamaica

Vintage Rum Sometimes it's best not to know how things are made, but I'm telling you anyway. Welcome to 'the dunder pit', the cesspool where Jamaican rum distillers grow their own bacteria, sourdough-style. Anything from distillation leftovers to rotten bananas and bat carcasses are left to fester, producing bacteria to add to the ferment and fast-track flavourful ester-compound [Glossary, p.16] formation. It explains the pungent Jamaican style, which is the specialist Islay malts of the rum world, divisive in their uniqueness. We're

If you like:
Banana & Brown Butter
[See 'Tropical Fruity', Fruity, p.51]
Black Butter & Muscovado Sugar
[See 'Buttery Creamy', Creamy, p.66]
Blonde Caramel & Dried Fig
[See 'Burnt Sweet', Sweet, p.57]

Try:
Beer: Bavarian Wheat [p.241]
Bourbon: Kentucky Straight [p.251]
Brandy: VSOP Cognac [p.177]

talking overripe banana notes only those overactive ester compounds *[Glossary, p.16]* can bring to the bottle.

Fortified Wine: Aged Tawny Port [p.168], Colheita Port [p.169], Cream Sherry [p.171]
Madeira: Malmsey [p.167]
Tequila: Añejo [p.190]

Martinique

Rhum Agricole Blanc Talk about the flavour police, Martinique has strict minimum requirements for the level of aroma compounds in their spirits. If these aren't met, what, do they lock you in the drinks-clink? Well, that would explain the expressive style of their particular *rhum*, with the French spelling, which is distilled from freshly pressed sugarcane juice, not molasses. Wild yeast produces a more fragile, funky-flavoured final product, with earthy chantarelle-mushroom mannerisms from the compound, mushroom alcohol. With sparse barrel contact, the Blanc version lives its best grassy, nutty, fruit-forward, cheesy life unchecked.

If you like:
Chantarelle & Apricot
[See 'Earthy Savoury', Savoury, p.90]
Cut Grass & Toffee
[See 'Grassy Herbaceous', Herbaceous, p.36]
Roast Chestnut & Bruised Apple
[See 'Nutty Baked', Baked, p.74]

Try:
Amaro: Cynar [p.224]
Brandy: VS Cognac [p.177]
Cider: Cask-Aged [p.186]
Fortified Wine: Fino Sherry [p.172]
Grain Spirit: Sweet Potato Shōchū [p.256]
Herb Liqueur: Green Chartreuse [p.213]
Orange Wine: Georgian [p.139]
Rum: Mojito [p.197]
Tequila: Añejo [p.190], Reposado [p.192]
White Wine: Vin Jaune [p.131]

Puerto Rico

Pina Colada I can't get Wham's 'Club Tropicana' out of my mind when I think of pina coladas, which must be an undiagnosed disorder. Translated as 'strained pineapple', pina colada accurately describes my head whenever George pipes up. The pina colada embodies the rum/pineapple/coconut trinity of tropical-island components, with the pineapple in the name bringing the brown sugar caramel, candyfloss and honey notes, mimicking the ester-rich *[Glossary, p.16]* flavour components of rum, particularly

If you like:
Coconut Cream & Pineapple
[See 'Tropical Creamy', Creamy, p.69]
Pineapple & Brown Sugar
[See 'Tropical Fruity', Fruity, p.52]

Try:
Mezcal: Joven [p.193]
Rum: Coconut [p.196], Pineapple [p.197]
Tequila: Reposado [p.192]
Whisky: Aged Japanese Single Malt [p.245]

its pineapple adjacency. Coconut's creamy lactones *[Glossary, p. 17]* neutralise pineapple's stingy bromelain enzyme *[Glossary, p.16]*, bonding over their shared coconut flavours.

PINA COLADA [Plant-Produced Drinks, Rum]

60ml White Rum
120ml Pineapple Juice
20ml Coconut Cream
10ml Single Cream
Pinch of Salt
Fresh Pineapple to garnish

Pulse white rum, pineapple juice, coconut cream, single cream and pinch of salt with a scoop of crushed ice, then pour into a tall glass and garnish with pineapple wedge.

Tea

China

Green Tea There's something a bit 'knit your own hot drink' about green tea; I'm not going to lie. Its lawn-green appearance comes from stopping tea leaf oxidation via steaming, or, as they do in China, pan-frying them in a massive wok. There's a major grassy flavour thread woven through green tea, via a compound called leaf aldehyde, which smacks of clipped grass, leaf shoots and kiwi fruit. It's a chemical also common to sea grapes, which share a pop of saline and a buttery, green note via aromatic compounds that usher in a complementary citrus component.

Green Tea Kombucha Fungus and fermentation have no place in tea, unless I forget to put my mug in the dishwasher for a few months. Well, now they do – kombucha's a thing, essentially sweetened tea fermented by a symbiotic culture of bacteria and yeasts, a floating tea fungus

If you like:
Foaming Butter & Green Tea
[See 'Buttery Creamy', Creamy, p.66]
Green Tea & Apple Cider Vinegar
[See 'Dried Herbaceous', Herbaceous, p.34]
Sea Grapes & Kiwi
[See 'Vegetal Minerally', Minerally, p.98]

Try:
Tea: Green Tea Kombucha [p.200],
Matcha [p.203]
White Wine: Picpoul de Pinet [p.129],
Vinho Verde [p.136]

If you like:
Dried Lime & Tomatillo
[See 'Fragrant Spicy', Spicy, p.102]
Green Tea & Apple Cider Vinegar
[See 'Dried Herbaceous', Herbaceous, p.34]

plug called a SCOBY *[Glossary, p.19]*. I know, cute name, but I'm trying not to gag at the concept. The bacteria feed off sugar to produce apple-cider-vinegary acetic acid *[Glossary, p.15]*, one of kombucha's mainframe flavours, with booze-free bubbles produced as a by-product. It can be sweet, fruity, floral, herbaceous, sour and sparkling, and flavoured with anything from ginger to mango.

Lapsang Souchong This is the brew that whisky-swigging heavy metallers might sip when they're not biting off bats' heads, or so I'm guessing. It's a black tea, coined the 'liquor of the tea world' with a pronounced smoky flavour that takes some acquiring. Translated as 'the small-leaf variety smoked by pine wood', 'lap' is pine and 'sang' is smoke. Lapsang Souchong is made by withering tea leaves over a pinewood bonfire, leaving them in barrels then stopping oxidation via another round of smoke-roasting. This intensive process invites in a pungent tobacco, paprika and black olive-adjacent, smoke-derived resinous aroma compound specific to pinewood and another with woody, citrusy, cardamom-like tones, both chemicals exclusive to this particular tea.

Oolong How can grazing your knee or being sent off to boarding school be 'character-building'? That's probably one for my next therapy session. Oolong tea leaves can relate; they've been tossed, bruised, rolled, compressed, oxidised, withered – you name it. In their case it's 'flavour-building', programming in new compounds for added complexity with each part of the painful process. Partial fermentation and oxidation create a halfway house between grassy and malty-

Try:
Cachaça: Caipirinha [p.194]
Coffee: Kenyan [p.205]
Rosé Wine: Sangiovese Rosé [p.142]
Rum: Mojito [p.197]
Tea: Green Tea [p.200]
Vodka: Bloody Mary [p.235]
White Wine: Mosel Kabinett Riesling Trocken [p.132]

If you like:
Dark-Fire Tobacco & Black Olive
[See 'Spicy Smoky', Smoky, p.84]
Mesquite & Cardamom
[See 'Woody Smoky', Smoky, p.85]
Pine Resin & Smoked Paprika
[See 'Woody Smoky', Smoky, p.86]

Try:
Amaro: Zucca Rabarbaro [p.225]
Mezcal: Reposado [p.194]
Red Wine: Crozes-Hermitage [p.149], Washington State Syrah [p.162]

If you like:
Cut Grass & Acacia Honey
[See 'Grassy Herbaceous', Herbaceous, p.35]
Jasmine & Caramel
[See 'Sweet Floral', Floral, p.30]
Nectarine & Oolong Tea
[See 'Creamy Fruity', Fruity, p.44]

Try:
Brandy: Peruvian/Chilean Pisco [p.179]
Coffee: Ethiopian [p.205]
Herb Liqueur: Yellow Chartreuse [p.214]

caramelly, also bringing in a honeyed note and those calling-card floral nuances that make Oolong so unique.

Orange Wine: South African Chenin Blanc [p.140]

Egypt

Peppermint Mummy's favourite herbal tea, literally – as the dried leaves have been found in Egyptian pyramids dating back thousands of years. Flavours revolve around peppermint's essential oil, which majors on menthol, a compound that messes with the cold receptors in our mouths, registering an icy blast on impact. Peppermint tea is usually blended with spearmint to bring in its balancing lemongrass-adjacent compound, which errs on the side of citrusy. Eucalyptol plays a major chemical role too, working its cooling, camphoraceous [Glossary, p.15], medicinal-aromatic magic, with earthy nuances of angelica and Thai basil.

If you like:
Candied Angelica & Thai Basil
[See 'Medicinal Spicy', Spicy, p.106]
Peppermint Tea & Lemongrass
[See 'Dried Herbaceous', Herbaceous, p.34]

Try:
Amaro: Fernet-Branca [p.224]
Anise Liqueur: Galliano [p.219]
Herb Liqueur: Bénédictine [p.212],
Crème de Menthe [p.213], Green Chartreuse [p.213]

England

Earl Grey If a drink was going to be named after me, it had better be something edgier than tea. Though for a nineteenth-century British prime minister, teabags are probably pretty on-brand. Earl Grey is a quirky one too; it's based around black tea leaves infused with bergamot orange peel's essential oil, which brings in a pronounced floral-citrus flavour profile from a suite of aromatic compounds, including bergamottin [Glossary, p.15]. Sour and overwhelming in the flesh, though I've been called worse, bergamot delivers a potpourri bowl of rose and lavender aromas over pomelo peel and a gentian root-like bitterness.

If you like:
Earl Grey & Blueberry
[See 'Dried Herbaceous', Herbaceous, p.33]
Gentian Root & Pomelo Peel
[See 'Bitter Spicy', Spicy, p.100]

Try:
Amaro: Suze [p.222]
Mixer: Indian Tonic Water [p.259]
Red Wine: Touriga Nacional [p.156]
Vermouth: Cocchi Americano [p.175]

Japan

Matcha It should be 'umm-matcha', followed by an umm-mindfulness bell chime and the swirl of a singing bowl, given its umm-meditation associations. I'll stop doing the 'um' thing now. Matcha's green tea leaves are covered by bamboo mats to shade them from direct sunlight, boosting the chlorophyll that gives matcha powder its vivid pea-soupy pigment. Shading also intensifies green tea's bounteous amino acids, which bring about matcha's marine-umami mannerisms, meshing with a creamy-tasting compound to make it a dead ringer for foaming seaweed butter.

If you like:
Beach Pebble & Thyme
[See 'Marine Minerally', Minerally, p.94]
Foaming Butter & Green Tea
[See 'Buttery Creamy', Creamy, p.66]

Try:
Red Wine: Nerello Mascalese [p.155]
Tea: Green [p.200]
White Wine: Assyrtiko [p.133], Chablis [p.126], Greco di Tufo [p.134], Muscadet Sèvre-et-Mains Sur Lie [p.128]

South Africa

Rooibos This probably sounds vain, but you know how clothes look better on you when you're sporting a tan? Likewise for grassy-looking rooibos, which, given some quality time under the African sun triggers the enzymatic oxidation process that invites in its characteristic flavours. We're talking honey-sweet, woody and perfumed, herbal-floral, vanilla, clove and toffee apple notes with a pop of mouth-puckering astringency from phenolic compounds *[Glossary, p.18]*. Leaf fermentation draws in compounds that essentially smell like smoked vanilla with botanical, almost beer-like malted-honey nuances from a natural chemical aptly named, maltol *[Glossary, p.18]*.

If you like:
Malt Biscuit & Heather Honey
[See 'Malty Baked', Baked, p.72]
Rooibos & Smoked Vanilla
[See 'Dried Herbaceous', Herbaceous, p.34]
Vanilla & Clove-Spiced Toffee Apple
[See 'Creamy Sweet', Sweet, p.60]

Try:
Brandy: VSOP Calvados [p.177]
Cider: Cask-Aged [p.186]
Fortified Wine: White Port [p.171]
Mezcal: Añejo [p.190]
Red Wine: Californian Pinot Noir [p.161]
Whisky: Drambuie [p.246], Japanese Single Malt [p.245], Rusty Nail [p.247], Speyside Single Malt [p.247]

USA

Echinacea The multitasking Swiss army knife of the herb world is basically a first-aid kit disguised as a cup of tea. Anything from sniffles to snake bites are a breeze for echinacea, although it's best to run it past a medical professional first. Made from mushed-up roots and rhizomes *[Glossary, p.18]* of the eponymous plant that trigger a bitter tongue tingle that tells you when it's working. Flavours are led by floral-camphoraceous *[Glossary, p.15]* lavender and rosemary notes, followed up by woody-spicy specifications, peppery and spearmint-citrusy compounds and a eucalyptus-adjacent chemical it shares with juniper.

If you like:

Echinacea & Malted Biscuit
[See 'Dried Herbaceous', Herbaceous, p.34]
Rosemary & English Lavender
[See 'Herbal Spicy', Spicy, p.105]
Spearmint & Juniper
[See 'Minty Herbaceous', Herbaceous, p.37]

Try:

Gin: Genever [p.228]
Herb Liqueur: Strega [p.215]
Red Wine: Corbières [p.148], Mencia [p.158]
White Wine: Torrontés [p.123]

Coffee

Brazil

Frank Sinatra was right, they do have a lot of coffee in Brazil, what with it being the world's largest producer of arabica coffee beans and all. Whether Frank tried it in Dunkin' Donuts or a swanky celeb hotspot, he'll have clocked Brazilian coffee's unique flavour profile, which is peanut buttery with low acidity and malty, bittersweet, burnt-popcorn notes. The nut-to-chocolate ratio of Brazil's beans are down to pyrazine compounds *[Glossary, p.18]* from roasting that can border on bitter, with their barely there acidity attributed to low-altitude growing.

If you like:

Dark Chocolate & Molasses
[See 'Roasty Sweet', Sweet, p.62]
Malted Loaf & Peanut Butter
[See 'Malty Baked', Baked, p.72]
Rwandan Coffee & Popcorn
[See 'Roasty Baked', Baked, p.76]

Try:

Beer: Chocolate Stout [p.239]
Coffee: Rwandan [p.207]
Nut Liqueur: Frangelico [p.254]
Sparkling Wine: Vintage Champagne [p.118]

Ethiopia

Just like England is for me, Ethiopia is the cradle of arabica beans, the world's most popular cultivar of coffee plant. It was clocked by Kaldi, a ninth-century goat herder, when his flock behaved erratically after munching on the plant's 'cherries', which any coffee junkie can relate to. Top-notch Ethiopian arabica should have aromas of jasmine, caramel and a distinctly fruity nuance, led by raspberries of all things. A compound called raspberry ketone delivers raspberry jam over woody-fruity black cherry, with a high-acid blueberry tang from elevated growing and red wine-like, bergamot viscosity.

If you like:

Black Cherry & Raspberry Jam
[See 'Floral Fruity', Fruity, p.46]
Earl Grey & Blueberry
[See 'Dried Herbaceous', Herbaceous, p.33]
Jasmine & Caramel
[See 'Sweet Floral', Floral, p.30]

Try:

Fruit Liqueur: Cherry Brandy [p.185]
Red Wine: Barolo [p.152], Californian Pinot Noir [p.161], Chianti Classico [p.153], Old-Vine Zinfandel [p.161], Primitivo [p.155], Touriga Nacional [p.156]
Tea: Earl Grey [p.202], Oolong [p.201]

Kenya

I've had it with coffee vernacular. I mean, who knew 'cup presence' was a thing? I'm only just getting my head around 'twisty crack' for goodness' sake, which means an inconsistent coffee blend in case you aren't a 'cafelier', or coffee expert. If it's anything like 'coffee charisma', Kenyan beans have got epic cup presence. Grown at lofty altitudes of 2,000 metres or more, they make a vibrant almost wine-like brew with boatloads of blueberry nuances. Volcanic soil elevates the bean's appley acidity, bringing in umami, lightly saline notes of tomatillo with the citrusy-woody leanings of dried lime.

If you like:

Apple Blossom & Coffee
[See 'Soft Floral', Floral, p.28]
Dried Lime & Tomatillo
[See 'Fragrant Spicy', Spicy, p.102]
Kenyan Coffee & Blueberry
[See 'Roasty Baked', Baked, p.75]

Try:

Beer: Coffee Stout [p.239]
Cachaça: Caipirinha [p.194]
Red Wine: Primitivo [p.155]
Rosé Wine: Sangiovese Rosé [p.142]
Rum: Mojito [p.197]
Tea: Green Tea Kombucha [p.200]
Vodka: Bloody Mary [p.235]
White Wine: Mosel Kabinett Riesling Trocken [p.132]

Mexico

When did successful people ever peak in high school? Mexico certainly didn't, discovering its coffee capabilities later on in life, in the eighteenth century, so it's still a relative newbie to the bean-scene. Mexican coffee majors on earthy notes of dark chocolate, molasses, white pepper and cinnamon from phenol compounds *[Glossary, p.18]*, which complement the way it's prepared over there. Request Mexican coffee and you'll be served their equivalent of an Irish coffee, with cinnamon, brown sugar, melted vanilla ice cream and a twist of tequila. I mean, when in Mexico . . .

If you like:
Dark Chocolate & Molasses
[See 'Roasty Sweet', Sweet, p.62]
Mexican Coffee & White Pepper
[See 'Roasty Baked', Baked, p.75]
Mexican Vanilla & Cinnamon
[See 'Creamy Sweet', Sweet, p.59]

Try:
Anise Liqueur: Sambuca [p.219]
Beer: Chocolate Stout [p.239]
Dessert Wine: Pineau de Charentes [p.163]
Fortified Wine: Bual Madeira [p.167]
Fruit Liqueur: Pacharán [p.186]
Nut Liqueur: Nocino [p.254]
Red Wine: Hermitage [p.150]
Tequila: Coffee [p.190], Reposado [p.192]

Nicaragua

Talk about parallel lives: the trauma endured by country and coffee bean has ultimately produced something great. Nicaragua's civil war, dictatorships, hurricanes, poverty and trade embargos mirror the picking, fermentation, milling and roasting that have delivered a coffee bean with complex nutty, vanilla, dark caramel, pome-fruit and citrusy characteristics. Less tenuous is the link between Nicaraguan coffee's mellow acidity and purity of flavours, which stem from the bourbon coffee plant, a mild variety of arabica that's shade-grown at high altitude, producing berries that require less roasting time for a cleaner, fresher, mildly aromatic cuppa.

If you like:
Lemon & Fresh Pear
[See 'Zingy Fruity', Fruity, p.52]
Nicaraguan Coffee & Dark Caramel
[See 'Roasty Baked', Baked, p.75]
Vanilla Pod & Roasted Pecan
[See 'Creamy Sweet', Sweet, p.60]

Try:
Beer: Coffee Stout [p.239]
Brandy: Peruvian/Chilean Pisco [p.179]
Coffee Liqueur: Espresso Martini [p.208]
Fortified Wine: Malmsey Madeira [p.167]
Red Wine: Rioja Gran Reserva [p.159]
Sherry: Oloroso [p.173]
Sparkling Wine: Crémant de Loire [p.119]
White Wine: South African Chenin Blanc [p.137], Vermentino [p.135]

Peru

The pressure's on to deliver top-notch coffee when you're home to one of the seven wonders of the world. That's Machu Pichu not Starbucks, though the latter did release a seasonal blend one year that put Peru on our general morning-coffee radar. Still, Peru doesn't spring to mind when we think of our morning reviver, which is a shame given its coffee's spectrum of flavours from honey, dark chocolate, malted milk and plum to orange blossom. Malty, fruity notes are nudged in via bean fermentation, with dark chocolate flavours from roasting-induced compounds, giving it a similar profile to Brazilian coffee.

If you like:
Dark Chocolate Mousse & Plum
[See 'Roasty Sweet', Sweet, p.62]
Orange Blossom & Honey
[See 'Soft Floral', Floral, p.29]
Peruvian Coffee & Malted Milk
[See 'Roasty Baked', Baked, p.76]

Try:
Beer: Brown Ale [p.238], Chocolate Stout [p.239], Coffee Stout [p.239], Dry Stout [p.241]
Brandy: Metaxa [p.178]
Dessert Wine: Mavrodaphne de Patras [p.165]
Fruit Liqueur: Curaçao [p.182]
Gin: Sakura Bee's Knees [p.228]
Mixer: Coca-Cola [p.260]
Red Wine: Argentinian Malbec [p.143], Pomerol [p.147], Uruguayan Tannat [p.160]
Sparkling Wine: Moscato d'Asti [p.121]
Whisky Liqueur: Drambuie [p.246]
White Wine: Condrieu [p.127]

Rwanda

For a country still in recovery, the land of a thousand hills sure makes a mean coffee bean. Creamy and silken with orange, white-chocolate and brown sugar notes, mine's a Rwandan coffee, please. Oh, to be blessed with near perfect coffee-growing conditions: high altitudes for slower ripening, regular rainfall, rolling hills, fertile volcanic soil and plenty of buttery bourbon, the coffee plant, not the booze. Dairy-like, white chocolate notes are a by-product of the bean-roasting process, with another of coffee's major compounds moonlighting as a key flavour component in popcorn.

If you like:
Rwandan Coffee & Popcorn
[See 'Roasty Baked', Baked, p.76]
Vanilla & Bitter Orange
[See 'Creamy Sweet', Sweet, p.59]
White Chocolate & Mocha
[See 'Roasty Sweet', Sweet, p.63]

Try:
Bourbon: Eggnog [p.249], Manhattan [p.251], Old-Fashioned [p.252]
Coffee: Brazilian [p.204]
Coffee Liqueur: White Russian [p.208]
Fruit Liqueur: Grand Marnier [p.182]
Mixer: Coca-Cola [p.260]
Nut Liqueur: Frangelico [p.254]
Sparkling Wine: Vintage Champagne [p.118]
Whisky: Baileys Irish Cream [p.243]

Coffee Liqueur

Belgium

White Russian No nineties bowling movie mention, no White Russian section. Simple. Favourite tipple of the Dude, *The Big Lebowski*'s protagonist, the White Russian is a one-stop shop for all the major food groups: alcohol, sugar, caffeine and fat. It's not just the diet that's balanced; flavour-wise, coffee liqueur softens vodka's edges, though it's a Black Russian until we've lobbed in the single cream or powdered creamer, if you're a practising 'Dudeist'. Kahlua majors on Mexican coffee for molasses and cinnamon notes with an injection of vanilla extract in the white chocolate and mocha-like cocktail.

If you like:
Rwandan Coffee & Popcorn
[See 'Roasty Baked', Baked, p.76]
White Chocolate & Mocha
[See 'Roasty Sweet', Sweet, p.63]

Try:
Bourbon: Eggnog [p.249]
Coffee: Brazilian [p.204], Rwandan [p.207]
Nut Liqueur: Frangelico [p.254]
Sparkling Wine: Vintage Champagne [p.118]
Whisky: Baileys Irish Cream [p.243]

Cocktail recipe

WHITE RUSSIAN [Plant-Produced Drinks, Coffee Liqueur]

40ml Vodka
30ml Coffee Liqueur
30ml Single Cream, shaken

Stir vodka and coffee liqueur together, then strain into an ice-filled tumbler and carefully lay cream over the top, stirring the cream to taste.

England

Espresso Martini A model walks into a bar and asks the waiter for something that will 'wake me up and eff me up'. That's the romantic little story of how the Espresso Martini came about, though it was the eighties in Soho, I suppose. Originally named the 'pharmaceutical stimulant', it's made from vodka, sugar syrup, a shot of ristretto and two types of coffee liqueur, Tia Maria and Kahlua. Ristretto is made from finer granules and

If you like:
Nicaraguan Coffee & Dark Caramel
[See 'Roasty Baked', Baked, p.75]
Peruvian Coffee & Malted Milk
[See 'Roasty Baked', Baked, p.76]

uses less water than espresso, dialling down the roasty bitterness while amplifying the acidity and dark-caramel notes, with the alcohol recalibrating coffee's breakfast connection.

Try:
Beer: Chocolate Stout [p.239], Coffee Stout [p.239], Dry Stout [p.241]
Coffee: Nicaraguan [p.206], Peruvian [p.207]
Whisky: Irish Coffee [p.244]

Cocktail recipe

ESPRESSO MARTINI [Plant-Produced Drinks, Coffee Liqueur]

50ml Vodka
30ml Espresso/Ristretto Coffee
10ml Sugar Syrup
10ml Coffee Liqueur
3 Coffee Beans to garnish

Shake vodka, espresso/ristretto coffee, sugar syrup and coffee liqueur with ice, strain into a Martini glass and garnish with coffee beans.

Flower Liqueur

France

Crème de Violette Bring up crème de violette and people will bang on about the Aviation cocktail, which is fair enough as it's a core ingredient alongside gin, Maraschino and lemon juice. But I'm banging on about this southern-French liqueur's flavour profile, which is made from macerating violet petals in neutral spirit or brandy. It's unflinchingly floral, though confusingly there's no cream in a 'crème'; which refers to the unctuous texture that comes through the addition of sugar. Ionone compounds *[Glossary, p.17]* are the chemical purveyors of violet's talcum-powdery, woody, sweet, rosy notes with its balancing bitterness – flavours that are similarly rambunctious in raspberries.

If you like:
Rose & Violet
[See 'Intense Floral', Floral, p.26]
Violet & Raspberry
[See 'Rich Floral', Floral, p.27]

Try:
Fortified Wine: LBV Port [p.169]
Red Wine: Argentinian Malbec [p.143], Beaujolais [p.146], Côte-Rôtie [p.148], Nero D'Avola [p.155]
Rosé Wine: New Zealand Pinot Noir Rosé [p.142]
Rum: White [p.197]
White Wine: Torrontés [p.123]

St Germain That genius phrase 'bartender's ketchup' nails St Germain, the elderflower liqueur mixologists lob into everything. It's made from alpine elderflowers that are picked in late spring

If you like:
Elderflower & Lemon Sherbet
[See 'Fruity Floral', Floral, p.24]
Mango & Elderflower
[See 'Tropical Fruity', Fruity, p.51]

and quickly macerated to preserve the nuanced mango over sweet blossom and piney-citrus flavours, and doing so, avoid any bitterness. Then there's the maceration in a grape eau-de-vie via a 'secret' family method, with the addition of sugar syrup giving it a viscosity that slows down the flow of liquid, allowing the flavours to linger for longer. That's just as well, given elderflowers' rose and lychee nuances which you want to stick around.

Salted Caramel & Lychee
[See 'Burnt Sweet', Sweet, p.58]

Try:
Anise Liqueur: Necromancer [p.221]
Dessert Wine: Rivesaltes Ambré [p.164]
Fruit Liqueur: Melon Ball Drop [p.184], Limoncello [p.184]

Drinks

Fruit-produced

Plant-produced

Herb-produced

Grain-produced

Mixers

England

King's Ginger It seems ginger has always been a royal trait, which isn't me being cheeky; I just mean the spice. Crafted for King Edward 'the caresser' to keep him warm during his topless Daimler jaunts, though I'm hoping he had a driver while he was drinking. Posh wine merchant Berry Brothers & Rudd whipped him up a vivifying liqueur by macerating root ginger and lemon rind in single malt whisky, sweetened with cane sugar. This is ginger in hellhound mode, all exposed teeth from its chilli-adjacent compounds, subdued by whisky's ginger-whispering malty notes and citrus's balancing twang.

If you like:
Australian Ginger & Cardamom
[See 'Zingy Spicy', p.110]
Baby Ginger & Linden Honey
[See 'Zingy Spicy', Spicy, p.111]
Dried Ginger & Lime
[See 'Zingy Spicy', Spicy, p.111]

Try:
Dessert Wine: Sauternes [p.164]
Mixer: Ginger Beer [p.259]
Rum: Dark 'n' Stormy [p.195]
Vodka: Moscow Mule [p.236]
White Wine: Auslese Riesling [p.131],
Spätlese Riesling [p.132]

Traditional Mead I never think about Friar Tuck, ever, so maybe it's because my mind is on monk-made drinks that I'm associating him with mead. Merry men aside, there's a primordial aura around this beverage, the oldest booze consumed by man, which predates beer or wine and is the alleged origin of the word 'honeymoon'. Mead's flavour spectrum veers from floral and fruity to smoky and spicy, depending on the botanical origin of the raw material. Fermentation retains honey-odorous alcohol compounds, triggering fruity ester formation [*Glossary*, *p.16*], while earthy, eucalyptus, medicinal-over-vanilla nuances stem from pollen-based compounds flown into honey on beeback.

If you like:
Manuka Honey & Custard Apple
[See 'Floral Sweet', Sweet, p.61]
Wet Earth & Eucalyptus Honey
[See 'Earthy Smoky', Smoky, p.83]

Try:
Amaro: Suze [p.222]
Mezcal: Añejo [p.193], Joven [p.193],
Reposado [p.194]
Orange Wine: South African Chenin
Blanc [p.140]

France

Bénédictine The monks are at it again. Not in that way. They're beavering away between matins and mass to unleash a

If you like:
Candied Angelica & Thai Basil
[See 'Medicinal Spicy', Spicy, p.106]

liqueur from undisclosed ingredients; it's all so delightfully *Da Vinci Code*. Not even chromatographic testing can decipher Bénédictine's closely cloistered components, so this is where trained eyes, ears, nose and mouth come into play. It definitely contains alcohol and around twenty-five herbs and spices, including mace, nutmeg, lemon balm, angelica, hyssop, cardamom, basil and cinnamon. Honey and saffron provide sweetness, pigment and balancing medicinal bitterness, mellowed by what I'm sensing to be exactly eight months' barrel-ageing.

Crème de Menthe No one's sipping liqueur to cure their heartburn, so when a nineteenth-century pharmacist invents a boozy drink it feels like a bit of a buzzkill. That said, minty compound menthol relaxes the muscles of our gastrointestinal tract, helping digest fatty foods, hence 'digestif', and don't get me started on what it does to the sphincter. So we're saying that Crème de Menthe is sweeter than peppermint tea, boozier than an after-dinner mint – where do we sign? Steeping Corsican mint leaves in grain alcohol brings its Grinch-coloured pigment into the viscous sugar-sweetened 'crème de' liqueur over a balancing pop of pine and lime notes.

Green Chartreuse I refuse to lead with 'Chartreuse, so good they named a colour after it'. Instead, like a neat shot of this iconic alpine liqueur, I'll begin by mentioning the instant herbal, woody, mentholated sucker punch to the palate that only 130 herbs, spices and flowers can deliver. It may sound like sipping on a boozy herb garden, mainly because it is. Botanicals are dried, crushed and mixed

Lavender Honey & Dried Rosemary
[See 'Floral Sweet', Sweet, p.61]

Try:
Fortified Wine: Dry White Vermouth [p.174]
Herb Liqueur: Green Chartreuse [p.213], Strega [p.215]
Tea: Peppermint [p.202]

If you like:
Christmas Tree & Preserved Lime
[See 'Fruity Spicy', Spicy, p.103]
Peppermint Tea & Lemongrass
[See 'Dried Herbaceous', Herbaceous, p.34]

Try:
Amaro: Fernet-Branca [p.224]
Anise Liqueur: Galliano [p.219]
Brandy: Pisco Sour [p.180]
Herb Liqueur: The Last Word [p.216]
Tea: Peppermint [p.202]
White Wine: Retsina [p.133]

If you like:
Candied Angelica & Thai Basil
[See 'Medicinal Spicy', Spicy, p.106]
Cut Grass & Toffee
[See 'Grassy Herbaceous', Herbaceous, p.36]

Try:
Amaro: Cynar [p.224]
Brandy: VS Cognac [p.177]
Herb Liqueur: Bénédictine [p.212]

DRINKS

in the monastery 'herb room' by the only two monks aware of the recipe at any time, which if you ask for it, they'll tell you is made from 'hamburger and goat's cheese' to throw you off the trail, so be warned.

Yellow Chartreuse The 'cone of secrecy' reminds me of those plastic contraptions worn by distraught-looking dogs, or is that the cone of shame? Either way, there's a lot of that going on with Chartreuse – secrecy around ingredients, not shame. Bartenders tend to use Yellow Chartreuse almost as a more complex version of sugar syrup in cocktails, given its mellow sweet, herbal profile from a blend of over a hundred herbs and spices, which is sweetened by acacia honey with its lightly eucalyptus leanings. Yellow Chartreuse also has a crowd-pleasing spearmint-citrusy hit. Well, even monks have bills to pay.

Germany

Jägermeister Nothing good comes from tipping herbal liqueur into a glass of energy drink. I mean, how is a responsible partygoer meant to curl up on the dance floor and get any kip with people flapping around like distressed eagles on uppers? Forgetting Jägerbombs for a minute, or hours if we're talking blackouts, Jägermeister blends a base spirit, water, sugar and caramel with the essential oils of fifty-six 'secret' spices, roots and herbs. Cinnamon, saffron, liquorice, juniper, anise, cardamom, ginger and orange are all supposed ingredients, collectively producing that black liqueur that is lovingly called *leberkleister* or 'liver glue' by Germans.

Rum: Mojito [p.197], Rhum Agricole Blanc [p.199]
Tea: Peppermint [p.202]
Tequila: Añejo [p.190], Reposado [p.192]

If you like:
Cut Grass & Acacia Honey
[See 'Grassy Herbaceous', Herbaceous, p.35]
Star Anise & Lemon Verbena
[See 'Fragrant Spicy', Spicy, p.102]

Try:
Anise Liqueur: Ricard [p.218]
Brandy: Peruvian/Chilean Pisco [p.179]
Fruit Liqueur: Limoncello [p.184], Pimm's [p.181]
Herb Liqueur: The Last Word [p.216]
Tea: Oolong [p.201]

If you like:
Aniseed & Sloe Berry
[See 'Fruity Spicy', Spicy, p.103]
Liquorice Root & Black Cardamom
[See 'Medicinal Spicy', Spicy, p.107]

Try:
Anise Liqueur: Ouzo [p.218]
Fruit Liqueur: Pacharán [p.186]
Red Wine: Graciano [p.158], Old-Vine Zinfandel [p.161], Uruguayan Tannat [p.160]
Rum: Black Spiced [p.196]

Italy

Strega 'Essential oil, toil and trouble' should be Strega's strapline, as allegedly it's named after the nineteenth-century witch that provided the recipe they still use today. You're welcome, herbal liqueur's marketing team, who haven't met a 'secret ingredient' strategy they didn't like. A bumblebee-yellow digestif liqueur made from seventy confidential ingredients, allegedly majoring on the essential oils of juniper and spearmint with bitter-honeyed, medicinal nuances and yellow pigment from saffron stigmas infused into the herbal distillate. Juniper's citrusy, resinous tones vibe with spearmint's lemony leanings, with hyssop and orris doubling down on Strega's minty-bitter profile.

If you like:
Orris Butter & Hyssop
[See 'Medicinal Spicy', Spicy, p.107]
Spearmint & Juniper
[See 'Minty Herbaceous', Herbaceous, p.37]
Star Anise & Lemon Verbena
[See 'Fragrant Spicy', Spicy, p.102]

Try:
Anise Liqueur: Ricard [p.218]
Fortified Wine: Dry White Vermouth [p.174]
Fruit Liqueur: Limoncello [p.184], Pimm's [p.181]
Herb Liqueur: Bénédictine [p.212], The Last Word [p.216], Yellow Chartreuse [p.214]
Tea: Echinacea [p.204]
White Wine: Torrontés [p.123]

HERB-PRODUCED

Norway

Aquavit While most of us are walking like an intoxicated John Wayne after a choppy sea voyage, aquavit thrives on squall-like conditions: the rougher, the better. Though I'm feeling woozy just writing this, the rollicking movements of the cargo ship transporting the spirit to new markets, with its seesawing temperatures expanding and contracting the oak barrels, further infuses flavour into the herbal distillate. Scandinavia's unique spirit centres around potato vodka infused with caraway, and to a lesser extent dill. Both herbs contain a compound called R-carvone *[Glossary, p.15]* that smacks of rye bread and citrus, while dill also brings in the anise-herbaceous mannerisms of its similarly fronded family member, fennel.

If you like:
Caraway & Dill Weed
[See 'Medicinal Spicy', Spicy, p.106]
Fennel & Lemongrass
[See 'Veggie Herbaceous', Herbaceous, p.40]

Try:
Anise Liqueur: Absinthe [p.216], Pernod [p.217], Necromancer [p.221]
Beer: Dry-Hopped IPA [p.239]
Bourbon: High-Rye [p.250]

USA

The Last Word In a plot twist, this isn't my last word. Sorry, not sorry. I'm free to ask long-winded questions like: have you seen what someone's done with a couple of maraschino cherries and lime wedges to turn this Prohibition-era cocktail into Baby Yoda, renaming it 'Baby Yoda's First Word'? While you google it, flavour-wise, we're dealing with a gin base spirit, Green Chartreuse, Maraschino and fresh lime juice for a harmony of anise-sweet, citrus-sour, cherry-stoney piney-juniper and herb flavours, garnished with a brandy-soused maraschino cherry, when it's not being used as one of Baby Yoda's eyes.

If you like:

Christmas Tree & Preserved Lime
[See 'Fruity Spicy', Spicy, p.103]
Morello Cherry & Almond
[See 'Floral Fruity', Fruity, p.47]
Star Anise & Lemon Verbena
[See 'Fragrant Spicy', Spicy, p.102]

Try:

Anise Liqueur: Ricard [p.218]
Brandy: Armagnac [p.175], Pisco Sour [p.180]
Fruit Liqueur: Kirsch [p.183], Limoncello [p.184], Maraschino [p.180], Pimm's [p.181]
Herb Liqueur: Crème de Menthe [p.213], Yellow Chartreuse [p.214]
Mixer: Cherry Coke [p.260]
Nut Liqueur: Amaretto [p.253]
Red Wine: Amarone [p.151]
Rosé Wine: Sangiovese Rosé [p.142]
White Wine: Retsina [p.133]

Cocktail recipe

THE LAST WORD [Herb-Produced Drinks, Anise Liqueur]

20ml London Dry Gin
20ml Green Chartreuse
20ml Maraschino
20ml fresh Lime Juice
Maraschino Cherry to garnish

Shake up London Dry Gin, Green Chartreuse, Maraschino and lime juice, then strain into a Martini glass and sink the maraschino cherry to the bottom as garnish.

Anise Liqueur

France

Absinthe There'll be no mention of severed ears, green fairies, golden-era Maxim's *de Paris* and Toulouse-Lautrec paintings in this section. Absinthe's psychotic reputation around France's belle époque bohemian set has been debunked,

If you like:

Fennel & Lemongrass
[See 'Veggie Herbaceous', Herbaceous, p.40]
Liquorice & Lemon Thyme
[See 'Spicy Sweet', Sweet, p.56]

frustratingly, with bad behaviour down to its super-high alcohol content back in the day. Wormwood, a key ingredient in absinthe, is a Mediterranean herb with a bitter profile that contains a compound called thujone *[Glossary, p.19]*, which can be psychoactive, hallucinogenic and lethal, though not in absinthe's minimal dosage *[Glossary, p.16]*. 'The trinity' gives absinthe a spiritual association, but refers to its mainframe flavours of green anise, grande wormwood and Florence fennel.

Pastis Stereotype trigger warning: I get flashes of rustic old French men playing pétanque in a village square when I think of pastis. Anyone else? It's a punchy aperitif centred around the compound trans-anethole *[Glossary, p.15]*, for an uncompromisingly bittersweet aniseed experience. Well, what do we expect? Its main ingredients are Chinese star anise and local liquorice root along with a number of Provençal herbs, including citrusy lemon thyme and melissa. From the regional word *pastisson* meaning 'mash-up', pastis is served with carafe tap water which is poured over the hydraphobic trans-anethole, turning it cloudy like a boozy snow globe.

Pernod Let me get this straight, Pernod was the original brand of absinthe in Parisian demi-monde café culture, later banned for its suspected incitement of poor behaviour. Pernod then pivoted to release a wormwood-free version, the drink we know today, which is lighter on liquorice than others in the anise liqueur pack. Talk about category disruption; there's got to be a business term for that – the kamikaze strategy perhaps? Produced

Wormwood & Elderflower
[See 'Bitter Spicy', Spicy, p.101]

Try:
Anise Liqueur: Arak [p.219], Ouzo [p.218], Pernod [p.217], Raki [p.220], Pastis [p.217], Necromancer [p.221]
Beer: Dry-Hopped IPA [p.239]
Fortified Wine: Cocchi Americano [p.175], Dry White Vermouth [p.174]
Herb Liqueur: Aquavit [p.215], Galliano [p.219]
Whisky: The Sazerac [p.248]

If you like:
Chicory & Liquorice
[See 'Bitter Herbaceous', Herbaceous, p.32]
Liquorice & Lemon Thyme
[See 'Spicy Sweet', Sweet, p.56]

Try:
Amaro: Zucca Rabarbaro [p.225]
Anise Liqueur: Absinthe [p.216], Arak [p.219], Ouzo [p.218], Pernod [p.217], Raki [p.220], Ricard [p.218]
Fortified Wine: Rosso Vermouth [p.175]
Whisky: The Sazerac [p.248]

If you like:
Fennel & Lemongrass
[See 'Veggie Herbaceous', Herbaceous, p.40]
Liquorice & Lemon Thyme
[See 'Spicy Sweet', Sweet, p.56]

Try:
Anise Liqueur: Absinthe [p.216], Arak [p.219], Necromancer [p.221], Ouzo [p.218], Pastis [p.217], Raki [p.220]
Beer: Dry-Hopped IPA [p.239]

by distilling fennel and star anise, then blended with another distillate of fourteen herbs and spices, including camomile, coriander and veronica, for its citrus-herbal, lemongrassy footnote.

Ricard When is pastis not Pernod? When it's Ricard. Some disagree, but basically both are pastis – Pernod from Paris, Ricard from Marseilles, though their rivalry was on the scale of Coca-Cola vs Pepsi, just to throw more brand names into the mix. They merged in the seventies, hence the libation leviathan Pernod Ricard came to be. Ricard has the infusion of significantly more liquorice root to differentiate it, which comes through in its yellower hue against Pernod's green, with a more complex flavour catalogue led by sweet compound trans-anethole *[Glossary, p.15]*, and a lemony touch from fennel's inflections of citrusy nuances.

If you like:
Herb Liqueur: Aquavit [p.215]
Whisky: The Sazerac [p.248]

If you like:
Chicory & Liquorice
[See 'Bitter Herbaceous', Herbaceous, p.32]
Star Anise & Lemon Verbena
[See 'Fragrant Spicy', Spicy, p.102]

Try:
Amaro: Zucca Rabarbaro [p.225]
Anise Liqueur: Pastis [p.217]
Fortified Wine: Rosso Vermouth [p.175]
Fruit Liqueur: Limoncello [p.184],
Pimm's [p.181]
Herb Liqueur: Strega [p.215], The Last Word
[p.216], Yellow Chartreuse [p.214]

Greece

Ouzo We've all been on holiday to Greece, poured a big morning glass of Evian and realised we're chugging neat Ouzo, right? Asking for a friend. Ouzo's monstrously high alcohol content has a requirement based in science, it prevents its leading alcohol-soluble, liquorice-flavoured phenol compound *[Glossary, p.18]* from busting out of its see-through solution. The emulsifying, milky influence that water has on anise-oil-based beverages is actually known as 'the ouzo effect' or 'louching', which literally means unclear or shady. Ouzeries pour it into a *kanoakia*, a highball glass, giving its supporting cast of cardamom, clove, fennel and cooling lemon thyme flavours space to shine.

If you like:
Fennel & Clove
[See 'Veggie Herbaceous', Herbaceous, p.39]
Liquorice & Lemon Thyme
[See 'Spicy Sweet', Sweet, p.56]
Liquorice Root & Black Cardamom
[See 'Medicinal Spicy', Spicy, p.107]

Try:
Anise Liqueur: Absinthe [p.216], Arak [p.219],
Pastis [p.217], Pernod [p.217], Raki [p.220]
Beer: Bavarian Wheat [p.241]
Herb Liqueur: Jägermeister [p.214]
Red Wine: Graciano [p.158], Old-Vine
Zinfandel [p.161], Uruguayan Tannat [p.160]
Rum: Black Spiced [p.196]
Whisky: The Sazerac [p.248]

Italy

Galliano Nice bottle, now what the hell do I do with it? This isn't an unreasonable reaction to the flute bottle of Galliano, which is too tall for standard cabinets, so there's no danger of it being stuffed to the back of one. Smart strategy, but how do we use this Day-Glo-yellow liqueur with lead flavours of vanilla and anise? Rolling pin, retro sculpture or lava lamp perhaps? Not while there's a classic cocktail to reinvent, anything from a Sazerac to an Old-Fashioned is reworked by Galliano's flavour toolkit of vanilla, star anise, juniper, lavender, cinnamon and peppermint tea.

If you like:
Fennel & Vanilla
[See 'Veggie Herbaceous', Herbaceous, p.40]
Peppermint Tea & Lemongrass
[See 'Dried Herbaceous', Herbaceous, p.34]
Spearmint & Juniper
[See 'Minty Herbaceous', Herbaceous, p.37]

Try:
Amaro: Fernet-Branca [p.224]
Anise Liqueur: Harvey Wallbanger [p.220]
Herb Liqueur: Crème de Menthe [p.213], Strega [p.215]
Mezcal: Joven [p.193]
Tea: Echinacea [p.204], Peppermint [p.202]
White Wine: Torrontés [p.123]

HERB-PRODUCED

Sambuca Remember when waking up with sticky elbows and scorched eyebrows was a thing? Ah, further education. That fast-approaching plastic tray held aloft by that well-meaning 'friend', laden with shot glasses you hoped weren't tequila. The good stuff is consumed 'con la mosca', where chewing coffee beans neutralises the sweetness, though don't flambé them unless charred coffee dust is your thing. Produced from star anise's steam-extracted trans-anethole-based essential oils [*Glossary, p.15*], sambuca is often blended with elderberries, from *Sambucus nigra*, for a bitter-fruity, sticky, woody-resinous liquorice and pepper-based experience, also served in coffee for an *ammazzacafè*.

If you like:
Liquorice & Prune
[See 'Bittersweet', Sweet, p.57]
Mexican Coffee & White Pepper
[See 'Roasty Baked', Baked, p.75]

Try:
Anise Liqueur: Ouzo [p.218]
Coffee: Mexican [p.206]
Nut Liqueur: Nocino [p.254]
Red Wine: Amarone della Valpolicella [p.151], Argentinian Malbec [p.143], Hermitage [p.150]
Tequila: Coffee [p.190]

Lebanon

Arak Not to be confused with aragh, the Armenian version of vodka, or 'aaarghh', the noise you make when you sip a neat

If you like:
Grains of Paradise & Wintergreen
[See 'Peppery Spicy', Spicy, p.108]

arak. Heck, the name even derives from the Arabic word for 'perspire', which makes sense given half of arak is pure alcohol. Based on fermented grape juice, it doesn't have to be nails-rough, higher-end versions are made from better quality Merwah grapes, which are less 'meh' than they sound. The wine is triple-distilled with aniseed, slowly, for maximum flavour-pull and rested in clay amphoras for a liquoricey, peppery and minty sipping extravaganza.

Turkey

Raki I've never milked a lion; you couldn't get close enough, which must be the point of Raki's nickname 'lion's milk'. It gives us an insight into the style of Turkey's flagship spirit, which rightly sounds a bit 'bitey'. Raki is the real deal when it comes to pure anise flavour, which is almost brandy-like in its production method. Crushed grapes and sun-dried raisins, or *suma*, are double-distilled with aniseed to extract its essence, rather than simply infused. This doubles down on two intensely liquorice-adjacent compounds, one a key element of fennel, the other of tarragon.

USA

Harvey Wallbanger How do you know when you're kitsch? When you're modelled on the Screwdriver cocktail, aka vodka and orange. The seventies wasn't exactly the belle époque of cocktail creation; I mean, chuck in tequila and we've got ourselves a Freddie Fudpacker cocktail. Let's face it, vodka, Galliano and orange juice with a soused cherry as garnish will have anyone banging their heads into walls,

Liquorice & Lemon Thyme
[See 'Spicy Sweet', Sweet, p.56]

Try:
Anise Liqueur: Absinthe [p.216], Ouzo [p.218], Pastis [p.217], Pernod [p.217], Raki [p.220]
Mixer: Dr Pepper [p.262]
Tequila: Reposado [p.192]
Whisky: The Sazerac [p.248]

If you like:
Chicory & Liquorice
[See 'Bitter Herbaceous', Herbaceous, p.32]
Liquorice & Lemon Thyme
[See 'Spicy Sweet', Sweet, p.56]

Try:
Amaro: Zucca Rabarbaro [p.225]
Anise Liqueur: Absinthe [p.216], Arak [p.219], Ouzo [p.218], Pastis [p.217], Pernod [p.217], Ricard [p.218]
Fortified Wine: Rosso Vermouth [p.175]
Whisky: The Sazerac [p.248]

If you like:
Fennel & Vanilla
[See 'Veggie Herbaceous', Herbaceous, p.40]
Sweet Orange & Cinnamon
[See 'Juicy Fruity', Fruity, p.48]

Try:
Fruit Liqueur: Pimm's [p.181]
Herb Liqueur: Galliano [p.219]

never mind the sozzled, sandal-clad surfer Tom Harvey that it was supposedly named after. Galliano's marketing department may have fabricated that story, but Harvey Wallbanger's flavour combination is bang on, showcasing a shared vanilla component, while complementing the anise and cinnamon-adjacent compounds housed in orange's essential oils.

Mezcal: Joven [p.193]
Red Wine: Mulled Wine/Glühwein [p.150]

Cocktail recipe

HARVEY WALLBANGER [Herb-Produced Drinks, Anise Liqueur]

50ml Vodka
100ml Orange Juice (with bits)
5ml Sugar Syrup
2 dashes Orange Bitters
Galliano

Stir vodka, orange juice with bits, sugar syrup and orange bitters into a glass, then carefully cover with a layer of Galliano.

Necromancer Before you order what's essentially the absinthe-based version of the Corpse Reviver, so potent it can wake up the dead, maybe consider your options. Morbid titles are a pattern with absinthe cocktails, from Death in the Afternoon, Obituary to Sleepy Hollow, like the black-and-yellow warning markings on hornets, which in practice only dare us to want them more. Drinking hornets is a bad option, especially when there's Lillet Blanc, St Germain, gin and lemon juice in a Necromancer, bringing soaring florals, herbaceous-style fruit, pine resin and a citrus-sherbet twang to absinthe's fennel-forward anise flavours.

If you like:
Elderflower & Lemon Sherbet
[See 'Fruity Floral', Floral, p.24]
Fennel & Lemongrass
[See 'Veggie Herbaceous', Herbaceous, p.40]

Try:
Anise Liqueur: Absinthe [p.216], Pernod [p.217]
Beer: Dry-Hopped IPA [p.239]
Flower Liqueur: St Germain [p.209]
Fruit Liqueur: Limoncello [p.184], Melon Ball Drop [p.184]
Herb Liqueur: Aquavit [p.215]

Cocktail recipe

NECROMANCER [Herb-Produced Drinks, Anise Liqueur]

Absinthe (if using gin)
20ml Gin
20ml St Germain
20ml Lillet Blanc
20ml Lemon Juice, freshly squeezed

Rinse a Champagne coupe with absinthe (if you're using gin), then shake up gin, St Germain, Lillet Blanc and lemon juice with ice and pour.

Amaro

France

Suze A word of warning: when you're next out harvesting gentian in the Auvergne, don't get it confused with its evil cousin, white veratrum; we don't want toxic on top of bitter. Once gentian roots are picked, they're stripped into cossettes, aka thin strips, left to macerate for a year in high-proof spirit, then pressed and blended with other herbs and sugar. It's the punchiest bitter beverage on the block, technically categorised as a 'gentiane aperitif' rather than an amaro. Suze has been creatively described as 'soil candy', given its mouth-puckering flavours of honey-drizzled wet earth, citrus and eucalyptus, but in a good way.

If you like:
Gentian Root & Pomelo Peel
[See 'Bitter Spicy', Spicy, p.100]
Wet Earth & Eucalyptus Honey
[See 'Earthy Smoky', Smoky, p.83]

Try:
Herb Liqueur: Traditional Mead [p.212]
Mezcal: Añejo [p.193], Joven [p.193], Reposado [p.194]
Mixer: Indian Tonic Water [p.259]
Tea: Earl Grey [p.202]
Vermouth: Cocchi Americano [p.175]

Italy

Aperol Spritz Who gives a monkey's if it's technically an aperitivo or an amaro, I'm filing Aperol in the guilty-pleasure category where it belongs. Aperol Spritz also has its roots in, well, hiding things, with the liqueur's candied-orange notes masking the accompanying basic sparkling wine, itself poured on top to offset Aperol's bitter infusion of orange rind, gentian, rhubarb and cinchona, aka quinine. Why the guilt? Well, there's something slightly 'newbie's first bitter drink' about Aperol's butterscotch-adjacent Insta-orange stabiliser wheels, versus the boss bitter beverages like Cynar and Zucca, though I'm a fan, but shhhh.

If you like:
Bitter Orange & Butterscotch
[See 'Juicy Fruity', Fruity, p.48]
Escarole & Orange
[See 'Bitter Herbaceous', Herbaceous, p.33]

Try:
Amaro: Averna [p.223], Campari [p.223]
Brandy: Sidecar [p.176]
Fortified Wine: Bual Madeira [p.167]
Fruit Liqueur: Cointreau [p.182], Grand Marnier [p.182], Triple Sec [p.182]
Mixer: Angostura Bitters [p.258]

APEROL SPRITZ [Herb-Produced Drinks, Amaro]

50ml Aperol
90ml Prosecco
30ml Soda Water
Orange Slice Half-moon to garnish

Pour Aperol, Prosecco and soda water into an ice-filled balloon-style glass, stir gently and garnish with orange slice.

Averna I respect amaro's hustle, pivoting from herbal tincture to bona fide mainstream tipple; now that's survival of the bitterest. It hasn't been easy – humans are deep-wired to swerve anything bitter-tasting and potentially toxic, from when our early ancestors were forageing for their five-a-day around the forest floor. Beverages like Sicily's Averna liqueur embottle the phrase 'be the change', steering our tastes towards their tongue-curlingly complex bitterness. There's still a fight-or-flight situation going on at the bar, but that's where Averna's gateway flavours of undisclosed bittersweet botanicals, including pomegranate and thyme over orange, come in.

If you like:
Escarole & Orange
[See 'Bitter Herbaceous', Herbaceous, p.33]
Wild Thyme & Pomegranate
[See 'Herbal Spicy', Spicy, p.105]

Try:
Amaro: Aperol Spritz [p.222]
Mixer: Angostura Bitters [p.258]
Red Wine: Chilean Carménère [p.144], Corbières [p.148]
Rosé Wine: Bandol Rosé [p.140]

Campari I don't want to alarm anyone, but you know Campari's red pigment? Right, that used to be produced by crushing cochineal insects into crimson-red carmine dye. Now they use artificial colouring, which doesn't give it as much body if I'm honest. Often used interchangeably with Aperol, Campari has way higher alcohol and more bitterness, with vivid notes of blood-orange peel, clove, cinnamon and cherry. Ingredients are kept cloak and dagger, though the bitter orange-adjacent chinotto fruit is a probable component, as is quinine over peppery, pine-like rocket notes from cascarilla bark.

If you like:
Blood Orange & Rocket
[See 'Bitter Spicy', Spicy, p.100]
Cinnamon & Blood Orange
[See 'Warm Spicy', Spicy, p.109]
Pink Peppercorn & Juniper
[See 'Peppery Spicy', Spicy, p.108]
Red Cherry & White Pepper
[See 'Floral Fruity', Fruity, p.47]

Try:
Amaro: Aperol Spritz [p.222], Negroni [p.224]
Fortified Wine: Rosso Vermouth [p.175]
Mixer: Cranberry Juice [p.261]
Red Wine: Crozes-Hermitage [p.149], Frappato [p.154], Gaillac Rouge [p.149], Graciano [p.158], Mulled Wine/Glühwein [p.150], Sangria [p.160]

Cynar Based on its bottle language, Cynar really doesn't want us to drink it: from the graphic of an armoured globe artichoke on the label and the cyanide-sounding name to the dark brown bittersweet, vegetal-tasting liqueur inside. It's actually pronounced *CEE-nar*, after the non-poisonous compound cynarin *[Glossary, p.16]* in its key ingredient, macerated artichoke leaves, which temporarily reconfigures how we perceive other ingredients, making them taste sweeter. Although Cynar amaro relies on the edible thistle for its vegetal vertebrae, it also houses an infusion of twelve other botanicals, including saffron, not unlike a medicinal caramelised, boozy, herbal tea.

Fernet–Branca Shooting Fernet-Branca is nicknamed 'the bartender's handshake', the industry wink that's a mark of respect among equals. There's even Fernet-Branca-branded 'challenge coins' to determine the most hardcore Fernet gladiators. Bartenders can be a sadistic bunch, revelling in the forced grimaces that come with Fernet's aggressively bitter profile, putting the 'win' in wince. It's the drinks equivalent of ordering offal instead of chicken on a menu, with a bitter profile from gentian and cedar, first-aid-kit flavours from myrrh and a mentholated moment from saffron, which morphs all mint-like in higher concentrations.

Negroni No wonder we mainline Negronis like we're thirsty guzzle-gannets; it's all based in science. Gentian is a key rooty ingredient in bitter amaro like

Rosé Wine: Bandol Rosé [p.140], Syrah Rosé [p.141]
Tequila: Paloma [p.191]

If you like:
Cut Grass & Toffee
[See 'Grassy Herbaceous', Herbaceous, p.36]
Globe Artichoke & Saffron
[See 'Bitter Spicy', Spicy, p.100]

Try:
Brandy: VS Cognac [p.177]
Herb Liqueur: Green Chartreuse [p.213]
Rum: Mojito [p.197], Rhum Agricole Blanc [p.199]
Tequila: Añejo [p.190], Reposado [p.192]

If you like:
Cedar & Saffron
[See 'Woody Smoky', Smoky, p.85]
Liquorice Root & Black Cardamom
[See 'Medicinal Spicy', Spicy, p.107]
Peppermint Tea & Lemongrass
[See 'Dried Herbaceous', Herbaceous, p.34]

Try:
Anise Liqueur: Galliano [p.219], Ouzo [p.218]
Herb Liqueur: Crème de Menthe [p.213], Jägermeister [p.214]
Red Wine: Graciano [p.158], Old-Vine Zinfandel [p.161], Uruguayan Tannat [p.160]
Rum: Black Spiced [p.196]
Tea: Peppermint [p.202]

If you like:
Escarole & Orange
[See 'Bitter Herbaceous', Herbaceous, p.33]

Campari, containing compounds that have been found to promote salivation and the production of digestive juices. Phew, we're off the hook. Duelling bittersweet nuances are key to Negroni's flavour chakra, which is kick-started by gin's juniper-citrusy jump leads, Rosso Vermouth's candied richness and Campari's bitter blast with a pop of pink pepper, wreathed in a spritz of orange-rind essence. It's an Americano cocktail for booze hounds basically, swapping soda for gin.

Pink Peppercorn & Juniper
[See 'Peppery Spicy', Spicy, p.108]
Seville Orange Marmalade & Grapefruit
[See 'Juicy Fruity', Fruity, p.48]

Try:
Amaro: Aperol Spritz [p.222], Averna [p.223]
Dessert Wine: Vin de Paille [p.164]
Fortified Wine: Rosso Vermouth [p.175]
Gin: Pink [p.226]
Mixer: Angostura Bitters [p.258]
White Wine: Grillo [p.135]

Cocktail recipe

NEGRONI [Herb-Produced Drinks, Amaro]

30ml London Dry Gin
30ml Campari
30ml Rosso Vermouth
Orange Twist or Slice to garnish

Pour London Dry Gin, Campari and Rosso Vermouth into an ice-filled tumbler, then stir and garnish with orange slice.

Zucca Rabarbaro Cue the 'doo-doo-doo-doo' *Twilight Zone* music, this is rhubarb, but not as we know it. That sounds both sinister and like a mash-up with *Star Trek*, if I'm honest; I'm always confusing my seventies sci-fi shows. *Rabarbaro* is rhubarb in Italian, which I dare you to pronounce without sounding like you've had a few. It's actually the dried underground rhizome *[Glossary, p.18]* of Chinese rhubarb that's used in this super-bitter beverage that brings all the smoky mesquite flavours to the yard, in a meeting of Chinese medicinal wisdom, cardamom, citrus peel and Italian amaro know-how.

If you like:
Chicory & Liquorice
[See 'Bitter Herbaceous', Herbaceous, p.32]
Mesquite & Cardamom
[See 'Woody Smoky', Smoky, p.85]

Try:
Anise Liqueur: Pastis [p.217], Raki [p.220], Ricard [p.218]
Fortified Wine: Rosso Vermouth [p.175]
Tea: Lapsang Souchong [p.201]

Gin

England

Gin & Tonic I'm not Steven Hawking, but we could go full lab-coat chemist on Gin & Tonic, if I understood the science. Let's just say, the laws of attraction apply to this classic pairing: mine for the drink and theirs for each other. Gin is vodka that's been infused with roots, berries, citrus, herbs, seeds and spices, with juniper as the breakout botanical, hence the name. The molecules in this aroma-rich mash-up are dead ringers for tonic water's bitter quinine-based chemistry, combining to form a sum of new flavours that are different from their individual parts.

If you like:
Lemon & Juniper
[See 'Zingy Fruity', Fruity, p.52]
Quinine & Lemon Oil
[See 'Bitter Spicy', Spicy, p.101]
Yellow Grapefruit & Juniper
[See 'Bitter Fruity', Fruity, p.42]

Try:
Fortified Wine: Dry White Vermouth [p.174]
Gin: Salty Dog [p.227], Tom Collins [p.230]
Mixer: Indian Tonic Water [p.259]

GIN & TONIC [Herb-Produced Drinks, Gin]

50ml London Dry Gin
Tonic Water
Lemon Wedge to garnish

Fill a highball glass with ice, pour in London Dry Gin, top up with tonic water, then garnish with lemon wedge and stir upwards from the bottom with a long stirrer.

Pink Gin Gin purists turn a similar shade of ballet slipper at the concept of pink gin – actually it's more like flame red with plumes of ear steam. Like ready-to-drink cocktails, pink gin is sneered at by the ginerati, who see it as an Insta-labradoodle bred by drinks corporations. Regular gin is flavoured with blushing items from raspberries and strawberries to pink grapefruit and rose petals, and those are the higher-end versions, but it's more about the optics with pink gin, so pour it into a ginormous balloon glass and don't get me started on gin purists' views on those.

If you like:
Pink Grapefruit & Strawberry
[See 'Bitter Fruity', Fruity, p.42]
Pink Peppercorn & Juniper
[See 'Peppery Spicy', Spicy, p.108]

Try:
Amaro: Campari [p.223], Negroni [p.224]
Fortified Wine: Rosso Vermouth [p.175]
Rosé Wine: New Zealand Pinot Noir Rosé [p.142], Provence Rosé [p.141]

Salty Dog Madonna described Lady Gaga's music as 'reductive', took a sip of her tea and said, 'Look it up'. So we did, and realised that the same could be said for cocktails. The Salty Dog is basically a classic Greyhound cocktail, containing gin and grapefruit juice, only with a salt-rimmed glass. That might sound like a minor tweak, but bear in mind that there's more to salt than its seasoning properties. Salt diminishes our ability to perceive bitterness, the ions [Glossary, p.17] blocking our tongue's bitter-taste receptors, morphing grapefruit's mouth-contorting compounds into something more balanced and . . . reductive.

If you like:
Yellow Grapefruit & Juniper
[See 'Bitter Fruity', Fruity, p.42]
Yellow Grapefruit & Sea Air
[See 'Bitter Fruity', Fruity, p.48]

Try:
Fortified Wine: Dry White Vermouth [p.174]
Gin: Gin & Tonic [p.226]
Tequila: Paloma [p.191]
White Wine: Rueda Verdejo [p.138],
Vermentino [p.135]

Cocktail recipe

SALTY DOG [Herb-Produced Drinks, Gin]

Salt
50ml London Dry Gin
Pink Grapefruit Juice
Splash of Soda
Lemon Slice and a Rosemary Sprig to garnish

Rim a highball glass with salt, fill it with ice, then add London Dry Gin and top up with pink grapefruit juice and a splash of soda. Stir and garnish with lemon slice and rosemary.

White Negroni I can't remember the last time I accidentally created a world-class cocktail. In fact, if I had a penny for every time that hasn't happened to me, I'd be rich. It was the case for British bartender Wayne Collins, though, when he couldn't find Campari or sweet vermouth to make a regular Negroni while in France, which he substituted for the bitter gentian-based beverage Suze and wine-based aperitif Lillet. The France-inspired flavour riff brought in a less aggressive bitterness, with flavours that pivoted around Suze's wildflower, earthy, herbaceous tendencies, like a mouthful of Alpine dandelions.

If you like:
Dandelion & Burdock
[See 'Medicinal Spicy', Spicy, p.106]
Endive & Honeysuckle
[See 'Bitter Herbaceous', Herbaceous, p.32]
Gentian Root & Pomelo Peel
[See 'Bitter Spicy', Spicy, p.100]

Try:
Amaro: Suze [p.222]
Beer: Australian Pale Ale [p.237]
Mixer: Dr Pepper [p.262], Indian Tonic Water
[p.259], Root Beer [p.262]
Tea: Earl Grey [p.202]
Vermouth: Cocchi Americano [p.175]

WHITE NEGRONI [Herb-Produced Drinks, Gin]

30ml London Dry Gin

30ml Suze

30ml Lillet Blanc

Lemon Twist or Slice to garnish

Pour London Dry Gin, Suze and Lillet Blanc
into an ice-filled tumbler, then stir and
garnish with lemon twist or slice.

The Netherlands

Genever Here's the answer to a question
no one asked: genever is the missing
link between whisky and gin. You're
welcome. The daddy of modern gin
is a herbal-malty hybrid, made with a
wine-malt spirit instead of neutral grain
alcohol. Genever, aka juniper, is the major
botanical flavouring that, along with spices
like coriander seed, delivers an earthy
balance of grain, camphoraceous [Glossary,
p.15] resin and woodiness. Genever is also
the origin of the phrase 'Dutch courage',
as it was drunk during the Anglo-Dutch
Wars in the sixteenth century, and that is
the answer to a question worth asking.

USA

Bee's Knees Sign me up for a Sakura
viewing party, or *hanami*; I'm down for
this blossom-frenzied Japanese knees-
up, especially while sipping Sakura Bee's
Knees cocktails. There's even a word for
nabbing the best spot; it's *basho-tori* in
case we need it. I'm not sure how it goes
down in Buffalo, New York State, where
the US's largest cherry-blossom festival
is held in parks where fallen petals are
collected, blended with roses and citrus
rind and made into Sakura gin. This is a
flip on the sweet-and-sour Prohibition-
era cocktail, where honey was introduced

If you like:

Echinacea & Malted Biscuit
[See 'Dried Herbaceous', Herbaceous, p.34]

Elderflower & Cereal
[See 'Fruity Floral', Floral, p.24]

Yellow Grapefruit & Juniper
[See 'Bitter Fruity', Fruity, p.42]

Try:

Beer: Belgian Wheat [p.237]

Fortified Wine: Dry White Vermouth [p.174]

Gin: Gin & Tonic [p.226], Salty Dog [p.227]

Tea: Echinacea [p.204]

Tequila: Paloma [p.191]

White Wine: Rueda Verdejo [p.138],
Vermentino [p.135]

If you like:

Cherry Blossom & Lemon
[See 'Soft Floral', Floral, p.28]

Orange Blossom & Honey
[See 'Soft Floral', Floral, p.29]

Try:

Brandy: Metaxa [p.178]

Coffee: Peruvian [p.207]

Fruit Liqueur: Curaçao [p.182]

Mixer: Coca-Cola [p.260]

Sake: Daiginjo [p.242]

Sparkling Wine: Moscato d'Asti [p.121]

to make bitter home-made 'bathtub' gin more palatable.

Whisky: Drambuie [p.246]
White Wine: Condrieu [p.127]

SAKURA BEE'S KNEES [Herb-Produced Drinks, Gin]

60ml Sakura Gin
25ml Lemon Juice, freshly squeezed
25ml Honey Syrup
90ml Honey (for the honey syrup)
60ml Water, just-boiled

Shake Sakura gin, freshly squeezed lemon juice and honey syrup (dissolve honey in just-boiled water and leave to cool) with ice. Strain into a Champagne coupe glass.

Dirty Martini Given their Bond association, it makes sense that Martinis are smooth assassins. They're pure alcohol, gin over vermouth; no wonder they cause people to fall asleep in high-end bar toilets, get lost in Hong Kong and wake up in their hotel room surrounded by McDonald's wrappers – so I've read. More *The Hangover* than *Casino Royale*, both gin and vermouth get their flavours from fruity esters *[Glossary, p.15]* and aromatic compounds in their botanical ingredients. Shaking with ice unleashes flavours that merge with olive brine's salt-distribution centre and lemon rind's bitter-citrus essential oils.

If you like:
Chicory & Green Olive
[See 'Bitter Herbaceous', Herbaceous, p.32]
Lemon & Juniper
[See 'Zingy Fruity', Fruity, p.52]
Lemon & Salt
[See 'Zingy Fruity', Fruity, p.53]

Try:
Fortified Wine: Fino Sherry [p.172]
Gin: Gin & Tonic [p.226], Tom Collins [p.230]
Tequila: Margarita [p.190], Slammer [p.192]

DIRTY MARTINI [Herb-Produced Drinks, Gin]

60ml London Dry Gin
15ml Dry Vermouth
Lemon-rind Twist to garnish (or 10ml Olive Brine and Green Olives)

To make a regular Martini fill a small (ideally metal) jug with ice, pour in London Dry Gin, dry vermouth and stir. Strain into a freezer-chilled Martini glass and garnish with a lemon-rind twist. Make it dirty with olive brine and trade the lemon twist for a green-olive-threaded toothpick.

Tom Collins 'Have you seen Tom Collins? Well, he just left, and he was talking some serious smack about you.' That's what people would say to each

If you like:
Lemon & Juniper
[See 'Zingy Fruity', Fruity, p.52]

other in the nineteenth-century Tom Collins prank, designed as a wind-up in the hopes that they would go from bar to bar looking for Tom Collins; even the newspapers were claiming bogus sightings of him. The notorious hoax, which allowed bartenders to prepare the seeker a drink when they asked for the non-existent troublemaker, would nowadays be settled by a 'keyboards at dawn' social media war. Little more than boozy lemonade, which I can say given Collins's rudeness, allows the gin to shine, preferably the sweeter Old Tom style that inspired the name.

Whipped Cream & Lemon Soda
[See 'Decadent Creamy', Creamy, p.68]

Try:
Gin: Dirty Martini [p.229], Gin & Tonic [p.226]
Sparkling Wine: Champagne Demi-Sec [p.117], Riesling Sekt [p.120]
Tequila: Slammer [p.192]
Vodka: Peach Martini [p.234]

Cocktail recipe

TOM COLLINS [Herb-Produced Drinks, Gin]

50ml London Dry/Old Tom Gin
25ml Lemon Juice, freshly squeezed
25ml Sugar Syrup
Chilled Soda
Fresh Lemon Wedge to garnish

Pour London Dry/Old Tom Gin, freshly squeezed lemon juice and sugar syrup into an ice-filled highball glass, top with chilled soda, stir and garnish with a fresh lemon wedge.

Drinks

Fruit-produced

Plant-produced

Herb-produced

Grain-produced

Mixers

Vodka

Canada

Bloody Caesar I don't know anyone who can say 'Worssessstersheeere sauce' without sounding like they've had too many Bloody Caesars, myself included. That's a fact not a challenge. The Canadian Bloody Mary was allegedly inspired by the flavour combo in spaghetti alle vongole, a dish it imitates via Clamato's blend of clam broth and tomato juice. Canada's almost national drink provides savoury umami nuances via the glutamic acid in tomato juice and the clam-chowder notes of Clamato, Worcestershire sauce's tamarind-based spices with a blast of Tabasco, sinus-clearing horseradish, a lemony-garnish zing and vodka's neutral-flavoured kickback.

If you like:
Chicory & Green Olive
[See 'Bitter Herbaceous', Herbaceous, p.32]
Pacific Oyster & Meyer Lemon
[See 'Marine Minerally', Minerally, p.94]
Worcestershire Sauce & Tomato Seed
[See 'Brothy Savoury', Savoury, p.89]

Try:
Fortified Wine: Fino Sherry [p.172]
Gin: Dirty Martini [p.229]
Vodka: Bloody Mary [p.235]
White Wine: Reuilly Sauvignon Blanc [p.130]

Cocktail recipe

BLOODY CAESAR [Grain-Produced Drinks, Vodka]

60ml Vodka
120ml Clamato Juice
15ml Lemon Juice, freshly squeezed
Few dashes Hot Sauce
10ml Worcestershire Sauce
Pinch Celery Salt
Pinch Paprika
Black Pepper
Sliced Celery and Lemon Wedge to garnish

Pour vodka, Clamato juice and lemon juice into a shaker with hot sauce, Worcestershire sauce, celery salt, paprika and a grind of black pepper. Roll rather than shake, then strain into an ice-filled glass and garnish with sliced celery and a lemon wedge.

England

Pornstar Martini Slow Comfortable Screw, Sex on the Beach . . . we've seen it all before with provocative cocktail names. Pearl-clutchers call it a Passion Fruit Martini, and it was invented by a London

If you like:
Elderflower & Cantaloupe Melon
[See 'Fruity Floral', Floral, p.24]
Passion Fruit & Vanilla
[See 'Tropical Fruity', Fruity, p.51]

mixologist who was partial to a vanilla and passion fruit flavour combo in desserts. A vanilla vodka base builds on texture via passion fruit purée and brightness from Passoã liqueur. We're supposed to slurp the passion fruit seeds with a teaspoon, then alternate sipping the cocktail with the accompanying Champagne 'money shot'. The flavour spectrum, ritual, theatre and risqué name has made the Pornstar Martini a legend in its own lunchtime.

Peach Blossom & Cream Soda
[See 'Soft Floral', Floral, p.29]
Yellow Bell Pepper & Passion Fruit
[See 'Sweet Herbaceous', Herbaceous, p.39]

Try:
Fruit Liqueur: Melon Ball Drop [p.184], Midori [p.185]
Mixer: Elderflower Cordial [p.258]
Sake: Junmai Ginjo [p.242]
Sparkling Wine: Bellini [p.120]
Vodka: Peach Martini [p.234]
White Wine: Bacchus [p.125], New Zealand Marlborough Sauvignon Blanc [p.136]

Cocktail recipe

PORNSTAR MARTINI [Grain-Produced Drinks, Vodka]

50ml Vanilla Vodka
20ml Passoã Liqueur
25ml Passion Fruit Purée
10ml Sugar Syrup
½ Passion Fruit to garnish
Shot of chilled Champagne/sparkling wine

Pour vanilla vodka, Passoã liqueur, passion fruit purée and sugar syrup into an ice-filled shaker and shake, hard. Strain into a coupe and garnish with passion fruit alongside a shot of chilled Champagne/sparkling wine.

France

Wheat Vodka I'm sorry, but I draw the line at elephant dung or human tears in my vodka. I'm more of an old-fashioned grain guy, or even potatoes, molasses, grapes, rice or oil-refining by-products. Unlike other spirits, vodka is about stripping out flavours, removing impurities that prevent it from being as smooth as Barry White at a Gillette convention. Given its neutral flavour and simple structure of ethanol and water, you could easily overlook the residual sweet, toasty graininess that comes with French wheat, the spice in rye or the creaminess crammed into corn vodka.

If you like:
Cherry Blossom & Lemon
[See 'Soft Floral', Floral, p.28]
Elderflower & Cereal
[See 'Fruity Floral', Floral, p.24]
Melba Toast & Cereal Milk
[See 'Toasty Baked', Baked, p.77]

Try:
Beer: Australian Pale Ale [p.237], Belgian Wheat [p.237]
Gin: Genever [p.228], Sakura Bee's Knees [p.228]
Sake: Daiginjo [p.242]
Whisky: American Wheat [p.249]

USA

Peach Martini You wouldn't catch me ordering a Peach Martini at a bar. No, ma'am, have you seen London cocktail prices? It would be a different story if someone bought me one; it's hard not to taste the appeal. Based around vanilla vodka, which veers from confectionary flavours to the more nuttily nuanced, though always with a cream-soda adjacency. Vanilla flavouring largely comes from a compound synthesised from petrochemicals, as the pods are so blooming spendy. Peaches contain lactone compounds [Glossary, p.17] with a natural dairy-cream element, while a pop of lemon juice and rosemary syrup curtail the cloying.

If you like:
Peach Blossom & Cream Soda
[See 'Soft Floral', Floral, p.29]
Whipped Cream & Lemon Soda
[See 'Decadent Creamy', Creamy, p.68]

Try:
Gin: Tom Collins [p.230]
Sparkling Wine: Bellini [p.120], Champagne Demi-Sec [p.117], Riesling Sekt [p.120]
Tequila: Slammer [p.192]
Vodka: Pornstar Martini [p.232]

Cocktail recipe

PEACH MARTINI [Grain-Produced Drinks, Vodka]

2 Peach Wedges
50ml Vanilla Vodka
15ml Lemon Juice, freshly squeezed
10ml Rosemary Syrup
Shot of Champagne (optional)

Muddle peach wedges at the base of a shaker, pour over vanilla vodka, lemon juice and rosemary syrup, then shake with ice and strain into a chilled Martini glass. Sip with a sidecar shot of Champagne, if you're feeling fancy.

Appletini When the Adam's Apple became a favourite of sorority sisters and Zach Braff's character, J. D., in *Scrubs*, they wisely changed the name to Appletini. The original glow-stick-green cocktail resembled something from Gotham City's chemical plant. Ah, West Hollywood in the nineties. Not a legitimate Martini, Sour Apple Liqueur was mixed with mediocre vodka and featured a lemon-soaked slice of green apple floating on top. These days you still get the herbaceous, fleshy green-apple notes from a glass rinse

If you like:
Granny Smith & Lemon
[See 'Crisp Fruity', Fruity, p.46]
Thyme Honey & Granny Smith
[See 'Floral Sweet', Sweet, p.61]

Try:
Cachaça: Caipirinha [p.194]
Sparkling Wine: Cava Brut Nature [p.122], English Non-Vintage [p.116], Riesling Sekt [p.120]
White Wine: Auslese Riesling [p.131], Clare Valley Riesling [p.124], Picpoul de Pinet [p.129], Vinho Verde [p.136]

of apple liqueur, calvados or cider for depth with a dash of the balancing tangy crab-appley, unripe grapey condiment, verjuice.

Cocktail recipe

APPLETINI [Grain-Produced Drinks, Vodka]

50ml Vodka
20ml Sour Apple Liqueur
15ml fresh Lime Juice
10ml Sugar Syrup
Green Apple Slice to garnish

Shake vodka, Sour Apple Liqueur, lime juice and sugar syrup with ice, then strain into a chilled Martini glass and garnish with apple slice.

Bloody Mary A bit like Hedy Lemarr, multitasking as Hollywood's most beautiful actress and inventing Wi-Fi in her spare time, I feel like the Bloody Mary is woefully underestimated. Its flavour synapses fire off hundreds of compounds, running the gamut of reactions ranging from heat, burn, sour, salty and umami. Tabasco's chilli-generated chemicals deliver the heat, vodka brings the burn, with black pepper's tingly terpene compound complementing Worcester sauce's salty dark spices. Tomato juice provides the overarching, fruity-umami flavour forum that lives for lemon juice's citric sting, which is soothed by celery's numbing properties.

If you like:
Dried Lime & Tomatillo
[See 'Fragrant Spicy', Spicy, p.102]
Soy Sauce & Dry-Roasted Peanut
[See 'Brothy Savoury', Savoury, p.88]
Worcestershire Sauce & Tomato Seed
[See 'Brothy Savoury', Savoury, p.89]

Try:
Cachaça: Caipirinha [p.194]
Coffee: Kenyan [p.205]
Grain Spirit: Baijiu Sauce Aroma [p.255]
Rosé Wine: Sangiovese Rosé [p.142]
Sake: Koshu [p.243]
Tea: Green Tea Kombucha [p.200]
Vodka: Bloody Caesar [p.232]

Cocktail recipe

BLOODY MARY [Grain-Produced Drinks, Vodka]

50ml Vodka
60ml Tomato Juice
5ml Amontillado Sherry
10ml fresh Lemon Juice
10ml Worcestershire Sauce
2.5ml Tabasco
Pinch Celery Salt, Paprika and Pepper
Celery Stick to garnish

Place a large scoopful of ice into a jug, pour in vodka, tomato juice, Amontillado sherry, fresh lemon juice, Worcestershire sauce, Tabasco, celery salt, paprika and pepper, then stir until the jug feels cold. Strain into a tall glass and garnish with a celery stick. Double up if you're sharing.

Cosmopolitan I've challenged myself not to mention the TV show, so here goes. The protagonist's favourite cocktail majors on cranberry and lime, an evolution of the citrus-booze-sugar bar staple, the Sour. She stopped drinking them when, as she rightly says, 'Everyone else started'. While bartenders scrap over who invented this modern-day classic, let's revel in the red fruit astringency and citrusy zing brought in by cranberry juice, which is reinforced by lime's bitter sting. This already sounds better than the water and food dye mocktails they drank on the set of *Sex and the City* . . . Doh!

If you like:
Cranberry & Lime
[See 'Sweet Fruity', Fruity, p.50]
Pink Grapefruit & Strawberry
[See 'Bitter Fruity', Fruity, p.42]
Ruby Grapefruit & Persian Lime
[See 'Bitter Fruity', Fruity, p.42]

Try:
Gin: Pink [p.226]
Rosé Wine: New Zealand Pinot Noir Rosé [p.142], Provence Rosé [p.141]
Tequila: Paloma [p.191]

Cocktail recipe

COSMOPOLITAN [Grain-Produced Drinks, Vodka]

40ml Lemon Vodka
20ml Triple Sec
40ml Cranberry Juice
15ml fresh Lime Juice
Dash of Orange Bitters
Orange Zest to garnish

Shake lemon vodka, Triple Sec, cranberry juice, fresh lime juice and a dash of orange bitters with ice, then strain into a chilled Martini glass and garnish with orange zest.

Moscow Mule You know the feeling when someone is having you on? Well, the Moscow Mule was invented by a barman at a British pub in Hollywood who was overstocked on ginger beer. Alarm bell number one: the name of the pub is the Cock & Bull. Two: his girlfriend had allegedly inherited a copper factory, hence the cocktail comes served in a copper mug. Seamlessly, as vodka touches copper, it starts to oxidise, enhancing the flavour of the vodka, zhuzhing up the bubbles and dialling down lime's acidity. I've just checked, and 'Gullible' is still in the dictionary.

If you like:
Australian Ginger & Cardamom
[See 'Zingy Spicy', p.110]
Cassia & Lime
[See 'Warm Spicy', p.109]
Dried Ginger & Lime
[See 'Zingy Spicy', Spicy, p.111]

Try:
Herb Liqueur: King's Ginger [p.212]
Mixer: Angostura Bitters [p.258], Cherry Coke [p.260], Coca-Cola [p.260], Ginger Beer [p.259]
Red Wine: Sangria [p.160]
Rum: Dark 'n' Stormy [p.195]

MOSCOW MULE [Grain-Produced Drinks, Vodka]

50ml Vodka	Pour vodka, fresh lime juice and sugar syrup
15ml fresh Lime Juice	into a copper mug and stir. Fill two thirds of
10ml Sugar Syrup	the mug with crushed ice, top up with ginger
Ginger Beer	beer and coronate with crushed ice, a dash of
Dash of Bitters and Mint Sprig	bitters and a mint sprig.

Beer

Australia

Pale Ale A stubby of pale ale is the booze equivalent of a cold shower on a scorching day, ideally tucked inside a koozie, the foam sleeve that supposedly keeps bottles cold. Without getting brand-specific I'm referring to Coopers in particular. That upfront malty thwack upon first sip, the light herbaceous, bitter, floral undertones, all based around the Pride of Ringwood hop variety that boasts super-high alpha acids. This brings them a unique bitterness that gives both Aussie and Pommy pale ales their particular roast plantain-like vegetal bite, which is offset by a balancing dollop of barley syrup.

If you like:
Barley Malt Syrup & Roast Plantain
[See 'Malty Baked', Baked, p.72]
Elderflower & Cereal
[See 'Fruity Floral', Floral, p.24]
Endive & Honeysuckle
[See 'Bitter Herbaceous', Herbaceous, p.32]

Try:
Beer: Bavarian Wheat [p.241], Belgian Wheat [p.237]
Bourbon: Kentucky Straight [p.251], Old-Fashioned [p.252]
Gin: Genever [p.228], White Negroni [p.227]
Vodka: French Wheat [p.233]

Belgium

Wheat Beer While Belgians aren't necessarily known for their wit, they are known for their *wit* beer, which technically means 'white'. The brewer's version of gin comes from medieval times, when wits were flavoured and preserved with spices like coriander, cumin, bitter orange peel and local herbs called 'gruit'. Aside from reminding me of Groot from *Guardians of the Galaxy*, we'll recognise those gruity, floral-sour tones from a pint

If you like:
Elderflower & Cereal
[See 'Fruity Floral', Floral, p.24]
Mandarin Orange & Lemon
[See 'Juicy Fruity', Fruity, p.48]

Try:
Beer: Australian Pale Ale [p.237], Bavarian Wheat [p.241]
Brandy: Sidecar [p.176]
Fruit Liqueur: Cointreau [p.182]

of Hoegaarden. It's referred to as 'white' due to its suspension of wheat and yeast proteins, which cause the beer to look hazy, or, well, white.

Gin: Genever [p.228]
Vodka: French Wheat [p.233]

England

Brown Ale We get it, it's brown in colour, though whoever named an ale category after such a lacklustre shade wants putting on a creative-thinking course. Largely associated with Blighty, there's a gamut of signature styles under the dishwater-dull brown ale umbrella. As a collective, they tend to be strong, malty and nutty with obvious notes of chocolate, honeycomb and molasses, hold the hops. Northern styles are higher in alcohol and lighter in colour, while southerners have a fruitier, more ester-rich *[Glossary, p.16]* flavour profile, maltier mannerisms and swing towards the sweeter end of the spectrum.

If you like:
Dark Chocolate Mousse & Plum
[See 'Roasty Sweet', Sweet, p.62]
Malted Honeycomb & Molasses
[See 'Malty Baked', Baked, p.73]

Try:
Coffee: Peruvian [p.207]
Dessert Wine: Mavrodaphne de Patras [p.165], Rutherglen Muscat [p.162]
Red Wine: Argentinian Malbec [p.143], Pomerol [p.147], Uruguayan Tannat [p.160]
Whisky: Irish Coffee [p.244]

Brown Porter Porters and stouts make me think of Sir Topham Hatt, the Fat Controller from *Thomas the Tank Engine*, don't ask me why. A mild brown, malt-based beer style, porters are sweeter and lighter-weight than stouts, in a 'bitter chocolate and burnt toffee layered over toasted hazelnuts and digestive biscuits' kind of way. Brown porters were popular with brawny eighteenth-century London river porters and dockers, hence the name. It's a heavier style than brown ale and lighter than stout, which uses toasted barley malt for those burley coffee flavours.

If you like:
Bitter Chocolate & Burnt Toffee
[See 'Roasty Sweet', Sweet, p.62]
Toasted Hazelnut & Digestive Biscuit
[See 'Nutty Baked', Baked, p.74]

Try:
Beer: Brown Ale [p.238], Stout [p.239]
Brandy: VSOP Cognac [p.177]
Fortified Wine: Marsala Sweet Superiore [p.168], Pedro Ximenez Sherry [p.174]
Nut Liqueur: Frangelico [p.254]
Sparkling Wine: Franciacorta Riserva [p.121], Mature Champagne [p.117], Vintage Champagne [p.118]
Tequila: Coffee [p.190]

Chocolate Stout In the words of Oscar Wilde, the one thing I cannot resist is temptation. Hence the term 'chocolate stout' accurately describes me after the Easter break. For easy access we can drink our dessert year-round, via a style created using darker aromatic 'chocolate malt' that's been roasted until it takes on an opaque pigment and malted-coffee flavours. Those naughty brewers are no strangers to cheekily adding in cocoa powder and nibs, working it early into the mash for depth and earthy flavours or later on into the ferment for the full-on chocolate show.

If you like:
Dark Chocolate & Molasses
[See 'Roasty Sweet', Sweet, p.62]
Peruvian Coffee & Malted Milk
[See 'Roasty Baked', Baked, p.76]

Try:
Beer: Dry Stout [p.241]
Coffee: Brazilian [p.204], Peruvian [p.207]
Whisky: Irish Coffee [p.244]

Coffee Stout Our morning cuppa is a frequent fixture in booze, from tequila and cocktails to our post-work pint. Brewers started experimenting with beans and beer in the nineties, given their parallel roasty, malty, fruity mannerisms, which give them a natural flavour affinity. Stout is a darker style of beer that lends itself to a coffee collaboration, with a robust flavour palate thanks to toasting malt at higher temperatures to bring in bitter-roasty, burnt-caramel notes. Coffee grounds enhance the existing espresso notes, which are layered over fruity fermentation-introduced compounds with the appealing aroma of apple blossom.

If you like:
Apple Blossom & Coffee
[See 'Soft Floral', Floral, p.28]
Nicaraguan Coffee & Dark Caramel
[See 'Roasty Baked', Baked, p.75]
Peruvian Coffee & Malted Milk
[See 'Roasty Baked', Baked, p.76]

Try:
Beer: Chocolate Stout [p.239], Dry Stout [p.241]
Coffee: Kenyan [p.205], Nicaraguan [p.206], Peruvian [p.207]
Coffee Liqueur: Espresso Martini [p.208]
Whisky: Irish Coffee [p.244]

Dry-Hopped IPA 'Timing is everything' and yet 'There's never a good time'. Thanks for nothing, self-help books. Beer brewers add hops to the brew kettle at the beginning, middle and end of the boil to create separate flavour effects. Hops are wildly aromatic and innately bitter, high in acids and essential oils, so introducing them later means less bitterness with inflated fruit aromas. Steeping dried hops

If you like:
Fennel & Lemongrass
[See 'Veggie Herbaceous', Herbaceous, p.40]
Yellow Grapefruit & Malt
[See 'Bitter Fruity', Fruity, p.43]

Try:
Anise Liqueur: Absinthe [p.216], Necromancer [p.221], Pernod [p.217]
Beer: Craft IPA [p.240], Grapefruit IPA [p.240]

in giant teabags is called dry-hopping, and it welcomes in fragrant oils and banishes the bitterness. It basically makes the hoppy notes pop, overlaying malty flavours with fennel, grapefruit and lemongrass notes.

Gin: Genever [p.228]
Herb Liqueur: Aquavit [p.215]

Grapefruit IPA I know it's genetic, but I find grapefruit too bitter without sugar. It turns out that some people are just more 'bitter blind' than others, so why do I like it in the context of beer then? That's a rhetorical question, as I won't understand the answer. Not all bitter flavours are processed via the same neural pathways, and IPA's sweet, malty backdrop and roasty bitterness complements grapefruit's musky-citrus profile. Grapefruit aromas in IPA are mimicked by the sulphurous thiol compounds *[Glossary, p.19]* given off by specific hop varieties, or by adding grapefruit peel to the boil.

If you like:
Cut Grass & Yuzu
[See 'Grassy Herbaceous', Herbaceous, p.36]
Yellow Grapefruit & Malt
[See 'Bitter Fruity', Fruity, p.43]

Try:
Beer: Craft IPA [p.240], Dry-Hopped IPA [p.239]
Fortified Wine: Dry White Vermouth [p.174]
Gin: Genever [p.228]

India Pale Ale What's the deal with 'high gravity' beer? Is it brewed in the air, on another planet, on a bungee rope? Nope, it just means there is a banquet of dissolved sugars, aka gravity, in the unfermented sugar-rich juice from the mashing and brewing process, aka the wort, for the yeast to eat, fermenting it into beer with ramped-up alcohol and flavours. These are the RuPaul's drag racers of the beer world, all intense 'notice me' flavours and exaggerated mannerisms. India Pale Ale is known as a beer with high 'original gravity', typically with mango's tropical pine-like characteristics and a bittersweet hoppy, elderflower flavour profile.

If you like:
Mango & Elderflower
[See 'Tropical Fruity', Fruity, p.51]
Yellow Grapefruit & Malt
[See 'Bitter Fruity', Fruity, p.43]

Try:
Beer: Craft IPA [p.240], Dry-Hopped IPA [p.239], Grapefruit IPA [p.240]
Gin: Genever [p.228]

Germany

Bavarian Wheat Beer I appreciate a supple pizza base, don't get me wrong, but not when I'm trying to brew beer. I don't make either very often to be fair, but the Germans do – hefeweizen, aka the term for unfiltered wheat beer, among others. Wheat is a tricky grain to brew given its proteins and starches try to bind together like stretchy bread dough, making it tough to extract their sugars. Wheat beer gets its signature clove-like notes from a particular phenol compound *[Glossary, p.18]* produced by a unique strain of yeast, which is combined with buttery banana flavours whipped up as by-products from fermentation.

If you like:
Banana & Brown Butter
[See 'Tropical Fruity', Fruity, p.51]
Elderflower & Cereal
[See 'Fruity Floral', Floral, p.24]
Fennel & Clove
[See 'Veggie Herbaceous', Herbaceous, p.39]

Try:
Anise Liqueur: Ouzo [p.218]
Beer: Australian Pale Ale [p.237], Belgian Wheat [p.237]
Bourbon: Kentucky Straight [p.251]
Gin: Genever [p.228]
Rum: Vintage Jamaican [p.198]
Vodka: French Wheat [p.233]

Ireland

Dry Stout *Good things come to those who wait.* Ah, Guinness slogans. From surfing horses to Rutger Hauer's 'pure genius' nineties ads that we weren't meant to understand. Dry stout, aka Irish stout, has that opaque pigmentation of its most famous branded incarnation, Guinness. Essentially a porter but with dark-roasted barley malt that's top-fermented with ale yeast rising to the surface, unlike lager yeast that sinks to the bottom. It may look like a pint of crude oil, but this full-bodied ale with roast-coffee and malted-milk notes retains a cheeky sweetness from unfermented sugars.

If you like:
Bitter Chocolate & Burnt Toffee
[See 'Roasty Sweet', Sweet, p.62]
Peruvian Coffee & Malted Milk
[See 'Roasty Baked', Baked, p.76]

Try:
Beer: Chocolate Stout [p.239], Coffee Stout [p.239], Dry Stout [p.241]
Coffee: Peruvian [p.207]
Fortified Wine: Marsala Sweet Superiore [p.168], Pedro Ximenez Sherry [p.174]
Tequila: Coffee [p.190]
Whisky: Irish Coffee [p.244]

Sake

Japan

Daiginjo I'm not one for labels, but it would be useful to know sake's preferred noun. What are we calling it, wine, beer, spirit? *Sake* translates as 'alcohol', so technically it's a fermented alcoholic drink made from rice, which isn't a tongue-tripper. Brewed like beer, with stylistic differences down to the level of rice polishing and yeast strain. The more polishing, the better, given sake is generally about purity and clean flavours, not complexity. Daiginjo is platinum-standard, its grains milled to half their original size for fewer impurities and diamond-cut notes of marzipan, cherry blossom and lemon.

If you like:
Cherry Blossom & Lemon
[See 'Soft Floral', Floral, p.28]
Lemon & Marzipan
[See 'Zingy Fruity', Fruity, p.53]

Try:
Gin: Sakura Bee's Knees [p.228]
Nut Liqueur: Amaretto [p.253]
Vodka: French Wheat [p.233]
White Wine: Soave Classico [p.135]

Junmai Ginjo Not to be dramatic, but sake is the beating heart of Japanese life; it's also rice, water, yeast and a mould called koji-kin *[Glossary, p.17]*, which bizarrely sounds like the *Karate Kid* sequel on Netflix. It's all about the starch at the heart of each rice grain, cue koji-kin, which is central to everything from soy sauce to miso soup. It grows on the rice grain, producing enzymes *[Glossary, p.16]* that break down the starch into sugar. Ginjo rice is super-polished, giving a clean ester-rich *[Glossary, p.16]* fruity aroma called ginjo-ka that is likened to fresh melon and white flowers.

If you like:
Elderflower & Cantaloupe Melon
[See 'Fruity Floral', Floral, p.24]
Yellow Peach & Star Anise
[See 'Creamy Fruity', Fruity, p.44]

Try:
Fruit Liqueur: Melon Ball Drop [p.184],
Midori [p.185]
Mixer: Elderflower Cordial [p.258]
Vodka: Pornstar Martini [p.232]
White Wine: Bacchus [p.125],
Rueda Verdejo [p.138]

Junmai-Shu Chill out and have a traditional ceramic *ochoko* cupful of sake, whichever style floats your *bōto*. My impressive kanji linguistic skills aside, diehard Junmai fans in the sake community defend it as the purest style.

If you like:
Sea Spray & Bread Dough
[See 'Marine Minerally', Minerally, p.95]
Tofu & Toasted Sesame Seed
[See 'Brothy Savoury', Savoury, p.89]

True, *Junmai* translates as 'pure', but it's all a bit political for something that's made to be enjoyed. While the Honjozo technique adds alcohol to accentuate the aromatics, Junmai-Shu is exclusively made from polished rice, koji-kin *[Glossary, p.17]* mould to kick-start fermentation, yeast and water. Junmai may not be fragrant, but it delivers a *hojun [Glossary, p.17]* saline-umami earthiness, which translates into flavours of tofu, dough and sesame seed.

Try:
Fortified Wine: Amontillado Sherry [p.171], Fino Sherry [p.172], Manzanilla Sherry [p.172]
Grain Spirit: Baijiu Sesame Aroma [p.255]
White Wine: Reuilly Sauvignon Blanc [p.130]

Koshu Charming. *Koshu* means 'old sake'. Would it have killed them to call it 'experienced'? A minimum of three years' ageing in tanks or ceramic jars warrants the Koshu title, so what does that make us then? In sake years we're talking prehistoric, given it's mostly a drink-me-fresh style of beverage. Containing more amino acids than any other booze, allegedly, as sake ages, complex chemical reactions make it heavier, more cloying, musty, funky and rich, lucky thing. Maple-cured smoky bacon, caramel, brothy, umami, nutty, clove, soy-sauce-like flavours creep in via age-induced compounds under higher storage temperatures.

If you like:
Olive Brine & Walnut Brittle
[See 'Brothy Savoury', Savoury, p.88]
Smoky Bacon & Clove
[See 'Meaty Savoury', Savoury, p.92]
Soy Sauce & Dry-Roasted Peanut
[See 'Brothy Savoury', Savoury, p.88]

Try:
Fortified Wine: Amontillado Sherry [p.171], Palo Cortado Sherry [p.173]
Grain Spirit: Baijiu Sauce Aroma [p.255]
Red Wine: Washington State Syrah [p.162]
Vodka: Bloody Mary [p.235]

Whisky

Ireland

Baileys Irish Cream Bartenders capitalise on Baileys' cream-curdling proclivities, mixed with lime juice in the gag-reflex-triggering Cement Mixer shot, or grenadine in the Brain Haemorrhage. Cream liqueurs are unstable, with a supporting cast of chemicals to stop this oil-in-water emulsion from separating.

If you like:
Crème Pâtissière & Praline
[See 'Decadent Creamy', Creamy, p.68]
White Chocolate & Mocha
[See 'Roasty Sweet', Sweet, p.63]

Baileys' flavours involve the complex interaction of compounds and textures from whisky, cream, cocoa and vanilla. Created in a lab by the father of my ex-boss, just to name-drop, who was looking to invent a best-selling drink that used up their slow-selling Irish whiskey and the spare cream from an Irish dairy plant. Waste not, want not.

Irish Coffee Done right, Irish coffee looks like a foaming île flottant in a tulip glass; done poorly and it's essentially a sad-looking latte. Basic Irish coffee, wearing its whippy cap of Anchor Squirty Cream, is light years away from piping-hot Peruvian coffee's honey-nutty notes, demerara sugar's molasses-rich, bittersweet scorched-caramel inflection, the malted sucker punch of fiery Irish whiskey soothed by the cooling tones of its malt-infused, creamy peak. Pro tips include pouring the cream over the back of a spoon, losing the novelty dash of crème de menthe for leprechaun vibes and no 'shamrock art'.

Try:
Bourbon: Eggnog [p.249]
Brandy: Advocaat [p.171]
Coffee: Rwandan [p.207]
Coffee Liqueur: White Russian [p.208]
Nut Liqueur: Frangelico [p.254]
White Wine: Meursault [p.127], White Rioja Reserva [p.138]

If you like:
Malted Honeycomb & Molasses
[See 'Malty Baked', Baked, p.73]
Peruvian Coffee & Malted Milk
[See 'Roasty Baked', Baked, p.76]

Try:
Beer: Brown Ale [p.238], Chocolate Stout [p.239], Coffee Stout [p.239], Dry Stout [p.241]
Coffee: Peruvian [p.207]
Dessert Wine: Rutherglen Muscat [p.162]

IRISH COFFEE [Grain-Produced Drinks, Whisky]

Cocktail recipe

Double Cream
30ml Irish Whiskey
15ml Demerara Sugar Syrup
60ml hot Filter Coffee

Pour piping-hot water into a latte glass and leave to sit, meanwhile, warm and froth your cream. Empty the glass, pour in Irish Whiskey, demerara sugar syrup, hot filter coffee and stir, then carefully overlay with the warm whipped cream, poured over the back of a spoon.

Irish Whiskey I'm a sucker for adverts, like the one where John Jameson wrestles a giant squid to rescue his barrel of whiskey. He grappled with an enormous hawk in another one, which means Jameson whiskey must be worth the risk. Well, if you like

If you like:
Clover Honey & Gingerbread
[See 'Floral Sweet', Sweet, p.61]
Malt Biscuit & Heather Honey
[See 'Malty Baked', Baked, p.72]

Irish whiskey's smooth profile, courtesy of drying the malt in a close kiln away from fire to avoid a smoky Scotch style, then, yes, a tussle with a titan is probably worth it. The combination of malted barley and mellower unmalted cereal grain with a triple distillation to banish the burn, weaves in super-smooth notes of honey, malted cereal and marmalade.

Malted Breakfast Cereal & Marmalade
[See 'Malty Baked', Baked, p.73]

Try:
Dessert Wine: Vin de Paille [p.164]
Tea: Rooibos [p.203]
Whisky: Drambuie [p.246], Japanese Single Malt [p.245], Rusty Nail [p.247]

Japan

Aged Single Malt Basically 'brat camp' for the young spirit, barrel-ageing brings in sixty per cent of a whisky's flavour. Immature characteristics of the 'new make' whisky are bred out by complex compounds extracted from the barrel, which vary depending on the wood and how it's been treated. Mizunara oak barrels bring in unique notes of Japanese temple incense and oriental spices like ginger, cinnamon and smoked vanilla. Pineapple and brown sugar notes appear after the very specific twenty-seven-year mark, as do creamy coconut inflections from the whisky lactone compound *[Glossary, p.17]*, which continue to intensify with age.

If you like:
Coconut Cream & Pineapple
[See 'Tropical Creamy', Creamy, p.69]
Gingerbread & Smoked Vanilla
[See 'Yeasty Baked', Baked, p.79]
Pineapple & Brown Sugar
[See 'Tropical Fruity', Fruity, p.52]

Try:
Grain Spirit: Sweet Potato Shōchū [p.256]
Mezcal: Joven [p.193]
Red Wine: Châteauneuf-du-Pape [p.147]
Rum: Coconut [p.196], Pina Colada [p.199], Pineapple [p.197]
Sparkling Wine: Mature Champagne [p.117]
Tequila: Reposado [p.192]

Single Malt Kudos to Japan for nailing the three Ts: tasty, trendy and *takai*, meaning expensive. The fourth T is for the tiny amount that is actually produced in Japan, the rest is repackaged Scotch, bourbon or other. Those of genuine Japanese provenance started out with a stylistic blueprint based on Scotch whisky, switching up the peaty profile as it wasn't a match with the domestic palate. Modern Japanese styles are closer to smoother Lowland and Speyside Scotch single malts, unctuously buttery, honeyed, biscuity and

If you like:
Cultured Butter & Fudge
[See 'Buttery Creamy', Creamy, p.66]
Malt Biscuit & Heather Honey
[See 'Malty Baked', Baked, p.72]
Vanilla & Clove-Spiced Toffee Apple
[See 'Creamy Sweet', Sweet, p.60]

Try:
Brandy: VSOP Calvados [p.177]
Cider: Cask-Aged [p.186]
Fortified Wine: White Port [p.171]
Red Wine: Californian Pinot Noir [p.161]

fudgy on the palate, best sipped with a splash of water.

Scotland

Coastal Beach parties always seem like such a good idea until you wake up rigid, reeking of seaweed and campfire smoke with sand in places you wouldn't care to share. That ship has sailed for me, though appreciating beach-party flavours in whisky is another kettle of fish. It's feasible that coastal whiskies take on briny, kelpy, iodine-rich flavours from maturation in dunnage warehouses *[Glossary, p.16]* facing the sea, the salty air also seeping into the barley during malting. Drying by peat fire doubles down on coastal notes, bringing in a whiff of beach bonfire and seashore funk.

Drambuie Thank Braveheart's beard they shortened *an dram buidheach*, Gaelic for 'the drink that satisfies', to Drambuie. That would have been a 'dram headache' to order in a bar. Not that I would, as aside from the Rusty Nail cocktail *[Whisky, p.247]*, it's not immediately obvious what the heck to do with it. On the rocks is the answer, given it's a sipping liqueur made from a blend of grain and malt whiskies, infused with spices including anise, orange peel and vanilla over Scottish-heather honey, which offsets its own sweetness with woody, floral, fresh-fruity accents.

Islay Malt You can never be prepared for Islay whisky, it's like skydiving or white-water rafting. Once you're done,

Tea: Rooibos [p.203]
Whisky: Drambuie [p.246], Irish Whiskey [p.244], Rusty Nail [p.247], Speyside Single Malt [p.247]

If you like:
Mesquite & Cardamom
[See 'Woody Smoky', Smoky, p.85]
Peat & Seashore
[See 'Earthy Smoky', Smoky, p.82]
Pepper Dulse & Burnt Orange
[See 'Vegetal Minerally', Minerally, p.97]

Try:
Amaro: Zucca Rabarbaro [p.225]
Mezcal: Reposado [p.194]
Tea: Lapsang Souchong [p.201]
Whisky: Islay Malt [p.246]

If you like:
Malt Biscuit & Heather Honey
[See 'Malty Baked', Baked, p.72]
Orange Blossom & Honey
[See 'Soft Floral', Floral, p.29]

Try:
Brandy: Metaxa [p.178]
Coffee: Peruvian [p.207]
Fruit Liqueur: Curaçao [p.182]
Gin: Sakura Bee's Knees [p.228]
Mixer: Coca-Cola [p.260]
Sparkling Wine: Moscato d'Asti [p.121]
Tea: Rooibos [p.203]
Whisky: Irish Whiskey [p.244], Japanese Single Malt [p.245], Rusty Nail [p.247]
White Wine: Condrieu [p.127]

If you like:
Mesquite & Cardamom
[See 'Woody Smoky', Smoky, p.85]

you're either gagging for another round or ticking it off the bucket list and running for the hills. It's whisky's notoriously smoky, tar-like, saline expression, brought on from drying malted barley in kilns that are powered by burning decomposed marine vegetation, i.e. peat. Rich in a compound that also gives shellfish their intense oceanic flavour, peat smoke infuses notes of iodine, asphalt, creosote, seaweed, tarred rope and antiseptic, which make it through distillation into the final blend.

Speyside Single Malt Speyside is the whisky equivalent of taking the Hollywood celebrity home tour. They may as well rename it 'Beverley Stills', with stars like Glenfiddich, Glenlivet and Macallan located there, which between them all make up over a third of the entire single malt Scotch market. In fact, half of Scotland's whisky distilleries are found in the triangular Highland region of Speyside, delivering a style of whisky considered to be the most complex. The heart of Scotch whisky production produces a lighter, sweeter style reminiscent of vanilla, tinned peaches, caramel, citrus and spiced apples.

USA

Rusty Nail Loud customers are the worst. I can relate to a Scottish bartender stirring a cocktail with a rusty nail in frustration over a vocal American. The guy got off lightly frankly, and unknowingly invented the name of a classic old-timey cocktail. The Rusty Nail's mellow, malty, honeyed, smoked vanilla flavours are thanks to Drambuie, which is mixed in with whisky for those who can't face the fiery bite. Drambuie's

Peat & Seashore
[See 'Earthy Smoky', Smoky, p.82]
Roasted Red Pepper & Samphire
[See 'Sweet Herbaceous', Herbaceous, p.39]

Try:
Amaro: Zucca Rabarbaro [p.225]
Mezcal: Reposado [p.194]
Tea: Lapsang Souchong [p.201]
Whisky: Coastal [p.246]

If you like:
Tinned Peach & Bitter Orange Zest
[See 'Creamy Fruity', Fruity, p.44]
Vanilla & Clove-Spiced Toffee Apple
[See 'Creamy Sweet', Sweet, p.60]

Try:
Brandy: VSOP Calvados [p.177]
Cider: Cask-Aged [p.186]
Fortified Wine: White Port [p.171]
Red Wine: Californian Pinot Noir [p.161]
Tea: Rooibos [p.203]
Whisky: Japanese Single Malt [p.245]

If you like:
Malt Biscuit & Heather Honey
[See 'Malty Baked', Baked, p.72]
Rooibos & Smoked Vanilla
[See 'Dried Herbaceous', Herbaceous, p.34]

Try:
Mezcal: Añejo [p.193]
Tea: Rooibos [p.203]
Whisky: Drambuie [p.246], Irish Whiskey [p.244], Japanese Single Malt [p.245]

blend of grain and malt whiskies, hay-like heather honey, herbs and spices, including anise, orange zest and cinnamon, nail the brief of sugar-coating blended whisky.

RUSTY NAIL [Grain-Produced Drinks, Whisky]

50ml Scotch Whisky
20ml Drambuie
Lemon Zest to garnish

Pour Scotch whisky into an ice-filled tumbler with Drambuie, then stir and garnish with lemon zest.

The Sazerac Any cocktail that requires two glasses, a technique and an absinthe rinse to prepare, I leave to professional bartenders. There's a reason why people do it for a living; besides, there's too much washing-up and where am I going to find Peychaud's Bitters? This is one of those cocktails. There's also the added pressure of the Sazerac being the official cocktail of New Orleans to consider. While mine inevitably taste Mardi gross, done properly rye whisky brings the signature spice and absinthe delivers the anise 'caress' with a dash of balancing bitters and zingy-herbal lemon oil.

If you like:
Cinnamon & Fennel Pollen
[See 'Warm Spicy', Spicy, p.110]
Liquorice & Lemon Thyme
[See 'Spicy Sweet', Sweet, p.56]
Star Anise & Lemon Verbena
[See 'Fragrant Spicy', Spicy, p.102]

Try:
Anise Liqueur: Absinthe [p.216], Arak [p.219], Ouzo [p.218], Pastis [p.217], Pernod [p.217], Raki [p.220], Ricard [p.218]
Fruit Liqueur: Limoncello [p.184], Pimm's [p.181]
Herb Liqueur: Strega [p.215], The Last Word [p.216], Yellow Chartreuse [p.214]

THE SAZERAC [Grain-Produced Drinks, Whisky]

10ml Absinthe
20ml Cognac
40ml Rye Whisky
10ml Sugar Syrup
2 dashes of Angostura Bitters (or 5 dashes of Peychaud's Bitters)
Lemon Rind

Add absinthe to a chilled lowball glass, then swirl and discard into shot glasses as optional chasers. Pour Cognac, rye whisky, sugar syrup, Angostura Bitters (or Peychaud's Bitters if you can find it) into a shaker with ice, stir rather than shake, and strain into the absinthe-rinsed glass with a twist of lemon rind.

Southern Comfort Look, I have
enough trouble with JLo, JLaw, BoJo
and ScarJo, I'm not shortening Southern
Comfort to SoCo. It's not just the name
that's tricky; the original recipe used
whisky and bourbon, which changed
to vodka and is now back to the 'new
original recipe' of whisky. For something
created in the Big Easy it sure is hard to
keep track of. Originally called 'cuffs and
buttons' after its ingredients of citrus peel
and cloves, it centres around the flavours
of a fruit concentrate, which I understand
is apricot, unless it's now peach . . .

If you like:
Chantilly Cream & Yellow Peach
[See 'Creamy Sweet', Sweet, p.59]
Dried Apricot & Candied Orange Peel
[See 'Spicy Sweet', Sweet, p.64]

Try:
Dessert Wine: Rivesaltes Ambré [p.164], Vidal
Ice Wine [p.163], Vin Santo [p.166]
Fortified Wine: Crusted Port [p.169], Palo
Cortado Sherry [p.173]
Sparkling Wine: Bellini [p.120]

Wheat Whisky Who hasn't wanted to
thump their fist down on the boardroom
table and say, 'I own fifty-one per cent of
this damn company'? Just me then. Wheat
whisky producers could probably relate,
given that figure applies to wheat whisky's
base ingredients, which are required to
contain that same minimum percentage of
wheat. It carries a massive flavour impact,
softening the spirit and rendering it milder
and more honeyed than rye's peppery
spice or corn's caramel richness. Ageing
in the obligatory brand-new charred oak
barrels infuses toasted coconut notes over
wheat's 'barely there' flavours of Melba
toast and creamy cereal milk.

If you like:
Cinnamon & Candied Rosemary
[See 'Warm Spicy', Spicy, p.109]
Melba Toast & Cereal Milk
[See 'Toasty Baked', Baked, p.77]
Toasted Coconut & Dried Spearmint
[See 'Tropical Creamy', Creamy, p.70]

Try:
Bourbon: Manhattan [p.251], Mint Julep
[p.252], Wheated [p.253]
Rum: Black Spiced [p.196]
Vodka: French Wheat [p.233]

Bourbon

England

Eggnog The 'nog' is the muggle version
of butterbeer, with a cheeky slug of
bourbon now Harry Potter fans are old
enough to drink. This booze-spiked Bird's
custard will trigger anyone with an eye
for healthy living with its composition

If you like:
Brown Butter & Nutmeg
[See 'Buttery Creamy', Creamy, p.66]
Crème Pâtissière & Praline
[See 'Decadent Creamy', Creamy, p.68]

of fat, sugar and alcohol. Its ingredients
include milk, egg and sugar, with a dash
of nutmeg for its cosy flavours of warm
spices and fragrant, roasty woodiness. Milk
fat is key to curbing the curdling, the
higher the better, meaning lower casein
concentrations to coagulate on contact
with booze's acidic influence.

White Chocolate & Mocha
[See 'Roasty Sweet', Sweet, p.63]

Try:
Brandy: Advocaat [p.179], VS Cognac [p.177],
VSOP Calvados [p.177], XO Cognac [p.178]
Coffee: Rwandan [p.207]
Coffee Liqueur: White Russian [p.208]
Nut Liqueur: Frangelico [p.254]
Whisky: Baileys Irish Cream [p.243]
White Wine: Meursault [p.127], White Rioja
Reserva [p.138]

EGGNOG [Grain-Produced Drinks, Bourbon]

Cocktail recipe

50ml Bourbon
10ml Sugar Syrup
25ml Full-fat Milk
1 Egg
Nutmeg

Pour bourbon, sugar syrup, milk and the
contents of a raw egg into an ice-filled shaker.
Shake, strain into another vessel, tip out the
ice, pour back into the shaker and dry-mix,
then strain into an ice-filled glass. Grate
nutmeg over the top for depth.

USA

High Rye Instead of high rye, let's start
with why rye? Stylistically rye grains
are the spice in the stew for bourbon,
breaking up corn's mellow caramel-like
sweetness with their baking spice-like
sassiness. Even the chemical structure of
the rye-grain kernel is unique, its cell walls
containing flavour compounds shared with
cinnamon, caraway, dill and anise, which
are unleashed in the milling and mashing
process and by yeast during fermentation.
Barrel oak mirrors rye's spicy chemical
configuration, building on them over time
and infusing them with its own coconut
notes from the creamy compound, whisky
lactone *[Glossary, p.17]*.

If you like:
Caraway & Dill Weed
[See 'Medicinal Spicy', Spicy, p.106]
Cinnamon & Candied Rosemary
[See 'Warm Spicy', Spicy, p.109]
Cinnamon & Fennel Pollen
[See 'Warm Spicy', Spicy, p.110]
Violet & Coconut
[See 'Rich Floral', Floral, p.27]

Try:
Bourbon: Manhattan [p.251], Wheated [p.253]
Herb Liqueur: Aquavit [p.215]
Rum: Black Spiced [p.196]
Whisky: The Sazerac [p.248],
Wheated [p.253]

Kentucky Straight The bluegrass state of Kentucky feels like a hotspot for hotel-trashing rockers knocking back Old-Fashioned cocktails and Mint Juleps. Tortured musicians aside, while bourbon gets its name from Bourbon County in Kentucky, it can now be made in any US state. It's like the Wild West, though, with straight bourbon as the only law-abiding style, with its minimum two years' ageing. Fruity ester compounds *[Glossary, p.16]* are the darlings of bourbon production, bringing forth those sought-after banana and roast-plantain notes, while barrel-ageing enriches the distillate with flavours of brown butter and barley malt syrup.

If you like:
Banana & Brown Butter
[See 'Tropical Fruity', Fruity, p.51]
Barley Malt Syrup & Roast Plantain
[See 'Malty Baked', Baked, p.72]

Try:
Beer: Australian Pale Ale [p.237], Bavarian Wheat [p.241]
Bourbon: Old-Fashioned [p.252]
Rum: Vintage Jamaican [p.198]

Manhattan I can't stand the word 'influencer', though it's fair to say that the Manhattan was one of the earliest influential cocktails. Just look at the number of iterations it's spawned, from the Rob Roy to all the others with 'Manhattan' in the title. Torch-wielding Manhattan purists, I hear you, but I'm sticking with the smoothness of bourbon over spicy rye whisky for the base spirit, though the latter is suspected to be the original. Rosso Vermouth's *[Fortified Wine, p.175]* botanical-saccharine mannerisms balance bourbon's caramel and vanilla components, and are reinforced by a dash of bitters and a twist of piney-woody orange zest.

If you like:
Cinnamon & Candied Rosemary
[See 'Warm Spicy', Spicy, p.109]
Vanilla & Bitter Orange
[See 'Creamy Sweet', Sweet, p.59]

Try:
Bourbon: High-Rye [p.250], Old-Fashioned [p.252], Wheated [p.253]
Coffee: Rwandan [p.207]
Fruit Liqueur: Grand Marnier [p.182]
Mixer: Coca-Cola [p.260]
Rum: Black Spiced [p.196]
Whisky: Wheat [p.249]

MANHATTAN [Grain-Produced Drinks, Bourbon]

Cocktail recipe

40ml Bourbon
25ml Rosso Vermouth
5ml Maraschino
2 dashes of Angostura Bitters
Orange Zest to garnish
Maraschino Cherry (optional)

Stir bourbon and Rosso Vermouth, Maraschino and Angostura Bitters, then strain into a chilled Martini glass, garnish with a twizzle of orange zest and an optional sunken maraschino cherry.

Mint Julep Who wouldn't want to be a member of the 'smash' family, for goodness' sake? It's actually a collective name for cocktails that spank ingredients to extract their essential oils, not unlike a pod of dolphins, a shiver of sharks or a cackle of hyenas, though what's the deal with a murder of crows? Mojitos and juleps use smashed mint, the latter with bourbon, sugar and crushed ice – don't forget the crushed ice. The official drink of the Kentucky Derby, the Mint Julep's sweet, toasty, herbal flavours are deeply synonymous with the Deep South.

If you like:
Cut Grass & Toffee
[See 'Grassy Herbaceous', Herbaceous, p.36]
Mint & Buttered Popcorn
[See 'Minty Herbaceous', Herbaceous, p.37]
Toasted Coconut & Dried Spearmint
[See 'Tropical Creamy', Creamy, p.70]

Try:
Amaro: Cynar [p.224]
Bourbon: Wheated [p.253]
Brandy: VS Cognac [p.177]
Herb Liqueur: Green Chartreuse [p.213]
Rum: Mojito [p.197], Rhum Agricole Blanc [p.199]
Tequila: Añejo [p.190], Reposado [p.192]
Whisky: Wheat [p.249]

Cocktail recipe

MINT JULEP [Grain-Produced Drinks, Bourbon]

6 fresh Mint Leaves
60ml Bourbon
15ml Sugar Syrup
Mint Sprig and Sugar to garnish

Shake mint leaves, bourbon and sugar syrup with ice, then strain into a julep cup or highball glass half filled with crushed ice. Stir and top up with yet more crushed ice, stir again and repeat until the glass is full. Garnish with mint sprig, sugar-dusted to taste.

Old-Fashioned Cocktails these days, they don't know they're born. Crack a book or double-click a web page and they'd see that their existence wouldn't be possible without the primitive life form that is the Old-Fashioned cocktail, like humans and early apes or amoebas, though I'm no biologist. Despite its forerunner status, the flavours in this stately Southern gentleman evolve depending on the style of whisky and bitters used in the mix. Bourbon brings in its usual smooth inflections of vanilla, plantain and barley malt syrup, with aromatic bitter-citrus accents the work of Angostura Bitters.

If you like:
Barley Malt Syrup & Roast Plantain
[See 'Malty Baked', Baked, p.72]
Vanilla & Bitter Orange
[See 'Creamy Sweet', Sweet, p.59]

Try:
Beer: Australian Pale Ale [p.237]
Bourbon: Kentucky Straight [p.251], Manhattan [p.251]
Coffee: Rwandan [p.207]
Fruit Liqueur: Grand Marnier [p.182]
Mixer: Coca-Cola [p.260]

OLD-FASHIONED [Grain-Produced Drinks, Bourbon]

50ml Bourbon

10ml Sugar Syrup

3 dashes of Angostura Bitters

Twist of Orange Zest to garnish

Stir bourbon, sugar syrup and Angostura Bitters together with ice, then strain into an ice-filled tumbler and garnish with orange zest.

Wheated Like the dad joke I'm about to make, why is bourbon such a corny beverage? Because it's mainly made of corn. Thanks and goodnight. It's a minimum fifty-one per cent to be exact; the rest is wheat, rye and barley, so it's unusual to find wheat flying solo as the secondary flavouring grain. The result is a 'wheater' with cream cracker-like candied flavours over corn's buttered–popcorn notes and mellow cinnamon inflections from new oak barrel-ageing. The iconic Pappy Van Winkle bourbon shows how well wheaters age, peaking later and holding their flavours for longer.

If you like:

Cinnamon & Candied Rosemary

[See 'Warm Spicy', Spicy, p.109]

Mint & Buttered Popcorn

[See 'Minty Herbaceous', Herbaceous, p.37]

Try:

Bourbon: Manhattan [p.251], Mint Julep [p.252]

Rum: Black Spiced [p.196]

Whisky: Wheated [p.253]

Nut Liqueur

Italy

Amaretto There's a lot to settle with amaretto, so let's start with the name. It's a play on the Italian word *amaro*, meaning 'a little bitter'. Frustratingly for romantics it has nothing to do with *amore*, though a few major brands have misleadingly hinted at a connection with 'bitter love'. Ingredient-wise, this liqueur is frequently flavoured with apricot stones, so what the heck's it doing in the nut liqueur section? The almond adjacency of apricot kernels, which share the marzipan-flavoured compound benzaldehyde *[Glossary, p.15]*, plus

If you like:

Lemon & Marzipan

[See 'Zingy Fruity', Fruity, p.53]

Morello Cherry & Almond

[See 'Floral Fruity', Fruity, p.47]

Try:

Brandy: Armagnac [p.175]

Fruit Liqueur: Kirsch [p.183], Maraschino [p.180]

Herb Liqueur: The Last Word [p.216]

Mixer: Cherry Coke [p.260]

Red Wine: Amarone [p.151]

Rosé Wine: Sangiovese Rosé [p.142]

the practice of using bitter almonds in Amaretto should explain why.

Frangelico Granted, it took me a minute to appreciate that Frangelico's bottle resembles a Franciscan friar. It even has the chord belt tied round the habit and everything, which I'm sure infringes a morality clause somewhere. Who cares? It's fun and loosely tied to a hermit monk called Fra Angelico, who was a drink innovator himself and would have enjoyed Frangelico's mocha, vanilla, cocoa butter and toasted-hazelnut flavours if he wasn't 600 years too late, given candied nuts and white chocolate work in anything, from Martinis to a nutty spin on Irish coffee.

Nocino Walnuts can be astringent so-and-sos. At best they taste like creamy, nutty teabags; at worst, bitter motor oil. Don't be put off Nocino though, an opaque Italian walnut liqueur made in the home-made style of sloe gin. So far, so romantic, though our pickers are on a deadline, as the walnuts must be harvested by the twenty-fourth of June when they're at peak fragrance and their cells are richest in essential oils. It also means the shells haven't hardened yet, allowing them to be sliced in half easily, bearing their bitter flavour compounds, which are tempered by steeping in vodka with sugar and orange zest.

Sake: Daiginjo [p.242]
White Wine: Soave Classico [p.135]

If you like:
Malted Loaf & Peanut Butter
[See 'Malty Baked', Baked, p.72]
Toasted Hazelnut & Digestive Biscuit
[See 'Nutty Baked', Baked, p.74]
White Chocolate & Mocha
[See 'Roasty Sweet', Sweet, p.63]

Try:
Beer: Brown Porter [p.238]
Bourbon: Eggnog [p.249]
Brandy: VSOP Cognac [p.177]
Coffee: Brazilian [p.204], Rwandan [p.207]
Coffee Liqueur: White Russian [p.208]
Sparkling Wine: Franciacorta Riserva [p.121], Mature Champagne [p.117], Vintage Champagne [p.118]
Whisky: Baileys Irish Cream [p.243]

If you like:
Mexican Coffee & White Pepper
[See 'Roasty Baked', Baked, p.75]
Walnut & Orange Zest
[See 'Nutty Baked', Baked, p.74]

Try:
Anise Liqueur: Sambuca [p.219]
Coffee: Mexican [p.206]
Fortified Wine: Malmsey Madeira [p.167], Palo Cortado Sherry [p.173]
Red Wine: Hermitage [p.150]
Tequila: Coffee [p.190]

Grain Spirits

China

Baijiu Sauce Aroma 'Liquid razor blades' is how President Nixon described sipping Baijiu, which wasn't used as its strapline. While visiting China, Nixon was shown how Baijiu could be set on fire, which he recreated for his daughter and allegedly almost burned down the White House. It's pronounced *bye-joe*, and is made via an ancient and complex process that gets scientists all aflutter. Cooked sorghum grain is fermented with qu, the Chinese counterpart to koji-kin *[Glossary, p.17]*, the Japanese mould that produces sake and soy sauce. A suite of aromatic compounds are generated, welcoming in the complex flavours of soy sauce, miso, peanuts, shiitake mushrooms and caramelised pretzel crust.

If you like:
Dried Shiitake & Caramel
[See 'Earthy Savoury', Savoury, p.90]
Red Miso & Pretzel Crust
[See 'Brothy Savoury', Savoury, p.88]
Soy Sauce & Dry-Roasted Peanut
[See 'Brothy Savoury', Savoury, p.88]
Tofu & Toasted Sesame Seed
[See 'Brothy Savoury', Savoury, p.89]

Try:
Grain Spirit: Baijiu Sesame Aroma [p.255], Sweet Potato Shōchū [p.256]
Sake: Junmai-Shu [p.242], Koshu [p.243]
Vodka: Bloody Mary [p.235]

Baijiu Sesame Aroma So, 'baijiu burps' are a thing – clearly the body's way of coping with a fiery shot of such psychedelic flavour complexity. This is a clear spirit produced from sorghum grain that's uniquely fermented without water, in a stone-lined, mud-bottomed pit with a depth and location that are key stylistic influences. Baijiu's intensity means that shot form is the popular way of consuming it. Sesame is a flavour subcategory, although sesame seeds aren't actually used in production, nor is there shared aroma chemistry; instead they're recreated via a collage of compounds with similar roasty, nutty, meaty mannerisms.

If you like:
Olive Brine & Walnut Brittle
[See 'Brothy Savoury', Savoury, p.88]
Red Pepper & Sesame Seed
[See 'Sweet Herbaceous', Herbaceous, p.38]
Tofu & Toasted Sesame Seed
[See 'Brothy Savoury', Savoury, p.89]

Try:
Fortified Wine: Amontillado Sherry [p.171], Palo Cortado Sherry [p.173]
Sake: Junmai-Shu [p.242], Koshu [p.243]

Japan

Sweet Potato Shōchū I'm easily confused, especially with so many Asian beverages beginning with the letter 'S', so I find the answer is to drink them all. Shōchū is similar to soju, Korea's answer to vodka, which are both stronger in alcohol than sake, with flavours dependent on whether they're made from rice, barley or sweet potato. Unlike sake, shōchū and soju are distilled, not brewed, though don't refer to shōchū as 'Japanese vodka' whatever you do. Sweet potatoes are fermented by sake's koji-kin fungus *[Glossary, p.17]*, bringing in umami miso and pretzel, earthy chestnut and bruised apple with smoky vanilla over sweet-spicy gingerbread.

If you like:

Gingerbread & Smoked Vanilla
[See 'Yeasty Baked', Baked, p.79]
Red Miso & Pretzel Crust
[See 'Brothy Savoury', Savoury, p.88]
Roast Chestnut & Bruised Apple
[See 'Nutty Baked', Baked, p.74]

Try:

Cider: Cask-Aged [p.186]
Fortified Wine: Fino Sherry [p.172]
Grain Spirit: Baijiu Sauce Aroma [p.255]
Orange Wine: Georgian [p.139]
Red Wine: Châteauneuf-du-Pape [p.147]
Rum: Rhum Agricole Blanc [p.199]
Sparkling Wine: Mature Champagne [p.117]
Whisky: Aged Japanese Single Malt [p.245]
White Wine: Vin Jaune [p.131]

Drinks

Fruit-produced

Plant-produced

Herb-produced

Grain-produced

Mixers

Caribbean

Angostura Bitters Bombard a dog with a truckload of toys and he swiftly loses his powers of selection. I can relate, as bitters give me choice-paralysis when I'm faced with every style under the sun, from celery, orange and pimento to Creole, mole, tiki and black walnut. In fairness, each brings a unique touch to tipples, but no one uses every blade in the kitchen to slice an orange. Angostura is the bitters equivalent of an all-purpose chef's knife, a multitasking bar seasoning that delivers a spiced rum-like flavour with cassia and lime bitterness to classic cocktails.

If you like:
Cassia & Lime
[See 'Warm Spicy', Spicy, p.109]
Escarole & Orange
[See 'Bitter Herbaceous', Herbaceous, p.33]

Try:
Amaro: Aperol Spritz [p.222], Averna [p.223], Negroni [p.224]
Mixer: Cherry Coke [p.260], Coca-Cola [p.260]
Red Wine: Sangria [p.160]
Vodka: Moscow Mule [p.236]

England

Elderflower Cordial There's something slightly Miss Marple about elderflower cordial; I imagine it sipped at the St Mary Mead village fete on her crime-busting day off. Much deserved, might I add, although, like Marple, elderflowers are less dainty than they first appear. Musky, bitter, herbaceous nuances lurk beneath the welcoming committee of melon, fresh pear, honey and blossom. It's made by steeping elderflower heads in sugar syrup, which is offset by citric acid for a balance of tartness. Wholesome aromas ultimately prevail, with elderflowers' spring-like honeysuckle flavours showing through, accompanied by rosy notes of village cricket and lawn tennis.

If you like:
Elderflower & Cantaloupe Melon
[See 'Fruity Floral', Floral, p.24]
Endive & Honeysuckle
[See 'Bitter Herbaceous', Herbaceous, p.32]
Lemon & Fresh Pear
[See 'Zingy Fruity', Fruity, p.52]

Try:
Beer: Australian Pale Ale [p.237]
Brandy: Peruvian/Chilean Pisco [p.179]
Coffee: Nicaraguan [p.206]
Fruit Liqueur: Melon Ball Drop [p.184], Midori [p.185]
Gin: White Negroni [p.227]
Sake: Junmai Ginjo [p.242]
Sparkling Wine: Crémant de Loire [p.119]
Vodka: Pornstar Martini [p.232]
White Wine: Bacchus [p.125], South African Chenin Blanc [p.137], Vermentino [p.135]

Ginger Beer Finding out that the ginger beer plant exists is the reverse of hearing that Santa isn't real. So, does it go next to the money tree or beside the spaghetti bush? It's actually the name for the yeast they originally used in ginger beer production, which happened to be a fairly alcoholic brew. Nothing quite as exciting for the soft drink, which is usually a carbonated beverage with ginger flavouring. That said, some high-end producers still employ authentic botanical brewing methods, infusing fiery compound gingerol *[Glossary, p.17]* via steeping milled ginger roots with herbs, citrus, sugar and yeast.

If you like:
Australian Ginger & Cardamom
[See 'Zingy Spicy', Spicy, p.110]
Dried Ginger & Lime
[See 'Zingy Spicy', Spicy, p.111]
Fennel & Ginger
[See 'Veggie Herbaceous', Herbaceous, p.39]

Try:
Herb Liqueur: King's Ginger [p.212]
Rum: Black Spiced [p.196], Dark 'n' Stormy [p.195]
Vodka: Moscow Mule [p.236]

India

Tonic Water Why did no one tell us we had bitter receptors in our gut as well as our mouth? So that's why I can't stomach tonic water on its own, with two sets of sensors for the bitter notes to get through. Tonic majors on quinine, the anti-malarial compound that rebranded itself as our favourite mixer. We have cinchona to thank for, well, everything really, as no tree bark has been more impactful in the world of tonics, bitters and aromatised beverages. Quinine in tonic is chemically attracted to gin's similarly shaped essential oil compounds, forming a flavour agregate that transcends their individual flavours, making bitter and botanical flavours the new yin and yang.

If you like:
Gentian Root & Pomelo Peel
[See 'Bitter Spicy', Spicy, p.100]
Quinine & Lemon Oil
[See 'Bitter Spicy', Spicy, p.101]

Try:
Amaro: Suze [p.222]
Gin: Gin & Tonic [p.226], White Negroni [p.227]
Tea: Earl Grey [p.202]
Vermouth: Cocchi Americano [p.175]

Spain

Vichy Catalan Full disclosure: I'm that guy who would drink Alka-Seltzer as a regular beverage, straight up. Ironically,

If you like:
Flint & Lemon Balm
[See 'Rocky Minerally', Minerally, p.96]

for something so super-refreshing, it's too intensely saline to offer much hydration, which is where Vichy Catalan comes in. It's the Champagne-standard sparkling water, or maybe Cava given it's from Barcelona, if you like your bubbly water with a whopping one gram of salt per litre. Though it can be an assault on the senses if you're expecting regular grassy water. That's because Vichy Catalan is high in dissolved minerals, which makes it a slam-dunk as sapid crushed ice to elevate cocktails.

Lemon Blossom & Sea Mist
[See 'Floral Soft', Floral, p.28]
River Stone & Alka-Seltzer
[See 'Rocky Minerally', Minerally, p.96]

Try:
Tequila: Margarita [p.190]
White Wine: Albariño [p.137], Chablis [p.126], Gavi di Gavi [p.134], Grillo [p.135], Pessac-Leognan [p.128], Pouilly Fumé [p.129], Puligny Montrachet [p.129], Sancerre [p.131], Soave Classico [p.135], Vinho Verde [p.136]

USA

Cherry Coke Not to brag, but it's 'Choke' to those in the know. Just saying. Now that's settled, the best part about Cherry Coke is knowing that no actual cherries were harmed in the making of it. Ingredients are kept within the lab walls, though cola flavours of nutmeg, vanilla, cinnamon, bitter orange and lime are matched with syrupy morello cherry and bitter-almond base notes, thanks to the compound benzaldehyde *[Glossary, p.15]*. It's the world's most used flavouring after vanillin, which isn't bad for a chemical that's used in nature to ward off predators via its ties to cyanide.

If you like:
Cassia & Lime
[See 'Warm Spicy', Spicy, p.109]
Morello Cherry & Almond
[See 'Floral Fruity', Fruity, p.47]

Try:
Brandy: Armagnac [p.175]
Fruit Liqueur: Kirsch [p.183], Maraschino [p.180]
Herb Liqueur: The Last Word [p.216]
Mixer: Angostura Bitters [p.258], Coca-Cola [p.260]
Nut Liqueur: Amaretto [p.253]
Red Wine: Amarone [p.151], Sangria [p.160]
Rosé Wine: Sangiovese Rosé [p.142]
Vodka: Moscow Mule [p.236]

Coca-Cola Whether writing about Coca-Cola is a career peak or trough, I'm down for it, and hopefully up to it. Why wouldn't I be? It's the world's best-selling caffeinated soft drink, with a secret formula based around the bitter, sweet, floral and spicy notes of vanilla, cassia, lime, bitter orange, lemon, orange blossom, coriander, coca leaves, nutmeg, caramel, zero cocaine and absurd amounts of sugar. I suspect ginger and lavender also

If you like:
Cassia & Lime
[See 'Warm Spicy', Spicy, p.109]
Orange Blossom & Honey
[See 'Soft Floral', Floral, p.29]
Vanilla & Bitter Orange
[See 'Creamy Sweet', Sweet, p.59]

Try:
Bourbon: Manhattan [p.251], Old-Fashioned [p.252]

feature, though I can't tell you why Coke tastes better in a glass bottle or what its chemical reaction is with Mentos.

Brandy: Metaxa [p.178]
Coffee: Peruvian [p.207], Rwandan [p.207]
Fruit Liqueur: Curaçao [p.182]
Mixer: Angostura Bitters [p.258], Cherry Coke [p.260]
Red Wine: Sangria [p.160]
Rum: White [p.197]
Vodka: Moscow Mule [p.236]
Whisky Liqueur: Drambuie [p.246]

Cranberry Juice While I appreciate that cranberries could help against UTIs, that's not appropriate information for a book about flavours. Let's shake it off, so to speak, and focus instead on cranberries' multifaceted flavour offering, with grassy, almondy, woody, blood-orange, floral, citrusy and piney characteristics all housed in one diminutive maroon berry. Where do they keep it all? In the skin mainly, in terpene compounds that also bring notes of pepper, clove, cinnamon and vanilla. Given cranberries' lightly tannic, super-tart and resinous mannerisms, the juice format usually comes with abundant sugar to make it more palatable.

If you like:
Cinnamon & Blood Orange
[See 'Warm Spicy', Spicy, p.109]
Cranberry & Lime
[See 'Sweet Fruity', Fruity, p.50]

Try:
Amaro: Campari [p.223]
Red Wine: Mulled Wine/Glühwein [p.150], Sangria [p.160]
Rosé Wine: Bandol Rosé [p.140]

Cream Soda Cream soda conjures up images of fifties-style American diners in my mind, not unlike those Edward Hopper paintings. Like my knowledge of art, a little goes a long way with vanilla, the flavour that puts the cream in cream soda. Studies have shown that adding vanilla flavouring to one per cent fat milk gives it a higher perceived creaminess than full-fat milk. This pricey spice, which is now synthesised from anything from cloves to beaver-bum glue, not only enhances our perception of dairy notes but of unctuous white chocolate-like textures as well, where perhaps there are none.

If you like:
Coconut Water & White Chocolate
[See 'Tropical Creamy', Creamy, p.70]
Cream Soda & Williams Pear
[See 'Decadent Creamy', Creamy, p.67]

Try:
Rum: Coconut [p.196]
Sparkling Wine: Bellini [p.120], Champagne Demi-Sec [p.117], Prosecco [p.122]

MIXERS

Dr Pepper In the words of the advert, 'What's the worst that can happen?' Well, we might need to wear our brown trousers, as prune juice is rumoured to be an ingredient. All we really know is that it's a blend of twenty-three secret components, though it could conceivably contain cherry, blackberry, almond, liquorice, caramel, clove, ginger, juniper, lemon, molasses, nutmeg, orange, plum, cardamom, allspice, birch and prickly ash. These would faithfully recreate Dr Pepper's nineteenth-century pharmacy aromas, led by the peppery, botanical, medicinal-style flavours. Oh, and it's actually prune-free, allegedly.

If you like:
Dandelion & Burdock
[See 'Medicinal Spicy', Spicy, p.106]
Grains of Paradise & Wintergreen
[See 'Peppery Spicy', Spicy, p.108]

Try:
Amaro: White Negroni [p.227]
Anise Liqueur: Arak [p.219]
Mixer: Root Beer [p.262]
Tequila: Reposado [p.192]

Root Beer Role-reversal alert: root beer is normally how I'd describe other drinks with peppery, medicinal flavours, so I'll have to find a way to describe root beer. Well, it has peppery, medicinal flavours, originally from the nutmeg and clove-like sassafras bark and the rich cola notes of ground-up sarsaparilla vine roots. Both contain a chemical of carcinogenic concern, so were replaced with artificial sassafras and flavour-alikes, with the line-up including dandelion, burdock, wintergreen, liquorice root, juniper and cloves, combined with a molasses syrup to give it a deep colour and burnt-sugar notes.

If you like:
Dandelion & Burdock
[See 'Medicinal Spicy', Spicy, p.106]
Liquorice Root & Black Cardamom
[See 'Medicinal Spicy', Spicy, p.107]

Try:
Amaro: Fernet-Branca [p.224], White Negroni [p.227]
Anise Liqueur: Ouzo [p.218]
Herb Liqueur: Jägermeister [p.214]
Mixer: Dr Pepper [p.262]
Red Wine: Graciano [p.158], Old-Vine Zinfandel [p.161], Uruguayan Tannat [p.160]
Rum: Black Spiced [p.196]

Bibliography

Books

Baker, Jokie & Clarke, Ronald J., *Wine Flavour Chemistry*

Briscione, James, *The Flavour Matrix*

Chartier, Francois, *Taste Buds & Molecules: The Art and Science of Food, Wine & Flavor*

Eriksson, C., *Understanding Natural Flavours*, pp.112–39

Farrimond, Dr Stuart, *The Science of Spice*

Gomez-Plaza, E., *Handbook of Fruit & Vegetable Flavors*

Hartings, Matthew, *Chemistry in Your Kitchen*

Horne, Thomas, *On Beer & Food: The Gourmet's Guide to Recipes and Pairings*

Jackson, Ronald, *Advances in Food Nutrition Research Volume 63: Speciality Wines*

Jackson, Ronald, *Wine Science: Principles and Applications*

Marsili, Ray, *Flavour, Fragrance and Odor Analysis,* Second Edition

McGee, Harold, Nose Dive: *A Field Guide to the World's Smells*

Patterson, Daniel & Aftel, Mandy, *The Art of Flavour: Practices and Principles for Creating Delicious Food*

Piggott, John, *Alcoholic Beverages: Sensory Evaluation and Consumer Research*

Segnit, Nicky, *The Flavour Thesaurus*

Stewart, Amy, *The Drunken Botanist*

Varnam, A., *Beverages: Technology, Chemistry & Microbiology*

Waterhouse, Sacks, Jeffery, *Understanding Wine Chemistry*

Webb, Tim & Beaumont, Stephen, *World Atlas of Beer*

Papers

Aprea, Eugenio *et al.*, 'Volatile Compounds of Raspberry Fruit'

Dixon, Jonathan & Hewett, Erroll W., 'Factors Affecting Apple Aroma/Flavour Volatile Concentration: A Review'

Lapalus, Emmanuelle, 'Linking Sensory Attributes to Selected Aroma Compounds in South African Cabernet Sauvignon Wines'

Manyi-Loh, Christy *et al.*, 'Volatile Compounds in Honey'

Masi, E. *et al.*, 'Characterization of Volatile Compounds in Mentha Spicata L. Dried Leaves'

Pino, Jorge Antonio & Quijano, Clara Elizabeth, 'Study of Volatile Compounds from Plum and Estimation of their Contribution to the Fruit Aroma'

Sawamura, M. & Lan-Phi, N. T., 'Chemical and Aroma Profiles of Different Cultivars of Yuzu Essential Oils'

Zhou, Meixue *et al.*, 'Analysis of Volatile Compounds and their Contribution to Flavor in Cereals'